THE DIGBY POEMS
A NEW EDITION OF THE LYRICS

The 24 short lyrics known as the Digby Poems are part of Oxford Bodleian MS Digby 102, a manuscript dating from the first quarter of the fifteenth century. They represent a challenge to the theory that vernacular religious writing was successfully stifled by the Church in this period.

In Helen Barr's new edition, the poems have been freshly transcribed and edited. The critical apparatus includes a full introduction, extensive annotation to each poem, and a glossary.

The edition also provides convincing new historical evidence for the provenance and authorship of the poems. Helen Barr shows that the sequence was written in the early years of Henry V's reign (c.1413–14), probably by a Benedictine monk eager to add his support for the Henrician new dawn.

The poems show strong support for war against France and for the proper conduct of parliamentary business. The poems are rigorous in their call for orthodox reform from within the Church. Throughout, the concerns of Church and State are inseparable from a fierce call for penitence, both collective and individual. Helen Barr's extensive annotation brings out not just the political significance of the poems but also their place in the tradition of devotional writing.

Helen Barr is Fellow and Tutor in English at Lady Margaret Hall, Oxford. She has edited and written on the Piers Plowman tradition, is author of *Socioliterary Practice in Late Medieval England* (2001), and co-edited *Text and Controversy from Wyclif to Bale* (2005) with Ann M. Hutchison.

EXETER MEDIEVAL TEXTS AND STUDIES

Series Editors: Vincent Gillespie and Richard Dance

Founded by M. J. Swanton
and later co-edited by Marion Glasscoe

The Digby Poems

A New Edition of the Lyrics

edited from
Oxford, Bodleian Library MS Digby 102

by Helen Barr

UNIVERSITY
of
EXETER
PRESS

Cover illustration: detail from Lydgate's *Fall of Princes*, HM 268 fo. 24v (reproduced by permission of the Huntington Library, San Marino, California).

First published in 2009 by
University of Exeter Press
Reed Hall, Streatham Drive
Exeter EX4 4QR
UK
www.exeterpress.co.uk

British Library Cataloguing in Publication Data
A catalogue record for this book is available from the British Library.

ISBN Paperback 978 0 85989 817 1
ISBN Hardback 978 0 85989 816 4

Typeset in Minion 10/13
by Carnegie Book Production, Lancaster

Printed in Great Britain by CPI Antony Rowe

Contents

Acknowledgements

The staff at Duke Humfrey in the Bodleian Library, Oxford, have been unfailingly helpful during the many times I consulted MS Digby 102, and I am grateful to The Huntington Library, San Marino, California, for permission to reproduce the image from HM 268 fo.24v, Lydgate's *Fall of Princes*, for the cover illustration of this edition. I also thank The News International Fund, and Lady Margaret Hall, Oxford, for generous help with research costs. James Cummings of the Oxford University Computer Services provided me with an electronic concordance and word index of my transcription of the text; a resource which has proved invaluable. I also want to thank Alistair Hodge for impeccable copy-editing, and Anna Henderson, editor at Exeter, for seeing this volume through the Press so efficiently.

Richard Jenkyns kindly helped me with some abstruse Latin, Simon Horobin with dialect, and Ralph Hanna with palaeography. Other friends and colleagues have generously discussed various aspects of these poems and made this edition better: Mishtooni Bose, Kantik Ghosh, Matthew Giancarlo, Gavin Hopps, Nicola McDonald, Jenni Nuttall, Nicholas Perkins, Vincent Quinn, Christopher Rovee, Annie Sutherland, and John Watts. I also want to thank Brantley Bryant and Ellen Rentz who were members of my graduate seminar when I was teaching at University of Columbia, New York. Their conversation about Digby and other late medieval literature gave me fresh insights. I am also immensely grateful to the two readers of the edition for their responses.

There are three people who deserve special thanks. Paul Strohm made it possible for me to spend four months at Columbia. This fabulous opportunity gave huge impetus to the preparation of this edition and I thank Paul for his extended conversation, his opening up of new intellectual possibilities for me, and the warmth of his encouragement both for this edition and for my work in general. Vincent Gillespie has been stalwart in seeing this work through to publication and I thank him for his astute reading of many sections of the edition, and for his forbearance when I subjected him to countless bursts of conversation about its progress. I have learnt a lot from our exchanges. Anne Hudson has been wonderfully encouraging all the while this work was growing, and I am deeply indebted to her rigorous reading of my initially hapless attempts to sort out the dialect and language, as well as clarification of all manner of textual peculiarities. This work would be so much the poorer without her extremely generous help. I hope that all traces of my foolish ignorance have been effaced; if any remain, I am wholly responsible.

And finally, warmest thanks to all my friends. Some of them would quail at the thought of having to read a single word of this, but their play has been important in speeding the work.

January 2009

Introduction

1. The manuscript

Oxford, Bodleian Library MS Digby 102 was written in the first quarter of the fifteenth century.[1] It contains an incomplete C text of *Piers Plowman* (fols 1a–97b);[2] 24 lyric poems (fols 98a–127b); the metrical paraphrase of the *Seven Penitential Psalms* by the anti-Lollard Carmelite friar Richard of Maidstone (fols 128a–136a),[3] and *The Debate between the Body and Soul* (fols 136a–139b).[4] All of the items are written out as prose. Despite changes in the colour of the ink, and sharpening of the pen, especially at fol. 128a, there is no conclusive evidence to suggest that the codex as a whole is not the work of one scribe.[5] A new quire is begun after the copying of *Piers* (fol. 98a), but thereafter, the remaining items were clearly intended to form part of a continuous sequence. The lyrics end at the bottom of fol. 127b. Maidstone's *Psalms* follow on from the lyrics in the same quire (fol. 128a).

---

[1]   Simon Horobin, '"In London and Opelond": The Dialect and Circulation of the C Version of *Piers Plowman*', *Medium Aevum* 74 (2005), pp. 248–69, at pp. 258–9, dates the MS to the first quarter of the fifteenth century and argues that one scribe is responsible for the whole codex. Ralph Hanna, in private communication, 20 April 2007, wrote that 'he would not want to date the MS later than 1430 and possibly a good deal earlier' (i.e. as early as 1400–10 potentially, and certainly there is no problem about it being second decade of the fifteenth century).

[2]   The text runs from Passus 2.159 to Passus 22.386.

[3]   See Valerie Edden ed., *Richard of Maidstone's Penitential Psalms* (Heidelberg: Winter, 1990).

[4]   This is edited (though not using Digby 102 as base text) in John W. Conlee ed., *Middle English Debate Poetry* (Michigan: East Lansing, 1991), pp. 18–49.

[5]   The description of the MS in George Russell and George Kane edd., *Piers Plowman: The C Version* (London: Athlone, 1997), p. 16, which is designated 'Y', is erroneous in several respects. They list 23 rather than 24 lyrics between fols 98a and 127b. They also state that there is an unmistakeable change of scribe at fol. 128a, after the end of *Piers Plowman*. While they are quite correct in noting the appearance of a rebus containing the letters H E R O N on fol. 97b and again on fol. 139b, their comment 'fol. 13a the date, 1420, apparently in the hand that numbered the quires', is misleading. Fol. 13a lacks such annotation, and I have not found it elsewhere in the MS.

The *Psalms* finish half way down fol. 136a and the body and soul debate is begun on the same folio. The formation of catch words (ink oval around the words and the words themselves crossed out in red) is the same throughout the codex. Line breaks are marked with a vertical line in red. In *Piers*, initial Passus capitals are blue and red; and in the lyric poems, stanzas are delineated with alternating blue and red paraphs. Poem titles are added in red. Two of them are missing (fols 119b–120a), which suggests that the titles were added later and two leaves turned over at once.

The collection of texts displays a 'rough unity, one dependent on informatively consistent thematic concerns'.[6] As a whole, the codex has a fiercely penitential focus. In contrast to the accompanying of *Piers* with dissident texts such as the avowedly Lollard *Pierce the Ploughman's Crede* in British Library MS Bibl. Reg.18.B.XVII and MS Trinity College Cambridge R.3.15, the Digby manuscript is demonstrably orthodox. Like those other codices which contain Maidstone's *Psalms*, the manuscript and especially the lyrics, contains devotional material which is pro-ecclesiastical and pro-sacerdotal. While the Digby codex differs significantly in scale and size from the Vernon manuscript, it shares very similar thematic concerns (as well as a copy of *Piers Plowman*).[7]

2. Previous editions of the Digby lyrics

The 24 lyrics were edited in their entirety by Joseph Kail in 1904.[8] A second volume which was to contain further annotation never appeared. Kail's introduction gives a brief overview of the first 18 poems of the sequence, focusing chiefly on those lyrics which appear to be topical; the more devotional pieces escape attention. Kail presents the lyrics as a chronological sequence, beginning in 1401 and ending in 1421 with Poem 18. He ties many of the poems, especially nos 1, 3, 4, 9, and 13, to the business of the parliament in a particular year. He dates Poem 14 to 1418 on

---

[6] Ralph Hanna, 'Miscellaneity and Vernacularity', in Stephen G. Nichols and Siegfried Wenzel, edd., *The Whole Book: Cultural Perspectives in the Medieval Miscellany* (Ann Arbor: University of Michigan, 1996), p. 44.

[7] The essays collected in Derek Pearsall ed., *Studies in the Vernon Manuscript* (Cambridge: Brewer, 1990) provide a comprehensive study of the manuscript as a whole and many of its contents: on the lyrics, see John Burrow, 'The Shape of the Vernon Refrain Lyrics', pp. 187–200 and John J. Thompson, 'The Textual Background and Reputation of the Vernon Lyrics', pp. 201–24. On the political significance of fifteenth-century miscellanies, see the essay by Philippa Hardman, 'Compiling the Nation: Fifteenth-Century Miscellany Manuscripts' in Helen Cooney ed., *Nation, Court and Culture: New Essays on Fifteenth-Century English Poetry* (Dublin: Four Courts Press, 2001), pp. 50–69.

[8] J. Kail ed., *Twenty-Six Political and Other Poems* (EETS OS 124, 1904). Kail adds two poems from Oxford, Bodleian Library MS Douce 322, 'Pety Job' and 'Parce Mihi, Domine'.

the grounds of 'some vague allusions to the fate of Sir John Oldcastle' (p. xx), and no. 16 to 1419 'because it contains references to the folly and to the assassination of John, Duke of Burgundy and Flanders' (p. xxi). The date of the poems is discussed more fully in section 4 of the introduction of the present edition (and in notes to the individual poems). I shall argue that Kail's historical readings, though highly influential on later editions and criticism, are misleading.

R.H. Robbins edited three of the poems (nos 3, 12, and 16) in his anthology of *Historical Poems*.[9] In each case, he preserves Kail's dating and his annotation reprises Kail's prefatory notes which record parallels between the poems and parliamentary business, and in the case of Poem 16, the murder of the duke of Burgundy. In his introduction, Robbins holds up Kail's dating of Poem 9 to 1410 as a prime example of how the turn to documentary record can 'help towards precise dating even of general moralising pieces' (p. xxiv),[10] and endorses Kail's chronological ordering of the sequence (p. xxix). Summing up the series, Robbins argues that they 'can best be regarded as occasional closet verse, written by some lesser religious dignitary for circulation among sober-minded laity and clergy who had a special interest and voice in practical politics' (p. xxix). As an after-thought, Robbins does note that 'in their religious-political subject matter and their form … the Digby series suggests the more numerous and better known Vernon-Simeon poems' (p. xxix).

Two further lyrics have been edited in more recent anthologies: Poem 3 by James Dean in an anthology of political writing,[11] and Poem 2 by John Conlee in an anthology of debate poems.[12] Dean recycles Kail's and Robbins' dating and annotation – his additional notes are discussed in my annotation to this poem. Conlee's editorial handling of Poem 2 is also discussed in the notes to Poem 2 in the present edition.[13]

---

[9] R.H. Robbins ed., *Historical Poems of the XIVth and XVth Centuries* (New York: Columbia University Press, 1959), pp. 39–53.

[10] See also R.H. Robbins, 'On Dating a Middle English Moral Poem', *MLN* 70 (1955), pp. 473–6; at p. 474.

[11] James Dean ed., *Medieval English Political Writings* (Michigan: TEAMS, 1996), pp. 153–8.

[12] Conlee, *Poetry*, pp. 210–15,

[13] There is also another version of Poem 16. Furnivall adds a characteristically laconic footnote to Kail's edition of the poem to say, 'I printed this, from my copy of the MS, in *Englische Studien* 1897, in forgetfulness of Dr. Kail. – F.J.F.', Kail, *Poems*, p. 69. Kail's response is not recorded.

3. Critical reception

There have been no studies of the Digby lyrics in their entirety, and little written on individual poems. Until very recently, it has been the more overtly political poems that have attracted attention. John Scattergood devoted generous space to the coverage of what he terms 'the important sequence in MS Digby 102' in his book on politics and poetry.[14] He discusses the Digby-poet's attitude towards Flanders, and his support for military action against France, and reprises Kail's interpretation of Poem 16 as a moralising review of the career of the duke of Burgundy (pp. 47–50 and pp. 69–70). Scattergood also draws attention to the concern in the series about keeping unlawful challenge to authority in check, paying heed to the dangers of internal division, and the commons' awareness of their financial importance (pp. 116–17 and p. 122). Scattergood's discussion of the grievances in Poem 9 follows Kail's dating of the poem to 1410; he concludes 'the attention given to these minor grievances would suggest that most of the major ones had ceased to seem important' (pp. 125–6). Scattergood's judicious discussion of the issues raised in the series in the context of analysis of better known political verse draws welcome attention to the significance of the poems, even if the temporal framework, derived from Kail's dating, can be challenged.

Janet Coleman also devotes significant space to the Digby series in her book on medieval readers and writers.[15] She discusses the second poem in the series as complaint literature infused with romance tropes before devoting broader analysis of Digby lyrics as examples of poems in the political complaint tradition, which use 'exhortatory generalities that are common to the "mirror for princes" genre' (pp. 95–9). Although Coleman acknowledges the presence of devotional items in the sequence, her focus is, once more, on the more overtly political pieces, especially those which recycle common tropes of good governance (pp. 100–3). She provides extensive commentary on the political concerns of Poem 3 (pp. 103–7). She observes that the poems are homiletic and prescriptive (p. 108), and that the poems are examples of 'relatively undistinguished late fourteenth-century type of admonitory poetry on the nature of good governance by kings and advisers, and the duties required of citizens in a just and peaceful realm' (p. 103). Kail's time-frame, and his parliamentary focus, are reproduced.

The audience of the poems is discussed briefly by Anne Middleton as part of her vigorous investigation into the reception of *Piers Plowman*. She characterises the audience as 'laymen of affairs and ... the ecclesiastics, regular and secular, who educated their children, counselled them and their king, and themselves

---

[14]   V.J. Scattergood, *Politics and Poetry in the Fifteenth Century* (London: Blandford Press, 1971), p. 17.

[15]   Janet Coleman, *English Literature in History, 1350–1400* (London: Hutchinson, 1981).

held positions in which they governed and dispensed justice'. She notes that the poems 'share some of the broadly ethical and devotional concerns of men of affairs, lay and ecclesiastical, at the coming of the Lancastrians'.[16] Once again, Kail's dating is influential. John Watts, in an important article on the role of the public in contemporary political discourse, discusses the Digby-poet's alignment of common voice with the commons, the declaration of truth, and with the agency of divine vengeance. Kail's marriage of particular poems to precise years of parliamentary discussion is bypassed, thus enabling the broader political inflection of the sequence to emerge.[17] Brantley Bryant's recent unpublished discussion of the preoccupation of the poems with the nuisance of 'singular profit' highlights the importance of the sequence in larger discussion of the discourses of economics in Middle English poetry.[18] Jenni Nuttall argues that Poem 13 of the sequence is part of an extended conversation about politics in early Lancastrian texts. The poem can be seen as an extension and alteration of Henry Beaufort's sermon rhetoric of the November 1414 parliament requesting financial aid for Henry V's French campaign.[19]

A rather different intervention into the Digby poems is represented by Vincent Gillespie's recent article on moral and penitential lyrics. Gillespie demonstrates how the penitential rigour of the devotional and moral lyrics in the sequence both continues a tradition of such writing and also has 'the potential to carry political freight ... if moral poetry is not susceptible of application to contemporary events, it has lost its power'.[20] Linking Digby more firmly with the minor poems of the

---

[16] Anne Middleton, 'The Audience and Public of *Piers Plowman*' in David Lawton ed., *Middle English Alliterative Poetry and its Literary Background* (Cambridge: Brewer, 1982), pp. 101–23; quotation from p. 108.

[17] John Watts, 'The Pressure of the Public on Later Medieval Politics' in Linda Clark and Christine Carpenter edd., *Political Culture in Late Medieval Britain*, Fifteenth Century IV (Woodbridge: Boydell, 2004), pp. 159–64. His investigation is further developed in 'Public or Plebs: The Changing Meaning of the Commons, 1381–1549' in H. Pryce and J. Watts edd., *Power and Identity in the Middle Ages: Essays in Memory of Rees Davies* (Oxford: OUP, 2007), pp. 249–51.

[18] Brantley L. Bryant, *Common Profit: Economic Morality in English Public Political Discourse, c.1340–1406* (unpublished Ph.D. dissertation, University of Columbia, New York, 2007), pp. 101–11.

[19] Jenni Nuttall, *The Creation of Lancastrian Kingship* (Cambridge: CUP, 2008), pp. 127–30.

[20] Vincent Gillespie, 'Moral and Penitential Lyrics' in T.G. Duncan ed., *A Companion to the Middle English Lyric* (Cambridge: Brewer, 2005), pp. 69–95; at pp. 91–3. One might contrast this remark to George Kane's dismissal of the so-called politicality of complaint literature, preferring instead, to see it as literature of moral instruction, 'Some Fourteenth-Century "Political" Poems', in Gregory Kratzmann and James Simpson edd., *Medieval Religious and Ethical Literature: Essays in Honour of G.H. Russell* (Cambridge: Brewer, 1986), pp. 82–91.

Vernon manuscript, and freeing them from the iron fist of the rolls of parliament, Gillespie shows how the penitential is also the political – and in so doing, also calls attention to the syntactical, lexical and stanzaic pointedness of poems,[21] showing that these poems are well crafted and sprightly.[22]

4. Date

i) *Parliamentary allusions*

It has been standard practice to date Middle English literary texts through identifying topical allusions: references (however cryptic), to contemporary events, persons or debates. But despite Kail's vigorous alignment of individual poems to contemporary parliaments or other events, it is extremely difficult to date these Digby poems with certainty. Part of the problem lies in the axiomatic, generalised temper of so much of the verse. This is not to suggest that such a temper cannot be topical – and indeed, I shall go on to argue that it is – but topical allusions, if indeed they are present, are much more difficult to determine in poetry whose texture is not particular but universal. Much of Kail's chronological dating of the series can be seen to arise from the editorial desire (or indeed, the felt editorial duty), to 'dock' the poems to something else, to give them credible historical weight and backing. It is a desire that permeates the study of anonymous texts: the quest for persons, names, and place puts a stop to the unruly generation of possible meanings and safely anchors the text to an originary source.

Notes to the individual poems in this edition reference and challenge Kail's dating. In order to avoid duplication of material, I will discuss only a handful of examples here. Kail dates Poem 1 to Henry IV's first parliament in 1400 on the grounds of the poem's treatment of justices, p. x. The alignment misses the fact that these comments are generic (see note to Poem 1/156ff., and lines 73ff.). Further, Kail suggested that line 81, 'Goddis bowe of wratthe on vs was bent' was a reference to the pestilence which haunted the western and northern parts of the country in 1399 (*Poems*, p. xi). But, as is characteristic of the poet's recycling of lines, the line is substantially repeated: it has already been used in Poem 1 at line 69 (see note) and recurs in Poem 12/87 (see note). Kail argued that Poem 12 dates from Henry V's reign. Can we be certain that in Poem 1, God's wrath refers to the 1399 pestilence, whereas in Poem 12 it refers to the threat of internal division at the start of Henry V's reign? While it is not impossible for the same diction to have different topical resonance in two different contexts, the repetition of line 81,

---

[21] Gillespie, 'Moral and Penitential Lyrics', pp. 92–3.

[22] James Simpson, *Reform and Cultural Revolution* (Oxford: OUP, 2002) writes of the Digby sequence, 'A new edition of these crisp and intelligent poems is needed', p. 218, n. 50.

and the generic (and biblical) nature of the trope[23] make it extraordinarily difficult to assign a particular year to Poem 1 with any confidence.

In fact, it is hard to assign any of the Digby lyrics to the reign of Henry IV. In each case where Kail attempts to do this, there are grounds for challenging his interpretation. Take Poem 3. Kail, dated the lyric to 1401 because he saw lines 138–41 to be a reference to the 1401 statute *De Haeretico Comburendo* which made provision for the burning of heretics (Robbins, *Historical Poems* and Dean, *Political Writings*, follow his lead). Unfortunately, there is no mention of either heresy, or, for that matter, of burning. The lines are a close paraphrase of Romans 13:4, and their diction is reprised in many other poems of the sequence (see further note to Poem 3/138–41, and also headnote to Poem 4). A further problem with Kail's parliamentary datings is that many of the criticisms raised in assemblies during the first decades of the fifteenth century were generic and repeated. Kail dated Poem 8 to 1408–9 because of parallel criticisms of the clergy in the seventh and eighth parliaments of Henry IV, *Poems*, p. xiv. Kail has his dates muddled here (see headnote to Poem 8), but the more substantive problem is that the criticisms he identifies as originating in 1408–9 had already been raised in 1401, 1402, and were again voiced in 1410 (see headnote). The same problem arises with his dating of Poem 9 to 1410 because of parallels between the comments of the poem and the business of that parliament, particularly complaints about the circulation of bad coinage, clipping and cheating. It is certainly the case that many of the specific comments in this poem map more closely onto this meeting of parliament than of any other between 1401 and 1419. But the abuses raised in this parliament were not new, nor was this the last time that such views were voiced. More substantively, the criticisms are commonplaces of pastoral instruction literature, and given the penitential focus of the poem, might be more pertinently read as pastoral rather than political allusions (see notes to lines 49–68).

ii) *The spectral two Johns*

There are two Johns who haunt the Digby series, their ghosts serving to pin down particular poems to particular events and years. One is Sir John Oldcastle; the other is John the Fearless, the duke of Burgundy. Kail dated Poem 14 to the beginning of 1418 because 'it seems to contain some vague allusions to the fate of Sir John Oldcastle, Lord Cobham' (*Poems*, p. xx). But, as Paul Strohm observes, 'more things were imagined about and for John Oldcastle than he could ever have performed'.[24]

---

[23]   Psalms 7:12: 'If he turn not, he will whet his sword; he hath bent his bow, and made it ready.' This is quoted by the author of *Gesta Henrici Quinti* during the account of Agincourt; see Frank Taylor and John S. Roskell edd. and trans. *Gesta Henrici Quinti* (Oxford: Clarendon Press, 1975), pp. 94–5.

[24]   Paul Strohm, *Theory and the Premodern Text* (Minneapolis: University of Minnesota Press, 2000), p. 132.

Modern historical accounts of the career of Oldcastle which draw heavily on Walsingham's chronicle paint a picture of Sir John, parliamentarian (1410–13), and seasoned soldier, as an older friend of Prince Henry, alongside whom he had fought. In 1413, however, when Oldcastle was accused of involvement in Lollard heresy, Henry, now king, had no option but to give Archbishop Arundel leave to proceed against Oldcastle for heresy. Oldcastle was imprisoned in the Tower, and, on examination took the opportunity to give a robust account of his heretical views. He was excommunicated and handed over to secular power for punishment, but managed to escape in October 1413 and went on to head a rebellion in early 1414. The uprising was successfully quashed and its participants summarily punished. Oldcastle evaded capture until November 1417, and after spending a brief time in the Tower under heavy guard, in December, he was sentenced to immediate execution and hanged.[25] The fascination, both medieval and modern, with details of the story can be traced both to a desire to present a scenario of Lollard menace successfully destroyed, and to a desire to psychologise Henry V, a new king who was shocked by the revelation that his friend was a heretic, and who was forced, reluctantly, to punish his old chum almost before the crown had settled firmly on his head.[26]

So, what of Kail's attraction to these events? These are the lines in question from Poem 14:

> Ʒif þou be kyngis chaunceller,
> Kepe þe crowne hool in stat;
> Ʒif þou be kyngis counselere,
> Loke no stones þerof abate.
> Ʒif oþer wolde make þe kyng þe hate,
> Or falsed ouer trouþe go,
> Tak þy leue, and kisse þe ʒate,
> Eche man be war er hym be wo.

(Poem 14/9–16)

---

[25] Account drawn from C.T. Allmand, *Henry V* (London: Methuen, 1992), pp. 294–303. Cf. Thomas Walsingham, *St Albans Chronicle*, ed. V.H. Galbraith (Oxford: OUP, 1937), pp. 70–89 and *Historia Anglicana*, ed. H.T. Riley (London: Longman, Roberts and Green, 1864), pp. 279–99 and pp. 327–8. See also Taylor and Roskell, *Gesta Henrici Quinti*, pp. 2–11.

[26] See, for example, Allmand's comment on Henry's reaction to the news that Oldcastle had confessed to owning heretical tracts: 'the king was deeply shocked by this revelation', and 'it was agreed that the king, as his friend, should be asked to see what he could do' (Allmand, *Henry V*, p. 295); and on Oldcastle's first imprisonment: 'whether out of friendship's sake or because, as Walsingham wrote, he did not want a sinner lost without some effort being made on his behalf, Henry granted Oldcastle forty days to consider his position. It was as far as he could go' (p. 296); and on the punishment of the rebels: 'these were the acts of a man who felt in command of events, who could act without vindictiveness in the hope of restoring normality as soon as possible' (p. 300).

Þe wyseman his sone forbed
Masouncraft, and all clymbyng,
And shipman craft for perile of dede,
And preuey in counseil be ney3 no kyng;
For his mysrulyng þou my3t hyng.
Þat shep my3te grese vnder þy to,
To fli3e to hy3e treste not þy wyng;
Eche man be war er hym be wo.

(Poem 14/41–8)

As the notes to individual lines indicate, these are sentiments that can be paralleled closely in Wisdom literature. That, in itself, of course, does not rule out the possibility that the poet has encoded topical resonance in timeless sagacity. But what of the precise diction in relation to 1419, the year to which Kail assigned the poem? He says this of lines 9–12, 'some advices of the 14th poem seem to involve a censure of the folly of a nobleman, who must have been a confidant and counsellor of the King (cf. ll. 9–12). He must have lost the favour of the prince by the tricks of his enemies (l. 10). From line 14 we may conclude that he underrated the intrigues of his adversaries, and that he trusted too much to the protection and to the benevolence of the sovereign. If the last stanza but one may be thought to refer to the attempt on the king's life, we have several circumstances which apply to Sir John Oldcastle. Even the kind of his death may be hinted at in line 45 *et seq.*' (*Poems*, p. xx). The slippage in the modality of this statement (propositional imperative 'must's yielding to conditional 'may's), is one indication of the fragility of the identification. Another is that the diction of the poem has nothing to do with benevolence, protection and favour (the Oldcastle/Henry friendship romance has seeped in here), and everything to do with the king's *officers*: his counsellors and chancellors, performing their duties correctly to defend the crown. The poem proceeds to warn sections of the political community in turn to discharge the duties of their responsibilities. The advice to shun intrigue and secret personal feuds is not identical to uprisings, public executions and religious dissent. The reference to hanging in line 45 is preceded by the king's 'mysrulyng'. If this is a reference to Oldcastle's hanging in 1417 it seems very odd for the poet to have described the heretical knight's execution as the result of a bad judgement on the part of the king, especially given the religious sensibilities of the poet (see section 5). There is a further issue. The diction of lines 9–16 recalls that of Poem 12:

3if sercle, and floures, and riche stones
Were eche a pece fro oþer flet,
Were þe crowne broken ones,
Hit were ful hard a3en to knet.

Auyse ȝow, er ȝe suffre þat fit;
Amende ȝe, þat mende mown.
ȝe þat ben wysest, cast ȝoure wyt:
Stonde wiþ þe kyng to kepe þe crowne.

(Poem 12/41–8)

A man myȝte be forborn
Fer fro a kynges place,
Wolde make a kyng to be forsworn
To lette þe lawe; it most not passe,
And make hym wene þat he grace,
And holy in condicioun,
And mayntene hym in his trespace,
While he pykeþ þe stones out of þe crowne.

(Poem 12/59–66)

As I shall argue below (and indeed, as Kail did), Poem 12 heralds a new king at
Easter; a correlation which points towards Henry V's coronation in 1413. The poem
calls for a robust defence of the crown and for each person to discharge their duties.
Lines 41–8 of Poem 12 are sufficiently close to those lines 9–14 of Poem 14 to make
it very difficult to assign one poem to 1413, and the other to 1418. I can see no
compelling evidence to date Poem 14 to 1418; in fact, I think it is impossible to date
it with any certainty at all. Lines 57–64 of Poem 12 are another matter. In contrast
to a poet such as Hoccleve, who unambiguously condemns Oldcastle's actions,[27] the
Digby poet is conspicuously non-specific about threats to Henry at the start of his
reign. But if the ghost of Oldcastle is to be found in the Digby poems, then this
stanza is as good a bet as any. It sketches a scenario of the danger of law being
set aside were a man to persuade the king of his holy condition, and instead of
being punished, being supported in his continual transgression while continuing
to encroach on royal authority. If we care to insert the cherished portrait of the
anguished young king being forced to punish his unholy friend in 1413, then it
could be hung in this stanza. Robbins certainly thought it could (see notes to
Poem 12/59–66).

The other John whose death has been used to date the poems is John the Fearless,
duke of Burgundy. In 1407 he instigated the murder of Louis, duke of Orléans,
the brother of the French king. Both Kail (*Poems*, p. xvii) and Robbins (*Historical
Poems*, p. 271), argue that Poem 12 refers to this event:

---

[27]   *Remonstrance Against Sir John Oldcastle*, in Thomas Hoccleve, *Minor Poems*, edd.
F.J. Furnivall and I. Gollancz, revised Jerome Mitchell and A.I. Doyle (EETS ES 61 and 73,
1970), pp. 8–24. See also notes to Digby Poem 13/145–52.

Loke of þyng þat ȝe bygynne:
Caste before how it wole ende:
Gostly, bodyly, what mowe ȝe wynne,
Eche man destroyȝe his best frend.
So dede Flaundres, how dede it wende,
Of noblay, þey han lore þe sown.

(Poem 12/81–6)

The diction needs to be observed carefully here. Is it really possible that the poet could have thought that Louis was John's best friend? Attention to the precise phrasing might give us pause for thought before emphatically claiming these lines as a topical allusion to Louis' murder. In the fourteenth and early fifteenth centuries there was almost constant turmoil in Flanders. As David Nicholas remarks, 'the chronology of military actions and civil discords is a numbing list of virtually annual foreign attacks or serious internal violence'.[28] There was civil war (1387–93) between the rival towns of Ghent and Bruges, which began from a dispute over canal construction in Bruges,[29] but there was also internal feuding within the various guilds of the towns. In 1407, following disturbances in Bruges within the weavers' guilds, a regulation was passed to control the use of banners used by the guilds in an attempt to control incitements to violence.[30] Poem 16 of the Digby series refers to 'craft' rising against 'craft' in its enumeration of the follies of Flanders (see note to line 60). The reference in Poem 13 to how those in Flanders destroy their best friends seems, to my mind, much more relevant to internal division and internecine artisanal feuds than to the murder of one royal prince by another from a different political dynasty.

The consequences of Louis' murder are relevant, however, to the topical resonance of the Digby poems, for it set France on the road to civil war, which eventually broke out in the winter of 1410–11. Following the assassination, hostilities between the Burgundians and the Orléanists intensified. Both parties sought help from England to bolster their cause. Between 1410 and 1414 there was a series of pacts and counter pacts between the various parties in whose negotiation both Henry IV and his son were directly involved. In 1412 an agreement was made between Henry IV, represented by his four sons, and the Armagnac faction at Bourges, which guaranteed to restore Aquitaine to the English, in exchange for which Henry was to defend the Armagnacs against the dukes of Burgundy. This prompted John, duke of Burgundy, to march against the Orléanists, and the alliance with England was renounced. A successful expedition against the French, which included the dukes of

---

[28]   David Nicholas, *Medieval Flanders* (London: Longman, 1992), p. 209.
[29]   Nicholas, *Medieval Flanders*, pp. 227–31.
[30]   Nicholas, *Medieval Flanders*, p. 342.

Clarence, York and Thomas Beaufort, resulted in the French dukes being anxious to buy the English out with considerable sums of money and treasure handed over.[31] In 1413 the English opened discussions both with the Burgundians and the Orléanists; the details remain obscure, but a series of truces was negotiated. On 8 October 1413 representatives of Charles VI received commissions to treat with Henry V, which led to a truce dated 24 January 1414 to operate for twelve months from 2 February. Until the summer Henry undertook further discussion both with the French king and with the duke of Burgundy. In July a detailed agreement between English ambassadors and the duke of Burgundy resulted in John the Fearless agreeing to support Henry V's claim to the French crown.[32] In 1415, on the eve of sailing on the Agincourt expedition, Henry dispatched copies of the 1412 Bourges agreement to the emperor and to the Council of Constance, 'so that all Christendom should know of the injuries that the French had inflicted on him'.[33] Poem 13/121–8 inveighs against truces and treaties in the context of urging military action against France, and it is possible that these remarks are influenced by knowledge of these negotiations.

Both Kail (*Poems*, p. xxi) and Robbins (*Historical Poems*, pp. 271–2) see Poem 16 of the series to refer to the murder of John of Burgundy by followers of Charles VI's son in 1419.[34] The poem is unambiguously about Flanders, as the first line emphatically declares: 'Loke how Flaundres doþ fare wiþ his folyhede!' (Poem 16/1). But, is it about the death of John? Kail writes (*Poems*, p. xxi), 'John of Burgundy lost not only his lordship (l. 62), but also his life: which was regarded as a punishment for the assassination of the Duke of Orleans (l. 63 *et seq*.)'. This is an interpretation that has been followed by commentators. Scattergood argues that this poem is 'a critical and moralizing review of the career of John the Fearless' (*Politics and Poetry*, p. 69). These are the lines in question:

> Here lord had part of þe foly þey were wounden ynne,
> Forthy he les his lordshipe and here fraunchise raft,
> Here enemys lawhen hem to skorne and seyn, for synne,
> Of here banere of grace God broken haþ þe shaft.
>
> (Poem 16/61–4)

Is death here? Line 62 comments that the lord of Flanders lost his 'lordshipe'. This is not necessarily equivalent to losing life. If 'lordshipe' be understood as

---

[31] E.F. Jacob, *The Fifteenth Century, 1399–1485* (Oxford: Clarendon Press, 1961), pp. 112–15; Walsingham, *St Albans Chronicle*, pp. 62–4.

[32] Jacob, *Fifteenth Century*, pp. 135–40.

[33] Taylor and Roskell, *Gesta Henrici Quinti*, p. 17.

[34] A modern account of the details is in Allmand, *Henry V*, p. 135. See also R. Vaughan, *John the Fearless: The Growth of Burgundian Power* (Woodbridge: Boydell, 2002).

'the position of a king or leader' (*Middle English Dictionary* (*MED*) 'lordship(e)' (*n*.); 3c), then Kail's reading is possible. But to my mind it is much more likely that 'lordshipe' means 'kingly power or authority' (*MED* 3b (cf. 1b)). The lord lost his lordly standing and Flanders lost their 'franchise', i.e. nobility of character (*MED*, 'fraunchise' (*n*.); 2a) through his actions. That their enemies laughed them to scorn (l. 63, and cf. note to Poem 12/147) suggests that the situation in Flanders is used in this poem to mock their reputation as a result of the civil dissent caused by their leader. Although Scattergood comments that the poem is a review of the career of John, he is closer to the mark when he observes how other poets 'saw the French situation as an example of what trouble civil disorder could cause in a kingdom which was badly led' (*Politics and Poetry*, p. 47). He quotes:

> Take hede how synne hath chastysed frauns
> Whan he was in hys fayrest kynde,
> How þat flaundrys hath myschaunys,
> ffor cause þe bysom ledeth þe blynde.
>
> 'The Bisson Leads the Blynde', ll. 69–72[35]

This poem, like Lydgate's 'A Ballade, in Despyte of the Flemynges',[36] is written later than Digby Poem 16, but what they all share is the use of 'dissolute Flanders' as a foil against which to counsel good government in England. Flanders is the glaring example of a kingdom gone wrong. It is important that the Digby poem is titled 'A *remembraunce* of Lij *folyes*' (my emphasis). It is a recollection of foreign civil disorder to sound a note of warning about contemporary conditions in England. The word 'folyes' is also important. Rather than an account of the career of one man, the poem is an example of the 'catalogue of fools' tradition of writing.[37] Invective combines with moralising to hold up the follies of Flanders as a mirror to English rule. As David Wallace has shown so trenchantly in his analysis of references to Flanders in the works of Chaucer, Flanders was a discourse, one which spoke 'most eloquently of the anxieties and desires of its English authors'.[38] The Digby Flanders poem (and the reference in Poem 13) are examples of exactly this discourse. If the poet is interested in recounting any details of John the Fearless, then he does so, not out of desire for a human portrait, but out of anxiety that the civil dissent in France will be a scenario that will happen in England. As I shall argue in Section 6, the social temper

---

[35]   Robbins, *Historical Poems*, 127–30/69–72.

[36]   In John Lydgate, *The Minor Poems of John Lydgate, Part II*, ed. H.N. MacCracken (EETS ES OS 192, 1934), pp. 600–1.

[37]   See B. Swain, *Fools and Folly during the Middle Ages and the Renaissance* (University of Columbia Press: New York, 1932), ch. 2.

[38]   David Wallace, 'In Flaundres', *SAC* 19 (1997), pp. 63–91; at p. 64.

of the Digby sequence is saturated with worry about internal division and a desire for harmonious wholeness. Poem 16 is a scathing account of the political nightmare which the poet does not want visited on English shores. Focus on John of Burgundy's death has distorted the political impact of the poem, and most probably, moved the compositional date of the sequence later than the majority of the poems suggest.

iii) *'Goddis champioun': topical allusion, or allusive topicality?*
Only one historical person is named in the series of poems:

> To Fraunce kyng Edward had queryle:
> Hit was his kynde heritage,
> And ʒe han þe same style,
> Wiþ armes of þe selue parage.
> And ʒit ʒoure querell dede neuere aswage
> Þat God haþ shewed in ʒoure manhede;
> On see, or land, on eche vyage,
> In dent of swerd God demed ʒoure dede.
>
> (Poem 13/113–20)

The 'kyng Edward' must be Edward III. 'Kynde heritage' (l. 114), asserts a natural right to the French crown. Edward's claim to the French throne rested on the rights of his mother Isabel, French wife of Edward II. The French sought to deny this claim on the base of Salic law which allegedly barred the succession of females to the throne.[39] But to which present king are these lines addressed? Isolated from other poems, it would not be impossible to see them as directed at Henry VI; in the context of the series as a whole, however, this seems unlikely. The address comes in a poem which urges the king to strengthen his borders and marches at home before making war on his enemy. The hostility towards truces in this poem has already been discussed, and suggests reference to the protracted negotiations between the Burgundians, Orléanists and the English in the years between 1410 and 1414. As the notes to this poem indicate, the lyric combines exhortations to end lawlessness with an unequivocal call to arms against France. There is no mention of any English victories against France in the sequence of poems; and given the triumphalist accounts of Harfleur and Agincourt in contemporary chronicles, such absence is significant.[40] All this suggests that the poet addresses Henry V at some point before the end of 1414. That the poet traces the king's lineage back to Edward III, stressing that he has the 'same style' and equal arms, might also be

---

[39]   Jacob, *Fifteenth Century*, p. 137.
[40]   Taylor and Roskell, *Gesta Henrici Quinti*, pp. 33–5, 82–103; and Walsingham, *Historia Anglicana*, II.305–15.

pointed. It confirms Henry as the true heir of Edward. Henry's father was son of John of Gaunt, Edward's third son. The deposed Richard II was the son of Edward, the Black Prince, first son of Edward III. Richard had left no heir to trouble the new Lancastrian kings, but Edmund, earl of March, could trace his ancestry back to Edward III via his grandmother Philippa, daughter of Edward's second son Lionel, duke of Clarence. Edward III's fourth son, Edmund, duke of York, had two sons, Edward, duke of York and Richard, earl of Cambridge. The earl of Cambridge, was of course, executed in 1415 for his part in the Southampton plot against Henry, though Poem 13 was probably written earlier.[41] The lines in Poem 13 on Henry's arms may simply be part of the assertion that he has a natural claim to the French crown; they may also, however, assert his legitimate hold on the English one.

Henry's crown is a topic that held some fascination for the poet. The poem which precedes the calls for war against France is a poem whose title 'God kepe oure kyng and saue the croune' stands as an accurate summary of its concerns.

> Glade in God, call hom 30ure herte!
> In ioye and blisse, 30ure merþe encres,
> And kepe Goddis lawe in querte.
> Þes holy tyme, lete sorwe ases;
> Among oure self, God sende vs pes.
> Þerto, eche man be boun
> To letten fooles of here res;
> Stonde wiþ þe kyng, mayntene þe croun.
>
> (Poem 12/1–8)

Poem 12 caps a liturgical sequence of poems which starts with the Lenten penitence of Poem 9 and moves to Easter in Poems 11 and 12. The present deixis of 'þes holy tyme' (l. 4) suggests a recent Easter. The calls for unity and peace 'among oure self' has both a theological inflection (see note to this stanza), and a political dimension. The refrain throughout the poem to 'mayntene þe croun' is bolstered by exhortations to all members of the political community to discharge their duties honourably and to avoid internal disputes. The poem concludes with an appeal to God to keep 'oure comely kyng' in his protection, and 'saue þe croun' (ll. 151–2). The combination of Easter and the king's crown must allude to Henry V. Henry's coronation took place on 9 April 1413, two weeks before Easter, which fell that year on 23 April. The coronations of the only other contenders for the allusion – Henry IV and Henry VI – fall well out of this time frame.[42] The poet

---

[41]   Allmand, *Henry V*, recounts the details of this episode, pp. 74–8.

[42]   Henry IV was crowned in September 1399 and Henry VI was crowned king of England in November 1422 and king of France in December 1430.

seizes on the theological significance of Easter as a time of rejoicing and corporate inclusion to herald what must have been a recently crowned new monarch.

There is another poem in the sequence which might allude to Henry's coronation within an Easter context. Poem 23 is an extended orthodox defence of the sacrament of the Eucharist. It contains the following stanza:

> A day is mad of solempnyte:
> Of þis table first ordynaunce is worschipful tolde;
> In þis newe kynges table now knowe we
> Newe estren endeþ þe olde;
> Newe thyng dryueþ old þyng fro his degre,
> Out of mynde, þe lasse of tolde;
> So soþfast sunne, by hys pousté,
> Dryueþ awey shadewe and striȝeþ colde.

> (Poem 23/25–32)

Once again, we appear to have a timely deictic reference to 'þis newe kyng' (l. 27) within the context of celebrating the solemn day of Easter (see note to line 23). The poet has created an elaborate political and theological pun in the correlation between the 'sothefaste sunne', that is Christ, conquering death and bringing new life, and the true son of Henry IV, the powerful new Henry, bringer of a glorious and fresh political dawn. 'Sunne' (l. 31) puns on the Son of God, the son of Henry IV, the natural sun, and the heraldic sun badge of Henry V. Henry's accession is paralleled to the Resurrection. The spiritual rebirth promised by Easter parallels the political rebirth promised by Henry's accession. The body of Christ in the Eucharistic feast suggests the political body incorporated in new hope and new joy.

To claim this topical allusion conclusively is problematic. Poem 23 is a metrical paraphrase of Aquinas's hymn 'Lauda Sion' which was composed for the feast of Corpus Christi. These are the lines of the hymn which correspond to the stanza just quoted:

> Dies enim solemnis agitur,
> in qua mensae prima recolitur
> huius institutio.
> In hac mensa novi Regis,
> novum Pascha novae legis,
> phase vetus terminat.
> Vetustatem novitas,
> umbram fugat veritas,
> noctem lux eliminat.

[The solemn day is enacted on which the original institution of this table is recalled. In this table of the new King the new Easter of the new law brings to an end the old Passover. Newness puts to flight oldness, truth puts to flight the shadows, light removes the night.]

('Lauda Sion', ll. 16–24)

'Þis newe kyng' is a direct translation from the Latin. The light and dark imagery of rejuvenation, and the new law of Christian Easter replacing the old are the words of Aquinas, not the Digby poet. The point of Aquinas's words is resolutely theological: the sacrament of the Eucharist replaces the Paschal feast celebrated in the Old Testament. The chief addition made by the Digby poet is in the elaboration of the light and dark imagery, and the introduction of the 'sunne'. The problem of interpretation here is whether the existence of the source text cancels out the possibility of political reference, or whether the poet saw the political resonance of the text he paraphrased. Is line 30 metrical padding, or a pointer to the contemporary political significance of Easter's new king? Poem 12 has already made the correlation between Easter and Henry; might the poet's addition of the polysemous pun have reestablished the connection? To my mind, the presence of a topical allusion could be argued either way. The allusive topicality of the poem as a whole is perhaps more substantial than the possible topical reference. The expansion of Aquinas's lines is of a similar temper to the description of Henry's coronation in the *Versus Rhythmici de Henrico Quinto*.[43] The identity of this work's author remains elusive, but internal references suggest that he was a Benedictine monk, and probably a member of the king's household. The description is not Eucharistic in tenor, but it does make comparison between Henry and Christ:

Te Regem vero Deus elegit, Deus unxit,
Et regum numero te Christi Passio junxit.

[God has indeed chosen you King, God has anointed you, and the passion of Christ has united you with the number of the Kings.]

(ll. 55–6)

The author gives the precise date of the coronation and stresses the radiance of the occasion. The glory of the table had never before been more splendid and Henry was like an angel:

---

[43]   *Versus Rhythmici de Henrico Quinto* in C.A. Cole ed., *Memorials of Henry V, King of England* (London: Longman, Brown, Green, 1858), pp. 63–75.

Curia regalis micat ornatu radiante,
Gloria mensalis non splendidior fuit ante.
Angelus in specie residebas, Rex decoratus,
Illa quippe die vultus tibi valde beatus.
Denique quod Christi laudi, quod Regis honori,
Rex bone, fecisti, simul et quod plebis amori.

[The royal court glitters with radiant adornment, the glory of the table was not more brilliant before. You sat an angel in appearance, an adorned king, indeed your face on that day was very blessed. In sum, what you did for the praise of Christ, what you did for the honour of the King, good king, and at the same time what you did for love of the people.]

(ll. 63–8)

The precise diction of *Versus Rhythmici* is not identical to that of the Digby poem, but both are forged out of common cultural materials. If Poem 23 does contain a clever reference to Henry V, it is significant that it is embedded in a paraphrase of a poem from the liturgy. The combination of the liturgical and the political is seen also at the end of *Versus Rhythmici*. The work concludes with a prayer for the king which is framed by excerpts from the liturgy of the nocturnal hours and the hours of the Virgin. As I shall argue in the next section, the strong presence of the liturgy in the Digby poems is politically significant.[44]

What might, then, be concluded from this examination of possible dateable references in the sequence? Poem 12, does, I think, point unambiguously towards Henry V, and to the early years of his reign. There is no other firm identification in the other poems to historical events or personages that can be conclusively established beyond 1414. But over and above the decoding of topical reference, the materials of the sequence of lyrics as a whole resonate profoundly with issues and actions of the early years of Henry V. While, in some ways, to suggest a date of 1413–14 for these poems represents an even narrower 'docking' of the poems than Kail's parliamentary and personage allusions, the twin theological and political importance of the series fits so comfortably into such a timeframe that it is hard (for this editor at least), to resist the desire to propose it. To substantiate this claim, the next section discusses the religious sensibilities of the lyrics.

---

[44]   The theological treatment of Henry V's coronation in Taylor and Roskell, *Gesta Henrici Quinti* is discussed in the final section of the introduction.

5. Religious sensibilities

i) *Heresy*

Throughout the sequence, the focus falls steadfastly on bolstering devotional orthodoxy within the individual and within the institutional church. Heresy is mentioned three times, but curiously the references are topically deracinated. Poem 1 characterises as 'heretikes' and out of the 'crede' (l. 126) those false thieves who want their heaven here on earth and then pay for it dearly amid the punishments of hell. In order to understand why God deals out mercy or punishment, man is urged to 'knowe thy self, loue God and drede' (l. 128). Poem 7 asks why human beings are bent on wickedness? The answer is denial of the existence of God, refusal to believe in heaven, purgatory or hell and 'anoþer heresy þere is/As best wiþoute soule to die' (ll. 79–80). The final reference to heresy is similarly vague:

> Thow may not knowe a cristen man:
> Þouȝ þu here hym say his crede,
> Þe ten comaudementis tan.
> [Þat] speke and do not þe dede,
> Ne serue God in loue and drede,
> Is heretyk out of fay.
> After ȝoure werkis ressauye þy mede;
> Þerof mon be no iour delay.
>
> (Poem 8/81–8)

None of these statements offers a conventional definition of heresy. The comments are curiously anodyne: the refusal to obey, or to believe, fundamental Christian teachings such as the existence of God. Particularly striking is the absence of any reference to the heresy which posed such a powerful challenge to institutional church authority in the later fourteenth and early fifteenth centuries. The lyrics make no explicit mention of Wycliffism, Lollardy, or any of their champions. Nothing in these lines suggests that the church was under attack from the dissemination of precise heretical ideas, ideas considered so dangerous that successive legislation had been passed in order to suppress them.[45] Rather, the references to heresy suggest that individual souls are in peril if they wilfully ignore basic Christian teaching.

One explanation, of course, for these anodyne comments is that the poems

---

[45]   The 1401 statute *De Heretico Comburendo* made provision for the burning of heretics. Archbishop Arundel's 1409 *Constitutions* attempted draconion censorship of heterodox views in its attempted policing of preaching, translation and the owning of books: see D. Wilkins ed., *Conciliae Magnae Britanniae et Hiberniae* (London, 1737), III.314–19.

are written after Archbishop Arundel's 1409 *Constitutions* and, as a result, are guarded in their expression of religious doctrine lest they breach the articles of this legislation. As is becoming increasingly clear, however, although the terms of the *Constitutions* provided for tight censorship of the expression of religious views, discussion of matters ecclesiological and theological was not uniformly stifled, nor could discussion take place only in code.[46] Further, an explanation for the deafening silence about Lollardy in the series based on censorship crumbles in the face of the outspoken denunciation of 'the sect' in various works written at the same time, or later than the poems. The *Gesta Henrici Quinti* opens with an explicit account of how Henry quashed the Oldcastle rebellion.[47] The *Versus Rhythmici* labels the Lollards as a 'gens perfida, frauda repleta' (l. 153) who attempted to plot the death of 'Henricum Quintum Regem' (l. 157) but the king, the warrior of the church, protector of the nation (l. 173), saved his people. Thomas Elmham's *Liber Metricus de Henrico V* identifies John Oldcastle with the 'Great Dragon' of Revelation 12:4 whose tail drew the third part of the stars to heaven: 'the satellite of hell … the Heresiarch or Arch-Lollard, John Oldcastle, whose stench is noted to have ascended most horribly to the nostrils of the Catholics even like that of a dunghill.'[48] Lines 31–49 of the poem present the foremost kingly duty of the king as preserver and defender of the true faith. These explicit statements of Henry's duty and resolve in combating named enemies of Holy Church are also found in Hoccleve's verse.[49]

The preacher of the macaronic sermons contained in MS Bodley 649, sermons which, as the appendix shows, have very much in common with the Digby lyrics, both in terms of their preoccupations and their temper, excoriates the perfidious practices of the Lollards in no uncertain terms. Lollards are 'the soldiers of Satan' and 'the messengers of the devil'. Lollardy itself is 'an accursed tornado

---

[46]   Nicholas Love's, *The Mirror of the Blessed Life of Jesus Christ* was written for Archbishop Arundel: see the edition by Michael G. Sargent (Exeter: University of Exeter Press, 2004), p. 7. The effects of Arundel's measures are discussed by Nicholas Watson, 'Censorship and Cultural Change in Late-Medieval England: Vernacular Theology, the Oxford Translation Debate, and Arundel's *Constitutions* of 1409', *Speculum* 70 (1995), 822–64; and for the view that robust criticism of the church was still possible post 1409, James Simpson, 'Saving Satire after Arundel's *Constitutions*: John Audelay's "Marcol and Solomon" in Helen Barr and Ann M. Hutchison, edd., *Text and Controversy from Wyclif to Bale: Essays in Honour of Anne Hudson* (Turnhout: Brepols, 2005), pp. 387–404.

[47]   Taylor and Roskell, *Gesta Henrici Quinti*, pp. 1–11.

[48]   Translation drawn from Cole's *Henry V*, introduction, p. xlix. The text reads, 'ortumque et occasum capitis jam confracti Draconis, cum cauda post se trahentis tertiam partem stellarum – illius videlicet, satellitis infernalis heresiarche, sive archi-Lollardi, Johannis de Veteri Castro (cujus putredo ad nares Catholicorum horribiliter ascendisse notatur', p. 82.

[49]   'O verray sustenour/And piler of our feith, and werreyour/Ageyn the heresies bittir galle', Hoccleve, *Minor Poems*, V.12–14, cf. Poem 4.

... generated by diabolical suggestions within a cloud of pride' and 'serpentine poison of hell'.[50] Why then, when closely contemporary writers are so blatant in their condemnation of the Lollards should the Digby poems fall so curiously silent? The answer is that the religious materials out of which the lyrics are crafted provide such a robust challenge and rebuttal of Wycliffite ideas that there is no need to mention dissident views by name. Rather than turning his fire on those who attack the church from outside, the preoccupation of the Digby poet is to rebuild the church from within. Rather than heaping burning coals on the head of the enemy, and thereby furnishing it with discursive space, the Digby poet ignores the foes of the church altogether. The sequence of lyrics performs, if you like, a kind of textual excommunication. There is no explicit space given to the Lollards within the walls of the lyrics. Instead, the poet builds a reformed church without dissident help; a church built out of penitence, sacramentalism, liturgy and purification.

ii) *Penance and devotion*

The whole sequence creates a robustly reformed institutional church, with the dispensation of penance as its founding principle.[51] The sequence opens with a fierce enjoinder to each person to know themselves, love God, and fear him, and concludes with a metrical paraphrase of the nine lessons and responses of the Office of the Dead. The sequence does not offer comfortable reading: there are frequent reminders of the fragility of the world and of human existence. The world is but a cherry fair, transitory, and a place where everyone, kings and the poor, must face up to their mortality and give reckoning to God (Poem 3/145–52). One day man is alive, the next day dead (Poem 4/198). 'Your life is but as a wind,' says the narrator in Poem 9; 'when it has blown its full, you will be forgotten. Therefore make your peace with God' (ll. 25–32). 'Don't be too proud in your prosperity; you don't know how soon you will have less. Don't be too sure of your health; you don't know how soon you will fall into sickness. Death claims each man for his own' (Poem 5/49–54). 'Think you will die, and you don't know when. Your plight is precarious, therefore fear and tremble. God will come on Doomsday and judge everyone according to

---

[50]   Patrick J. Horner, ed., *A Macaronic Sermon Collection from Late Medieval England: Oxford MS Bodley 649* (Toronto: PIMS, 2006), pp. 140; 84, 302–4, 236.

[51]   In many ways, the lyrics can be seen to take up the project of reforming the church that fails so cataclysmically in *Piers Plowman*. This is not to suggest that the lyrics are a direct response to Langland's poem, but that in their placing after *Piers* in Digby, they can be seen to provide a radical reformist remedy to the catastrophic finale of the preceding poem. If the central effort of *Piers* is to imagine the construction of a reformed church with the dispensation of penance as its legitimising cornerstone, then that effort implodes irretrievably at the end; see James Simpson, 'Grace Abounding: Evangelical Centralization and the End of *Piers Plowman*', *YLS* 14 (2000), 49–73.

their works. The good run to the bliss of heaven; the wicked shall burn in Hell in endless torment. Death shall feed them' (Poem 22/57–64).

Fear and abjection are the poet's besetting themes. The reader of these poems has the terror of judgement thumped home (Poem 7/18; 8/102, 10/189, 24/97–104). Readers are enjoined to think on their sins, and to reflect on what they have done since they were born (Poem 22/41). Time and again they are reminded that each deadly sin is a deadly knife (Poem 7/105; 21/127) and not to sin out of presumption. Everything is numbered in God's sight, even the least step (Poem 1/134). Nothing can be hidden from God (Poem 1/95; 4/153-4). Humankind is nothing more than a stinking mess 'sulpid in sin' (Poem 11/74; 21/105–6). The body is worms' meat, a sack of sin (Poem 7/5/160), a description to which the poet was much attracted. Think deep in your heart, says the narrator of Poem 22, of what matter you were formed. You were made out of filthy seed and entered the world through the gateway of sin. I know no fouler filth then when you were fed inside your mother. You were brought out in a sack of filth, in horrible wretchedness and stinking sin (Poem 22/1–8). It comes as no surprise that the poet expands the lines from the Office of the Dead in Poem 24; the speaker says to stink and rottenness, 'you are my father and mother', and, to the worms, 'you are my brother and sister' (ll. 267–71).

This penitential severity is accompanied by exhortations to reflect on human guilt. Woven into the sequence are devotional lyrics which offer searing meditation on the agony of Christ's passion and human complicity in his suffering as the consequence of sin. In Poem 10, Christ speaks directly to the reader: 'have you any notion of the torment I suffered at the hands of the cruel Jews in order to release your souls of darkness? I suffered death and harrowed Hell … Can you tell me whether I might do more; and yet while I am your friend, you are my foe. Where I make peace, you make discord; where I love, you hate, and stick me outside the gate' (ll. 57–70). 'Despite all my suffering, you still revisit your sin and dwell therein' (l. 80). Man's ingratitude to Christ through persistent sinning is conveyed through graphic and crisp repointing of common devotional tropes. The spear wound in Christ's side becomes a sword that pierces through Christ's heart and the spleen. Christ reminds the reader, 'I hadde þe poynt, and ȝe þe hylt' (ll. 26–7). The spear wound is then conflated with the fatal bite of the apple in the Garden of Eden to produce the densely imaginative and theological accusation, 'ȝe boten an appyl þat þirled my brest' (l. 32).

Meditation on Christ's passion does modulate into a gentler key in other lyrics. In the Easter lyric of Poem 11, Christ warns the reader that they will have to give account on the Day of Judgement for his sacrifice (here, imagined as a loan (l. 110)). At the same time, however, the wounds borne by Christ and his bearing of human sins in heart and thought brought about reconciliation between God and humankind (ll. 101–4). Poem 17 urges the reader to love God on account of the great love he showed humankind in his Passion. The lyric closes with the traditional image of Christ's body as a charter: the parchment as Christ's skin written with the red blood of his wounds, and sealed with true love to guarantee the heritage of human salvation. The name of Jesus is likened to a plant called 'trewe loue'. Its leaves were the hands and feet of Christ and human love was to him so dear that his heart was pierced with a spear. If a soul that is sick applies that plant, then spiritual health will be restored (Poem 17/185–92).

Mercy is promised – but at a cost. Pithily put in Poem 17, 'And we þenke to amende, he profreþ to kys' (l. 15). For all his extended reflection on the starkness of human abjection, the poet does show us a God who actively wants to redeem his defouled creation. For that to happen, humankind must actively make amends for its sin. Reconciliation with God is only possible through penance. The reader is enjoined to make amends or else to suffer the consequences (Poem 9/5/115/135; 17/84/178; 19/28; 24/329/342). Repentance is urged in the most fervent tones (Poem 17/75/95; 19/52/74). As penance, the reader is advised to perform the seven works of mercy and offer alms to the poor and needy (Poem 7/69/72/89/114; 9/5; 17/95 and 19/96), and to give account to God for misdeeds by reckoning up sins before God does his own accounting on Doomsday (Poem 1/29/35; 3/151; 7/83; 9/92; 10/196/210; 11/110; 21/148 and 24/231). The God of the Digby poems is a fierce God; but the hope of mercy is proffered to those who are truly contrite and actively penitent.

iii) *Defence of the sacraments*
All this may suggest a focus on individual penance and merit, but it is a crucial aspect of the religious sensibility of these lyrics that the practice of penance is rooted inexorably within the institutional church. Poem 9 is an orthodox defence of the sacrament of confession.

> This holy tyme make 30w clene;
> Burnysche bry3t 30ure soules blake!
> Fro 30w to God, let þe prest be mene
> To do penaunce and synnes forsake,
> Wiþ almes dede amendes make.
> And repentaunce may grace gete,
> In goode werkis wysely wake,
> And wiþ God of pes Y rede 3e trete.
>
> (Poem 9/1–8)

Kail interpreted 'holy tyme' as a reference to Easter, but the obligation for each parishioner to make confession to their parish priest specifies *before* Easter. As *Speculum Sacerdotale* explains: there are four Lenten seasons in the year; three are optional, but not the 'one *afore* Paske, the whiche is comen to *alle men*' (my emphasis), p. 74/24–5.[52] Far from an Easter poem, this is a series of injunctions to repent before receipt of the Eucharist on Easter Sunday, and a call to penitence which can be paralleled in many pastoral and confession manuals.[53]

The diction is more pointed than a call for penitence, however, simply because one is foul and doomed to die. There is an insistence on *oral* confession, and the presence of the priest and his role as an essential mediator between sinners and God is ostentatiously repeated. The word 'prest' appears six times, a frequency conspicuously more dense than in any other poem. The first appearance is in the first stanza just quoted. The remaining instances are in lines 34, 42, 83, 95 and 186. As the notes to these lines demonstrate, the details of the call for oral confession here can be paralleled in pastoral manuals: the concern to make a full confession; not to falsify the record, and to carry out whatever penance the priest has enjoined. But while the materials of the poem are forged out of the penitential literature of the institutional church, their repetition is distinctive. The injunction to shrive 'wel' (l. 34) is followed by three commands to confess everything to the priest (ll. 44, 83 and 185). The role of the priest in prescribing penance – a delicate job which is given detailed treatment in pastoral literature[54] – is referenced in lines 185–86, where the parishioner is urged to follow the priest's teaching and to carry out penance properly. And while confession was required only once a year, here the poet urges the parishioner to call the priest more often (l. 95), lest he forget some of his sins and imperil his soul.

Why so much repetition? There is an absent addressee, an absent enemy which this poem seeks to combat. The over-determination of the poem calls up the opposite of what is being strenuously asserted here: the spectre of Wycliffite views of penance: contrition which does *not* require the presence of a parish priest as intermediary to hear oral confession. One of the clearest expositions of this Wycliffite teaching is seen in the *Testimony of William Thorpe*. Purportedly a record of the examination for heresy of the Lollard William Thorpe by the archbishop of Canterbury, a debate is set up, not just between Arundel and Thorpe, but with a straw man, a nameless person whom, it is said, Thorpe tried to persuade out of his orthodox thinking on the sacrament. These are the straw man's words:

'Þou3 God for3eue men her synnes, 3it moten men be asoylid of preestis, and do þe penaunce þat þei enioynen to hem'. (ll. 1881–3)[55]

---

[52]   Edward H. Weatherly ed., *Speculum Sacerdotale* (EETS OS 200, 1936).

[53]   See notes to individual lines.

[54]   Frederick J. Furnivall ed., *Handlyng Synne* (EETS OS 123, 1903), II.349–96; Weatherly, *Speculum Sacerdotale*, pp. 63–94.

[55]   *The Testimony of William Thorpe* in Anne Hudson ed., *Two Wycliffite Texts* (EETS OS 301, 1993).

A clearer summary of the position of Digby Poem 9 would be hard to find. Thorpe's views are, of course, to the contrary. He argues that while priests can counsel sinners to live well and abandon their sinful ways, only God can absolve sin: 'þo preestis þat taken vpon hem to asoyle men of her synnes blasfemen God, siþ it parteyneþ oonly to þe lord God to assoyle men of alle her synnes' (ll. 1897–9).[56] It is precisely against such pernicious views that Digby Poem 9 preaches. As I shall argue in Section 9, the Digby poet is not a lone voice in the reign of Henry V asserting the need for institutional penance to combat the heretical views of the Lollards which so threatened to weaken the sacramental power of the church.

There is a similar manoeuvre in Poem 23. It is titled in the manuscript 'Of the sacrament of the altere'. Despite Arundel's legislation, the rubrication of the manuscript blazons the fact that the subsequent poem will engage in discussing the very sacrament which has been seen by modern commentators as the litmus test in distinguishing orthodoxy from heresy.[57] It is discussion of exactly this kind of topic that Arundel's *Constitutions* was designed to police and to suppress, reserving such subjects only for discussion in Latin among the clergy.[58] Poem 23 is a paraphrase and expansion of the hymn 'Lauda Sion' which, in 1246, Pope Urban IV asked Thomas Aquinas to write in honour of Christ for the new feast of Corpus Christi. As in Poem 9, the poet forges the materials for his verse from the liturgy of the church. While the poet paraphrases most of the hymn, there are significant reversals of order and also embellishments which are discussed in notes to individual lines. The overall purpose is the use of 'Lauda Sion' to pen an emphatic defence of the orthodox view of the sacrament of the Eucharist. The additions to the source make it crystal clear that the poem is an attempt to assert true church doctrine and to fend off oppositional views. The poem insists on the necessity of both the teaching, and the clergy, of the institutional church.

There is no equivalent to the opening stanza in the 'Lauda Sion':

> I wole be mendid ʒif Y say mys:
> Holychirche nes noþer tre ne stones;
> Þe hous of preyers God nempned þys –
> Boþe goode men and wikked ressayueþ at ones;

---

[56] *The Twelve Conclusions of the Lollards* states that oral confession to a priest is a 'feynid power of absoliciun' which 'enhaunsith prestis pride', Anne Hudson ed., *Selections from English Wycliffite Writings* (Cambridge: CUP, 1978), p. 27/115–16.

[57] Paul Strohm, *England's Empty Throne: Usurpation and the Language of Legitimation, 1399–1422* (Yale: New Haven and London, 1998), pp. 45–53.

[58] Wilkins, *Conciliae Magnae*, III.314–19. For the problems in controlling the expression of views on what was a delicately difficult topic, see Gary Macy, 'The Dogma of Transubstantiation in the Middle Ages', *JEH* 45 (1994), pp. 11–41.

> Þere as gadryng of goode men ys,
> Is holychyrche of flesch and bones;
> Prestes are lanterne hem to wysse
> Þe wise weyes to heuene wones.

(Poem 23/1-8)

The spur for this stanza is the reference to Sion in the preface from Aquinas'
poem; the Digby poet equates Sion with a definition of the contemporary church.
The anxious disclaimer of line 1 is an indication that the poet is venturing into
potentially difficult territory both in discussing the sacrament of the Eucharist, and
also in offering a definition of what constitutes Holy Church. The remark in line 2
sails close to Wycliffite dismissals of the materiality of the church on earth and
the gathering of good men in lines 5–6 also chimes rather closely with Wycliffite
diction.[59] Initial diffidence notwithstanding, it becomes clear from the poem as a
whole that these opening lines preface an exposition of the true doctrine of the
sacrament of the Eucharist by locating such discussion *within* the church. Line 3,
with its echo of Christ's words from Matthew 21:13, 'my house shall be called the
house of prayer', marks out the church as a congregation of the spiritually upright
rather than a den of thieves. The statement that priests are a 'lanterne' (l. 7) reprises
the description of priests as 'lanterns of light' in Poem 8/62 and Poem 21/153. The
phrase is one that is often used in Wycliffite texts, and its occurrence, both here
and elsewhere in the Digby sequence, suggests an appropriation of diction used
more often in unorthodox contexts to stress the importance of the robust spiritual
guidance of the clergy of the institutional church.[60] There is no mention of priests
in 'Lauda Sion'.

Priests are also introduced at two further points in the paraphrase:

> When þou to chirche gost
> To resceyue God, wisely go;
> [...] Suppose þe prest haue but on ost,
> Breke it and parte to twenty and mo,
> As moche is þe leste cost
> As in þe grettest pece of þo.

---

[59]   'But howeuere we speken in diuerse names or licknessis of þis holi church, þei techen
nouȝt ellis but þis oo name, þat is to seie, "þe congregacioun, or gedering togidir of feiþful
soulis þat lastingli kepen feiþ and trouþe, in word and dede, to God and to man, and
reisen hir lijf in siker hope of mercy and grace and blisse at her ende, and ouercoueren, or
hillen, þis bilding in perfite charite that shal not faile in wele ne in woo"', *The Nature of
the Church*, Hudson, *Wycliffite Writings* p. 116/21–7.

[60]   This point is expanded in Section v.

Deme all yliche, lest and most,
Quaue not, ne drede, not to sen hit so.

(Poem 23/81–8)

There is no exact equivalent to this stanza in 'Lauda Sion'. The poet adds in references to church attendance and the priest. Line 85-7 expands 'Lauda Sion' ll. 54-7: 'fragmento' (part) and 'totus' (whole) become 'twenty and mo' and the poet introduces 'moche', 'lest' and 'grettest' to emphasise that in the breaking of the bread at the Eucharist Christ's body remains whole in every part. The added reassurance in line 88, that while the host is broken, God's body remains intact, combats the heretical view that if Christ's physical body is present in the bread, then it is dismembered when the priest confects the sacrament.[61] The countering of unorthodox views of the Eucharist is located within a scenario of a parishioner watching a priest performing the miracle of the Eucharist while attending communion in church. There is also no exact equivalent to lines 65–72 in 'Lauda Sion':

While obley in yrnes or boyst ys stoken,
Hit nys but bred and sengyl bake;
Whanne þe prest to hit Goddis wordis hath spoken,
Crystys quyk body vndir bred o cake.
Þou3 it a þousand peces seme broken,
Nes parted ne wasted, but al holl take.
In byleue of holychirche, who wyl hym 3oken,
A3en þis non argument may make.

(Poem 23/65–72)

The expansion of this stanza emphasises the sacramental role of the priest in confecting (performing) Christ's body when he speaks 'Goddis wordis', that is, the restatement of Christ's words at the Last Supper in the liturgy. 'Lauda Sion' does not mention the role of the priest at all. The assertion that Christ's body is physically present in the bread, though is not broken when the sacrament is confected, counters contrary views, and does so explicitly within the context of the liturgy. The last two lines of this stanza are also highly significant. They are completely without trace in Aquinas's hymn. '3oken', although used for rhyme, makes adherence to 'byleue of holychirche' with some force (l. 71). 'A3en þis non argument may make' completes the stanza but, given there is no counterpart in 'Lauda', this is surely a clear sign of the direction of the poem's remarks; to defend true doctrine and the authority of the institutional church against dissenters.

---

[61] For Wycliffite views on the Eucharist, see A. Hudson, *The Premature Reformation* (Oxford: OUP, 1988), pp. 281–90.

These concluding statements are part of the textual dynamic of the poem as a whole. In a fashion very similar to the over-determined references to priests as intermediaries in poem 9, the word 'byleue' is used nine times in the poem alongside other references to faith which has been taught: 'byleue of herte' (l. 46) 'bok of oure byleue' (l. 50), 'good byleue' (l. 56), 'byleue of holychirche' – 'gostly byleue' (l. 96) as well as lines 71–72 already quoted. 'Byleue' appears four times in the penultimate stanza, lines 113–20. The poet adds a verse of liturgical quality to his source which reasserts that the miracle of the Eucharist cannot be apprehended through bodily senses; Christ's present body in the bread can be understood by faith alone. The insistence that the discussion of the poem is in accordance with faith, in keeping with the belief of holy church, can clearly be seen to fend off arguments to the contrary. What is said in the poem constitutes 'true' belief, and therefore, by extension, anything different must be false. Once again, the mobilisation of diction appears to wrest back discursive territory from the Lollards.[62]

What the poem attempts is nothing less than a systematic defence of the miracle of transubstantiation in the Eucharist. Simultaneously it forms a hearty rebuttal of the Wycliffite contestation of the sacrament. Wyclif argued that the priest blesses, consecrates, and confects the sacrament, the efficacious sign of Christ's Body; he does not confect Christ's body itself: 'Christ is in the host as in a sign, otherwise the host would not be a sacrament; but he is not really and truly there according to his whole humanity.'[63] By contrast, as we have seen, this Digby poem builds on Aquinas's words to assert categorically that God's physical body is present in the sacrament after the priest has confected. While the poet never mentions the presence of Christ's Galilean Body, he goes out of his way to combat arguments that the miracle of transubstantiation is impossible. The plenitudinous body of Christ in the sacrament is stressed, buttressed by reference to the doctrine of Holy Church:

> Lore is ȝouen to cristen men:
> Into flesch passeþ þe bred,
> As holychirche doþ vs kenne;
> Þe wyn to blod þat is so red.
> Þou seest not fleschly þou takest þenne,
> Þy byleue of herte makeþ þe fast fro ded;

---

[62] 'Byleue' is a very common word in Wycliffite texts, standing either on its own, or prefixed by 'true' or 'false', see e.g. *EWS* II.86/110; 135/8; 159/155; 328/6–7; 330/51; Gloria Cigman ed., *Lollard Sermons* (EETS OS 294, 1989) 1.306; 2.676; 3.152; F.D. Matthew ed., *The English Works of Wyclif Hitherto Unprinted* (EETS OS 74, 1880, 2nd revised edn, 1902), p. 19; 159; 207.

[63] John Wyclif, *De Eucharistica*, ed. J. Loserth (London: Trübner, 1892), p. 115. For Wyclif's position on the sacrament, see David Aers, *Sanctifying Signs* (Notre Dame: University of Notre Dame Press, 2004), pp. 53–65.

Wiþouten ordre of þynges to renne,
By tokene and word þat he bede.

Wiþouten help of ordre of þyngis
Þe bok of oure byleue is lent,
Vnder dyuerce spices only tokenynges,
Þou3 þe spices fro hym be went;
Not durked ne hyd, but ri3t shynynges,
Þou3 fleschly sy3t fro hym be blent;
Þe soule haþ ioye and mery synges
When good byleue seeþ þe sacrament.

(Poem 23/41–56)

These two stanzas are a close paraphrase of 'Lauda Sion', ll. 31–39. Aquinas's words are used to defend orthodox belief that the bread and the wine are turned into Christ's body and his blood. Simultaneously they work to fend off Wycliffite arguments that the consecrated host is a sign – a manifestation of Christ's passion – and that bread and wine do remain on the altar after the Host has been broken. Line 49 is an addition to 'Lauda Sion', and restates the miracle of transubstantiation: each species of bread and wine is annihilated and becomes instead Christ's body and his blood. The reference to 'holychirche' in line 43 expands on the hymn, to stress that the doctrine of transubstantiation has the authority of the institutional church. 'Byleue of herte' (l. 46), paraphrases 'fida' (faith) but is part of the added chain of references to the acceptance of orthodox doctrine. 'Þe bok of oure byleue' in line 50 is added to the source and once again stresses institutional authority for the doctrine expounded. The poet's handling of Aquinas's theological arguments is tracked in the notes to the individual lines.

Informing the whole poem, is the orthodox belief that one of the reasons why God's flesh and blood is invisible to human eyes is to increase the merit of human faith.[64] The tenor of the whole poem, even if derived chiefly from 'Lauda Sion' is reminiscent of a passage in Nicholas Love's *Mirror*, a work written in 1410 at the express command of Archbishop Arundel. Here is the passage which extols the mystery of the sacrament and defends the Real Presence against the logic of human reason, human sight, and the natural order of things:

Þe sacrament of þe autere dewly made by virtue of cristes wordes is
verrey goddus body in forme of brede, & his verrey blode in forme

---

[64]   See Aers, *Sanctifying Signs*, pp. 4–7. Aers discusses the sermons of Thomas Brinton, the writings of the Carmelite friar Roger Dymock, pastoral literature and English devotional writing.

of wyne, & þouh þat forme of brede & wyne seme as to alle þe bodily
wittes of man brede and wyne in his kynde as it was before, neuerles
it is not so in soþenesse, bot onely goddus flesh and blode in
substance, so þat þe accidents of bred & wyne wonderfully &
myraclesly aȝeynus mannus reson, & þe commune ordre of kynde bene
þere in þat holi sacrament without hir kyndely subiecte, & verrey
cristies body þat suffrede deþ vpon þe crosse is þere in þat sacrament
bodily vnder þe forme & liknes of brede, & his verrey blode vndur likeness
of wyne substancially & holely, without any feynyng or deceit, & not
onely in figure as þe fals heretike seiþ.

(p. 151/31–p.152/1)

The theological doctrine of Poem 23 is identical to this formulation by Love. The
Digby poet wants to preserve the miracle of the sacrament and defend its sanctity
against those who would see Christ's presence at the Eucharist 'onely in figure'.
But the purpose of the Digby poet goes further than a lesson in academic theology
and an address to personal devotion.

> In sted of þat oure soules to glade
> We reseceyue oure housel God o blisse.

(ll. 127–8)

These final two lines have no counterpart in 'Lauda'. The poem comes to rest on a
note, quite literally, of present-day incorporation. That the poem closes with an image
of communal receipt of the sacrament is not accidental. It brings the poem full circle.
While the opening stanza, as I have discussed above, lives a little dangerously in its
articulation of corporate solidarity as the definition of a spiritually sound church, the
concept of a unified body of Christ 'al holl' is extremely important to the political
resonance of the poem. The poem proclaims the belief that the consecrated host
constitutes Christ's 'corpus mysticum', that is the Church. The Digby poet identifies
adherence to the belief of the Real presence in the Eucharist with membership of
the true Christian church, Christ's body. Devout belief in the sacrament of the altar
makes each and every member of the community part of the mystical body of Christ.[65]
The communal receipt of communion encapsulates a contemporary body of Christ
united in belief and devotional orthodoxy.[66]

---

[65]   Cf. Aquinas's comment that the sacrament signified 'the unity of the mystical body of
Christ which is an absolute prerequisite for salvation, because outside of the Church there is
no salvation', Thomas Aquinas, *Summa Theologiae* (London: Blackfriars, 1964–81), III.73.3.

[66]   Studies which explore the political and communal significance of the sacrament
include Aers, *Sanctifying Signs*; Miri Rubin, *Corpus Christi: The Eucharist in Late Medieval*

iv) *The liturgy*

It is also no accident that the poet chooses Aquinas's hymn as the basis for his poem, given its use for the liturgy of the Eucharist on the Feast of Corpus Christi. The institutional and communal performance of these words also stresses the corporate church united in the articulation of orthodox belief. The poem forms part of an important liturgical strain in the sequence as a whole. Poems 9 to 12 form a mini-sequence which moves from Lenten preparation to the celebration of Easter and the receipt of the Eucharist in Poem 12. Poem 9 is, as I have argued, forged out of the penitential handbooks of the church designed to prepare the parishioner and the priest for full confession and penance before taking communion. Poem 10 makes substantial use of the liturgy for Good Friday, in particular Christ's reproaches delivered from the cross to upbraid humankind for their ingratitude. (These are discussed in more detail below.) Following on from the fierce Lenten penitence of Poems 9 and 10, we move to the solemn feast of Easter Day in Poem 11. Once again, there is liturgical referencing. Line 2 of the poem runs: 'Now Alleluya is vnloken'. During Lent, the Alleluya was not sung at the Mass. Its return at the Easter Mass signalled the joy of Christ's resurrection.

Poem 21 may also have been influenced by knowledge of liturgical practice. It is a metrical paraphrase of the Beatitudes from the Sermon on the Mount. The poet alternates the anaphoric (initially repetitive) 'blessed be' narrative structure of Matthew's gospel with the 'cursed be' formulae of Moses' words to the people of Israel in Deuteronomy 27:15–25 and 28:16–19. The Beatitudes passage formed the basis for the Gospel reading for the Feast of All Saints (1 November), and was also one of the Gospels appointed for a Feast of several martyrs. The liturgical resonance of the biblical text is entirely appropriate to the poems' extended concern with the kinds of behaviour which may earn spiritual reward and those which will reap eternal damnation. The liturgy is explicitly used as the basis of the final poem in the sequence. Poem 24 is a metrical paraphrase not only of the nine lessons of the Office of the Dead, but also its responses and versicles, especially those at the close of the office. The sequence of poems ends with a communal recitation and reflection on morality, sin, penance and the need for spiritual reform if there is to be any hope of salvation.

Quite literally, the Digby poet builds the church into his poems and creates an incorporated church community. This ecclesiology also bears political resonance. Henry V's enthusiasm for promoting liturgical practice has been well documented. As Jeremy Catto observes, 'Henry V's emphasis on the forms of public worship

---

Culture (Cambridge: CUP, 1991); Sarah Beckwith, 'Ritual, Church, and Theatre: Medieval Dramas of the Sacramental Body' in David Aers ed., *Culture and History, 1350–1600* (Hemel Hempstead: Harvester Wheatsheaf, 1992), pp. 65–89, and Sarah Beckwith, *Christ's Body: Identity, Culture, and Society in Late Medieval Writings* (New York: Routledge, 1993).

is striking'.[67] Lydgate appears to have written translations of the 'Eight Verses of St Bernard' for the king's use at Mass, and of 'Benedic anima mea domino' in the chapel at Windsor at the request of the dean while the king was at evensong.[68] After Henry's accession, Thomas Arundel was replaced by Henry Chichele as archbishop of Canterbury. He and his fellow bishops introduced an emphasis on corporate worship, with more ceremonies, new feasts and cults, more elaborate music and emphasis on public processions. New occasional offices were introduced which offered frequent opportunities for corporate expression of personal contemplative prayer or devotional meditation. These new offices included 'The Five Wounds', 'The Crown of Thorns' and meditations on the Passion.[69] The inclusion of the devotional lyrics in the Digby sequence might owe something to this movement. The liturgical strain of the poems can be seen as part of the broader concern to focus on public forms of corporate devotion as a means of bolstering the orthodoxy of the church and countering the subversive threats of Lollardy. Chichele and his bishops championed the use of the Sarum rite in an attempt to create a standardisation of liturgical practice throughout the kingdom. Catto notes that the Sarum Use was 'a subject of conscious pride ... in the early years of the fifteenth century, and ... attests the vitality and importance of public communal worship in the church's response to Lollardy'.[70] The strong presence of the liturgy in the Digby poems, its devotional and penitential lyrics, its use of pastoralia, and its insistence on the sacramental authority can all be seen to be part of the building of a new reformed church with Henry V at its head. This resurgent church militant in the Digby poems is built with robust rigour to silence any threats that might come to it from outside. And a vital part of this rebuilding concerns restoration of those inside – the clergy.

v) *Reform*

So outspoken are many of the Digby poems for the need to weed out corruption in the church, there are no grounds for thinking that the poet's voice was cauterised through fear of reprisals from Arundelian legislation. Religious malpractice is criticised robustly, and sometimes in a vein which would not be out of place in some 'left-wing' Lollard texts. Poem 17 is titled 'Loue that God loueth'. The first stanza enjoins the audience to love what God loves and hate both day and night anything that God hates (ll. 1–8). Not surprisingly, the hate list develops to include covetousness, the performing of office for reward, fleshly pursuits, and the delight

---

[67]   Jeremy Catto, 'Religious Change under Henry V' in G.L. Harriss ed., *Henry V: The Practice of Kingship* (Oxford: OUP, 1985), pp. 97–116; at p. 107.

[68]   Derek Pearsall, *John Lydgate (1371–1449): A Bio-bibliography* (Victoria: University of Victoria, 1997), p. 17. The information derives from a comment made by the bibliographer John Shirley.

[69]   Catto, 'Religious Change', p. 109.

[70]   Ibid., pp. 108–9.

in worldly goods which 'in heuene comeþ nou3t' (l. 64). More surprising are the following remarks:

> For gold and syluer and precyous stones,
> Swetnes of floures, erþely bewte,
> Þe shrynes wiþ all seyntes bones,
> In heuene were foul felþe to se.
>
> (Poem 17/65–8)

The designation of shrines and saints' bones as foul filth might have delighted a Lollard,[71] but it is quite clear from the overt defence of church teaching on the sacraments that the writer of these poems did not share the more polemical views promulgated by Wycliffism. In his concern to whip corruption and to purify the church, some of the targets are coincident with those set up by Lollard reformers, but they are also characteristic of the reform of the church under Henry V.[72] These Digby poems can be seen as part of a more widespread move to reclaim the moral high ground from Wycliffite reformers. There is nothing to fear from honest and robust criticism of the abuses in the Church; the church will only be strengthened thereby, and the common people, so dependent on the proper discharging of ecclesiastical responsibility, will be all the better for it.

The fourth poem addresses the time-worn problem of honest truthtelling in a world which favours the flatterer. All the estates are addressed, from the king to the commons and the church attracts a particularly stinging charge:

> Thou3 holy chirche shulde fawtes mende,
> Summe put hem of for mede;
> And summe wiþ maystri3e hem defende,
> That holy chirche stant of hem drede.
> Þo þat rechelesly sowe here sede,
> Here lond of vertues ligge ful lay.
> Þe holy chirche þe corn shulde wede;
> For cowardis þey dar not say.
>
> (Poem 4/137–44)

---

[71] There is a frequent emphasis in Lollard works on practical good works rather than honouring images, e.g. Matthew, *Works of Wyclif*, p. 7/24ff; 279/14ff.; Cristina von Nolcken ed., *The Middle English Translation of the Rosarium Theologie* (Heidelberg: Winter, 1979), pp. 99/12–27 and Hudson, *Wycliffite Writings*, p. 84/29–42.

[72] For accounts of the efforts of Henry, Chichele and the bishops to reform the church from within, see Catto, 'Religious Change' and Allmand, *Henry V*, pp. 257–305.

It is the duty of the church to correct misdeeds and bring the sinner to repentance. In the view of this writer, the church is negligent in so doing, partly because it fears reprisals from the powerful.[73] The lines interleave several texts from parables about sowing in Matthew's gospel (see note to these lines). The image of separating the cockle from the corn (l. 143) is used in a variety of Middle English texts to describe the intrusion of heretics into the true belief of the Church (see note to the line).[74] The pointing of the Digby verse, however, rather than targeting the heretics, as is more customary, places the responsibility of weeding the church's clean corn firmly in the hands of the clergy. The suggestion here is less of heresy than clerical indulgence of sin. The stanza exploits biblical diction to suggest that the result of the church's laxity in punishing sin is moral barrenness, an aridity relevant not just to the individual, but to the 'lond' (l. 142). The threat to the church is not from dissidence but from negligence. The land will be fallow unless the clergy have the moral courage properly to discharge their duties and bring sinners, however powerful they may be, to account.

Elsewhere in the sequence, the writer is unreservedly critical of those priests who fail to take their responsibilities seriously, and who consequently imperil the very souls for which they have charge. One of the most sustained examples is in Poem 8:

> Who takeþ cure, he bereþ charge
> By Goddis lawe þe folk to preche.
> Þey make conscience large,
> Take tyþe and nyl not teche.
> Crist his postles tauȝt in speche
> Fro worldis worschip to wende away,
> Gostly and bodyly þe soules to leche,
> And bad hem make no iour delay.
>
> Worldis good nes not holichirche,

---

[73] Cf. 'The Office of Curates' in which the Wycliffite writers complain that corrupt clergy are protected by 'helpe of lordes' so that their superiors cannot correct them. 'His souereyn schal not dore correcte him for drede of his temperaltees & wraþþe of lordis; þus lordis ben made schildis of synne for a litel money or worldly seruyce of wickid curatis, þat riȝtwisness may not forþ in her vertuouse lyuynge', Matthew, *Works of Wyclif*, p. 155.

[74] Wycliffite writers also appropriated the image to their own ends, e.g. 'All þoo þat haue be and beþ, and schul be into þe Day of Doom, pursueris of true cristen peple, ben of þe generacioun of Caym: and alle þoo þat han be pursued for the loue of God, and ben now, and schul be into þe Day of Doom beþ of þe generacioun of Abel. And, as Crisostom seiþ ... þe cockel schal growe amonge þe good whete into þe dai of ripe' Cigman, *Lollard Sermons*, 2.699–705.

Richesse and worschep Y ȝow forbede,
Þe folk is cherche, in hem ȝe worche,
Here noo oþer to don þy dede.
Þat doþ þe dede is worþy mede;
Þu mayst not serue two lordis to pay,
Þat on he serueþ in loue and drede,
Þat oþere he serueþ wiþ iour delay.

Who ressayueþ benefys for richesse and ese,
To haue his lyuyng in sykernes,
Raþere þan serue God to plese
He ressayueþ hit omys.
For riȝt [fol. 106a] as Iudas dede kys
Ihesus, and after hym betray,
So þey gyle þe soules fro blisse;
Of Goddis seruyce make iour delay.

(Poem 8/17–40)

There is nothing guarded in these sentiments. The first two stanzas are uncannily reminiscent of the satirical portrayal of fraudulent priests which is the backstory to Chaucer's portrait of his virtuous Parson.[75] The obligation to preach is disregarded, tithes are gathered, but no teaching is offered and Christ's instructions to his apostles are blithely ignored. The second stanza voices a criticism which appears again and again in these poems; that members of holy church are far too concerned with worldly goods at the expense of the people to whom they should minister. Responsibility, a key concern of the sequence as a whole, is stressed with the word 'charge' (l. 16); see also Poem 9/171. The appeal to God's law to assert the clergy's duty to preach (l. 18) chimes with Wycliffite calls for the primacy of preaching over all other clerical duties.[76] The remark is part of a sustained pattern in which appeals for church reform are couched in diction used more commonly by Lollards. In order to outflank and bypass heretical complaint about the institutional church, the Digby poet beats the dissidents at their own game by stealing their language and robbing it of its heterodox power. The criticism of priests' exacting tithes

---

[75] *The General Prologue*, A. 477–528 in Larry D. Benson ed., *The Riverside Chaucer* (Oxford: OUP, 1988). See also Jill Mann, *Chaucer and Medieval Estates Satire* (Cambridge: CUP, 1973), pp. 55–66.

[76] See Matthew, *Works of Wyclif*, pp. 55–57; 111/9ff.; p. 188/1; T. Arnold ed., *Select English Works of John Wyclif* (Oxford: Clarendon Press, 1869–71), p. 130/16ff; p. 145/9; p. 202–03; M.L. Swinburne ed., *The Lanterne of Light* (EETS OS 151, 1917), p. 55/10ff; *Jack Upland*, p. 64/232ff in P.L. Heyworth ed., *Jack Upland, Friar Daw's Reply and Upland's Rejoinder* (Oxford: OUP, 1968).

without instructing their parishioners was a complaint voiced by the commons in parliament (see headnote to this poem) but it is also generic. The Wycliffite position on tithing was more extreme; that parishioners have the right to withhold tithes from sinful priests (see notes to line 20). Once again, the Digby poet can be seen to wrest back territory from the Lollards. Tithing was a contentious issue: church law made the payment of tithes obligatory.[77] The Digby poet defends the orthodoxy of tithing, but demands that clerics honour the payment of tithes by ensuring that they teach their parishioners. The problem is not with the system of the institutional church; the problem is with individual negligent priests.

Lines 21–3 explicitly draw on the bible: Christ's commandments to his apostles (see note to the lines). These gospel texts, especially the injunction to take nothing for the journey when the apostles set out, are frequently used in Wycliffite texts to call for the disendowment of the church, and also to inveigh against the temporal possessions of the friars.[78] Lines 30–2 draw on the gospel injunction that no man can serve two masters (see note to the lines). Once again, these texts were pressed into service in Wycliffite polemic to argue for the disendowment of the church.[79] The poet re-appropriates dissident polemic to urge the need for the priests to reform themselves from within. Arguments over benefice (l. 33) have a long history (see headnote to Poem 8 and also note to this line). The poet's quarrel is not with benefices in and of themselves but with those who abuse the privilege. Lax priests, in a striking condemnation, are likened to Judas, betraying Christ with a kiss (see note to lines 37–38). The image of betrayal is significant; it suggests defection and treachery from within the ranks. If the church is to be purged of corruption, then it is the responsibility of those from inside its walls to do it. Such cleansing will pull the rug from the feet of those outsiders whose attack is on the very foundation of the church.

Diction characteristic of Lollard polemic is also reappropriated in later lines of this poem: '3oure rule is groundid in charyte/As li3t of lanterne to lede þe way' (Poem 8/61–2). 'Ground' and its derivatives are used liberally by Wycliffites to question whether the contemporary church is based in apostolic purity.[80] 'Charity' is wielded with dissident force to suggest that the contemporary church is rooted

---

[77] '3e schul tythe truly, for to kepe 3ou sekerly out of þe artycle of cursyng', A. Brandeis ed., *Jacob's Well* (EETS OS 115, 1900), p. 37/5–6.

[78] E.g. Hudson, *Wycliffite Writings*, p. 121/52–86.

[79] The sixth conclusion of The Lollard Disendowment Bill runs 'for temperalte and spirituelte ben to partys of holi chirche, and þerfore he þat hath takin him to þe ton schulde nout medlin him with þe toþir, *quia nemo potest duobus dominis seruire*', Hudson, *Wycliffite Writings*, p. 26/65–7 and p. 152, n.62–72.

[80] E.g. 'Þei clouten falsehed to þe trouþe wiþ miche vngroundid mater', Hudson, *Wycliffite Writings*, p. 118/108; cf. Matthew, *Works of Wyclif*, p. 337; Arnold, *Wyclif*, III.244/13, 248/16, 255/24, 353/15; Swinburne, *Lanterne*, 59/8, 65/11.

not in holy love, but in greed for temporal possession.[81] The phrase 'liȝt of lanterne' – or lantern of light – drawn from the conclusion to Matthew's Sermon on the Mount, is often used to describe the ideal clergy (see note to line 62). It is reused in the Digby sequence (Poem 21/153–6, 23/7–8). It is also a phrase pressed into service by Lollard writers to expose how far the contemporary clergy have fallen from their pristine foundation.[82] The Digby poet wrests the formulation back into the legitimate hands of the church to insist on the necessity of reform. If I am correct in seeing the deliberate redeployment of Lollard diction in the Digby poems, then what it represents is an attempt to seize the reforming ground back from the dissidents and wield their characteristic modes of expression with all the force of orthodoxy by asserting that the office of priesthood is essential to the spiritual welfare of the people. Put simply 'þe folk is cherche' (l. 27).

The criticism of the clergy in Poem 8 prepares the way for the focus on penance in Poem 9; this is a poem which, as we have seen, spells out the need for parish priests to be 'mene' between God and their parishioners through proper administration of the sacrament of penance. But it is not only the people who must 'burnysche bryȝt' their 'soules blake' (l. 2). So must the priests. A bishop must heal his flock from within, and parish priests must do their utmost to fulfil the responsibilities with which they have been entrusted:

> ȝif a clerk haue, þurgh hap,
> Cure of soules, or bischopriche,
> He hat not bischop – he hat a by shap;
> Make oþere after his werkis like,
> To kepe his shep fro helle tike,
> In folde go amonge hem blete,
> Saf and sounde brynge hem ylyk
> Bytwen God and hem to trete.

(Poem 9/153–60)

---

[81] For Wycliffite usage of 'charity' see e.g. Hudson, *Wycliffite Writings*, p. 116/26 where the true congregation of the church is likened to a 'bilding in perfite charite that shal not faile in wele ne in woo', and 'Of Faith, Hope and Charity', where the seventh condition of charity is stated to be that it seeks not selfish ownership of goods, but 'sekiþ worschip to god profyte to his chirche', Matthew, *Works of Wyclif*, p. 354/11–13.

[82] The most sustained example is the text Swinburne, *Lanterne*. See also *Mum and the Sothsegger*, l. 1749 in Helen Barr ed., *The Piers Plowman Tradition* (London: Everyman, 1933) and *The Plowman's Tale*, l. 969–70 in W.W. Skeat ed., *Chaucerian and Other Pieces: The Complete Works of Geoffrey Chaucer* (Oxford, 1897). Gower also uses the image in *Vox Clamantis*, III.1070–80 in *The Complete Works of John Gower: the Latin Works*, ed. G.C. Macaulay (Oxford; Clarendon Press, 1902).

This is one of the most ingenious stanzas in the whole sequence. It takes the form of a witty turn on the pastoral trope that can be traced back to the words of Christ to Peter, 'feed my sheep' (John 21:17) and is taken up in many pastoral manuals (see notes to the lines). Line 155 contains the pun on which this stanza depends: 'bischop … by shap'. Kail printed 'byshap' but there is clearly a space in the MS between 'by' and 'shap'. The sense of both of these words is far from certain (for *MED* references see note to line 155). What is clear, however, is that the sound of 'bischop' is translated into 'by shap'; and concomitantly, the meaning of 'bishop', a leader of the church, is redefined. The distance of hierarchy is dismantled. The sense of the stanza is that if any cleric happen to have pastoral cure of souls, or to become a bishop, he is not called a bishop; he is called a fellow sheep/shape/creation. In order to set an example to others he needs to go into the sheepfold among his flock, bleating alongside them, and protect them from the hound of hell. A proper cleric shelters his sheep from evil by being an intermediary 'bytwen God and hem' (l. 160). The distinctive turn on pastoral imagery locates the responsibility for the welfare of parishioners firmly on the shoulders of parish priests. It stresses the need for humility and for stringent vigilance.

As the poem progresses, the narrator is unequivocal in spelling out the responsibilities of the clergy:

> Benefice of holychirche first was graunted
> For prestis holy lyf to lede;
> Dryue out synne, suffre non be haunted,
> Here non oþer to do his dede;
> Þe werkman is worþy his mede,
> In felde, in toun, and in strete.
> Teche vnwys, helpe hem þat nede,
> Byfore God for hem to trete.
>
> In wordis, þey sayn þey wil do wel;
> Take cure of soules as worthi clerkis,
> And resceyue þe charge euery del
> To wasche synful soules serkis;
> Þey preue hemself fooles in werkis,
> Wiþ holy water nele no parischen wete.
> Caste away antecrist merkis!
> Goþ wiþ God of pes to trete!
>
> (Poem 9/161–8)

The plea for a return to first principles ('first', l. 161) would not look out of place in a Lollard tract. It is a further example of the writer calling for the reform of the priesthood from within the institutional church. Line 164 repeats line 28 in

Poem 8 and mobilises the conventional opposition between a true shepherd and a hireling to urge the clergy not to perform their duties for financial gain but out of due care for their flock. The injunction is bolstered by reference to Luke 10:17 and Timothy 5:18, a text already cited in Poem 2/40 in the context of condemning the preference for ill-gotten reward and favour to honest work. The injunction for priests to 'teche vnwys' (l. 167) repeats the exhortation of Poem 8 (see also note to 9/167), and the diction of lines 171–4 deploys a conventional image of the priest's penitential duties to his parishioners (see notes to the lines). The presence of so many tropes which are staples of pastoral literature shows the poet using the penitential handbooks of the church as a conduct book for the clergy.

The stern imperatives of the narrative voice in lines 175–76 are an index of the poet's fervour for reform, and once more steal a march on Lollard territory. The command to cast away 'antecrist merkis' picks up on characteristic Wycliffite diction. Many Lollard texts figure the Pope as Antichrist. The contemporary corrupt church is the church of Antichrist, in direct opposition to the true church, which is the congregation of saved souls.[83] In the Digby poet's reference to Antichrist, it is not the church itself that is in league with the devil, only those corrupt priests who fail to discharge the duties of the institutional church.

Even more strident than these imperatives is the excoriation of negligent clergy in Poem 10. The poem is an example of a popular kind of religious lyric in the 'complaint of Christ' tradition, where the crucified Christ enumerates the sufferings accumulated in dying to redeem humans who, nevertheless, persist in their sinful ways. The origins of these poems were the speeches of God in Lamentations 1:12, Micah 6:3 and Isaiah 5:4 (see headnote to Poem 10). These biblical texts formed part of the Easter liturgy, and were known as the *Improperia*, or Good Friday reproaches. They also provided an authority and structure for the complaint of Christ at the Last Judgement. What is singular in Digby's treatment of this type of lyric is the direction of Christ's complaint. Other lyrics of this type show Christ addressing the individual human soul. But in lines 99–140 of Poem 10, there is a sudden – and startling – switch of address. The guns are turned on the clergy. Their urgent reform, especially their abuse of temporalities, is here put into the mouth of God. In verse which reprises the antitheses of the *Improperia*, God accuses the clergy of the abuse of temporal possession (see notes to individual lines), and then promises vengeance of the most terrifying kind:

> And ȝe defoule my holy place,
> Þat turneþ þe chirche out of his gyse.
> Holy chirche is spirytuall grace,
> Þe duwe dette, deuyne seruyse.

---

[83] See note to Poem 9/175.

Þey calle me as he þat no God was,
Þat cure of soules don despise;
Fro hem Y wole turne my face,
And calle hem as fooles, out casten fro wyse.
Þat sellen soules for temperal getyng,
Þey maken skourges to here owe betyng.
Here good dayes ben wastyng,
And þey to helle hastyng,
To be wiþ fendes chastyng,
Fulfille on hem my thretyng.

(Poem 10/127–40)

Drawing on biblical text (see note to line 133), the stanza is as forthright as it is possible to be against those who despise 'cure of soules' (l. 132). Damnation will be theirs. Line 136 conflates the proverb about making a rod for one's own back with reference to Christ's scourging before his crucifixion. The image dramatises how corrupt clergy will bring eternal punishment on their own heads.

The liturgy in poem 10 is turned full force on the clergy; the topoi of devotional meditation are used to calumniate sinful priests. Traditional advice and formulae from pastoralia and biblical text are pressed into service to insist on the need for the church to weed out corruption. There is no overt confrontation with the Lollard attack on the church from outside. Instead, the poet appropriates characteristic Wycliffite script to show that the spiritual reform of the realm lies in the hands of the church itself. Whether it anticipates it, or is part of it, the Digby reform agenda chimes with archbishop Chichele's determination in the convocation of 1416 to sweep away the dust of negligence in the contemporary church.[84]

There is, however, one aspect of the Digby poet's reformist agenda which contrasts strikingly with Wycliffite polemic: the treatment of the friars. Wycliffite texts characteristically frame the friars as limbs of Antichrist, or they are figured as bastard branches of the contemporary church.[85] The fraternal orders are an excrescence, and as *Pierce the Ploughman's Crede* terms it, 'put in' by the devil's stupidity.[86] There is only one reference to friars in the Digby sequence, and it is not uncomplimentary. Poem 10 begins with an account of the reluctance of humankind to hear rebuke of their sins. On account of pride, they think themselves equal to God, and at a sermon will ask a friar to make it short or else shut up (Poem 10/1–6).

---

[84] Wilkins, *Conciliae Magnae*, iii. 352, 378.
[85] See *EWS*, I.380–81/53–68 and 512/75–85; Matthew, *Works of Wyclif*, p. 364 and Arnold, *Wyclif*, III.184. This trope is discussed in Helen Barr, *Socioliterary Practice in Late Medieval England* (Oxford: OUP, 2001), pp. 139–41.
[86] *Pierce the Ploughman's Crede*, lines 505–6.

Monks do not escape so lightly. The whole of Poem 18 is devoted to urging proper observance of the monastic rule. The imbalance in the treatment of private religions in the sequence merits some reflection. Might a friar have been responsible for composing the sequence? There are certainly other examples of texts which are probably written by friars which interrogate clerical corruption and call for reform.[87] Might the presence in the sequence of a poem which seems so critical of monasticism alongside such robust excoriation of corruption in the regular clergy signal fraternal one-up-manship? As I shall argue in the final section of the introduction, such an authorial context seems unlikely, but this still begs the question as to why this series of lyrics should include a poem devoted wholly to the reformation of monastic practice.

Kail saw Poem 18 as indebted to proposals for the reform of the Benedictine orders in 1421 (see headnote to Poem 18). Certainly many of the concerns addressed in the poem are similar to the proposals to which no lesser person than Henry V pledged his support. But, as with Kail's docking of poems to parliamentary texts, the wedding of this poem to a particular document might miss a larger topical resonance. Henry V championed the role of monasticism in the church. The new monasteries of Sheen and Syon were not established until 1415, but contemporary chroniclers are unanimous in declaring that in 1414 Henry had turned his mind to the establishment of these new foundations, with a third projected.[88] In fact, preparations for the Brigittine order at Syon can be seen to have started as far back as 1407.[89] Henry's desire for monasticism to offer a 'powerhouse of prayer' for the good of the realm is as likely a spur for the Digby poet's inclusion of a poem which stressed the importance of a reformed monastic order as the partisan pen of a friar, or the awareness of a particular topical occasion. As I shall argue in the last section of this introduction, there are compelling reasons for seeing the Digby poems as emerging from a Benedictine context. Just as in his comments about the regular clergy, the poet insists on the need for reform within the church; moreover, pointed remarks about monastic negligence in Poem 18 are expressed by a writer from within their ranks rather than by a disgruntled outsider contemptuous of their existence. To give this argument full force, however, we need to turn to the more overtly secular and governmental concerns of the Digby poet – and to the much neglected area of his poetic practice.

---

[87]   P.H. Barnum ed., *Dives and Pauper* (EETS 275, 1976 and 280, 1980) and sermons preserved in MS Longleat 4, see Anne Hudson and H.L. Spencer, 'Old Author, New Work: The Sermons of MS Longleat 4', *Medium Aevum* 53 (1984), pp. 220–38.

[88]   Walsingham, *Historia Anglicana*, II.300; Taylor and Roskell, *Gesta Henrici Quinti*, p. 13.

[89]   See David Knowles, *The Religious Orders in England*, vol. 2 (Cambridge: CUP, 1957), pp. 157–82.

6. Social temper

i) *Making the political body whole*
Throughout the sequence, *what* the poet says is inseparable from *how* he says it. The declarative statements of the lyrics, their use of figurative diction, and the position of narrative voice accumulate to model a political realm that functions in co-operative harmony. Just as the poems build, from the church's institutional materials, a reformed institution that is grounded in Christ's 'holl' body, so too, they build a whole state out of the component parts of each of its members.

Consider the following stanza from Poem 3:

> To wete ȝif parlement be wys,
> Þe comoun profit wel it preues.
> A kyngdom in comouns lys,
> Alle profytes, and alle myscheues.
> Lordis wet neuere what comouns greues
> Til her rentis bigynne to ses.
> Þere lordis ere pore comons releues,
> And mayntene hem in were and pes.

(Poem 3/97–104)

On one level, this is a ringing endorsement of the business of parliament to redress the grievances of the commons by listening to parliamentary complaints.[90] There is an ardent defence of the role of the commons, but to take the axiomatic statement of line 99 out of context would be to misrepresent the poetic agenda of this poem and the sequence as a whole. Throughout, there is a passionate concern with the plight of the poor, and exhortations to those in positions of power – whether the king, the clergy, or nobility – not to plunder poor men's goods and thereby abuse the responsibilities with which they have been entrusted.[91] But, emphatically, the poems do not champion the role of the commons (whether in the parliamentary sense, or in the sense of the third estate more broadly),[92] at the expense of other estates. This is clear from the stanza just quoted.[93] In order to ensure 'comoun profit' (line 98 – and see note to the line), it is important that the commons are

---

[90] Coleman, *Literature in History*, pp. 103–7.
[91] Poem 1/122/145–56, 4/150, 8/14/65–8, 9/157–60, 10/197–208, 21/73–80.
[92] Cf. Watts' discussion cited in footnote 17..
[93] It also emerges from the repetition of the word 'eche' in the lyrics. The very first word of the first lyric is sounded time and again to stress the importance of each and every member of the political community playing their part in ensuring the common profit of the whole.

not exploited. The lords of the realm are stated to be ignorant of the grievances of the commons until their rents begin to dry up. The narrator urges the nobility to relieve the poverty of the commons and to succour them in war and peace. The political note that is sounded is one of mutual cooperation: one group supporting another that is more vulnerable. The commons are a source of income for the whole community, and to ensure that income, their role in the political body must be respected.

Far from advancing the case of a particular group,[94] or a particular cause, the poet is keen to stress that the good of the whole takes precedence over that of the individual. There are repeated calls for wholeness and the avoidance of fragmentation and for public good to be put ahead of private interest. The fate of the kingdom lies not so much in the commons, but in commonality. The poems urge this strenuously in the statements made throughout the sequence, and they also model such commonality in their poetic temper. Throughout, the poetic voice is not particularised, but common; not markedly topical, but generic; not identifiable with a particular group, or even a particular position or person, but speaking for all, from a position of time-honoured common sense. There is a political edge to this poetic temper, but not the one that has usually been seen in these poems, partly as a result of Kail's editorial practice of nailing individual poems to successive parliamentary assemblies.

The prevailing speech acts of the lyrics are propositional truth-statements. Overwhelmingly, the narrative voice is declarative, modulated with exhortation. The poet gives us a rare insight into his social agenda in Poem 3:

> I speke not in specyale
> Of oo kyngdom the lawe to telle;
> I speke hool in generale
> In eche kyngdom the lawe to telle.
>
> (Poem 3/49–52)

Specifics are avoided. The concern to 'telle' ... (stressed by repetition) 'hool' creates a poetic voice which is a model of wholeness rather than individuality. This is a vocal positioning which is commensurate with overt statements that avoid singularity and embrace corporate cooperation.

Close examination of the verbal temper of the sequence highlights clusters of diction which reveal recurrent concern with this issue. One such cluster centres on the use of the word 'singulere' or 'singulerte':

---

[94]   To this concern to respect the role of the commons might be compared the championing of the cause of knighthood (Poem 13/143–52) and the contemplative work of monks (Poem 18/145–52).

And synguler profit by fals assent	(1/4)
And syngulere profit ys aspi3ed	(5/28)
For syngulere profyt eche a dele	(17/37)
For synguler profyt of temperalte	(8/60)
For synguler profyt þou wolde haue	(14/52)
Syngulerte is sotyle þefte	(13/81)
For synguler profyt is sotyll theft	(21/60)
For defaute of iustice and singulere to wynne	(16/59)
For synguler wynnyng to his astate	(21/93)

'Singularity' can be translated as anything that profits an individual at the expense of the good of the larger community, such as private interest, private gain or private motivation. The repetition of the denunciation makes it abundantly clear that singular profit is to be condemned, but what is also noteworthy is that these rebukes are delivered to a broad range of addressees: Poem 1 to the King; Poem 5 in a kingdom; Poem 17 a human sinner; Poem 8 priests; Poem 14 the king's subjects; Poem 13 scornful fools; Poem 21 those who steal from the poor, and warring subjects; and Poem 16 the state of Flanders. The treatment of singularity shows how the poet returns again and again to a specific theme, but changes the mode of address in order to extrapolate a wholeness of applicability. Singular profit is damaging precisely because of its singularity; the sweep of poetic address is inclusive and covers the spectrum of human society, and also human relationships with God. The near verbatim repetition of the term 'sotyle þefte' is an example, both of the poet's propensity for propositional truth statements, and also for the repetition of axioms which is common throughout the sequence; both exemplify the poetic concern to speak 'hool in generale'.

Another lexical cluster that is very dense in the sequence centres on avoidance of 'debate' and internal war. Again, the range of reference is inclusive. The narrator warns against making debate with friends, debate between neighbours, debate within the kingdom, debate among ourselves, each man debating with each other, making debate with God, debate among the limbs of the human body, and by extension, debate within the body politic.[95] Poem 4 provides a representative example:

> God made oo lawe for eche astate,
> Riche and pore in al degre.
> Do no wrong, ne debate,
> But as þou wolde men dede by þe.
> For God hym self þis wrot he,
> Betok to Moyses in his lay;

---

[95] Poems 4/149/243; 5/25; 6/21; 8/59; 10/67; 11/39; 12/33; 15/125; 17/106; 20/80 and 21/91.

> Be Goddis childre in charyte,
> As God doþ in the gospell say.

(Poem 4/241–8)

An image of corporate wholeness: each estate, rich and poor, living according to the one law given by God, is juxtaposed with the admonition to 'do no wrong ne debate' and bolstered by biblical authority from the gospel of Luke and Paul's letter to the Romans (see notes to Poem 4/241–54). The dense lexical clusters around wholeness and unity are accompanied with directives to avoid internal war and dissent.[96] Poem 14 contains some of the pithiest assertions: 'Kepe þe crowne hool' (l. 10), and those in positions of authority are bidden to 'loue al crafty folk yliche' (l. 35).

The sequence is peppered with one-liners of the same political stripe as those just quoted, but there are four poems, especially, which take corporateness as their prevailing subject. One is Poem 23 on the sacrament of the altar, which I have analysed in the previous section. Another is Poem 11, entitled 'God & man ben made atte on'. The refrain 'at on' picks up on the title and, rather like the repetition of singular profit, debate and internal war, is sounded in a number of contexts.[97] There is the reconciliation of man and God through the Eucharist celebrated at Easter (Poem 11/1–8); the reconciliation between each member of the parish in the act of communion; a harmony which draws directly on the direction in pastoral handbooks for each communicant to have resolved any differences between themselves and any other person before receiving the sacrament (Poem 11/25–32, and see notes); and harmony between body and soul in order not to offer debate with God (Poem 11/33–40). One of the reasons for the presence of three poems which explicitly reference Easter is that it is a time of unity and incorporation, signalled, of course, by Christ's resurrection, his Eucharistic body, and the act of communion. That the poet marks the Easter-tide coronation of Henry V, then, in Poem 12, can be seen as an integral part of the social temper of the lyrics. The holy time of Easter (Poem 12/4) is a time for peace among ourselves, to which 'eche man' is disposed (l. 6, *my emphasis*). The poem is entitled 'God kepe the croun and saue the kyng'. The refrain urges defence of the crown, and the crown itself is used as a metonym of wholeness:

> What doþ a kynges crowne signyfye
> Whan stones and floures on sercle is bent?
> Lordis, comouns, and clergye

---

[96]   Poem 2/67; 12/125; 15/142; 16/29; 20/93 and 21/90.

[97]   Unusually, there is a density of rhyme on the same word 'on' in this poem. Elsewhere, there is as much variety on rhyme words, including those in refrain position, as possible. The re-sounding of 'on' chimes with the agenda of the poem to assert oneness. See headnote to Poem 11.

To ben all at on assent.
To kepe þat crowne, take good tent
In wode, in feld, in dale, and downe:
Þe leste lyge man wiþ body and rent –
He is a parcel of þe crowne.

(Poem 12/11–16)

As in Poem 13, the poet shows concern for the most vulnerable member of the political community, 'þe leste lyge man' (l. 15), but the key words are 'all at on assent' (l. 14). The image of the circle of the crown is used to figure unbroken allegiance and agreement in every part of the realm (hence the list in line 14), and among its every member. This is the ideal; it soon yields in the poem to anxious concerns over its reality:

What signyfyeþ þe stones aboute?
Richesse, strengþe, and gret bounté;
Oure townes, and castels, þe reme wiþoute –
Þey are oure stones of gret pousté:
In pes, þey kepe all þis contre.
Holynes, contemplacioun,
God let hem neuer skaterid be,
And saue þe kyng, and kepe þe crowne.

(Poem 12/17–24)

Ȝif we among oure self debate,
Þan endeþ floure of chyualrie.   (ll. 33–4)

Ȝif sercle, and floures, and riche stones
Were eche a pece fro oþer flet,
Were þe crowne broken ones,
Hit were ful hard aȝen to knet.   (ll. 41–4)

To kepe þe crowne, God graunte ȝow grace,
And let it neuere be tobroken.   (ll. 49–50)

The poet is supremely aware of the power of political symbolism to create a model of desire that cannot stand up to human contentiousness, ambition and rivalry, whether projected or past. The Digby poet is not alone in fastening on the convenient symbolic circle of the crown as an image of seamless unity (see notes to lines 9–24), but in comparison with his near contemporary poets, his is the voice most protractedly anxious about its rupture. Poem 12 begins with gladness and rejoicing – but it ends with the diction of 'werre ... among vs', 'fi3t ... among oure self', 'shent', 'lorn', and 'skorn' (ll. 125–52).

The most extended example of the poet's concern for unity is seen in Poem 15. It is entitled in the manuscript 'the descryuyng of mannes membres' and takes the form of a description of the individual parts of the human body in the familiar image of the body politic which derives ultimately from St Paul's letter to the Corinthians 12:14. This trope is used in a variety of texts, whether overtly political or not (see headnote). What is distinctive about the Digby poem is the precision of its detail and the inclusiveness of the broadest possible range of estates and persons within estates. The head, predictably, is likened to the king, but even with this conventional trope, the poet manages a mini-allegory within an allegory:

> The heued, Y likne to a kyng,
> For he is lord souereyn of al;
> Haþ foure to his gouernyng:
> Mouþ, and nose, and eyen wiþal,
> Eryn fayre to his heryng.
> To serue, þe brayn is pryncypal,
> Chef of counseil, ymagenyng
> To caste before, er after fal.
>
> (Poem 15/9–16)

The head is put in charge of four of the five senses and the function of the brain, in the mini-household allegory, is likened to the primary need for counsel. As the poem unfolds, as many parts of the body as possible are enumerated and made to bear the figurative associations of a representative cross section of all classes of society. The narrator associates the neck with justice, man's chest with the priesthood, the shoulders and the backbone with lords and knights; hands are the squires, and the fingers are yeomen; the ribs are lawyers, the thighs merchants, the legs craftsmen, the feet ploughmen; and the toes are true labourers who travail whatever the weather despite being hungry. The narrator warns that:

> Toes helpeþ man fro fal to ryse;
> He may not stonde þat haþ no toon,
> Lepe, ne renne, ne ryde in syse,
> Wrastle, ne fy3te, ne put þe ston.
> 3if seruaunt þe maystere refuse,
> Þe seruaunt lyuyng sone were gon;
> And maystres, þou3 þey ben wyse,
> Wiþout seruant lyue not alon.
>
> (Poem 15/73–80)

Although we are reminded that a body cannot stand up after a fall without toes, the second half of the stanza also stresses the mutual interdependence of servant and master. Just as the poet does not champion the commons (however much he is keen to stress their importance) over and above the other estates, so here, while the body cannot function without toes, the toes need to work with, not against, their superiors. What drives the poem is a vision of co-operation, and hence its enumeration of body parts which go unmentioned in other treatments of this trope.

In a dramatic twist, however, right after this stanza, the poem suddenly explodes into a heated argument between the stomach, the mouth, the ears, eyes, hands and feet. The static idealism of human body parts neatly mapped on the members of a political community is shattered once that body leaps into action, or rather speech. A cacophany ensues:

> Þe wombe preyed þe mouþ to blynne,
> 'þou etest and drynkest þat Y ake!'
> 'To slepe', quod þe eyȝe, 'we may not wynne;
> Þe wrecched wombe so doþ vs wake!'
>
> 'We dulle of heryng!' quod þe ere,
> 'We dase for dronken!' quod þe eyȝe,
> 'I wende but o mone þere were,
> And me þouȝte two Y seyȝe!'
> Quod þe handis, 'Fro mouþ may we not vs were!'
> Quod þe mouþ, 'Y drank while y myȝte drye!'
> 'Allas!' quod þe feet, 'all we bere,
> And ȝoure bargayn dere abye!'

(Poem 15/85–96)

> Þe mouþ in anger he dede saye,
> 'Þes þre dayes do ȝour best;
> Al þat tyme, nyȝt ne daye,
> No mete ne drynk come in my brest'.

(Poem 15/101–4)

> Quod þe eren, 'Oure heryng is at þe laste'.
> Quod eyen, 'We dase and waxe blynd'.
> Quod handes and feet, 'Oure strengþe is paste'.
> Quod brayn and herte, 'Vs wantes mynde'.
>
> Quod þe mouþe, 'ȝe playne whyle y ete,
> And while Y faste, ȝe make gret doel'.

Quod handes and feet, 'Also we gete
Þat þou spendest eche a deel;
We may play, swynke, and swete,
While mouþe in mesure makeþ his mele.

(Poem 15/109–18)

The sinews of the stanza form are stretched to accommodate rapid-fire speech that is often very witty: for example, the eye, dazed with drink, complains that he thought that there was only one moon in the sky. Thanks to the actions of the stomach and mouth, he thinks he sees two. The repetition of 'quod' at the start of lines 109–18 is an aural recreation of successive, but far from petty, accusations and counter-accusations. The poem moves from controlled enumeration of harmonious members, each bearing their part, to unregulated quarrelling that comes close to simply noise (or it would do, had the poet not such a keen ear for witty repartee).[98]

The mouth and stomach appear to be the particularly guilty parties, but in character with the poet's desire to value the contribution of all members of a political community, as the analogy develops, it is clear that simple fasting; i.e. preventing the mouth and stomach from action, is not enough to remedy this situation. While the mouth refrains from eating for three days, this so weakens the ears, eyes, hands feet, brain and heart that the body is useless. Measure is necessary so that the body can work in complete harmony; each body part contributing his part to the greater good of the whole organism. The narrator chips in to give his gloss on his extended analogy:

I likne a kyngdom in good astate
To stalworþe man, my3ty in hele;
While non of his lymes oþer hate,
He is my3ty wiþ anoþer to dele.
3if eche of his lymes wiþ oþer debate,
He waxeþ syk, for flesch is frele;
His enemys wayte, erly and late,
In his feblenesse on hym to stele.

And hed were fro þe body stad,
Noþer partye were set at nou3t;
And body wiþoute armes sprad,
Were armes wiþoute handis ou3t;

---

[98] On the alignment of political dissent with senseless noise see John M. Ganim, 'Chaucer and the noise of the people', *Exemplaria* 2 (1990), pp. 71–88.

> Ne handis, but þey fyngres had,
> Wiþoute fingere what were wrouȝt?
> Þes lymes makeþ hed ful glad –
> And al þe body, and it be souȝt.
>
> (Poem 15/121–36)

There is actually no need for the narrator to step in and moralise his poem. That he provides this gloss of unequivocal morality, however, is in keeping with the poetic temper of the lyrics overall. The warring voices are tamed and contained in a univocal declaration of cooperative corporation. Line 125 states the recurrent concern to avoid debate. The poem models harmonious corporateness both by providing extended description of a fully functioning body politic and by settling a multi-vocal dispute with universally accepted wisdom spoken through a voice which knits up the discord. An annotator has written 'Nota bene' in the margin adjacent to this stanza.

ii) *Figurative diction*

The extended analogy of Poem 15 shows the poet cross-fertilising the trope of the body politic with a dramatic scenario which, while it also has a political legacy, has much in common with debates between the body and soul (see headnote to Poem 15). Metaphor and simile do not scale imaginative and poetic heights in the Digby poems, but the use of figure performs important socio-theological work. As with the example of Poem 15, time and again the Digby poet couches his declarative statements in diction that has a double valency. Yoked together in metaphor are the spiritual and the earthly, the theological and the political. Commensurate with the concern for making all 'at on', the diction of the poems fuses into one that might be thought to be separate spheres of action.

One such place where this is seen is in Poem 9. Varying use is made of the refrain 'with God of loue and pes ȝe trete'. The meaning of 'trete' is not straightforward. One sense is to plead, or to entreat, but, not entirely separable from this, is the sense of 'to negotiate, especially terms of peace' (see headnote to Poem 9). This is particularly evident in lines 17–20:

> Ofte han we treted wiþ God o trewe,
> And sayde no more synne we wolde,
> And euery ȝeere we breke it newe,
> Thre dayes no trewes wiþ hym nele holde.

The importance of not falling back into sin is stressed in *Speculum Sacerdotale* where true penance is said to be sorrow, thinking on one's misdeeds, making confession 'and no more to be in wille for to falle ther-to a-ȝeyn' (p. 65/17–19). The lines in Digby are noteworthy, however, for framing this twice as a broken truce with God. I have not been able to find a comparable use of 'trete' in these senses in a penitential, or broadly spiritual, context.[99] The more straightforward secular use of 'trete' is used in Poem 13 where the poet urges the king not to make truces or arrange treaties with France. To do so would be to 'trete ʒour self out of ʒoure riʒt' (l. 140). War is the only viable option (see headnote to Poem 13 and notes to lines 129–44). In the context of making rightful claim to the French crown, truces are condemned. But in the context of penitential behaviour, making a truce with God is encouraged. The double-valency of the figurative diction in Poem 9 models the harmonious reconciliation of the human world within itself and the human world to God. 'Treting' brings human beings into harmony with each other, and simultaneously, brings human souls into concord with God.

As part of the penitential focus of the lyrics, humankind is urged to think on their sins, and reminded that at the Day of Judgement, they will need to give account to God of all that they have done since they were born. The poet regularly figures this fierce message with diction drawn from human accounting and financial management. Christ's sacrifice for human beings is figured as a loan (Poem 11/110); the human soul as God's 'rent' (Poem 7/87). In order to face up to God's 'rekenyng' on Doomsday, human beings must 'rekene' their own sins. They are reminded not to fall into 'arerage', or arrears, in accounting for their sins; here the poet presses legal diction into service.[100] Some of the most frightening images of the series create the scenario of devils writing down the works of the sinner (Poem 1/87), counting his sins (Poem 4/235), burning the rolls, or record, of 'rerage' (Poem 11/111) and fiends who appear on Judgement Day reading the roll of sin, bearing a tally stick which shows the 'countretayle' of unrepented sins (Poem 4/236 and Poem 24/393). Just as human beings are urged to be scrupulous in their financial dealings with each other, not to take other men's goods, and most especially not to rob the poor, so are they enjoined to be meticulous in giving account of the record of their sin. As the image of the tally-stick shows so well, there is no margin for erroneous miscalculation, and, as the poet is prone to point out, nothing escapes the sight of God.[101] The series ends on precisely this note. Humankind will have to give account of everything they have done, right down to the least twinkling of the eye (Poem 24/412). The poet's last words are: 'the leste bargayn þat he dede bye' (l. 418).

Relationships between humankind and God are often figured in diction which resonates with earthly government, the keeping of law, and the waging of war.

---

[99] The figure is also used in Poem 3/152. See also note to Poem 9/17–20.

[100] For 'rekene' see Poem 9/92; 10/210; 21/148; 24/231. 'Rekenyng' 1/29/35; 7/83; 10/196; 14/31; 16/125 and 'rerage' 8/100 and 9/103. And see notes to these lines for the legal diction.

[101] See Poems 1/95; 4/153; 12/93/95 and 14/71.

Poem 5 figures those who abandon truth and live falsely as rebels against God's law. Having no fear of God, they rob and murder in order to fill their coffers. Those who forsake wisdom and behave wilfully have the sword of vengeance drawn against them (ll. 33–40). The sinner who 'ryse[s]' against God's law is likened to a criminal who rebels against secular authority. The diction of secular servage and allegiance is also reregistered in a spiritual context to present humankind with a choice: either hold to God's law, or fetch up as the slave of the devil. Human beings are warned to keep out of the 'daunger' (power) of the fiend (Poem 4/39); they are cautioned against ending up as the devil's 'knaue' (Poem 1/55; Poem 4/109 and Poem 17/142). The wicked soul is the devil's 'soget' (Poem 17/165) and in his 'seruage' (Poem 17/142 and Poem 20/182). Poem 5 laments that once man was 'angels pere' and has now become 'soget to fendis' (l. 21). The concern for proper government and rightful allegiance seen in the more uniformly secular lyrics of the series also nourishes the diction which describes the government and destiny of the human soul.

As has been discussed above, the lyrics show an almost obsessive apprehension about internal dissension in the political realm, and a zeal for repelling enemies abroad. Once more, this secular diction is present in lyrics which discuss God's relationship to humankind. The anxiety about the political consequences should 'we among oure self debate' (Poem 12/33) has its counterpart in the statement that 'we ben vnkynde wiþ God debate' (Poem 11/39) and God's accusation to the human soul that, instead of giving Him love, it holds 'debate' (Poem 17/106). Poem 3 ends with a stanza which stresses the importance to a kingdom of good name and good life. Sin is the cause of all grievances. Every kingdom hangs in God's balance and since humankind has free will, they have the choice to choose their destiny: 'to haue wiþ God werre or pes' (Poem 3/161–8). God is often figured as a military leader who either protects his friends or wreaks vengeance against his enemies (Poem 10/46/173). The Digby poet is not original in using this diction, but he does so emphatically. The more devotional lyrics show Christ pleading with humankind: I am your friend but all you desire is to be my enemy (Poem 10/66/125 and notes to the lines). God explains that his sacrifice on the cross was to make friends of his enemies (Poem 19/31). Humankind is warned against following sinful behaviour which will make God their 'ful foo' (Poem 1/106) and encouraged to think on how God makes provision for the protection of his friends (Poem 3/109/157/159).

The diction of friend versus foe has an especially acute double valency in Poem 11. The feast of Easter is a time of rejoicing because God 'on oure enemys haþ vs wroken' (l. 4). God's victory over the enemy of the fiend is a traditional image (see note to the line) but as the poet develops this image it is hard not to see a secular counterpart to his diction:

> Man, and ȝe holde my lawe,
> All þyn enemys shal þe drede;

And þou stonde of me non awe,
Þyn enemys outeray þe in dede.
For þere as I my frendis lede,
Þey shul not sporne at stok ne ston;
In all here werkis, þey shal wel spede,
Ȝif God and man be wel at on.

Myn enemys Y shal reue here syȝt;
Ȝeue syknes, and drede, pouert and wo.
My frendis, Y ȝeue syȝt and myȝt,
Richesse, strengþe, ouer here foo.
Hem thar not drede where þey go;
Here wele and worschip in euery won.
Siþ ȝe be syker, kepe ȝow so,
Now God and ȝe are wel at on.

(Poem 11/81–96)

On one level these stanzas promise reconciliation between God and human beings if mankind obeys God's law. But on another level, especially given the Easter coronation of Henry V, there is also the suggestion that these lines are relevant to the realm of England. Prosperity and renown will follow if the nation is obedient to God's law; God will offer protection within and wreak terrible vengeance on its enemies without. The spiritual import of conquering the enemy of sin also suggests the promise of conquest over secular enemies. None of this is made explicit, but especially when the mini-sequence of Poems 9–13 builds to create a model of corporate unity both for the secular realm, and between human beings and God, the diction of war and peace has a resonance in Poem 11 which exceeds a narrowly spiritual reference.

One final cluster of diction which has both an earthly and spiritual valency centres around the household. As Jenni Nuttall, has shown, household narratives were an especially important trope in urging reform in political poetry written in the reign of Henry IV.[102] One of the key functions of a household was to offer hospitality, especially for poor visitors.[103] Early fifteenth-century poems often show households violating this principle by expelling poor visitors, or treating them

---

[102]   Jenni Nuttall, 'Household Narratives and Lancastrian Poetics in Hoccleve's Envoy's and Other Early Fifteenth-Century Middle English Poems' in Cordelia Beattie, Anna Maslakovic and Sarah Rees Jones edd., *The Medieval Household in Christian Europe: Managing Power, Wealth and the Body* (Turnhout: Brepols, 2003), pp. 91–106.
[103]   Felicity Heal, *Hospitality in Early Modern England* (Oxford: Clarendon Press, 1990), pp. 1–22.

shabbily – especially if they happen to be truthtellers. The most graphic instance of this is the ejection of Wit in *Richard the Redeless*, where he is actually kicked out of the household by a courtier who wears piked shoes (III.232).

A variation on these tropes is used in Digby. In an encomium on the resilience of truthtelling, the poet writes:

> Trouþe secheþ non hernes ther los is lamed;
> Trouþe is worschiped at euery des.
>
> (Poem 3/5–6)

Space is socially significant in household narratives. In *Mum and the Sothsegger*, the 'sothesegger' is nowhere to be seen in the tables in the hall at the banquet, but has dined earlier with Drede in a 'chambre' (ll. 827–38). Truthtelling is banished from the central public place of the hall; intimidated into a private chamber. In Digby the image is reversed in this moment of optimism in Poem 3. Truth does not lurk in corners but is worshipped at every dais. Line 6 figures an ideal household with truth in prominent position at the apex of public space, the dais in the hall.

The spaces of the household are also used by the Digby poet in writing about human treatment of God. Just as the sinful man fails to perform the works of mercy by allowing those who are 'herberles' to lie outside (Poem 6/38), so too human ingratitude towards God's sacrifice on the cross is figured as refusing Him hospitality. God is figured as a guest who is treated shabbily by his human hosts. They throw him outside the gate (Poem 10/69), or take him in only for one night and then turn him out in the morning (Poem 10/121–3). This image is used again in Poem 11/65–8. God complains that folk used to be happy to receive him 'ymydde here brest' but eject him in the morning and turn his palace into a nest of devils. The human heart is a household inhospitable to God. Proper hospitality is an important thread of the poems. The reader is urged to grant no hospitality to what God hates (Poem 17/7–8) and to keep God within 'ʒoure ynnere gate' (Poem 11/36). Man's refusal to allow God to rest in his proper household place, instead placing him beyond the perimeter, is a wilful choice which has drastic consequences. Those who exult in sin and encourage others to do so are described as locking the gates of heaven against themselves, and purchasing hospitality in hell (Poem 21/45–8). And God's reproach to man that they 'stick him' outside the gate in Poem 10 is transposed in Poem 17 into God's terrifying ultimatum: give me your love, or

> My face wiþ loue shalt þou not se,
> But steke þe wiþoute heuene ʒate,
> Fro alle vertues and charyte,
> Wiþ helle houndes in endeles date.
>
> (Poem 17/109–12)

The poet's use of figurative diction centred on the household articulates proper patterns of both social and spiritual behaviour. Correct management of household space cherishes both truthtellers and the needy – and God. Human inhospitality will earn a terrifying punishment; those who offer God only temporary refuge, or turn him out of the gates, will be locked outside the gates of heaven and become the permanent guests of the hounds of hell.

iii) *Narrative voice*
The declarative statements and figurative diction of the poems are part of a social temper which models corporate unity and spiritual concord between humans and God. In the same fashion, the poet creates a narrative voice that is common, communal and consensual. Looking for the particularly pertinent, or searching for individuality violates the carefully constructed poetic persona of these political lyrics. There are few instances where an opinion is placed into the mouth of an 'I'. Even where this occurs, the 'I narrator' is not an individual; he is a mouthpiece for conventional wisdom; the already said, the often-said; for commonly received moral truths. The truth of old proverbs is explicitly called upon in Poem 3:

> Old speche is spoken ȝore:
> What is a kyngdom tresory?
> Bestayle, corn stuffed in store,
> Riche comouns, and wyse clergy;
> Marchaundes, squyers, chiualry
> That wol be redy at a res,
> And cheualrous kyng in wittes hyȝe
> To lede in were, and gouerne in pes.
>
> Among philosofres wyse,
> In here bokes men writen fynde
> Þat synne is cause of cowardyse.

> (Poem 3/65–75)

The reference to 'old speche … spoken ȝore' and the books of wise philosophers are an important key to the poetic quality of the narrative voice. The words of the narrative voice are forged from earlier speech and wise books. Individual lines can be paralleled extensively in wisdom literature, common proverbs, biblical citations and penitential manuals. Further, the narrator recycles what he has already said: numerous individual lines within the poems are re-used, sometimes within the same poem, sometimes in much later poems in the sequence. Many of these repetitions are verbatim, or with small changes such as in the use of pronouns, grammatical form, or the ordering of the line. Alongside this are repetitions of phraseology, and as I have illustrated above, clusters of diction. Notes to the poems record this repetition, but to give a picture of the poetic texture this creates as a whole, here is a snapshot of the repetition of lines and phrases from the first poem of the sequence:

Eche man be war that bereth astate	(1/1)
Eche man wot that bereth estate	(1/97)
That ouere puple haue astate	(8/57)

Man, knowe thy self, loue God and drede	(1/8
cf. 1/9/16/32/88/96/104/112/120/128/136/144/160/168)	
Man, knowe thy self, and lerne to dye	(7/title)
Man, knowe þy self and lerne to dye.	(7/8)
To knowe 3oure seluen now bygynne;	(9/12)
What þou art knowe þy self wel	(22/9)

That ouer puple hast gouernaunce.	(1/10)
That ouer puple han gouernaunce,	(5/41)
Ouer cite or town hast gouernaunce	(14/34)

Make vnyte ther was distaunce.	(1/13)
Gouerne the puple in vnyte	(1/21)
To gouerne puple in vnyte	(3/130)
To gouerne þe puple in vnyte	(8/63)
All 3oure reme in vnyte	(13/106)
In vnyte togydre so	(20/18)

The puple is Godes, and not 3oures	(1/19)
Þe puple is Goddis and no3t 3oures	(13/51)

In the comaundements that God bede.	(1/22)
Do þe comaundement þat he bede.	(3/106)
Do comaundementis þat God bed;	(7/63)
And do þe comaundementis þat Y bede	(19/112)

God wole haue rekenyng ywys	(1/29)
God wole haue rekenyng	(1/35)
Þerof God wole rekenyng craue	(7/83)
To 3elde rekenyng of Goddis lon	(11/110
cf. 10/196; 14/31; 16/125)	

Thy getyng, thy holdyng, thy spendyng mys.	(1/31)
Þy getyng, þy holdyng, þy spendyng mysse;	(8/7)
Man of his owen hath no thyng;	
Man is Goddis, and al God sent.	(1/33–4)
Al is Goddis and so be ȝe	(3/132)
Al is Goddis and he is lent	(7/82)
For worldly wys is gostly nys,	(1/45)
Þis worldly wysdom is gostly nys	(8/77)
Folowe mesure in euene syse,	(1/61)
Set mesure in euene assise	(3/13)
Man synne not in ouerhope;	(1/129)
Man synne not in ouerhope.	(7/97)
In ouerhope be not to bold	
In synne for to haue mercy	
Let not wanhope in þe be old	(20/201–3)
Fle fro fooles and folwe wise	(1/167)
Folowe fooles, and fle fro wyse.	(6/28)
Fle all folly and folwe þe wise	(22/72)

The saturation of the narrative voice of the poems with the sagacity of wisdom literature, biblical quotation, and common proverb can be seen in the following examples from Poem 1.

> Eche man wot that hath wyt,
> These worldes goods beth not his;
> Alle is Godes: he oweth hit,
> And land and see, and pyne and blis.   (25–8)

Cf. Ecclesiasticus 11:14, 'Prosperity, adversity, life and death, poverty and riches come of the Lord'

> Serue God for helle drede;
> Fle fro synne and al vys.   (41–2)

Cf. Zupitza, *Proverbis of Wysdom* 244:3–4, 'The fyrst proverbe to begynne/Drede god and fle fro synne'; and 'Love god and fle fro synne,/And so may thow hevyn wynne' (247:137–8).

> And fooles erande may not spede.   (46)

Cf. Proverbs 26:6, 'He that sendeth a message by the hand of a fool cutteth off the feet and drinketh damage'.

> Richesse and hele maketh wylde men raue
> That to vertues take non hede.
> Er thy soule be fendes knaue,
> Knowe thy self, loue God and drede.   (53-6)

Cf. Proverbs 11:4, 'Riches profit not in the day of wrath: but righteousness delivereth from death'.

> For God seeth thurgh euery bore.   (95)

Cf. Ecclesiasticus 40:19, 'The works of all flesh are before him and nothing can be hid from his eyes'

> The man withoute charitee
> May neuere wynne heuen blisse.
> As thou wolde men dede for the
> Do thou so liche; eche man haue hisse.   (113-16)

Cf. Luke 6:30-1, 'Give to every man that asketh of thee; and of him that taketh away thy goods ask them not again/And as ye would that men do to you, do ye also to them likewise'.

> To wene no mercy thou hauen myght.
> Alle thyng is nombred in Goddis sight: (133-4)

Cf. Job 14:5, 'Seeing his days are determined, the number of his months are with thee; thou hast appointed his bounds that he cannot pass' and Wisdom 11:20, 'thou hast ordered all things in measure, weight and number'.

> Who that takeþ fro pore to eke with his,
> For that wrong is worthy wo.   (145-6)

Cf. Proverbs 22:16, 'He that oppresseth the poor to increase his riches, and he that giveth to the rich shall surely come to want'.

> That ȝeueth to that liȝe or go
> Mete or drynke, herborwe or wede,   (149-50)

Cf. Matthew 25:35-6, 'For I was an hungered, and ye gave me meat: I was thirsty, and ye gave me drink: I was a stranger, and ye took me in/Naked, and ye clothed me'.

He is a fool that doth answere
To a man er tale be told;   (153–4)

Cf. Ecclesiasticus 11:8, 'Answer not before thou hast heard the cause'

Er charitee in hert wexe cold,   (159)

Cf. Matthew 24:11–12, 'And many false prophets shall rise, and shall deceive many/And because iniquity shall abound, the love of many shall wax cold'.

Old horded hate maketh wratthe to rise,   (165)

Cf. Proverbs 10:12, 'Hatred stirreth up strifes: but love covereth all sins'.

Fle fro fooles and folwe wise.   (167)

Cf. Proverbs 9:6, 'Forsake the foolish and live; and go in the way of understanding'

Space alone prohibits a more comprehensive account of how the poetic temper of the lyrics is sedimented with recycled old lore. The Digby poems are an echo-chamber of the already said. The speech acts produced by the narrative voice are overwhelmingly admonitory; the narrative persona created is that of a weathered sage who speaks timeless wisdom. There is, however, a very timely edge to this narrative fashioning.

Distinctions between the moral and the topical in the discussion of 'political' poetry are beside the point in considering the Digby poems.[104] Of course they are moral – as the catalogue of axiomatic statements above demonstrates beyond doubt. But why should this not simultaneously have political capital? It is not just the use of marked vocabulary or references to arcane events buried in chronicles that makes texts political. What appears normative – bland even – has just as much potential to harbour political energy as discourse that is angular, aggressive and distinctive. And, more to the point, its political force is easier to overlook precisely because this discourse has the appearance of 'naturalness' or normativity. Adopting a timelessly moral common sense temper performs an act just as social

---

[104]   Cf. Kane's dismissal of the so-called politicality of complaint literature, footnote 20 above.

and political as referring to an event that can be traced in the parliament rolls. What the social temper of these Digby poems *does* is to create a model of political community whose legitimacy, harmony and time-honoured existence is difficult to question, built as it is on assertive time-worn common sense. The narrative voice of the lyrics forges a sphere for public address[105] and it also fashions a stable political community. As the discussion of corporate unity above has shown, the poems are riddled with anxiety lest this stability be shattered, but the poet does his best to build a political community with *common* sense as its foundation.

As David Lawton has demonstrated in a seminal essay on the poetic texture of fifteenth-century poetry, this kind of voice was especially characteristic of the early years of Henry V's reign.[106] The Digby poems fall outside the scope of Lawton's study, but they can be seen to be very much part of this social discourse. What the sequence fashions as a whole is a political realm united through common profit, with a reformed church at its heart, and with Henry V at its head. While the social temper of the Digby poems might appear 'dull', the political positioning of this discourse has timely bite. The platitudes are nothing less than the depersonalised voicing of radical conservatism.

7. Poetics

For all the dependence on the already-said, these lyrics are not dull. Although the poet works with commonplace and convention, frequently these are treated with no little agility and wit. Further, the poet works within demanding stanza forms. The eight-line stanza is the poet's staple. Thirteeen lyrics have an ababbcbc rhyme scheme with refrain.[107] Nine lyrics use an eight-line stanza without refrain rhyming abababab.[108] Two poems have stanzas of fourteen lines which rhyme abababab-ccdddc.[109] Within such stringent schemes, the poet is capable of great variety of voice, and an extremely supple use of the verse form.

Poem 6 reverses the tropes of 'learn to die' lyrics (see headnote). There is a

---

[105]   Anne Middleton identifies a particular kind of poetic voice which creates an idea of public poetry, 'the adoption of a common voice to serve the common good where there is a constant relation of speaker to audience within an ideally conceived worldly community. The poetic voice is offered as a common voice in essentially public terms', 'The Idea of Public Poetry in the Reign of Richard II', *Speculum* 53 (1978), pp. 94–114 reprt. in Stephanie Trigg ed., *Medieval English Poetry* (London: Longman, (1993), pp. 24–46; at p. 25. Middleton's essay concerns literary texts written before 1400, but her remarks are entirely pertinent to the Digby poems.

[106]   David Lawton, 'Dullness and the Fifteenth Century' *ELH* 54 (1987), 761–99.

[107]   Poems 1, 2, 3, 4, 5, 6, 7, 8, 9, 11, 12, 13 and 14.

[108]   Poems 15, 17, 18, 19, 20, 21, 22, 23 and 24.

[109]   Poems 10 and 16.

muscular energy in the series of improper injunctions that comprise this poem. Crisp one-liners such as 'Do as þou þou3t neuere to dye' (l. 14) are contained in stanzas where subtle variation in metrical stress may be seen to recreate a sense of the recklessness which the poem ironically encourages:

> Day and ny3t walke late
> At cokes hostry and tauerne.
> Þou3 þu no man oþere hate,
> Go not ere þu make debate.
> To lewed, lettred, and clergye,
> Do no reueraunce to non astate;
> Þan men wole drede þe bodylye.
>
> (Poem 6/18–24)

The poet achieves a canny riff on metrical stress within the tight regulation of the demands of the rhyme scheme. Here, the initial trochees of lines 18, 21, and 23 craft an insouciance of tone which is in keeping with the devotional pitch of the lyric as a whole. Also characteristic of the poet's deft touch is the use of shorter metrical lines which create an abruptness of address. Line 18 here, with its predominant Old English monosyllables, is one such example. The polysyllabic, Latin/French 'reueraunce' of line 23 foregrounds the correct decorous behaviour which the diction of the rest of the stanza boldly flouts.

Poem 20 takes the form of an inversion of the 'Complaint of Christ' religious lyric. Instead of Christ rebuking humankind for failing to return His love, and for continuing in a life of sin, here the body makes a formal complaint against Christ to God. Jesus is accused of having stolen the body's soul. The poem adroitly re-positions religious, legal and literary tropes. The complaint trope is blended with traditional body and soul debate motifs. The gendering of the soul as female and the body as male creates the opportunity for ironising the narrative voice of the body. For instance, the soul's exhortations to the body to give up its worldliness are framed as the scolding rebukes of a shrewish wife:

> Wolde Y be proud, she biddeþ be meke,
> Wolde Y be gloton, she biddeþ me faste,
> Þere Y wolde take, she biddes me eke,
> Wolde Y be lyther, she biddis be chaste,
> 3if Y fy3te, she biddes ley forþ my cheke,
> Þere Y am slow, she biddis be haste.
> Here answere is not to seke,
> To speke to here my wynde Y waste.
>
> (Poem 20/49–56)

The comic force of the stanza derives partly from the invocation of a domestic spat with body and soul figured respectively as hen-pecked husband and contrary wife, and partly from a superbly controlled use of inverted chiasmus. The poet combines the use of heavy rhyme (all on phonetically stopped consonants), and the avoidance of elevated diction, with a clever series of oppositions which create a double sound pattern within the stanza. The anaphoric 'biddeþ' and 'wolde' thump out a scenario of frustrated discord – but the key to the dexterity of the stanza lies in the breaking of this pattern in the final two lines. The pattern of volition followed by rebuke modulates into two lines without caesura and without antithesis: the rebuttal of aspirant sinful behaviour deflates into a weary admission of defeat. The resounding oppositions collapse into slack, self-pitying submission. The formulaic 'wynde Y waste' (used also Poem 12/51), with the alliteration falling on phonetically unstopped syllables brings the recalcitrant antitheses of the first six lines of the stanza to a feeble close.

Modulation of tone and voice in the series are often the result of such metrical accomplishment. A later stanza in the same lyric shows the poet's adeptness in creating verisimilitudinous verbal exchange through the counterpoint of grammatical and metrical structures:

> She repreueþ me my dagged cloþes,
> And longe, pyked, crakowed shon;
> Vpbreyde[þ] me my grete oþes,
> And sayþ Y breke Goddis bone.
> Þat me is lef, all she loþes.
> I seye, 'Oþere men so don!'
> She seyþ, 'Þey go to helle woþes –
> Wole to wende wiþ hem to wone!'
>
> (Poem 20/137–44)

Vocal argument erupts into the stanza with the petulant recreation of the injured voice of the body in line 142. The brevity of the bland and lightweight self-defence cuts into the metrical regularity of the previous lines. The callowness of the body's self-justification is exposed through the almost stichomythic response of the soul. Quick as a flash, and with anaphoric refutation 'she sayþ', the morally threadbare and peevish excuse of the body is cut down to size as a recipe for eternal damnation.

As the series develops, the narrator's voice inhabits a number of different persons and positions: the stern wise sage; the flatterer and the labouring man in Poem 2; plotting 'executours' in the same poem; the various members of the body politic, as discussed above – and God. Some of the tautest writing in the sequence comes in poems which are voiced by God. The poet uses the fourteen-line stanza of Poem 10 to telling effect with God's reproaches to sinful humankind:

God seiþ, 'Man, Y made þe of nouȝt,
And put the in to paradys,
Of erþely þynges þat Y wrouȝt
To neme þat neded to þyn eys.
I lent þe fre wil and þouȝt,
Warnyng of foly to be wys;
At þe tre of wysdom foly þu souȝt,
And ȝaf for an appyl þe most of prys.
Þe same mouþ þat þe appyl gnewe,
In þat mouþ þe holy croys grewe,
Wheron Y dyed for ȝoure gylt.
Þurgh þe herte, and þurgh þe mylt;
I hadde þe poynt – and ȝe, þe hylt!
Ȝoure heritage Y bouȝt ȝow newe.

(Poem 10/15–28)

The reasoned argument of lines 15–22 draws on entirely conventional diction which is used elsewhere in the lyrics. But it is given a bitter edge by the turn in the stanza to the ccdddc rhymes. The trope of 'felix culpa' is fused with the legend of the holy cross made from the wood from the pips of the apple bitten in the Garden of Eden. The image is compacted into two lines bound by the sound of the anaphoric 'mouþe' and the rhyme of 'gnewe/grewe'. The introduction of new rhyme words foregrounds their impact. The poet uses the successive ddd rhymes to intensify man's ingratitude for Christ's sacrifice. The rhymes are all monosyllabic and phonetically stopped, sounds all the more forceful for their repetition and antithetical patterning. While the spleen (mylt) does not usually figure among Christ's body parts, the rhyme sets up the devastating image of the spear wound as a sword plunged into Christ's body, with mankind holding the hilt. The last line, detached from the immediate rhyme and syntax, and without internal sound patterning, makes all the more pointed Christ's redemption for those who put him to death.

Internal sound patterning is used in other lyrics with rhetorical virtuosity:

Ȝif þou sette loue in þat degre
To loue God, for he þe wrouȝt,
Þan make þou hym as he dede þe,
Þan loue for loue euene is brouȝt.
Ȝif þou loue God, for he made þe fre,
Þat dyȝed for the, to blisse þe bouȝt,
þan dyȝe þou for hym as he dyȝed for þe;
Ȝut heuene blisse þou quytest hym nouȝt.

(Poem 17/41–8)

The sentiments have a long history, but the poet puts them to work by matching rhyme and rhetorical stress. The usual practice of the poet is to use different rhyme words in each stanza, though there are some exceptions as I discussed above, in the case of 'on' in Poem 11. Here the poet repeats the rhyme of 'þe', a repetition which is not, I think, the result of the poet's defeat by the 'skarsete of rhyme'. The anaphoric repetition of the second person pronoun, together with the anaphora and polyptoton of 'loue' and 'dyȝe', heaps up the guilt on the reader. The diction is plain, which adds to the force of the lines; and once again, the poet controls the architecture of the whole stanza with a deftness which scores an important theological point. As in the example quoted from Poem 10, the last line is semi-detached. Here the detachment results from the absence of internal sound patterning that has dominated the preceding lines, and also from the appositive syntax. The last line, coming to rest on 'nouȝt', is a stinging reminder of man's inability to equal God's love.

The tightness of the stanza form, far from being a constraint on the poet, is used to orchestrate the sense. This is especially seen in places where the verse is based on axioms:

> What may thy richesse þe auayle
> Whan þu art to deþe dryue?
> Thy wynd is layd, þu mayst not sayle,
> Þouȝ þu lete out bonet and ryue.
>
> (Poem 7/25–8)

The taunting question of lines 25–26 is answered by a pithy sententia whose force is accented through the use of assonance in line 27. The image of being driven towards death is answered with a figure whose sound patterning underscores the uselessness of human endeavour. Letting out sails avails nothing when there is no wind. The move from abstract to more concrete diction enables the poet to quicken what might otherwise be a series of dreary dead platitudes, as in Poem 5:

> And on þy strengþe be not to bold,
> Ne skorne no pore, ne feble of elde;
> For lyue long, ȝe mon be old,
> In feblenes to hoke and helde;
>
> (Poem 5/57–60)

The timeless moral injunctions are given bite by the sudden introduction of the feeble attempt to stoop and bend (l. 60). Of course, the hendiadys facilitates the rhyme, but it works for its place in making vivid the decrepitude of old age. The supplementing of rhyme with dissonance lends a crispness to what otherwise might be simply time-worn.

Sound reinforces sense in other ways. In places, the lyrics move into densely alliterative diction, for instance line 2 of Poem 9, 'Burnysche briȝt ȝoure soules blake'. The ringing exhortation results from the combination of alliterative and metrical stress, coupled with the variation on long vowel sounds. In Poem 10, within the demands of an even more tightly constructed stanza form, the verse suddenly explodes into alliterative denunciation with God's injunction 'Not to fostre þe as a swyn/Þy foule flesche in fylþe to fede' (Poem 10/201–2). The poem on the follies of Flanders uses alliteration in its opening lines to establish a tone of invective close to that of 'flytyng':

> Loke how Flaundres doþ fare wiþ his folyhede!
> Durste no man dygge after trouþe wiþ no manere toles;
> To wynne wrongly wele, wod þey gan wede,
> But werkis of wys men were cast vnder stoles.
>
> (Poem 16/1–4).

This tone is reinforced by the use of metrically shorter lines in the dddc rhymes of the stanza, for instance:

> Who so wil not knowe his awen astat,
> Ne deliuere chekkys er þat he be mat,
> He shal haue worldis wondryng,
> And his soule hyndryng,
> And ay in paynes pondryng,
> To mende þanne is to late.
>
> (Poem 16/107–12)

Once again, the move into figurative diction with the image drawn from chess saves the lines from blandness. The metrical pattern of alternating the dentally stopped c rhymes with the disyllabic d rhymes lends energy to the warnings. As so often, the syntactical semi-detachment of the last line of the stanza sums up the moral with pithy directness.

Repetition and balance are used in a number of ways in these lyrics to vary tone and voice and to reinforce declarative statements. I have discussed the liturgical quality of the penultimate stanza of Poem 23 above. Poem 21 uses an antithetical structure of alternating the 'blessed be' formula drawn from Matthew's Sermon on the Mount with the 'cursed be' invective from Deuteronomy (see headnote). There are many lines in the series whose vigour is the result of antithesis: 'Þat ȝe hyde, ful bryȝt Y se' (Poem 10/92); 'To endeles werre, or endeles pes' (Poem 3/136), and 'Today is quyk, tomorwe is fay' (Poem 4/198). The refrain poems use variation on the last line of each stanza to punch home their moral message, but even within this there is inflection and modulation of tone. Poem 12 has as its refrain the urgent call to 'kepe þe croun', but, just as in the second stanza (quoted above, pp. 45–6) where the last line is varied to describe the least liege man as a part of the crown, so too, in the call to beware of foreign enemies in the fourth stanza, the poet introduces variety into the refrain:

> By3onde þe see, and we had nou3t,
> But all oure enemys so ney3e vs w[o]re,
> Þou3 all here gold were hider brou3t,
> I wolde set hit at lytel store.
> Oure enemys wolde coke þerfore,
> Wiþ ordynaunce, and habergeoun:
> Wynne þat, and wel more:
> Oure landes, oure lyues, þe reme, þe crowne.
>
> (Poem 12/25–32)

The sudden reduction of syllables in line 31 voices the starkness of enemy threat; the anxiety is registered keenly by the asyndeton (absence of grammatical connectors) on the refrain in the last line; the list concluding ominously with the link word 'crowne'.

One final example shows how the repetition of grammatical inflection subtly reinforces propositional statement:

> At domesday no man shal be excusyd:
> Lord, ne lady, mayde ne knaue,
> For wykked counsel scholde be refusyd,
> And after good counsayle craue.
> After warke þat þay vsed,
> I shal hem deme or saue:
> Þe sauyd excusyd, þe dampnyd accusyd,
> As thay deseruyd echon haue.
>
> (Poem 24/402–10)

The separation of the goats from the sheep in this, the penultimate stanza of the sequence, is underscored by the sound patterning: assonance in lines 403 and 409; asyndeton in line 403; the antithesis of line 409, and more subtly, throughout, by the repeated 'yd' endings of past participles and participle adjectives, a sound that is reinforced through its use in rhyme position. The repetition is not mere ornamentation. In a stanza which presses home the message that each person shall be judged according to what they have done, the ultimate worth of accumulated deeds is emphasised by the insistent sounding of the past tense.

8. Provenance

MS Digby 102 is one of a group of five manuscripts containing a *Piers Plowman* C Text which Simon Horobin analysed in an article in 2005. These were manuscripts which had previously been used to support the theory that Langland returned to Malvern in his declining years in order to revise the B version of his poem. Horobin shows that while these manuscripts do contain South West Worcestershire (SWW) forms, these should be attributed to the exemplar rather than to the scribe.[110] They are inherited from a common exemplar, and in each case that Horobin examines, such SWW forms appear alongside other non-western spelling features. Horobin argues that rather than Worcestershire, the more likely provenance of these manuscripts is London. This is suggested by Eastern dialect layers and extralinguistic features such as handwriting, layout and ordinatio. Horobin argues that the dialect of these manuscripts showed that Londoners tolerated a much broader range of dialect variation than has generally been accepted, and also that the practice of literatim copying was still buoyant.[111]

These conclusions are entirely supported by analysis of the dialect of the Digby poems in MS Bodley 102.[112] Their dialect is not identical to that of the preceding *Piers* text, though they do share some of the same forms.[113]

	Piers	*Digby*
after	aftur	after, aftur
again	aȝeyn	agayn, aȝayn[114]
against	agaynes, aȝen, aȝenes, aȝennes, aȝeyn	agaynes, aȝen, aȝens, aȝenst, aȝeyn, aȝeyns[115]
any	eny (ony)	any, eny[116]
are	beth	ar, are, aren, arn, ben, beth[117]
but	bote	bot, but

---

[110] Horobin, 'In London and Opelond', pp. 252–3.

[111] Ibid., pp. 263–5.

[112] Space prohibits an exhaustive analysis of the dialect; I have chosen representative examples from the whole corpus of lyrics.

[113] The table adds to the items catalogued by Horobin, 'In London and Opelond', p. 260, from the profile in *LALME*, LP7770, III.561.

[114] *agayn* (4/103, 20/3); *aȝayn* (11/67, 19/30).

[115] *agaynes* (10/86); *aȝen* (1/75, 4/3, 23/72); *aȝens* (3/33; 24/34/146); *aȝenst* (13/76); *aȝeyn* (24/230/259); *aȝeyns* (18/56).

[116] *any* (4/200); *eny* (8/58; 14/97).

[117] *ar* (4/117, 12/66, 24/197); *are* (19 examples); *aren* (24/99); *arn* (1/126); *ben* (47 examples); *beth* (1/26).

	Piers	*Digby*
each	eche, vche	ech, eche
ere	ar (are)	er(e)
fire	fuyr	fire
from	fram	fram, fro, from[118]
good	good	good
her	here	here
high	hiȝe	hey, hiȝe, hyȝe
if	yf	ȝif
man	man	man, mon
many	many, mony, moneye	many, mony(e)
might	myhte	myght, miȝt, myȝt
much	mochel, much	moche, muche, myche, mochil[119]
not	nat, nauht	noght, noȝt, not
own	owen, owne	own, owe, owen, awen[120]
saw	seyh	seyȝe
say	segge	say, sey
shall (sg.)	shal	schal, shall
shall (pl.)	shal	schul, schulle, schullen
she	sche, she	sche, she
should	scholde	scholde, schuld(e), shuld
sin	synne	synne
since	sennes sethe, sethen	sen, siþ
strength	strenghe, strength	strengþ, strengþe, strengthe
such	such(e)	such(e)
than	then, thenne	than, thanne, þan, þanne
their	here (hyre)	here
them	hem	hem
these	thes, this	þes, thes, these
though	thow (thogh)	thouȝ, þouȝ, thow
through	thorw, thorowe	thurgh, þurgh
was	was	was, wes[121]
which	whiche, wiche, whuche	whiche, whyche, whoche[122]

---

[118]   *fram* (24/383); *fro* (136 examples); *from* (11 examples).

[119]   *moche* (29 examples); *muche* (2/head); *myche* (18/159); *mochil* (20/193).

[120]   *awen* (2/34; 7/120; 12/130; 16/107; 20/167/194, 21/34, 21/120); *owe* (10/136); *owen* (23 examples); *own* (7/81).

[121]   *was* (37 examples); *wes* (3/142).

[122]   *whiche* (2/18, 5/43); *whyche* (23/19); *whoche* (3/36).

	Piers	*Digby*
while	while, whiles	while, whule, whyle[123]
will (sg.)	wol(e)	wil, will, wille, wole, wolle
will (pl.)	wol, wolle, wolleth	wil, will, wol, wole, wolen
work (n.)	werk	warke, werk, worke[124]
work (v.)	worche	worche
yet	ȝut	ȝet, ȝit, ȝut[125]

While the same scribe was responsible for copying both of these texts, the differences in spelling suggest that he copied literatim rather than imposing his own orthography on the texts.[126] It is also striking that there is much more variety in spelling in Digby than in the *Piers* text. LALME locates the manuscript to Worcestershire, and certainly, many of the forms are compatible with such a location. But with the exception of *whoche* (the only instance is Poem 3/36) and *whule* (only at Poem 14/26), SWW spellings are not ubiquitous (compare *fuyr* in *Piers* with *fire* in Digby). Indeed, the range of spelling features in the Digby poems suggests a rather different provenance, one that is not compatible with the *LALME* geographical grid location method. The Digby lyrics show a particularly rich example of mixed orthography. This is especially noticeable (though not exclusively) in words which appear in rhyme. There is an eccentric choice of forms which show the poet raiding possible – and impossible – spellings. South Western (SW) orthography does feature: e.g. *despuse* (Poem 5/35), though the -u- form is not recorded in *MED*. Elsewhere in Digby the form is *despi/y/se* (Poem 6/26, 10/132, 22/70, 24/289). Might the *despuse* spelling have resulted from a crossover with *dispuse*? In Poem 9 *dure* (l. 71) rhymes with *hire, sire* and *fire*. A [u] form is possible in rhyme with *fire* and *hire*, both deriving from OE [ȳ], but not *sire*. In Poem 11 *refuse* (l. 41), rhymes with *rise, blis* and *kys*. This is an inexact rhyme all round. Even if *kys* (OE *cyssan*) could have a rounded vowel, it would be long and therefore not a perfect sound match with OF *refuse*. That *rise* derives from OE [i] and *blis* OE [y] adds further confusion. In Poem 21/61, *gultless* appears in the middle of the line; the Western spelling is not needed for rhyme. In Poem 1/166, the form is *gilteles* and *giltles* in Poem 9/126; both are in the middle of the line.

As these examples show, the spelling of words is eclectic. Throughout the sequence the same words are spelled in different dialect forms. Sometimes the variation can be attributed to the need to find a rhyme word, but this is by no means always the case. Alongside the presence of Western dialect forms are many

---

[123]   *while* (15 examples); *whule* (14/26); *whyle* (3/125, 11/69, 15/113, 22/69).
[124]   *warke* (24/407); *werk* (69 examples); *worke* (24/413).
[125]   *ȝet* (7/87; 16/83); *ȝit* (3/41, 12/133, 17/49, 20/63); *ȝut* (1/39, 7/39, 10/77, 17/13, 18/182).
[126]   The rare occasions when the scribe miscopied a dialect spelling are discussed below.

Eastern spellings.[127] In Poem 7/61 *telyeþ* appears in the sense of tills, cultivates. The word is not in rhyme position. *Dreuen* is used in Poem 11/12. Elsewhere the form is *dryue(þ)* (Poem 7/26, 3/120, 23/29).[128] In Poem 20/72 *spettes* in the sense of 'spits' appears outside rhyme position. *Besynesse* is the spelling of Poem 15/28 and 18/13 (cf. *besye* 19/85 and *besyen*, 16/42). Poem 17/68 has *felþe* and 22/5 *fylþe*. Poem 17/49 has Eastern *byhende* in rhyme position, while in the same poem, line 171, the form is *byhynde*. In Poem 12, Eastern spelling is used in the *flet … knet* rhyme of lines 42–4 (cf. Poem 20/25/27), but elsewhere *knyt* appears in rhyme position (Poem 1/59, 5/13, 10/85, 15/18). In Poem 12/106 and 13/17, the formula *lyf* and *leme* is used; the second in rhyme position. There are no other examples of 'limb' (sg) in the sequence. The plural spelling is always *lymes* see Poem 15/39 etc. and 19/76. In Poem 13/82 *blende* is the Eastern spelling of 'blind' (vb). The form secures rhyme, as it does when the same verb is used Poem 5/20. As an adjective, and always in rhyme position, the form is *blynd(e)* (Poem 3/77, 4/215, 5/7, 9/26, 10/13, 15/110, 17/134, 23/39).[129] In Poem 24/61 *nesse* rhymes with *kesse*. This is the only example of the Eastern spelling of this verb. Elsewhere, the form is *kys(se)*, e.g. Poem 1/163 ,1/119, 8/37, 11/47, 17/15, 18/84 and 19/30.

The same pattern of variation is seen in the strong presence of Northern features. There are a number of present participles with Northern spelling: *blasande* (Poem 2/12); *vnwetand* (Poem 4/213); *berkand* (Poem 2/238) and *plesande* (Poem 20/75).[130] None of these is a rhyme word. Similarly, Northern spellings occur, sometimes seemingly at random, at other times, to furnish rhyme. In Poem 24/362/407 *warke* appears for no obvious reason.[131] It is not used for rhyme, and elsewhere, apart from *worke* (Poem 24/413), the form is *werk* (e.g. Poem 4/154, 8/76, 13/94, 14/23; 18/136, 24/41). In Poem 7/37 *hattere* is not in rhyme position, nor *haldeþ* (Poem 9/65), nor *awen* (Poem 16/107); nor *ham* (Poem 24/210). *Hame*, however, is used in Poem 2/23 to rhyme with *name* and *fame*. Such variation is characteristic. In Poem 9/108 *þrawe* rhymes with *lawe, sawe* and *drawe*. But in Poem 14/78, *thro* is the form, rhyming with *wo*. In Poem 9/172, Northern *serkis* secures rhyme on *werkis* and Poem 10/39

---

[127]   While I use the term 'Eastern', 'i/e' variation is common in London and SE Midland texts in the early fifteenth century.

[128]   The poet may be taking advantage here of a rarer form of 'dreven' from OE 'dræfan', a verb related to 'drifan' but originally with a distinct meaning, see *MED* 'dreven' (v.); 1 and (v.); 2. Later, these forms were often confused.

[129]   Similar to the case of 'dreven', the poet may be taking advantage of a rarer form. *MED* 'blenden' (v.) from OE 'blendan' is related to 'blindan' but originally with a distinct meaning. See *MED* 'blenden' (v.); 1.

[130]   These 'Northern' forms are also characteristic of East Midlands and East Anglia, as well as Northern, see *LALME* 4:105. They are also found in London; see Simon Horobin, *The Language of the Chaucer Tradition* (Cambridge: Brewer, 2003), p. 140.

[131]   The form is rare, but scattered in the East Midlands, see *LALME* 4:89.

sare rhymes with *bare* and *spare*. Elsewhere in rhyme position, the form is *sore*: see Poem 12/114, 19/11/73, 20/106, 21/33, 24/387. In Poem 15 the poet rhymes *hondes*, *brondes* and *stondes* (ll, 36–40), and *handes* with *wandes* and *standes* (ll. 58–64) (cf. Poem 4/194–6, 18/81–3).[132] In Poem 16/86 *knawe* is used to rhyme with *awe, lawe* and *drawe*; but elsewhere the form is *knowe* (e.g. Poem 1/8 etc.; 4/46, 7/8, 8/81, 9/12). In Poem 19/62 the Northern form of the preposition 'to', *tille* rhymes with *ylle, spille* and *wille* and Poem 20/44 rhymes *pertille* with *wille* and *skille*.

In Poem 6/41, the MS reads *seruant*. It is the only place where the scribe has not copied a Northern spelling which is needed for rhyme. While *seruaunt* is the spelling at Poem 6/2, 9/130, 15/77/78, 20/36 and 21/147; (*seruant* at Poem 2/40 and 15/80), none of these is in rhyme position. In order to rhyme with *hand* in Poem 6, the poet must have originally written *seruand*, a form chiefly found in the North and the North East (though there are examples from West Midlands). In Poem 15/7 the MS reads *vnbende*. The rhyme words are *kynde, wynde* and *mynde*. Given the propensity for exact eye-rhymes, the poet's original must have been 'vnbynde'. Similarly with the MS reading *nelle* in Poem 18/52, it is likely that the scribe miscopied. The rhymes are *skille, fulfille* and *wille*. Throughout the sequence both *nel* and *nyl* forms are used, but only in Poem 18 is the Eastern spelling found at the end of the line. Is it a scribal error for *nylle* which is the spelling used in rhyme Poem 10/8? There is another instance of possible confusion in Poem 21/60, where *theft* rhymes with *thrifte, gyft* and *wyft*. While 'theft' is spelt consistently thus in the lyrics (Poem 13/81, 15/23), it is odd that eye-rhyme is not sustained in Poem 21 given the presence of *wyft* for *weft* at the end of the stanza (l. 64). There are some other places where eye-rhyme is not maintained.[133] For example, in Poem 13/1 *ysse* is the only example of this form of the 3rd singular present *is* in the whole sequence. The form is clearly confected in order to secure eye-rhyme with *mysse* (l. 3) but elsewhere there is inconsistent concern to achieve this effect with *mys* or *mysse* (see Poem 14/57–59, 17/178–80, 19/28–30, 23/1–3, 24/342–44).

Apart from these examples, the scribe appears to have copied rhyme words precisely. The range of dialect variety is promiscuously wide, and yet the scribe has kept up with, what are, in some instances, rather peculiar forms. In Poem 10/87 the spelling *pyt* is used to secure the rhyme. If this has the sense of 'put', it is the only example of the verb in rhyme position and elsewhere *put* is the usual form, e.g. Poem 3/25, 4/138/196. It is likely that it is a form of 'picchen', in the sense of

---

[132] Throughout, there is variation in the 3sg. *pres.* of verbs. The -es form alternates with -eth, sometimes for the sake of rhyme, sometimes without apparent reason, e.g. Poem 12/73–80 where *sechep, þenkeþ* and *stondes* all appear in the middle of the line. Chaucer uses -s forms only in *The Reeve's Tale* or to facilitate rhyme in *Book of the Duchess* 73, 258 and *House of Fame*, 426.

[133] As in the SW spellings 'use' which rhyme with words spelt –'ise' discussed above.

'thrust'. No infinitive form of the verb is listed in *MED* 'picchen' (*v.*), though the past participle 'ipeʒt' is recorded. In Poem 11/3 *mest* is used for rhyme (cf. Poem 24/10/12). Elsewhere (e.g. Poem 3/28, 4/35, 10/22, 12/60, 13/75 etc.), the form is *most* and used in rhyme position in Poem 23/87. The poet is not above mischievous invention in furnishing rhyme words for his exacting stanza forms. In Poem 10/23 the poet eschews the usual weak form of the preterite 'gnawed' and writes *gnewe*. *MED* 'gnauen' (*v.*) does list 'gneue' as a possible preterite singular of OE 'gnagan' with past participle 'gnogen' but even if this is the source, it shows the poet raiding unusual spelling forms in order to complete the rhyme. In Poem 13/113 *queryle* is a confected spelling to secure rhyme with *style* (l. 115). Elsewhere the form is *querel(l)* (see Poem 3/87, 9/139, 13/96, 13/117, 21/116/123). This is another example of the eclectic selection of forms for rhyme, with assonance, and/or approximate rhymes seeming to be entirely acceptable. In Poem 14/45 *hyng* rhymes with *clymbyng, kyng* and *wyng*. When the verb is used elsewhere, the form is *honge(þ)* (Poem 3/165 and 16/83). *MED* does list 'hyng' as a spelling of the infinitive of the verb, suggesting influence from Old Norse, but once again the choice of form is distinctive, and departs from the spelling one might expect given the form of the verb elsewhere in the sequence. In Poem 15/22 *het* could be a confected past participle from *MED* 'highten' (*v.*); 2b 'to adorn' 'honour', with the sense that if a man is invested with the order of knighthood then he is honoured with a collar (badge of office). More likely, perhaps, is that it is a form of 'hitten' in the sense of 'to touch'. *MED* 'hitten' (*v.*); 1f; there are no other uses of this verb in the sequence, so it is not possible to compare the poet's choice of forms. In Poem 22/15 the spelling of the infinitive *kele*, 'to become cool', secures rhyme with *wel, whel* and *fele*. Here the poet appears to have chosen this form of from OE 'celan'; see *MED* 'kelen' (*v.*) rather than from OE 'colian'; see *MED* 'colen' (*v.*); 1.

From the evidence assembled, the most likely provenance for these poems is London. The range of dialect diversity which the poet embraces and which the scribe reproduces is far wider than that of the scribes whom Simon Horobin analyses in his work on the language of the Chaucer tradition. Yet the dialect features of the Digby poems are consistent with his argument that the London dialect in the later fourteenth and early fifteenth centuries permitted great variation, and that dialect forms which were later stigmatised were as yet unmarked by such sociolinguistic connotations'.[134] While both Chaucer and Hoccleve had occasional recourse to Northern and Eastern dialect when stuck at the end of a line,[135] for all his injunctions against plunder, the Digby poet is a profligate pilferer of all manner

---

[134]   Horobin, *Language of Chaucer*, p. 140.
[135]   E.g. 'kisse/kesse' variation in Chaucer, and the rhyme of 'sittand' and 'hand', see Horobin, *Language of Chaucer*, p. 50 and Hoccleve's rhyming of 'herte' with the Eastern form of OE 'astyrian', 'asterte', ibid, p. 121. See also footnote 132 above.

of spelling forms. A London provenance for these poems is commensurate with the poet's knowledge of parliamentary business and international affairs. It also sits comfortably with the poet's evident championing of the new reign of Henry V. The presence of SW Midland forms in poems whose dialect diversity suggests a London provenance also suggests that the Digby poet had more in common with William Langland than simply having had his lyrics follow *Piers Plowman* in the only manuscript that preserves them. Might the Digby poet also have been in London and in 'opelond'?

Speculative though the suggestion is, it derives support from the extensive parallels between the Digby lyrics and the macaronic sermons composed in the reign of Henry V, preserved in Oxford, Bodley MS 649.[136] The author of these sermons was clearly a Benedictine monk. As Horner argues, 'while the name of this preacher remains uncertain, allusions within the sermons make clear his Benedictine affiliation and his university training at Oxford. References to historical events also suggest that most of the sermons were composed around the time of Henry V's reign, many of them after the Lollard uprising of 1414 led by Sir John Oldcastle.'[137] The collection as a whole shows an orthodox preacher passionate to explain and defend Church doctrine on the sacraments, especially the Eucharist and penance. The preacher is also at pains to emphasise the divinely ordained role of the clergy in theological investigation and liturgical activities and devotes considerable attention to practical pastoral theology in his discussions of how confessors should treat penitents. The reform of sinful priests is urged; there is open denunciation of the Lollards, and vivid exhortations to his listeners to unite themselves with Christ's suffering on the cross; the sermons include brief devotional lyrics. Furthermore, the sermons call for a harmoniously functioning political body. There is sustained criticism of flattery, robbing the poor, oppressing the commons and internal dissent. And there is overt support for the 'heavenly soldier' Henry V both against France, and against the Lollards. Every note that is sounded in the lyrics is sounded in the sermons, save that Lollards are cold-shouldered by the poet and denounced vehemently by the preacher.

Some of the Bodley sermons are also found in another Oxford manuscript, Bodleian, MS Laud Misc.706. An 'ex libris' on fol. 181v states that the manuscript belonged to John Paunteley, monk of St Peter's in Gloucester, 'sacre pagine professor' at Oxford 1410 and author of the funeral sermon in 1412 of Abbot Walter Froucester at St Peter's.[138] While the attribution of the macaronic Bodley sermons to Paunteley cannot ultimately be proved, their Benedictine provenance is beyond doubt, and it

---

[136]   Horner, *MS Bodley 649*.

[137]   Patrick J. Horner, '"The King Taught us the Lesson": Benedictine Support for Henry V's Suppression of the Lollards', *Mediaeval Studies* 52 (1990), pp. 190–220; at p. 191.

[138]   See Horner, *MS Bodley 649,.*p. 5.

is exactly such a provenance which provides the most likely explanation also for the authorial milieu of the Digby poems. The appendix charts the extensive parallels between the concerns of the Digby poems and those of the macaronic sermons. The coincidence in the use of proverbs and figurative expressions is especially striking. The annotation to the poems shows that the poet's use of proverbial expression can be paralleled in other texts. But I have not found another single work in which so many of the *same* proverbs feature. There is also variation in the dialect forms in the English parts of the sermons. In Sermon 4 the religious lyrics rhyme 'brith' with 'withe' (p. 151) and then 'wy3t' with ''bry3t' (p. 153). There is also evidence of Northern spelling, e.g. 'qwytter' (whiter) (p. 283). Such extensive connections between the Digby lyrics and the sermons are unlikely to be a matter of coincidence. They may not have been composed by the same monk; John Paunteley may have had no hand in either. But to suggest that the Digby poems were written by a Benedictine monk from Gloucestershire who attended Oxford, and who was present in London is far from fanciful. The abbot of St Peter's Gloucester, Hugh of Morton, is expressly recorded as one of the receivers of petitions at the 1416 Westminster parliament (*PROME*, March 1416, item 7). I have been unable to find out any further details about either Paunteley or Morton.[139] But even without being able to excavate a lived life behind either of these two names, what does emerge very clearly is the kind of authorial milieu we can construct for the Digby lyrics. A university-trained monk with access to public occasion and parliamentary politics, whether first-hand or by report from his brothers, is exactly the kind of figure to have been in a position to pen both the political and the religious dimensions of these poems.

And the possible connections with the Benedictine house at Gloucester also have a timely resonance for the political and religious positioning of the poems. The presence in the sequence of Poem 18, which urges monastic reform together with the championing of Henry V, suggests that the Digby poet was part of an axis of Benedictine support for the monarch. Henry had turned to Benedictine writers even before he became king. Lydgate tells in the Prologue to his *Troy Book* that Henry, 'the worthy prynce of Walys' 'me comaunded the drery pitus fate/Of hem of Troye in englysche to translate' (ll. 102–6).[140] The envoy to the book, written with Henry now king, places Henry among the Nine Worthies and compares him with scriptural and classical heroes and rulers.[141] In occasional poems, Lydgate praised Henry V as 'Goddis knyght' and 'Goddes chaumpyon'.[142] As I have mentioned

---

[139]   Neither John Paunteley nor Hugh of Morton is listed in the History of the University of Oxford.

[140]   John Lydgate, *Lydgate's Troy Book*, ed. Henry Bergen (EETS ES 97, 103, 106, 1906).

[141]   Lydgate, *Troy Book*, p. 877, lines 36–49.

[142]   'A Defence of Holy Church' in *The Minor Poems of John Lydgate, Part I: Religious Poems*, ed. H.N. MacCracken (EETS ES 107, 1911), no. 10, lines 26 and 69.

above, Lydgate also provided the king with translations of Latin texts for use in the liturgy.

The Digby poet's theological imagery in celebrating Henry's coronation is of the same temper as that found in the *Versus Rhythmici*, an extensive praise poem written by an anonymous monk of Westminster who served in some capacity in the king's household. Thomas Elmham, a monk of St Augustine's, Canterbury, thought to be responsible for the *Gesta Henrici Quinti*, written in 1418, also invests Henry's coronation with scriptural significance, likening the new king Henry to the newly born Christ child, not only anointed at his coronation, but an Epiphanic defender of the church and the saviour of the kingdom.[143] All of these Benedictine works show unequivocal support for Henry both as secular monarch and champion of the church against the seditious threat of the Lollards.[144]

To furnish forth a name and a place for the writer of these Digby lyrics would be highly desirable; perhaps the ultimate editorial 'docking' of a text to an originary external antecedent in order to authorise its significance.[145] But if we must seek an author for these poems,[146] despite their careful cultivation of a common rather than individual poetic voice, then a Benedictine monk who was part of the cultural milieu of the pro-Henrician writing of the order is as likely a candidate as any.[147] To provide a more specific local habitation and a name would be to venture into territory more imaginative than proper.

---

[143]   Taylor and Roskell, *Gesta Henrici Quinti*, pp. 1–4.

[144]   As argued persuasively by Horner, 'Benedictine Support'.

[145]   To produce an author for these lyrics is an act which mobilises the 'author function': see Michel Foucault: 'The author is therefore the ideological figure by which one marks the manner in which we fear the proliferation of meaning' in 'What is an author?' in David Lodge ed., *Modern Criticism and Theory: A Reader* (London: Longman, 1988), pp. 196–210; at p. 209. Compare the comment in Barthes' essay 'The Death of the Author': 'To give a text an Author is to impose a limit on that text, to furnish it with a final signified, to close the writing. Such a conception suits criticism very well, the latter then allotting itself the important task of discovering the Author (or its hypostases: society, history, psyche, liberty) beneath the work: when the Author has been found, the text is 'explained' – victory to the critic' in Roland Barthes, *Image, Music, Text*, ed. and transl. Stephen Heath (Glasgow, Fontana, 1979), p. 147.

[146]   Cf. Scattergood's comment that 'if an image of the author is necessary, it must be derived from the verses themselves', *Politics and Poetry*, p. 17.

[147]   This Benedictine bolstering of Henry might be compared with what Pearsall describes as the 'trinity' of Chaucer, Gower and Lydgate regularly invoked in the fifteenth century as part of the foundation myth of English poetry and the English language – and by extension, the English nation, Derek Pearsall, 'The Idea of Englishness in the Fifteenth Century' in Helen Cooney ed., *Nation, Court and Culture: New Essays on Fifteenth-Century English Poetry* (Dublin: Four Courts Press, 2001), pp. 15–27; at p. 24.

Appendix: Parallels between the Digby lyrics and the Macaronic sermons in MS Bodley 649

	Bodley 649	*Digby*
i. Religious views		
Imperative of oral confession to a parish priest	pp. 45, 90, 126, 146, 164, 202, 332, 352, 438	Poem 9
Orthodox defence of sacrament of Eucharist	pp. 168, 332, 422	Poem 23
At Eucharist all should be in charity with each other	p. 392	Poem 11/25–32
Reform of clergy; proper use of temporal goods	p. 112	Poem 8/25ff.
Truthful preaching aligned with spiritual honesty	p. 160	Poem 4/57ff.
Clergy to live better; choose the right path	p. 474	Poem 8, 10, 21/153–60
Clergy urged to instruct parishioners in solid faith	p. 192	Poem 8, 9
Clergy not looking after sheep	p. 346	Poem 9/153–60
Monastic reform	p. 528	Poem 18
ii. Devotional tropes		
Charter of Christ	p. 84	Poem 17/180–84
'Undo the dore of your heart'	p. 226	Poem 11/36
Christ's heart pouring out love/suffering	pp. 82, 370, 376, 478	Poem 17/198
Christ's rebukes to ungrateful man	pp. 196, 376	Poem 10, 11
Jesus gathering herbs to cure sickness	p. 146	Poem 17/185–92
Christ's passion restoring Adam's defouled image	p. 200	Poem 17/24; 19/5–8
Oaths tearing Christ's body	p. 196	Poem 19/73–76

	Bodley 649	Digby
iii. Penitential tropes		
Devil's rolls of sin	p. 82	Poem 4/235, 11/111, 24/393
Soul in thrall to the devil	p. 82	Poem 1/44, 4/109, 5/21, 17/142/165
No matter how strong or beautiful you will die	p. 122	Poem 4/145-52, 7/1-32
Miserable, transient world compared to the sea	pp. 262, 418, 518	Poem 4/1-8
Signs of death; body as a shadow or leaves	p. 310	Poem 5/1-8, 24/177-84
Worldly honour a slippery thing	p. 524	Poem 4/225-58
Know thyself	pp. 515-16	Poem 1, 7, 22
Man as sack of sin and filth	p. 470	Poem 7/5-8, 22/4-8
Today a doughty warrior tomorrow a dead one	p. 524	Poem 4/193-96
Fear justice but not despair	p. 338	Poem 1/129, 7/97, 20/201-02
Torments of hell	p. 312	Poem 24/323-40
Perform the works of mercy	p. 160	Poem 17/33-34
Church sanctuary as place to know contrition	p. 328	Poem 10/71-76
iv. Political/social comments		
Henry V as saviour of realm	pp. 462, 522	Poem 13/121-68
Henry V's white garment of purity at coronation	p. 156	Poem 23/29-32
Ship of state analogy	pp. 270, 418, 520	Poem 1/65
Formerly all nations honoured and feared the English	pp. 216, 528	Poem 12/121-28
Kingdom as one body; healthy if not destroyed	p. 438	Poem 15
Storms of dissension destroy a kingdom	p. 522	Poem 13/145

	Bodley 649	*Digby*
Avoidance of slander and private detraction	pp. 86, 142	Poem 1/161–68, 3/18–24, 4/35–36
God's displeasure at envy and discord	pp. 220, 438	Poem 12/29–36/87–88/145–52
False flatterers cherished as wise men of counsel	pp. 142, 246	Poem 2, 4/73–82/143–52
Importance of justice for rulers	p. 180	Poem 1/6, 9/65–72, 14/33–40
Do not accept favour or gifts	p. 182	Poem 1/8–16, 1/61, 3/9–16/25–32/97–104, 17/17–24
Warnings against oppression of commons	p. 182	Poem 3/97–104, 13/33–40/117
Plain soldiers are vilified	p. 246	Poem 2/44–48
Criticism of false merchants, weights and measures	p. 250	Poem 9/52–60
Criticism of false coin	pp. 400–02	Poem 9/52–56
Oppression of those who dare speak the truth	p. 322	Poem 2, 4
Criticism of false executours	p. 342	Poem 4/229–40
Criticism of snatching goods from the poor	p. 322	Poem 1/122/145–56, 4/50, 8/14/165–68, 9/157–60, 10/197–208, 21/73–80

v. Proverbs

Fly not too high	p. 168	Poem 14/47
False flatterer as weather vane	p. 88	Poem 2/57–58
Stepping over a straw	p. 142	Poem 4/89–90
Seeing two moons in the sky as the result of over-indulgence	p. 242	Poem 15/91–92
Currying favel	p. 246	Poem 4/190
Guile dressed in flateris wede	p. 322	Poem 4/12, 13/30
The more worship, the more vnworship	pp. 468, 518	Poem 14/1–4
Sea of prosperity ebbing and flowing	p. 526	Poem 4/1–4

Abbreviations and select bibliography

Abbreviations
CUP—Cambridge University Press
EETS—Early English Text Society
ELH—English Literary History
EWS I—Hudson, A. ed., *English Wycliffite Sermons*, vol. 1 (Oxford: Clarendon, 1983)
EWS II—Gradon, P. ed., *English Wycliffite Sermons*, vol. 2 (Oxford: Clarendon, 1988)
JEH—Journal of Ecclesiastical History
LALME—McIntosh, A., Samuels, M.L. and Benskin, M. edd., *A Linguistic Atlas of Late Medieval English* (Aberdeen: University of Aberdeen Press, 1986)
MED—Kurath, H., Kuhn, S.M. and Lewis, R.E. edd., *Middle English Dictionary* online (Ann Arbor: University of Michigan Press, 1952–2001; http://quod.lib.umich.edu/m/med/)
MLN—Modern Language Notes
OED—Oxford English Dictionary
OUP—Oxford University Press
PROME—Given-Wilson, C. ed., *The Parliament Rolls of Medieval England* (Leicester: Scholarly Digital Editions and The National Archives, 2005)
SAC—Studies in the Age of Chaucer
YLS—*Yearbook of Langland Studies*

Location of commonly cited works
Confessio—cited from Gower, *English Works*
The Crowned King—cited from Barr, *Tradition*
In Praise of Peace—cited from Gower, *English Works*
Mirour—cited from Gower, *French Works*
Mum and the Sothsegger—cited from Barr, *Tradition*
Pierce the Plowman's Crede—cited from Barr, *Tradition*
Richard the Redeles—cited from Barr, *Tradition*
Vox—cited from Gower, *Latin Works*

References to individual Canterbury Tales are from Benson, L.D. ed., *The Riverside Chaucer* (Oxford: OUP, 1988)

Quotations from the Bible are taken from *Douay-Rheims Catholic Bible*: http://www.drbo.org

Quotations from Thomas Aquinas, 'Lauda Sion' are from www.preceslatinae.org/thesaurus/Hymni/LaudaSion.html

Select bibliography

Primary sources

Andrew and Waldron, *Pearl Poems*—Andrew, M. and Waldron, R. ed., *The Poems of the Manuscript* (Exeter: Exeter University Press, 1987)

Arnold, *Wyclif*—Arnold, T. ed., *Select English Works of John Wyclif*, 3 vols (Oxford: Clarendon Press, 1869-71).

Aquinas, *Summa Theologiae*—Aquinas, Thomas, *Summa Theologiae* (London: Blackfriars, 1964-81)

Barr, *Tradition*—Barr, H. ed., *The Piers Plowman Tradition: A Critical Edition of Pierce the Ploughman's Crede, Richard the Redeles, Mum and the Sothsegger and The Crowned King* (London: Everyman, 1993).

Barnum, *Dives and Pauper*—Barnum, P.H. ed., *Dives and Pauper* (EETS OS 275, 1976 and 280, 1980).

Benson, *The Riverside Chaucer*—Benson, L.D. ed., *The Riverside Chaucer* (Oxford: OUP, 1988).

Blunt, *Myroure*—Blunt, J.H. ed., *The Myroure of oure Lady* (EETS ES 19, 1873).

Brandeis, *Jacob's Well*—Brandeis, A. ed., *Jacob's Well* (EETS OS 115, 1900).

Brinton, *Sermons*—Brinton, T., *The Sermons of Thomas Brinton, Bishop of Rochester*, ed. M.A. Devlin (London: Royal Historical Society, 1954).

Brown, *Religious Lyrics XV*—Brown, C. ed., *Religious Lyrics of the XVth Century* (Oxford: Clarendon, 1939).

Brown, *Secular Lyrics*—Brown, C. ed., *Secular Lyrics of XIVth and XVth Centuries* (Oxford: Clarendon Press, 1952).

Brown, *English Lyrics*—Brown, C. ed., *English Lyrics of the XIIIth Century* (Oxford: Clarendon Press, 1950).

Brown, *Religious Lyrics XIV*—Brown, C. ed., *Religious Lyrics of the XIVth Century* 2nd edn, revised G.V. Smithers (Oxford: Clarendon, 1952).

Bryant, *Common Profit*—Bryant, B.L., *Common Profit: Economic Morality in English Public Political Discourse, c.1340-1406* (unpublished Ph.D. dissertation, University of Columbia, New York, 2007).

Cigman, *Lollard Sermons*—Cigman, G. ed., *Lollard Sermons* (EETS OS 294, 1989).

Cole, *Henry V*—Cole, C.A. ed., *Memorials of Henry V, King of England* (London: Longman, Brown, Green, 1858).

Conlee, *Poetry*—Conlee, J.W. ed., *Middle English Debate Poetry* (Michigan: East Lansing, 1991).

Dean, *Political Writings*—Dean, J. ed., *Medieval English Political Writings* (Michigan: TEAMS, 1996).

Edden, *Maidstone's Psalms*—Edden, V. ed., *Richard of Maidstone's Penitential Psalms* (Heidelberg: Winter, 1990).

Elmham, *Liber Metricus*—Elmham, T., *Liber Metricus de Henrico V* in C.A. Cole, ed., *Memorials of Henry V, King of England* (London: Longman, Brown, Green, 1858).

Embree and Urquhart, *The Simonie*—Embree, D. and Urquhart, E. eds., *The Simonie*, (Heidelberg: Winter, 1991).

Erbe, *Mirk's Festial*—Erbe, T. ed., *Mirk's Festial* (EETS ES 96, 1905).

Fein, *Pety Job*—Fein, S. ed., *Pety Job* (Michigan: TEAMS, 1998).

Furnivall, *Political, Religious and Love Poems*—Furnivall, F.J. ed., *Political, Religious and Love Poems* (EETS OS 15, 1866).

Furnivall, *Vernon Poems*—Furnivall, F.J. ed., *The Minor Poems of the Vernon Manuscript Part II* (EETS OS 117, 1901).

Furnivall, *Handlyng Synne*—Furnivall, F.J. ed., *Handlyng Synne* (EETS OS 123, 1903).

Furnivall, *Hymns to the Virgin and Christ*—Furnivall, F.J. ed., *Hymns to the Virgin and Christ* (EETS OS 24, 1867; reprint 1973).

Given-Wilson, *Parliament Rolls*—Given-Wilson, C. ed., *The Parliament Rolls of Medieval England* (Leicester: Scholarly Digital Editions and The National Archives, 2005).

Gower, *French Works*—Gower, J., *The Complete Works of John Gower: the French works*, ed. G.C. Macaulay (Oxford: Clarendon, 1899).

Gower, *English Works*—Gower, J., *The English Works of John Gower*, ed. G.C. Macaulay (EETS ES 81, 1900).

Gower, *Latin Works*—Gower, J., *The Complete Works of John Gower: the Latin works*, ed. G.C. Macaulay (Oxford: Clarendon Press, 1902).

Gradon, *Ayenbite*—Gradon P. ed., *Ayenbite of Inwyt* (EETS OS 23, 1866; reprint 1965).

Gradon, *Sermons*—Gradon, P. ed., *English Wycliffite Sermons*, vol. 2 (Oxford: Clarendon, 1988).

Gray, *Religious Lyrics*—Gray, D. ed., *A Selection of Religious Lyrics* (Oxford: Clarendon, 1975).

Hanna and Lawton, *The Siege of Jerusalem*—Hanna, R. and Lawton, D. eds, *The Siege of Jerusalem* (EETS OS 320, 2003)

Heyworth, *Reply and Rejoinder*—Heyworth, P.L. ed., *Jack Upland, Friar Daw's Reply and Upland's Rejoinder* (Oxford: OUP, 1968).

Hoccleve, *Regement*—Hoccleve, T., *The Regement of Princes*, ed. F.J. Furnivall (EETS ES 72, 1899).

Hoccleve, *Minor Poems*—Hoccleve, T., *Minor Poems*, edd. F.J. Furnivall and I. Gollancz, revised Jerome Mitchell and A.I. Doyle (EETS ES 61 and 73, 1970).

Holmstedt, *Speculum Christiani*—Holmstedt, G. ed., *Speculum Christiani* (EETS OS 182, 1933).

Holthausen, *Vices and Virtues*—Holthausen, F. ed., *Vices and Virtues Part I* (EETS OS 89, 1888).

Horner, *MS Bodley 649*—Horner, P.J. ed., *A Macaronic Sermon Collection from Late Medieval England: Oxford MS Bodley 649* (Toronto: PIMS, 2006).

Horstmann, *Altenglische Legenden*—Horstmann, C. ed., *Altenglische Legenden* (Heilbronn: Verlag von Gebr. Henninger, 1881).

Horstmann, *Vernon Poems*—Horstmann, C. ed., *The Minor Poems of the Vernon Manuscript Part I* (EETS OS 98, 1892).

Hudson, *Wycliffite Writings*—Hudson, A. ed., *Selections from English Wycliffite Writings* (Cambridge: CUP, 1978).

Hudson, *Wycliffite Sermons*—Hudson, A. ed., *English Wycliffite Sermons*, vol. 1 (Oxford: Clarendon, 1983).

Hudson, *Wycliffite Texts*—Hudson, A. ed., *The Testimony of William Thorpe* in *Two Wycliffite Texts* (EETS OS 301, 1993).

Hudson, *Lollard Preacher*—Hudson, A. ed., *The Works of a Lollard Preacher* (EETS OS 317, 2001).

Julian of Norwich, *Revelation*—Julian of Norwich, *A Revelation of Love*, ed. Marion Glasscoe (Exeter: University of Exeter Press, 1976).

Kail, *Poems*—Kail, J. ed., *Twenty-Six Political and Other Poems* (EETS OS 124, 1904).

Littlehales, *The Prymer*—Littlehales, H. ed., *The Prymer, or The Lay Folk's Prayer Book* (EETS Part I, OS 105, 1895; Part II, OS 109, 1897).

Love, *Mirror*—Love, N., *The Mirror of the Blessed Life of Jesus Christ*, ed. Michael G. Sargent (Exeter: University of Exeter Press, 2004).

Lydgate, *Troy Book*—Lydgate, J., *Lydgate's Troy Book*, ed. Henry Bergen (EETS ES 97, 103, 106, 1906).

Lydgate, *Poems I*—Lydgate, J. *The Minor Poems of John Lydgate, Part I: Religious Poems*, ed. H.N. MacCracken (EETS ES 107, 1911).

Lydgate, *Fall of Princes*—Lydgate, J. *The Fall of Princes*, ed. Henry Bergen (EETS ES 121-4, 1918-19).

Lydgate, *Poems II*—Lydgate, J. *The Minor Poems of John Lydgate, Part II*, ed. H.N. MacCracken (EETS OS 192, 1934).

Matthew, *Works of Wyclif*—Matthew, F.D. ed., *The English Works of Wyclif Hitherto Unprinted* (EETS OS 74, 1880, 2nd revised edn, 1902).

McIntosh, A., Samuels, M.L. and Benskin, M. edd., *A Linguistic Atlas of Late Medieval English* (Aberdeen: University of Aberdeen Press, 1986).

Morris, *Cursor Mundi*—Morris, R. ed., *Cursor Mundi V* (EETS OS 68, 1878; reprint 1966).

Myers, *Documents*—Myers, A.R. ed., *English Historical Documents 1327-1485* (London: Eyre and Spottiswoode, 1969).

Nelson Francis, *Vices and Virtues*—Nelson Francis, W., *The Book of Vices and Virtues* (EETS OS 217, 1942).

Nolcken, *Rosarium Theologie*—Nolcken, C. von ed., *The Middle English Translation of the Rosarium Theologie* (Heidelberg: Winter, 1979).

Offord, *Parlement*—Offord, M.Y. ed., *The Parlement of the Thre Ages* (EETS OS 246, 1959).

Peacock, *Myrc's Instructions*—Peacock, E. ed., *Myrc's Instructions for Parish Priests* (EETS OS 31, 1868).

Panton and Donaldson, *Destruction of Troy*—Panton G.A. and Donaldson, D. edd., *The 'Gest Hystorial' of the Destruction of Troy* (EETS OS 39, 1869 and 56, 1874).

Pearsall, *Piers C-Text*—Pearsall, D. ed., *Piers Plowman: The C-Text* (Exeter: University of Exeter Press, 1994).

Robbins, *Historical Poems*—Robbins, R.H. ed., *Historical Poems of the XIVth and XVth Centuries* (New York: Columbia University Press, 1959).

Russell and Kane, *Piers C*—Russell, G. and Kane, G. edd., *Piers Plowman: The C Version* (London: Athlone, 1997).

Schick, *The Temple of Glass*—J.Schick, ed. *Lydgate's Temple of Glass* (EETS ES 60 1891)

Schmidt, *Piers B*—Schmidt, A.V.C. ed., *The Vision of Piers Plowman: A Complete Edition of the B Text* (London: Everyman, 1987).

Schmidt, *Piers Parallel Text*—Schmidt, A.V.C. ed., *Piers Plowman: A Parallel Text Edition of the A, B, C, and Z Versions* (London: Athlone, 1995).

Shepherd, *Ancrene Wisse*—Shepherd, G. ed., *Ancrene Wisse, Parts Six and Seven* revised edn (Exeter: University of Exeter Press, 1991).

Skeat, *Chaucer*—Skeat, W.W. ed., *Chaucerian and Other Pieces: The Complete Works of Geoffrey Chaucer* (Oxford: Clarendon Press, 1897).

Statutes of the Realm—*Statutes of the Realm*, 10 vols (London: Eyre and Strahan, 1810-22).

Swinburne, *Lanterne*—Swinburne, M.L. ed., *The Lanterne of Light* (EETS OS 151, 1917).

Taylor and Roskell, *Gesta Henrici Quinti*—Taylor, F. and Roskell, J.S. edd. and trans., *Gesta Henrici Quinti* (Oxford: Clarendon Press, 1975).

Trigg, *Wynnere and Wastoure*—Trigg, S. ed., *Wynnere and Wastoure* (EETS OS 297, 1990).

Walsingham, *St Albans Chronicle*—Walsingham, T., *St Albans Chronicle*, ed. V.H. Galbraith (Oxford: OUP, 1937).

Walsingham, *Historica Anglicana*—Walsingham, T., *Historia Anglicana*, ed. H.T. Riley (London: Longman, Roberts and Green, 1864), vol. 2.

Weatherly, *Speculum Sacerdotale*—Weatherly, E.H. ed., *Speculum Sacerdotale* (EETS OS 200, 1936).

Wilkins, *Conciliae*—Wilkins, D. ed., *Conciliae Magnae Britanniae et Hiberniae*, vol. 3 (London, 1737).

Wright, *Poems and Songs*—Wright, T. ed., *Political Poems and Songs* (Rolls Series, London, 1859–61), 2 vols.

Wyclif, *De Eucharistica*—Wyclif, J., *De Eucharistica*, ed. J. Loserth (London: Trübner, 1892).

Zupitza, 'Proverbis of Wysdom'—Zupitza, J. ed., 'Proverbis of Wysdom', *Archiv* 90 (1893), pp. 241–68.

Secondary sources

Aers, *Sanctifying Signs*—Aers, D., *Sanctifying Signs* (Notre Dame: University of Notre Dame Press, 2004).

Alford, *Glossary*—Alford, J.A., *A Glossary of Legal Diction* (Cambridge: Brewer, 1988).

Allmand, *Henry V*—Allmand, C.T., *Henry V* (London: Methuen, 1992).

Barr, *Socioliterary Practice*—Barr, H., *Socioliterary Practice in Late Medieval England* (Oxford: OUP, 2001).

Barthes, *Image*—Barthes, R., *Image, Music, Text*, ed. and transl. Stephen Heath (Glasgow: Fontana, 1979).

Beckwith, 'Dramas'—Beckwith, S., 'Ritual, Church, and Theatre: Medieval Dramas of the Sacramental Body' in *Culture and History, 1350–1600*, ed. D. Aers (Hemel Hempstead: Harvester Wheatsheaf, 1992), pp. 65–89.

Beckwith, *Christ's Body*—Beckwith, S., *Christ's Body: Identity, Culture, and Society in Late Medieval Writings* (New York: Routledge, 1993).

Bennett, 'Nosce te ipsum'—Bennett, J.A.W., '"Nosce te ipsum": Some Medieval Interpretations', in *J.R.R. Tolkien: Scholar and Storyteller*, edd. M. Salu and R.T. Farell (Ithaca, 1979), pp. 138–58.

Blamire, *Defamed and Defended*—Blamires, A., ed., *Woman Defamed and Woman Defended* (Oxford, 1992).

Catto, 'Religious Change'—Catto, J., 'Religious Change under Henry V' in *Henry V: The Practice of Kingship*, ed. G.L. Harriss (Oxford: OUP, 1985), pp. 97–116.

Coleman, *Literature in History*—Coleman, J., *English Literature in History: 1350–1400* (London: Hutchinson, 1981).

Cooney, *Essays on Poetry*—Cooney, H. ed., *Nation, Court and Culture: New Essays on Fifteenth Century English Poetry* (Dublin: Four Courts Press, 2001).

Dobson, *The Peasants' Revolt*—Dobson, R.B., ed., *The Peasants' Revolt of 1381* (London, 1983).

Duffy, *Altars*—Duffy, E., *The Stripping of the Altars: Traditional Religion in Late Medieval Culture* (Cambridge: CUP, 1991).

Embree, 'The King's Ignorance'—Embree, D., 'The King's Ignorance: A Topos for Evil Times', *Medium Aevum* 54 (1985), pp. 121–26.

Ganim, 'Chaucer'—Ganim, J.M., 'Chaucer and the noise of the people', *Exemplaria* 2 (1990), pp. 71–88.

Gillespie, 'Moral and Penitential Lyrics'—Gillespie, V., 'Moral and Penitential Lyrics' in *A Companion to the Middle English Lyric*, ed. T.G. Duncan (Cambridge: Brewer, 2005), pp. 69–95.

Hanna, 'Miscellaneity'—Hanna, R., 'Miscellaneity and Vernacularity', in *The Whole Book: Cultural Perspectives in the Medieval Miscellany,* edd. S.G. Nichols and S. Wenzel (Ann Arbor: University of Michigan, 1996).

Harriss, 'Parliament'—Harriss, G., 'The Management of Parliament', in *Henry V: The Practice of Kingship*, ed. G. Harriss (Oxford: OUP, 1985), pp. 137–58.

Hodges, *Chaucer and Costume*—Hodges, L.F., *Chaucer and Costume* (Cambridge: Brewer, 2000).

Horner, 'Benedictine Support'—Horner, P.J., '"The King Taught us the Lesson": Benedictine Support for Henry V's Suppression of the Lollards', *Mediaeval Studies* 52 (1990), pp. 191–220.

Horobin, *Language of Chaucer*—Horobin, S., *The Language of the Chaucer Tradition* (Cambridge: Brewer, 2003).

Horobin, 'In London and Opelond'—Horobin, S., '"In London and Opelond": The Dialect and Circulation of the C Version of *Piers Plowman*', *Medium Aevum* 74 (2005), pp. 248–69.

Hudson, *Premature Reformation*—Hudson, A., *The Premature Reformation* (Oxford: OUP, 1988).

Hudson and Spencer, 'Sermons of MS Longleat'—Hudson, A. and Spencer, H.L., 'Old Author, New Work: The Sermons of MS Longleat 4', *Medium Aevum* 53 (1984), pp. 220–38.

Jacob, *Fifteenth Century*—Jacob, E.F., *The Fifteenth Century 1399–1485* (Oxford: Clarendon Press, 1961).

Kane, 'Political Poems'—Kane, G., 'Some Fourteenth Century "Political" Poems', in *Medieval Religious and Ethical Literature: Essays in Honour of G.H. Russell* edd., G. Kratzmann and J. Simpson (Cambridge: Brewer, 1986), pp. 82–91.

Knowles, *Religious Orders*—Knowles, D., *The Religious Orders in England* (Cambridge: CUP, 1948–59), 3 vols.

Lawton, 'Dullness'—Lawton, D., 'Dullness and the Fifteenth Century' *ELH* 54 (1987), pp. 761–99.

Lodge, *Modern Criticism*—Lodge D. ed., *Modern Criticism and Theory: A Reader* (London: Longman, 1988).

Macy, 'Dogma'—Macy, G., 'The Dogma of Transubstantiation in the Middle Ages', *JEH* 45 (1994), 11–41.

Mann, *Chaucer and Satire*—Mann, J., *Chaucer and Medieval Estates Satire* (Cambridge, CUP, 1973).

Middleton, 'Public Poetry'—Middleton, A., 'The Idea of Public Poetry in the Reign of Richard II', *Speculum* 53 (1978), pp. 94–114 reprt. in *Medieval English Poetry*, ed. Stephanie Trigg (London: Longman, 1993), pp. 24–46.

Middleton, 'Audience and Public'—Middleton, A., 'The Audience and Public of *Piers Plowman*' in *Middle English Alliterative Poetry and its Literary Background*, ed. D. Lawton (Cambridge: Brewer, 1982), pp. 101–23.

Nicholas, *Medieval Flanders*—Nicholas, D., *Medieval Flanders* (London: Longman, 1992).

Nuttall, 'Narratives and Poetics'—Nuttall, J., 'Household Narratives and Lancastrian Poetics in Hoccleve's Envoy's and Other Early Fifteenth Century Middle English Poems' in *The Medieval Household in Christian Europe: Managing Power, Wealth and the Body*, edd. C. Beattie, A. Maslakovic and S. Rees Jones (Turnhout: Brepols, 2003), pp. 91–106.

Nuttall, *Lancastrian Kingship*—Nuttall, J., *The Creation of Lancastrian Kingship* (Cambridge: CUP, 2008).

Owen, *Connection*—Owen, L.V.D., *The Connection between England and Burgundy during the First Half of the Fifteenth Century* (Oxford: Clarendon, 1909).

Pearsall, *Vernon*—Pearsall, D., ed., *Studies in the Vernon Manuscript* (Cambridge: Brewer, 1990).

Pearsall, *Lydgate*—Pearsall, D., *John Lydgate (1371-1449): A Bio-bibliography* (Victoria: University of Victoria, 1997).

Pearsall, 'Englishness'—Pearsall, D., 'The Idea of Englishness in the Fifteenth Century' in *Nation, Court and Culture: New Essays on Fifteenth Century English Poetry*, ed. H. Cooney (Dublin: Four Courts Press, 2001), pp. 15–27.

Peck, *Kingship and Common Profit*—Peck, R.A., *Kingship and Common Profit in Gower's Confessio Amantis* (Carbondale: University of Illinois Press, 1978).

Powell, 'Restoration'—Powell, E., 'The Restoration of Law and Order' in *Henry V: The Practice of Kingship*, ed. G. Harriss (Oxford: OUP, 1985), pp. 53–74.

Rubin, *Eucharist*—Rubin, M., *Corpus Christi: The Eucharist in Late Medieval Culture* (Cambridge: CUP, 1991).

Robbins, 'Dating'—Robbins, R.H., 'On Dating a Middle English Moral Poem', *MLN* 70 (1955), pp. 473–76.

Scattergood, *Politics and Poetry*—Scattergood, V.J., *Politics and Poetry in the Fifteenth Century* (London: Blandford Press, 1971).

Simpson, 'Grace Abounding'—Simpson, J., 'Grace Abounding: Evangelical Centralization and the End of *Piers Plowman*', *YLS* 14 (2000), pp. 49–73.

Simpson, *Reform*—Simpson, J., *Reform and Cultural Revolution* (Oxford: OUP, 2002).

Simpson, 'Marcol and Solomon'—Simpson, J., 'Saving Satire after Arundel's *Constitutions*: John Audelay's "Marcol and Solomon"' in *Text and Controversy from Wyclif to Bale: Essays in Honour of Anne Hudson* edd. H. Barr and A.M. Hutchison (Turnhout: Brepols, 2005), pp. 387–404.

Steiner, *Culture*—Steiner, E., *Documentary Culture and the Making of Medieval English Literature* (Cambridge: CUP, 2003).

Strohm, *Social Chaucer*—Strohm, P., *Social Chaucer* (Cambridge, Mass.; London: Harvard University Press, 1989).

Strohm, *Language of Legitimation*—Strohm, P., *England's Empty Throne: Usurpation and the Language of Legitimation 1399-1422* (Yale: New Haven and London, 1998).

Strohm, *Theory*—Strohm, P., *Theory and the Premodern Text* (Minneapolis: University of Minnesota Press, 2000).

Swain, *Fools and Folly*—Swain, B., *Fools and Folly during the Middle Ages and the Renaissance* (New York: University of Columbia Press, 1932).

Vaughan, *Burgundian Power*—Vaughan, R., *John the Fearless: The Growth of Burgundian Power* (Woodbridge: Boydell, 2002).

Wallace, 'In Flaundres'—Wallace, D., 'In Flaundres', *SAC* 19 (1997), pp. 63–91.

Watson, 'Vernacular Theology'—Watson, N., 'Censorship and Cultural Change in Late-Medieval England: Vernacular Theology, the Oxford Translation Debate, and Arundel's *Constitutions* of 1409', *Speculum* 70 (1995), pp. 822–64.

Watts, 'Politics'—Watts, J., 'The Pressure of the Public on Later Medieval Politics' in *Political Culture in Late Medieval Britain*, Fifteenth Century IV, edd. L. Clark and C. Carpenter (Woodbridge: Boydell, 2004), pp. 159–64.

Watts, 'Commons'—Watts, J., 'Public or Plebs: The Changing Meaning of the Commons, 1381–1549' in *Power and Identity in the Middle Ages: Essays in Memory of Rees Davies*, edd. H. Pryce and J. Watts (Oxford: OUP, 2007).

Whiting, *Proverbs*—Whiting, B.J., *Proverbs, sentences and proverbial phrases: from English writings mainly before 1500* (Cambridge, Mass: Harvard University Press, 1968).

Woolf, *Religious Lyric*—Woolf, R., *The English Religious Lyric in the Middle Ages* (Oxford: Clarendon Press, 1968).

Yunck, *Lineage*—Yunck, J.A., *The Lineage of Lady Mede* (Indiana: Notre Dame, 1971).

The lyrics from MS Digby 102

Poem 1. Loue God and drede

The poem as a whole can be seen as an extended treatment of the biblical text, 'The fear of the Lord is the beginning of wisdom' (Proverbs 1:7). The narrative voice is akin to that of the speaker in biblical wisdom literature. This opening poem shares many ideas and expressions with Poem 7 and Poem 22, and is close in tenor to a nine-stanza lyric in the Vernon Manuscript (Furnivall, *Vernon Poems* II.672–5), which also uses the phrase 'vche mon ouȝte him-self to knowe' (line 12) as the refrain of the poem. The focus is chiefly religious, urging an awareness of sin, mortality, and the need to be ruled by conscience, but those in power do not escape examination: 'Knowe þi flesch, þat wol rote;/For certes, þou maiȝt not longe endure;/And nedes dye, hennes þou mote/Þei þou haue kyngdam and Empyre' (ll. 73–6). Compare also the remarks on the importance of the king taking counsel in Hoccleve, *Regement*, 4852–3, 'Bygynnyng of wisdom is, god to drede;/What kyng dredith god, is good and iust'.

1. Loue God and drede

Eche man be war, that bereth astate,
Of counseil of double entendement;
Of tyrauntrye and preuey hate;
And synguler profit by fals assent,
And ȝong to ȝyue iugement.   5
In evenhede lawe ȝe lede,

1] The bearing of public office and its responsibilities is a key concern of these poems. Line 1 is repeated almost verbatim at line 97; cf. also Poem 8/57. Compare also Poem 3/138–41 and 8/17.

2] **double entendement** is repeated at line 71. Truth-telling counsellors are described in contemporary literature as having plain, not 'double' speech, e.g. 'pleine and bare', Gower, *Confessio*, VII.2350. The importance of honest counsel is a staple of advice to princes in literature, e.g. Gower, *In Praise of Peace*, 141–7; *Mum and the Sothsegger*, 31–3; Hoccleve, *Regement*, 4859–956 and especially line 4915, 'In auxenge eeke of reed, ware of fauel'.

4] **synguler profit** occurs five more times in a secular context, see Poem 5/28, 14/52, 17/37, 21/60. The poet also condemns 'synguler wynnyng' (Poem 21/93) and the singular profit of temporality (Poem 8/60). The concept of 'singularity' – individual profit or gain – is diametrically opposed to the poems' concern with corporate wholeness and responsibility. 'Singuler profit' is a phrase used with some regularity in the Rolls of Parliament. There is particularly dense usage between 1380 and 1394 and then again between 1401 and 1411. After 1411, the next instance is not until 1425. The contexts range from the private interest of the owners of stanks and wells (*PROME*, January 1401: Item 97), drapers (September 1402: Item 36), abuse of the wool staple (November 1411: Item 33) and barring passage on the River Severn (November 1411: Item 47). In each case 'singuler profit' is seen to conflict with the greater good of the common realm, e.g. 'nemy pur commune profit' (October 1404: Item 60); 'a nulle avauntage de vous tresgracious seignur eniz damage commune a tout le roialme' (January 1410: Item 49) and 'a tresoutrageouse damage detout vostre dit roialme en commune' (November 1411: Item 33). The collocation 'singuler profit' is attested only twice in *MED* 'singler(e)' (*adj.*); 3a: in Rymer's *Foedera* (1418) and in Chaucer's *House of Fame*, l. 310. It is highly likely that the use of this phrase, and its contexts in the Digby poems, is influenced by parliamentary discourse.

5] This line may be deficient. Elsewhere, 'ȝong' occurs only as a group noun for young people in formulaic collocations with 'olde' (Poem 9/23, 13/131, 14/65 and 17/121). The sense of line 5 is that those in office ought to guard against the pronouncements of the young. This is a standard topos of advice to princes in literature, see Hoccleve, *Regement*, 4943–56, especially line 4947, 'Ware of yong conseyl, it is perilouse'.

6] **lawe** many closely contemporary poems assert that the primary function of a king is to maintain law, Gower, *Mirour*, 2234–6, 23077–9; *Vox*, VI.613–14 and *Confessio*, VII.2704–8, 2714–24; Schmidt, *Piers Parallel Text*, B.Prol.141–2, 'Dum rex a regere dicatur nomen

Worche be good auisement.
Man, knowe thy self, loue God and drede.

Drede God and knowe thy selue,
That ouer puple hast gouernaunce.   10
Noght for the loue of ten or twelue
Brynge not a Comone in greuance;
Make vnyte ther was distaunce,
Weye o lawe in euenhede
Bytwen fauour and vengeaunce.   15
Man, knowe thy self, loue God and drede.

Eche mannys gouernours
Of hous, or lordshipe, or cite,

---

habere/Nomen habet sine re nisi studet iura tenere.' Another version of this statement
appears at the end of 'On the Times', Wright, *Poems and Songs*, I.278.

8]   The **knowe thy self** refrain anglicises the phrase 'nosce te ipsum': 'know thyself'.
Originally a Socratic motto, the phrase acquired a variety of interpretations in the Middle
Ages, see Bennett, 'Nosce te ipsum'. Bennett notes that by the end of the fourteenth
century the phrase had become a 'preacher's commonplace', p. 151. Self-knowledge was
seen as a remedy against Pride, e.g. Morris, *Cursor Mundi*, 2750–2 and a prerequisite for
wisdom, e.g. *The Monk's Tale*, B.3329, 'Ful wys is he that kan hymselven knowe'. It is a
phrase used also in explicitly regnal contexts: e.g. the advice given to the triumphant
Roman Emperor in Gower's *Confessio*, VII.2386–9, '... Tak into memoire/For al this
pompe and al this pride/Let no justice gon aside,/Bot know thiself, what so befalle'. The
narrator of *Richard the Redeless* tells the deposed King Richard II that he came to the
kingship 'er ye youre-self knewe' (I.119); in contrast to the good knights who 'knowe
well hem-self' (III.200).

11]   **ten or twelue** is formulaic and the numbers are clearly used for rhyme, cf. Poem 12/99,
but there is an analogue in the November 1411 parliament, *PROME*: Item 47 where, in the
context of lawlessness on the River Severn, the king is asked to consider the 'heynous
mieschief avantdit, qe serroit suffert pur singuler profit de duzze ou vynt persones'.

12]   **Comone** in the sense of common weal. The Digby poet preserves the singular form
for this sense. As an adjective, the form is 'como[u]n': see Poem 3/98, 4/17, 4/19, 4/155,
4/207. The plural 'comouns' means the 'commons' as distinct from the lords and the
clergy: see Poem 12/11. See Introduction, pp. 42–3 for further discussion of this important
nexus of terms.

13]   The importance of the king governing in **vnyte** is seen also at line 21; an issue repeated
verbatim in Poem 3/130, 8/63, 13/106 and cf. 20/18.

14]   The importance of administering even-handed justice recurs at line 164 and Poem
3/12–13, 12/111 and 13/71. It is a commonplace of advice to princes in literature, e.g.
Hoccleve, *Regement*, 2479–80, 'Who-so it be that Iustice verray/Desireth folowe, first
mote he god drede'.

The puple is Godes, and not ʒoures –
Thow they be soget to ʒoure degre,   20
Gouerne the puple in vnyte
In the comaundements that God bede.
And ʒe wole lyue in charite,
Knowe thy self, loue God and drede.

Eche man wot that hath wyt,   25
These worldes goods beth not his;
Alle is Godes: he oweth hit,
And land and see, and pyne and blis.
God wole haue rekenyng ywys
Of men and cloth, the leste shrede;   30
Thy getyng, thy holdyng, thy spendyng mys.
Man, knowe thyself, loue God and drede.

Man of his owen hath no thyng;
Man is Goddis, and al God sent.
God wole haue rekenyng   35

19]   The line is repeated at Poem 13/51. Poem 3/131 inserts 'ne ryches' after 'puple'. The advice
to the king is developed in the following two stanzas to apply to every individual, as part
of the widespread vision of the sequence in which every member of the realm, from the
king downwards, is seen to bear responsibility for the health of the political community.

28]   Cf. Ecclesiasticus 11:14, 'Good things and evil, life and death, poverty and riches, are
from God.'.

29, 35]   **rekenyng** cf. Poem 7/81–4 and 11/110–13. In each case, the poet conflates the political
and the spiritual. In this poem there is play on the senses of measuring cloth (*MED*
'rekenyng' (*n.*); 2b), and the Last Judgement (*MED* 'rekenyng' (*n.*); 3). There were several
measures passed in the parliaments of the first two decades of the fifteenth century to
attempt to regulate the measurement of cloth, e.g. *PROME*, Henry IV January 1410: Item
69, 'Also, the commons of your realm declare that whereas by a statute and ordinance
made in your realm in the seventh year of your gracious reign [1406], all short cloths
made in the parts of the west country in your realm should measure twenty-eight yards
in length along the crest, and each dozen of cloths should be fourteen yards long along
the crest, and striped cloths should be made to the same length along the edge: that is,
the whole cloth twenty-eight yards, and the dozen fourteen yards.' The spiritual sense
of reckoning in giving account to God is common in religious tracts, e.g., 'for god wole
haue rekennynge of eche dede, of eche word, & of eche þouʒt, & of eche ʒifte', Matthew,
Works of Wyclif, p. 33, and 'And siþ Crist haþ lent ech man here al þat he haþ, and wole
axe of þis streite rekenynge, how he dispendiþ it, to ech man of þis world may þis parable
be applied', Arnold, *Wyclif*, I.23.

33–4]   The same sentiment recurs at Poem 3/132 and 7/82.

Of ryht and wrong; how it is went.
Man, not nys thyn; alle God lent,
And borwed thyng mot home ful neede;
And ȝut thy soule is Goddis rent.
Quyte that wele in loue and drede.   40

Serue God for helle drede;
Fle fro synne and al vys.
And ȝe loue God for heuen mede,
ȝyue Hym thyn hert fro fleschly delys,
For worldly wys is gostly nys,   45
And fooles erande may not spede.

38]   **borwed thyng** for the proverbial phrase, cf. Pees's complaint against Wrong in Schmidt,
Piers Parallel Text, 'He borwed of me bayard and broughte hym hom nevere' (B.IV.53,)
and Piers's statement of clean accounts when he makes his will, '... my dettes are quyte;/I
bare hom that I borwed er I to bedde yede' (B.VI.98–9). See also Poem 9/129.

39]   **Goddis rent.** The poem continues the play of earthly and spiritual management,
cf. Poem 7/87 and 24/186. I have not found the exact collocation elsewhere but other
works warn of the dangers of cultivating worldly goods at the expense of others, and
the consequent danger to the soul, which is the property truly only of God. Cf. Gradon,
Ayenbite, 144/19, 'Þeruore zayþ oure lhord þet þe kingdom of heuene is hare ... ase þe
ilke þet beginþ to onderuonge þet frut and þe rentes hou hi ssolle by y-blissed ine þe
oþre wordle.' In *The Childe of Bristowe* (Horstmann, *Altenglische Legenden*, pp. 315–21),
the eponymous hero is able to save his father from the torments of hell only by making
restitution for all his ill-gotten gains: 'To make god my foo,/To sle my soule it were routhe/
Any science that is trouthe/Y shal amytte me ther-to;/For to forsake my soule helthe/For
any wynnyng of worldes welthe.' (p. 316). In Schmidt, *Piers Parallel Text*, Piers plays on
the notion of debt, property and the Last Judgement when he makes his will: 'He shal
have my soule that best hath deserved/And defende it fro the fend, for so I bileve/Til I
come to hise acountes as my crede me telleth/To have a relees and a remission – on that
rental I leve' (B.VI.87–90). The Friar in *The Summoner's Tale* is given a satirical twist on
the notion of the soul as God's rent in his self-calumniating admission of the abuse of
the sacrament of confession: 'I walke and fisshe Cristen mennes soules/To yelden Jhesu
Crist his propre rente' (D.1820–1). See also Poem 17/25.

40]   **Quyte,** cf. Poem 7/88 and 9/132.

41–2]   Cf. Zupitza, 'Proverbis of Wysdom', 'The fyrst proverbe to begynne/Drede god
and fle fro synne' (244:3–4); and 'Love god and fle fro synne,/And so may thow hevyn
wynne' (247:137–8). Whiting, *Proverbs*, lists other variations on this proverbial phrase,
G.215, p. 235.

44]   **fleschly delys,** cf. line 58 and Poem 17/51, 18/73 and 20/171.

45]   The line is repeated almost verbatim at Poem 8/77.

46]   **fooles erande,** cf. Proverbs 26:6, 'He that sendeth words by a foolish messenger, is
lame of feet and drinketh iniquity'.

In begynnyng to be wys,
Knowe thyself, loue God and drede.

And 3e wole wyte, thus mowe 3e lere
What man pursueth his soule to saue.   50
3if hym be lef of God to here,
He ableth hym self mercy to haue.
Richesse [fol. 98b] and hele maketh wylde men raue
That to vertues take non hede.
Er thy soule be fendes knaue,   55
Knowe thy self, loue God and drede.

That man that wole be gouerned by wyt,
Fle fro foly and worldis delys;
Loke his charge, how it is knyt,
And take conseil that is wys.   60
Folowe mesure in euene syse,
Lete no falshed blome ne sede.
And lawe be kept, no folk nyl ryse;
Than seruest God in loue and drede.

53–5]   Cf. Proverbs 11:4–5, 'Riches shall not profit in the day of revenge: but justice shall
    deliver from death. The justice of the upright shall make his way prosperous: and the
    wicked man shall fall by his own wickedness.'
55]   **fendes knaue** the same phrase is used at Poem 4/109 and 17/142 and is part of sustained
    diction which positions the soul either as servant to an aristocratic God or in thrall to
    devils.
60]   Gower singles out counsel as the most important attribute of kingship: 'For conseil
    passeth alle thing./To him which thenkth to ben a king' (Confessio, VIII.2109–10). The
    stress on the role of good counsel is an emphasis in keeping with the sentiments of
    contemporary poems, e.g. Gower, In Praise of Peace, 141–7; Hoccleve, Regiment, 4936–49
    and 4953–6.
62]   **falshed blome ne sede**, cf. Poem 13/142, 'Lete falsed growe tyl he sede'.
61]   **euene syse**, cf. line 164, and Poem 3/13.
63]   **lawe be kept**, cf. the narrator's advice to Prince Henry in Hoccleve, Regiment to observe
    the laws: 'lawe is bothe lokke and key/Of suerte; whil law is kept in londe,/A prince in his
    estate may sikir stonde' (2777–9) and Gower, Confessio, VII.2759–64, 'If lawe stonde with
    the riht,/The poeple is glad and stant upriht./Wher as the lawe is resonable,/The comon
    poeple stant menable,/And if the lawe torne amis,/The poeple also mistorned is.'
64]   The line is repeated Poem 3/15.

Whanne a fool stereth a barge,   65
Hym self, and al the folke is shent.
There as conscience is large –
By wrath or mede – the doom is went.
The bowe of Goddis wrath is bent
On hem that deth not that God bede.   70
War wordes of dowble entendement;
Knowe thy self, loue God and drede.

зif a kyngdom falle a chaunce
That al the rewme myght greue,
Aзen that make an ordinaunce   75
To kepe зow euere fro suche myscheue,
And chastise hem that matere meue.
Make othere take ensaumple treuth to hede;
Who so is wys hys werkys preue.
Loue God, and зe thar not drede.   80

65]   **stereth a barge**. The idiomatic phrase draws on the traditional comparison between a ship and the state. 'The Song on the Death of Edward III 1377', Robbins, *Historical Poems*, pp. 102–6, bases its whole narration on the comparison, likening the various parts of the ship to the various classes of the realm and showing how well the ship sailed under Edward. The analogy was also used in a macaronic sermon delivered shortly before Henry V departed to France in 1421. It is preserved in the macaronic sermons of Horner, *MS Bodley 649*, pp. 270, 418 and 520. In other contexts the analogy illustrates a realm in disarray, e.g. *Richard the Redeless*, IV.71–82, where chaotic parliamentary proceedings are described in an extended analogy in which the 'maister' of the 'barge' does not know how to steer it in a storm. Gower uses the ship of state image in *Vox*, I.1593–2078 to dramatise the danger and confusion at the time of the uprising in 1381.

67]   **conscience** is used in the legal sense of the ability to judge right from wrong, Alford, *Glossary*, p. 34.

69]   **bowe … is bent**, cf. the wrath of God against Jerusalem described in Lamentations 2:4, 'He hath bent his bow like an enemy: he stood with his right hand as an adversary'. See also notes to line 81.

72]   Cf. line 2.

73–80]   Kail, *Poems,* suggested that these lines referred to the Cirencester plot against Henry IV in 1400. It is more likely that the sentiments are generic, but if they are topical, then a later timeframe is more plausible, see Introduction, p. 18, and cf. Hoccleve, *Regement*, 2796–803, 'swich vnbuxumnesse/Suffred, vs make wol of seurte lame./Who-so may þis correct, is worthi blame/Þat he doth naght, alasse! Þis suffraunce/Wol vs destroye by continuance./Is ther no lawe þis to remedie?/I can no more; but, and this forth growe,/This londe shal it repent and sore abye'.

78]   **matere meue**: to put forth a plea or make a petition, Alford, *Glossary*, p. 102.

79]   Cf. Poem 5/47 and 13/164.

Goddis bowe of wratthe on vs was bent;
There we thenke al to lyte.
His ȝerde of loue on summe is lent,
With swerd of vengeaunce, he summe doth smyte.
The brydell with teeth thay byte 85
That of God taken non hede;
Or fendys alle ȝoure werkys wryte –
Man, knowe thy self, loue God and drede.

Why pore men don riche reuerence,
Two skylles Y fynde therfore: 90
To tyrauntes don hem greuaunce
To rewe and aȝen restore.
Goode men, for loue they worshipe more
That don hem good and help at nede;
For God seeth thurgh euery bore. 95
Man, knowe thy self, loue God and drede.

Eche man wot that bereth estate
Why they hit resceyue, and to what wyse.
Worship for drede is preue hate:
Suche worship of frendes men schold refuyse; 100
In loue and drede, worshipe the wyse,
Be suget to resoun in lengthe [fol. 99a] and brede;
For God seeth thurgh eche mysse.
Man, knowe thy self, loue God and drede.

81] Cf. line 68 and Poem 12/87. Kail, *Poems*, suggested that line 81 was a reference to the pestilence which haunted the western and northern parts of the country in 1399 (p. xi) but argues that Poem 12 dates from Henry V's reign. Kail's identification of Poem 1 with 1399 is unstable. See Introduction, pp. 6–7.

87] The image of devils reading, writing or counting human sins recurs at Poem 4/235, 11/111, 18/120 and 24/392.

95] Cf. Ecclesiasticus 39:24, 'The works of all flesh are before him and nothing can be hid from his eyes'.

97] Cf. line 1.

99ff] Cf. Hoccleve, *Regement*, 'to hem longith it, for goddes sake,/To wayue cruelte and tyrannye,/And to pitee, hir hertes bowe & wrye,/And reule hir peple esily and faire:/It is kyngly, be meeke and debonaire' (3384–8) and 'Prudence hath leuer loued be þan drad;/Ther may no prince in his estate endure,/Ne ther-yn any while stande sad,/But he be loued, for loue is armure/Of seurete.' (4782–6).

103] Cf. line 95 and Poem 12/93 and 14/71.

As long as man doth wrong,   105
He maketh God his ful foo.
The more he dwelleth theryn long,
To his soule he encreseth woo.
Er he fele het, Y rede say 'hoo!' –
Er his soule glowe as glede.   110
Haue heuene or helle; chese of two.
Man, knowe thy self, loue God and drede.

The man withoute charitee
May neuere wynne heuen blisse.
As thou wolde men dede for the   115
Do thou so liche; eche man haue hisse.
For all that euere is goten mysse
Mot be rekened a drope ȝe shede.
Thes worldis good and thou mon kysse.
Man, knowe thy self, loue God and drede.   120

False men bye helle ful dere:
That taken with wrong are Goddis theues;
They han here heuene in this world here,
After in helle, huge myscheues.
What they byleue, here werkys preues;   125
Arn heretikes, and out of the crede.
Why God doth loue, why God doth greues:
Man, knowe thy self, loue God and drede.

106]   **ful foo**, cf. the converse formula with **frend** Poem 3/105.
110]   **glowe as glede** is formulaic, cf. Poem 13/14.
111]   Cf. Poem 10/154.
113–16]   Drawn from Luke 6:30–1, 'Give to every one that asketh thee, and of him that
     taketh away thy goods, ask them not again. And as you would that men should do to
     you, do you also to them in like manner.'
116]   **hisse**: the spelling of the third possessive pronoun indicates a concern for eye-rhyme.
     The same form is used Poem 17/28 and 18/158.
119]   **kysse**: *MED* records no examples of 'kissen' in the sense of 'kiss goodbye to', to lose
     by kissing, but presumably this must be the sense. The earliest recorded example of the
     verb in this sense given by OED kiss (*v.*) 4. *trans.* with *adv.*, *prep.*, or *compl* is 1606,
     Shakespeare, *Ant. & Cl.* III. x. 7 'We haue kist away Kingdomes, and Prouinces'.
126]   **heretikes**: See Introduction, p. 19.

Man, synne not in ouerhope;
Thou wynnest not Goddis mercie with fight;   130
Hit wolde brynge the in wanhope
To wene no mercy thou hauen myght.
Alle thyng is nombred in Goddis sight:
The leste tryp that euere ȝe trede;
His mercy is medled with his right.   135
Man, knowe thy self, loue God and drede.

Mannes conscience wil hym telle:
Riche and pore, fool and wyse,
Whether he be worthi heuene or helle
To resceyue after his seruyce.   140
Eche man auyse hym that is wys,
Pore and prynce, styf on stede,
Or vyces ouer vertues rys.
Man, knowe thy self, loue God and drede.

Who that takeþ fro pore to eke with his,   145
For that wrong is worthy wo.
Another richer than he is
Of the same shal serue hym so.
That ȝeueth to that liȝe or go
Mete or drynke, herborwe or wede,   150
God sendes ynow to tho
That louen God and hym wolen drede.

129]   The line is identical to Poem 7/97 and the sentiment is repeated Poem 8/47 and
20/201.

133]   Cf. Job 14:5, 'The days of man are short, and the number of his months is with thee:
thou hast appointed his bounds which cannot be passed', and Wisdom 11:21, 'thou hast
ordered all things in measure, and number, and weight'.

145]   Cf. Proverbs 22:16, 'He that oppresseth the poor, to increase his own riches, shall
himself give to one that is richer, and shall be in need.'

149]   The poet draws on the description of the Last Judgement, Matthew 25:35–6, 'For I
was hungry, and you gave me to eat; I was thirsty, and you gave me to drink; I was a
stranger, and you took me in: Naked, and you covered me: sick, and you visited me: I
was in prison, and you came to me.' The trope of the 'works of mercy' is also used in
Poem 17/36 and ironically Poem 6/38.

He is a fool that doth answere
To a man er tale be told;
But after the dede deme there;   155
Lete not lawe be fauoured ne sold;
Suche maken fals men be bold,
And false men myghte stroye a thede.
Er charitee in hert wexe cold,
Man, knowe thy self, loue God and drede.   160

3if a man do a-nother mys,
Neighbores shuld hem auyse;
The trespasour amende and kys,
Do bothe parties euene assise.
Old horded hate maketh wratthe to rise,   165
And ofte gilteles blod to blede.
Fle fro fooles and folwe wise.
Man, knowe thy self, loue God and drede.

153]   Cf. Ecclesiasticus 11:8, 'Before thou hear, answer not a word: and interrupt not others
in the midst of their discourse.' **Answere** is a legal term: a defence in response to a
charge or accusation, Alford, *Glossary*, p. 6. **tale** is the plaintiff's account in a legal suit,
Alford, *Glossary*, p. 151.

156ff]   The injunctions to administer law equitably and to make peace between warring
parties were used by Kail, *Poems,* to date the poem to the complaints against justices in
the first parliament of Henry IV's reign. The remarks, however, are generic, see Gower,
Confessio, VII.2754–6, 'For if the lawe of covoitise/Be set upon a jugges hond/Wo is the
poeple of thilke lond' and the exemplary tales which follow which show the disasters that
ensure when law is bought and sold. Cf. Conscience's criticisms of how Mede corrupts
the law in Schmidt, *Piers Parallel Text,* B.3.155–62, and *Mum and the Sothsegger,* 1141–8.
The narrator quotes from Canon Law at line 1148b 'Fauor et premium timor et odium
peruertunt verum iudicium'.

159]   **charitee … wexe cold,** cf. Matthew 24:12, 'And because iniquity hath abounded, the
charity of many shall grow'. The poet draws the image from Christ's prophecy of the
signs of the Last Judgement. Cf. Poem 22/31.

163]   **amende:** to correct or reform, Alford, *Glossary*, p. 5.

164]   **assise:** a trial in which sworn assessors or jurymen decide questions of fact, Alford,
Glossary, p. 145.

165]   Cf. Proverbs 10:12, 'Hatred stirreth up strifes: and charity couereth all sins'. Cf.
Lydgate, *Fall of Princes,* 'Whan eueri man drouh to his partie/Of old hatreede to kyndle
new envie' (2265–6).

167]   Cf. Proverbs 9:6, 'Forsake childishness, and live, and walk by the ways of prudence'.
See also Poem 22/72.

Poem 2. Mede and muche thank

The poem takes the form of a debate between two unnamed speakers who stand respectively for the principles of performing service for the sake of recognition or acknowledgement, and serving a lord for material reward and gain. The poem has been edited more recently than Kail, *Poems*, by John Conlee in *Middle English Debate Poetry*. He names the speakers 'Soldier' and 'Courtier', taking his cue from the use of the word 'trauaylyng man' (l. 9). While the speaker who argues against service for gain clearly does act on military service (ll. 29–31), his social role is larger than this: he stands for the principle of active work and wise counsel in contrast to the flattering words and luxurious posturing of the extravagantly dressed courtier. In contrast to Kail, who assigned the last four stanzas to the honest working man, Conlee assigns lines 65–72 and 81–8 to the courtier. He remarks that Kail's assignment of speech breaks up the established pattern of alternation of speakers: 'Lines 65–72 seem to be a direct response to the soldier's extreme indictment of the courtier in the previous stanza, and the activities described in lines 67–70 clearly apply to one engaged in soldiering. Furthermore, unexpected reversals of this kind are not unusual in debate poetry, a poetic stratagem sometimes referred to as "wrongfooting" the audience' (p. 214). Conlee's reading is attractive and produces a sophisticated poem which debates the merits of 'mede' with a nuance of the kind seen in *Piers Plowman*. My hesitation in following Conlee, and, instead, maintaining Kail's assignment of speakers, is based on viewing this poem in the context of the Digby sequence as a whole. Given the persistent criticism of flattery and singular profit, and repeated calls for truth and common good and wise counsel, I think it unlikely that the poem would give the last word to the sycophantic courtier. Line 85, with its emphasis on serving 'selue' is a condemnation entirely consonant with criticism of self-serving throughout the Digby poems. The narrative voice becomes aligned with that of the 'trauaylyng' man (l. 9).

2. Mede and muche thank

In blossomed buske I bode boote,
In ryche array, with ryches rank,
Fayre floures vnder foote;
Sauour to myn herte sank.
I sawe two buyrnes on a bank;   5
To here talkyng I tok hede:
That on preysede moche thank,
That other held al with mede.

That on a trauaylyng man had ben,
He was but in mene array;   10
That other clothed in gawdy gren,
Blasande briȝt, embrowdid gay.

1] **blossomed buske**: the evocation of a pleasant woodland setting with fresh smelling flowers and a first person narrator is suggestive of the formulaic lines of a 'chanson d'aventure', a genre of Old French poetry in which the typical plot is the meeting of a young man and woman in the countryside. There follows: either attempted seduction, or a lament from the woman about how she has been treated either by lover or husband. The 'chanson' setting is used in a number of Middle English poems to introduce debate poems, most notably *The Owl and the Nightingale*, but also *The Thrush and the Nightingale*. The debate poem *Merci Passith Ritwisnes* (Conlee, *Poetry*, pp. 200–9) begins in a very similar fashion to this poem: 'Bi a forest as y gan walke/With-out a paleys in a leye,/I herde two men togidre talke,/I þouȝte to wite what þei wolde seie.' (ll. 1–4). In Digby, the speaker drops from sight after these opening lines. The alliteration of lines 1–3, which marks the literary formality of the opening, is not sustained.

2] **array** refers to the verdure of the wood.

7] **moche thank**, in the sense of non-material gratitude or acknowledgement. Cf. Poem 16/76 where the speaker of wise counsel 'gete[s] no þonk but harm and shame'. God's acknowledgement of good deeds, and standing with truth, is seen also at Poem 13/16. The speaker who addresses the king in *The Crowned King* asks only for thanks and not reward, 'To pike a thonk with pleasaunce my profit were but simple' (l. 48).

8] **mede** has a range of senses throughout the sequence, see glossary. The majority of examples are pejorative, with the sense of material reward sliding into selfish corruption, but the more neutral sense of plain reward is also seen in lines 40 and 80; cf. Poem 1/43, 4/11 and 7/71. The complexity of the semantic tussle over the senses of 'mede' in Schmidt, *Piers Parallel Text*, B.III, however, is not represented in the sequence.

9] **trauaylyng**, in the sense of willing to work, including being prepared to face danger for his lord.

11–12] **gawdy gren … embrowdid gay**, cf. Youthe in Offord, *Parlement*, ll. 122–9, whose extravagant costume is also green, woven with gold and richly embroidered. Chaucer's

'Loo, felow, chese y may
To ryde on palfrey or on stede.
Shewe forth moche thonk, Y the pray;   15
Loo, here Y shewe sumwhat of mede.'

'Syr, I see thou hast richesse;
How thou hit get, whiche is thy fame,
In corage and prowesse,
After thy dede resceyue thy name,   20
Other in worshipe, or in shame.
Men wol the deme after thy dede:
Thy fer trauayle, or cochour at hame,
How serued thou to haue that mede?'

Squire is embroidered like a meadow full of flowers, *General Prologue*, A.89–90; and the lusty Yeoman is also clothed in green, l. 103. Green costume has a number of associations: youthful excess, promiscuity, newness, and in social terms, disorder, thoughtlessness, inconstancy, Hodges, *Chaucer and Costume*, p. 67, n.49. Cf. the contrast between the extravagantly dressed flattering courtiers and Wit the truthteller in *Richard the Redeless*, III.133–238.

12] **blasande**, the Northern form of the present participle, not used here to secure rhyme, is one of several indications of the mixed spelling forms in the poems.

13] **felow** indicates the courtier's contempt for what he sees as the lowly social status of the poorly clad man; see *MED* 'felau' (*n.*); 5b. This contrasts to the respectful use of **Syr** in line 17.

14] **palfrey ... stede**, a fine riding horse or war horse.

15] **the**: the courtier consistently addresses the honest man with the inferior form of the second person pronoun, apart from **3e**, see note to l. 31.

17] **Syr**: the honest man uses a respectful title to the courtier, but his use of second person pronouns vacillates between the respectful **3e** and the familiar **thou**, possibly to indicate the slippery social status of the courtier.

18] **How thou hit get**, part of the sequence's sustained concern with rightful and wrongful gain and profit, see Poem 1/31, 8/7, 8/67, 10/135, 19/34. This temporal theme is modulated into a spiritual context in the discussion of gaining admission to heaven.

20] **After thy dede**, cf. Isaiah 59:18, 'As unto revenge, as it were to repay wrath to his adversaries, and a reward to his enemies: he will repay the like to the islands. According to their deeds, accordingly He will repay.' This line is repeated verbatim at Poem 6/58 and 14/7, and there are modulations of this commonplace at Poem 7/103, 13/8/16/56/80 and 19/103. See also *The Wife of Bath's Tale*, III.158 and 1170.

23] **fer trauayle ... cochour**. This antithesis captures the honest man's willingness to put himself in danger for his lord while the courtier pleases himself at home with servile flattery in small matters, a contrast discussed by Yunck, *Lineage*, pp. 272–3. A similar scenario is dramatised in *Mum and the Sothsegger*, 264–76. **hame**: the Northern form is used for rhyme. Elsewhere **hom(e)** is the form Poem 1/38, 12/1, 20/77 apart from **ham** Poem 24/210, which is not in rhyme position.

'I plese my lord at bed and bord,   25
þou3 Y do but strype a stre,
And florische fayre my lordis word,
And fede hem forth with "nay" and "3ee".
Whan trauaylyng men fare euele on see,
In fight, in preson, in storme and drede,   30
With moche thonk than mery 3e be,
And Y wole make me mery with mede.'

'Flateryng is the fendis scoles;
3oure awen werkys preueth 3ow nys.
3e skorne lordes and make hem 3oure foles,   35
To playe and lawhe at 3oure delys.
Do for a lord, and he be wys,
Trewe trauayle shal not lese his dede;
To vertuous lord al worship lys:
The trewe seruant is worthy his mede.'   40

'Say, felowe, what doth the greue
My glosyng, flateryng, play and daunce?
Shulde my souerayn aske the leue
Whom hym list to auaunce?
Thou getest the thonke with spere and launce,   45
Ther-with [fol. 100a] thou myght the clothe and fede;

26] **strype a stre** strip a straw, i.e. vain and useless activity. The expression is proverbial, based on the sense of 'straw' as a worthless object; see *MED* 'strau' (*n.*); 2a.

30] A variation on this line occurs at line 52.

31] **3e be**: the switch to the plural second person pronoun refers back to **men** (l. 29), but also produces the requisite form of the verb 'be' to fit the rhyme scheme.

33] **fendis scoles**, method of learning associated with the devil. The idea is commonplace; see *MED* 'scole' (*n.*); 2.2. The plural form facilitates the rhyme.

39] Cf. Poem 13/136 where it is remarked that when 'gloser' and 'flaterer' are admitted, 'worship' is never won.

40] Cf. Luke 10:7 and 1 Timothy 5:18, 'the labourer is worthy his hire/reward'. The poet translates the biblical 'labourer' as **trewe seruant**, whereas at Poem 9/165 the line runs 'The werkman is worþy his mede'. **mede** translates the Vulgate's 'mercede', and is used here in a non-pejorative sense as 'deserved reward'. The quotation is also used in Schmidt, *Piers Parallel Text*, B.II.123.

42] **glosyng** as distinct from truthtelling is excoriated throughout Poem 4, where, at line 78, it is stated that glosers should not 'go so gay'. The gloser and the flatterer are linked in Poem 7/22 and 16/5 states that glosers counsel lords to accept 'mede'.

I, gloser, wil stonde to my chaunce,
And mayntene my men al with mede.

My flateryng, glosyng, not me harmes;
I get loue and moche richesse   50
When wel faryng men of armes
In fight, in presoun, and distresse.
When thou art old and feble Y gesse,
Who wole the fynde fode or wede?
Lete moche thonk than thy mete dresse,   55
And Y wole make me mery with mede.'

'I likne a gloser in eche weder
To folwe the wynd as doth the fane;
ȝe begeten hony togedere –
To stroyȝe that cometh the drane.   60
Me thenkeþ þere wit is wane,
To stroiȝe the hony and foule hit shede,
Gloser hath brought faytour lane
To halle and chamber, to lordes, for mede.

48] **mayntene.** The practice of maintaining followers with livery and financial incentives
has a long history of criticism in parliaments in the late fourteenth and early fifteenth
centuries, and measures were passed to try to regulate the practice (*Statutes of the
Realm*, II.74–5, II.113). Maintenance attracts hostile commentary in a number of poems,
e.g. Schmidt, *Piers Parallel Text*, B.II.53–66 and III.153–69; *Richard the Redeles* Passus II;
Mum and the Sothsegger, 243–54 and 788–844. In Digby honourable maintenance is seen
to be the support of the poor commons, Poem 3/104.

58] **fane**: the weather vane is a proverbial symbol of fickleness and mutability, see especially
The Crowned King, where the king is advised to secure wise counsellors, and to shun the
flatterer 'for he that fareth as a faane folowyng thy wille/Worche thou well or woo, he woll
the not amende' (111–12); cf. *The Clerk's Tale*, IV.995–6, 'O stormy peple! Unsad and evere
untrewe!/Ay undiscreet and chaungynge as a fane!' and Lydgate, *Troy Book*, 1.3509.

59–64] In a shift into personification allegory, 'Gloser' and 'Faytour' (wastrel) are seen to
gather honey together which the drone then destroys. The narrator glosses the drone as
the lean 'faytour' – wastrel – introduced by the gloser into the hall. The sense is very
condensed and it is possible that the repetition in lines 60 and 62 is an indication of
scribal corruption. A more extensive account of drones as social parasites is seen in
Mum and the Sothsegger, 982–6, 1044–63. *Pierce the Ploughman's Crede*, 726–9 likens
the parasitic friars to drones.

59] **hony** has the connotation of 'honied' or fraudulent words, *MED* 'honi' (*n.*); 2b: cf.
Hoccleve, *Male Regle*, 221.

64] Cf. *Richard the Redeless*, III.126, where fashionable courtiers are 'feete into chambris'.

Thy wikked speche come fro ferre;   65
Euel thou spekest, worse dost mene.
Thou woldest euere more were werre
For profyt and pilage thou myght glene.
Cristen blod destroyed clene,
And townes brent [as] a glede.   70
Thy conscience is ful lene;
Thou noldest not come ther but for mede.

In wikked lyuer no good counsayle;
Is coward of kynde, ny3t and day.
Good lyuere dar fende and assayle,   75
And hardy in dede brou3t to bay.
I wolde thou were brou3t to assay,
At nede, a wys counseil to rede;
Were thou as hardy as thou art gay,
3e were wel worthy to haue good mede.   80

Thenketh the not it doth the good,
Whan thou out of thy bed dost swerue?
3e clothe 3ow and do on 3oure hod,
At tyme of day thy mete dost kerue.
Why dost thou thy seluen serue?   85

67–72]   The characterisation of the courtier as a war profiteer who, nonetheless, is unwilling
   to risk his life for his king is strikingly reminiscent of the discussion of the profiting
   from war in the altercation between Mede and Conscience, Schmidt, *Piers Parallel Text*,
   B.III.175–208.
70]   **as a glede**. The MS reads 'on a glede'. It is possible to understand 'glede' as an open space;
   see *MED* 'glade' (*n*.); 1; but in other poems, **glede** means coal; see *MED* 'glede' (*n*.); 2, and is
   used in similes of burning Poem 1/110 and 13/14; a sense which better fits the line here.
74]   Cf. Poem 13/135, 'for wynnyng þey counselled to cowardys'.
75]   Cf. Poem 3/84 where a good counsellors 'dar fende and assayle'.
77]   **assay**: in the legal sense of being examined in a trial, Alford, *Glossary*, p. 10.
83–4]   The image of the flatterer clothing himself and carving for himself cunningly
   reregisters the usual practice of a lord giving a hood and clothing for a retainer, and
   a retainer carving before his lord, as at the end of *The Summoner's Tale* where Jankin
   carves before the lord of the manor and receives a hood in return for solving the problem
   of the mathematical division of the fart.
85]   **seluen**, to serve one's self rather than the common good and profit is akin to working
   solely for singular profit, see note to Poem 1/4. Cf. *Mum and the Sothsegger*, 163 where
   courtiers who shun plain-speaking counsel are said to 'speke of thaire owen spede', and
   270 where the narrator tells Mum that he 'serues thy-self, and no man elles'.

I trowe thou do it for gret nede –
For hunger and cold, elles myghtest thou sterue.
This preueþ thou seruest al for mede.'

86–8] The plain speaker turns the tables on the flatterer by pointing out that, for all his fine apparel and words, the flatterer serves **mede** simply out of the **nede** to fend off starvation.

Poem 3. Treuth, reste and pes

In addition to Kail, *Poems,* this poem is edited in R.H. Robbins, ed., *Historical Poems of the XIVth and XVth Centuries* (New York: Columbia, 1959), pp. 39–44 (notes pp. 268–70), and in James Dean, ed., *Medieval English Political Writings* (Michigan: TEAMS, 1996), pp. 153–8. Both later editors follow Kail in dating the poem to 1401. Kail advances detailed support from parliamentary discussions of that year (pp. xi–iii) which Robbins and Dean follow. Likewise, Kail's claim that lines 138–44 were written in favour of the 1401 statute *De Haeretico Comburendo* (*Statutes of the Realm,* II.125–8) are upheld by the later editions. The latter claim is tenuous; see notes to lines 137–44. The difficulty of assigning a precise date to this poem stems from the generic and commonplace nature of its sentiments. As the writer states in line 49, his criticism is not specific, but general. There are numerous parallels with lines in other Digby poems and other Middle English social poetry. While a date for this poem in the early years of the first decade of the fifteenth century cannot conclusively be ruled out, the axiomatic statements about a well-ordered kingdom are consonant with the anxieties and hopes at the start of the reign of Henry V. Indeed, there are substantial echoes of Poem 3 in Poems 12 and 13, poems which almost certainly refer to the beginning of Henry's rule. On the problems of dating, see further, Introduction, p. 7. The generic statements of the poem, and its moralising, bears comparison to wisdom lyrics such as those found in *Vernon* e.g. 'Who says the sooth, he shall be shent', Furnivall, *Vernon Poems* II.683–6, and 'Truth Ever is Best', Furnivall, *Vernon Poems* II.699–701.

3. Treuth, reste and pes

For drede ofte my lippes Y steke,
For false reportors that trou[th]e mys famed;
ȝut charitee chargeth me to speke:
þouȝ trouþe be drede, he nys not ashamed,
Trouþe secheþ non hernes ther los is lamed,   5
Trouþe is worschiped at euery des.
In that kyngdom ther trouþe is blamed,
God sendes vengeaunce to make trouþe haue pes.

Trouþe is messager to ryȝt,
And ryȝt is counseille to iustice;   10
Iustice in Goddis stede is dyȝt.
Do euene lawe [fol. 100b] to fooll and wyse,
Set mesure in euene assise,
The riȝte weye as lawe ges.
And lawe be kept, folk nyl not ryse;   15
That kyngdom shal haue reste and pes.

1] The narrator is initially presented as a truthteller, though this focalisation drops from
view. The diction recurs in Poem 4/113; 4/117 and 13/100.
2] **trou[th]e**. The MS reads 'trouhte'. This is the only instance of this spelling in the entire
sequence and I have emended. **mys famed**, the defamation of truth, is a commonplace,
cf. Poem 12/73 and *Mum and the Sothsegger*, 175–92.
4] Cf. similar diction Poem 12/75.
5] **hernes**, cf. Poem 4/157 and 12/74.
8] **vengeaunce**. God's vengeance on lawless kingdoms is a recurring motif in the Digby
sequence, see Poem 1/84, 4/115/119, 5/39, 9/105, 12/148, 13/84, 14/87. A similar trope is used
in *Richard the Redeles*, III.351 where, after the silencing of truth, and the expulsion of
Wit the truthteller from the king's court, God intervenes.
9–16] The sentiments of this stanza are very similar to those of Poem 12/65–72.
12] Cf. Poem 1/6/14.
13] Cf. Poem 1/61 and 13/71.
14] Cf. Poem 9/67.
15] The line repeats, near-verbatim, Poem 1/63 and anticipates line 27 in this poem.
15–16] Cf. *Mum and the Sothsegger*, 224–5, 'Hym graunte of his grace to guye wel the
peuple/And to reule this royaume in pees and in reste.'
16] The line is repeated at line 32.

3if suche a tale tellere were,
To a kyng apayre a mannys name,
The kyng shulde boþe partyes here,
And punysche þe fals for defame.   20
Þan fals men wolde ases for blame,
For falshed, body and soule it sles.
Falshed endes ay in shame,
And trouþe in worschipe and in pes.

Whanne lawe is put fro ri3te assise,   25
And domesman made by mede,
For fawte of lawe 3if comouns rise,
Þan is a kyngdom most in drede.
For whanne vengeaunce a comouns lede,
Þei do gret harm er þey asses.   30
Ther no man oþer doþ mysbede,
That kyngdom shal haue reste and pes.

Whan craft riseþ a3ens craft,
In burgh, toun, or cite,
Þey go to lordes whan lawe is laft,   35
Whoche party may strengere be,
But wyse men þe sonere se.
By witles wille þey gedre pres,
Or lordis medle in foly degree.
Let lawe haue cours in reste and pes.   40

3it þere is þe þridde distaunce
Bryngeþ a kyngdom in moche noy3e:
Ofte chaunge of gouernaunce,
Of all degree, lowe and hy3e.

17–24]   Cf. Poem 13/9–16.
19]   **boþe partyes**, cf. Poem 15/44.
25–32]   Cf. Poem 1/63/156, 9/57–60/65–8, 12/60, 13/25–32, 14/60 and 16/53.
33]   **craft … a3ens craft**, cf. Poem 16/60 in the later poem, the reference is to Flanders. It is unclear whether there is reference to specific artisanal strife (see Introduction, p. 11), or whether the line in both poems is a generic axiom which warns against internal division.
42]   **noy3e**: the spelling may be scribal. Throughout the sequence, there is a concern to create eye-rhymes. *MED* does record the form 'ni3e'; see 'noi' (*n*.).

A kyng may not al aspie: 45
Summe telle hym soþ, summe telle hym les.
Þe whete fro þe chaf ȝe tryȝe,
So mowe ȝe leue in reste and pes.

I speke not in specyale
Of oo kyngdom the lawe to telle;   50
I speke hool in generale
In eche kyngdom the lawe to telle.
Also is writen in þe gospelle,
A word þat God hym seluen ches:
Raþere þan fiȝte, a man go selle   55
On of his cloþes, and biȝe hym pes.

A worþi knyȝt wol worchip wynne;
He wil not ȝelde hym þouȝ me þret,
But raþere as malice doþ bygynne,
Quenche hit at þe firste het.   60

45-6] **kyng may not al aspie**. The ignorance of the king is identified as a topos of counsel literature, see Embree, 'The King's Ignorance', p. 121. See also Embree and Urquhart, *The Simonie*, 313–24 and *Mum and the Sothsegger*, 133–42.

47] A biblical image, see Jeremias 23:28, 'The prophet that hath a dream, let him tell a dream: and he that hath my word, let him speak my word with truth: what hath the chaff to do with the wheat, saith the Lord?' and Matthew 3:12, 'and he will thoroughly cleanse his floor and gather his wheat into the barn; but the chaff he will burn with unquenchable fire', Matthew 13:30, 'Gather up first the cockle, and bind it into bundles to burn, but the wheat gather ye into my barn'. Proverbial use of this phrase is seen in a number of Middle English texts, e.g. Gradon, *Ayenbite*, 210/30; *The Man of Lawe*, B.701; *The Nun's Priest*, B.4633; Gower, *Confessio*, Prol.844 and Lydgate, *Troy Book*, Prol.151.

52] **telle**. The more usual poetic practice is to rhyme on different words, and it is possible that **telle** is an example of dittography (caught from line 50). While a word such as 'spelle' would also fit the sense, there remains the possibility that there is deliberate repetition of the practice of telling, in the sense of telling truths, and therefore I have not emended the text.

55-6] No Gospel verse corresponds exactly to these lines. It is possible that the poet has conflated elements of the following verses: Matthew 19:21, 'If thou wilt be perfect, go sell what thou hast, and give to the poor, and thou shalt have treasure in heaven: and come follow me' and Luke 22:36, 'But now he that hath a purse, let him take it, and likewise a scrip, and he that hath not, let him sell his coat and buy a sword'.

59-62] Cf. Ecclesiasticus 28:12–14, 'For as the wood of the forest is, so the fire burneth: and as a man's strength is, so shall his anger be, and according to his riches he shall increase his anger. A hasty contention kindleth a fire: and a hasty quarrel sheddeth blood: and

For, and ȝe lete it growe gret,
Hit brenneþ breme as fyre in gres.
Lawles nouellerye loke ȝe lete;
So mowe ȝe lyue in reste and pes.

Old speche is spoken ȝore: 65
What is a kyngdom tresory?
Bestayle, corn stuffed in store,
Riche comouns, and wyse clergy,
Marchaundes, squyers, chiualry
That wol be redy at a res,   70
And cheualrous kyng in wittes hyȝe
To lede in were, and gouerne in pes.

Among philosofres wyse,
In here bokes men writen fynde
[fol. 101a] Þat synne is cause of cowardyse.   75
Wel lyuyng man, hardy of kynde,
Wikked lyuere, graceles blynde –
He dredeþ deþ – þe laste mes.
Þe good lyuere haþ God in mynde,
Þat mannys counseil makeþ pes.   80

What kyng that wol haue good name,
He wol be lad be wys counsayle;
Þat loue worschip and dreden shame,
And boldely dar frende and assayle.

a tongue that beareth witness bringeth death. If thou blow the spark, it shall burn as a
fire: and if thou spit upon it, it shall be quenched: both come out of the mouth.'
60]   firste het. Dean, *Political Writings*, following Robbins, *Historical Poems*, glosses this
as 'go'. Kail, *Poems*, does not provide a gloss. Elsewhere in the sequence 'het' means
'heat' Poem 1/109, 15/69, and this fits the sense here.
62]   fyre in gres: a proverbial image, cf. *The Wife of Bath* D.487–8, '... in his owene grece I
made hym frye/For angre and verray jalousye', and Schick, *The Temple of Glass*, 349–50,
'Thus is he fryed in his owene gres/Torent and torn with his owene rage'.
71–2]   cheualrous kyng: a description consonant with the image of the king in Poem 12.
77/79]   Cf. Poem 2/73–5.
78]   mes. Kail, *Poems*, glosses this as 'adversity', and Robbins, *Historical Poems,* as 'mass,
sacrament'. Dean, *Political Writings*, observes that the idea is 'that death is the final rite
of passage for the soul'. I have glossed it as 'affliction'; see *MED* 'mes' (*n.*); 1b.
81–2]   Cf. Poem 1/60.
84]   Cf. Poem 2/75.

Þere wit is, corage may not fayle,   85
For wysdom neuere worschip les.
Corage in querell doþ batayle,
And ende of batayle bygynneþ pes.

Defaute of wit makeþ long counsayle;
For witteles wordes in ydel spoken.   90
Þe more cost, þe lesse auayle;
For fawte of wyt, purpos broken.
In euyl soule, no grace is stoken,
For wikked soule is graceless:
In good lyuere, Goddis wille is loken,   95
Þat mannys counsell makeþ pes.

To wete ȝif parlement be wys,
Þe comoun profit wel it preues:
A kyngdom in comouns lys,
Alle profytes, and alle myscheues.   100
Lordis wet neuere what comouns greues
Til her rentis bigynne to ses.
Þere lordis ere pore comons releues,
And mayntene hem in were and pes.

Make God ȝoure ful frend;   105
Do þe comaundement þat he bede,

94]   'Nota' is written in the margin of the MS next to this line.
97]   Cf. Poem 13/1-8 and *Mum and the Sothsegger*, 133.
98]   **comoun profit**. This is the only use of the precise phrase in the sequence, although
      the poems are saturated with warnings to adhere to this principle, cf. note to Poem 1/4.
      The idea is explored in Middle English social poetry by Peck, *Kingship and Common
      Profit*, and see also Alford, *Glossary*, 'commune profit', pp. 32-3. Hoccleve expresses
      the need for the king to love common profit rather than his own advantage or delight,
      Regement, 1147-8; cf. 2295.
99-104] **in comouns lyes**. Taken out of context this statement could be seen to endorse a
      radical view of the political community. But, in keeping with the sequence as a whole,
      the poet is keen to stress the mutual interdependence of all the estates in the realm, cf.
      Poem 3/68-72. In mind here is the fiscal importance of the commons. The king and the
      lords rely on grants and rents to secure the well-being of the realm, and to sustain it in
      times of attack. These lines should be viewed alongside Poem 12/137-44. Cf. also Poem
      13/41-52 and *The Crowned King*, 60-74.
105-12] This stanza appears to draw on Old Testament narratives which describe
      God's protection of his chosen people so long as they obey his commandment, e.g.

Þou3 all þe worlde a3en 3ow wend,
Be God 3oure frend, 3e thar not drede:
For þere as God his frendis lede,
He saueþ hem boþe on lond and sees.   110
Who so fi3teþ, God doþ þe dede:
For God is victorie and pes.

What kyngdom werreþ hym self wiþ ynne,
Distroyeþ hym self, and no mo.
Wiþoute, here enemys bygynne   115
On eche a syde assayle hem so.
Þe comouns, þey wil robbe and slo,
Make fyere, and kyndel stres,
Whan ryches and manhode is wastede and go;
Þan drede dryueþ to trete pes.   120

The world is like a fals leman,
Fayre semblaunt, and moche gyle.
Wiþouten heire dyeþ no man,
God is chief lord of toun and pyle.
God makeþ mony heire in a whyle,   125
For God ressayueþ eche reles;
God kan breke hegge and style,
And make an hey wey to pes.

God made lordis gouernoures
To gouerne puple in vnyte.   130

Deuteronomy 11:22-3, 'For if you keep the commandments which I command you, and do them, to love the Lord your God, and walk in all his ways, cleaving unto him, the Lord will destroy all these nations before your face, and you shall possess them, which are greater and stronger than you', and cf. Deuteronomy 6:1-5.

113-16]   Internal dissension could be located in many contexts: the divisions after the deposition of Richard II, the threats and attacks from a variety of external enemies during Henry IV's reign, compounded by factionalism among the nobility, or the threats of this continuing in Henry V's reign. See further, Introduction, pp. 8-9. There is nothing that conclusively ties these lines to the start of Henry IV's reign and to the 1401 parliament. There are similar sentiments expressed elsewhere in the Digby sequence, Poem 5/25-32 and especially 12/33-40/121-36. The concern in Poem 3 with internal dissension and foreign threat resonates especially strongly with Poems 12 and 13.

121]   Cf. Poem 4/227-8.

130]   Cf. Poem 1/21 and 8/63.

Þe puple, ne ryches, nys not ȝoures:
Al is Goddis, and so be ȝe.
Eche day ȝe may ȝoure myrrour se,
Eche man after oþer des;
ȝoure auncetres arn gon – after schal ȝe,   135
To endeles were, or endeles pes.

Eche kyng is sworn to gouernaunce
To gouerne Goddis puple in riȝt.
Eche kyng bereþ swerd [fol. 101b] of Goddis vengeaunce
To felle Goddis foon in fiȝt,   140
And so doþ euerons honest knyȝt.
That bereþ þe ordre as it wes:
The plough, þe chirche to mayntene ryȝt,
Are Goddis champyons to kepe þe pes.

The world is like a chery fayre,   145
Ofte chaungeþ all his þynges.
Riche, pore, foul and fayre,
Popes, prelates, and lordynges:
Alle are dedly, and so ben kynges.
Or deþ lede ȝow in his les,   150

131-2]   Cf. Poem 1/19/27/34, 7/82 and 13/51.

134-6]   Cf. Poem 7/17 and 22/57.

139-41]   There is no sound evidence for seeing these lines as a reference to the 1401 statute *De Haeretico Comburendo* (*Statutes of the Realm*, II.125-8) which made provision for the burning of heretics – not least because the poem makes no mention of burning. See similar sentiments also at Poem 12/105-8. Far from being a topical reference, the lines are a paraphrase of Romans 13:4, 'For he is God's minister to thee, for good. But if thou do that which is evil, fear: for he beareth not the sword in vain. For he is God's minister: an avenger to execute wrath upon him that doth evil.' Elsewhere in the sequence God's foes are nameless enemies against which wars are waged, Poem 21/86 and, more frequently, sinful human beings, 10/66/125, 19/45 and 24/132. This poem plays out an antithesis of being God's friend, or God's enemy lines 105/108/109/158-60, an antithesis which is seen at many other points in the sequence: Poem 9/141, 13/87, 17/55/167, 20/214 and 24/99. See also note to lines 105-12 above.

145]   **chery fayre**, a phrase which often indicates the transitoriness of human existence, e.g. 'Make Amends for thy Sins', Horstmann, *Vernon Poems* II.727-30/85-6, 'Þis world nis but a chirie feire/Nou is hit in sesun, nou wol hit slake'; Gower, *Confessio*, Prol.454, 6891, and Hoccleve, *Regement*, 1289.

Arraye by tyme ȝoure rekenynges,
And trete wiþ God to gete ȝow pes.

What bryngeþ a kyngdom al aboue
Wys counseil and good gouernaunce?
Eche lord wil other loue,   155
And rule wel labourrers sustynaunce.
God makeþ for his frendis no destaunce,
For God kan skatre þe grete pres.
God for his frendis maþ ordynaunce,
And gouuerneþ hem in werre and pes.   160

Good lyf is cause of good name;
Good name is worthi to haue reueraunce.
[…]
Synne is cause of greuaunce.
Eche kyngdom hongeþ in Goddis balaunce –   165
Wiþ hym þat holdeþ, wiþ hym þat fles.
Ȝe haue fre wille: chese ȝoure chaunce
To haue wiþ God werre or pes.

151]   Cf. Poem 7/83, 11/110 and 24/231.
158–9]   Cf. note to lines 105–12 and Ecclesiasticus 12:4, 'God will repay vengeance to the
    ungodly and to sinners, and keep them against the day of vengeance', and Deuteronomy
    32:43, 'for he will revenge the blood of his servants: and will render vengeance to their
    enemies, and he will be merciful to the land of his people'.
158]   God's ability to **skatre** his enemies is seen also Poem 10/144.
161]   Cf. Ecclesiasticus 41:15, 'Take care of a good name: for this shall continue with thee,
    more than a thousand treasures precious and great', and Zupitza, 'Proverbis of Wysdom',
    224:12, 'Pride goþe bifore, and after comeþ schame;/ȝe, wele is hym þat haþe a good
    name'. See also Whiting, *Proverbs*, p. 423, N.12 for variations on this proverb.
163]   A line is lacking in the MS.
165–8]   Cf. Poem 9/105–12 where, as here, the poet draws parallel the fate of an individual
    sinner and a sinful kingdom. The poem concludes with a series of pithy sententiae in a
    sustained example of the use of moral discourse to urge political stability.
167–8]   Cf. Poem 11/61–2.

Poem 4. Lerne say wele, say litel, or say noȝt

Kail, *Poems*, suggested that this poem originated in 1404 because in the February parliament of that year the commons asked the king to remove from court four persons who displeased them. Kail saw this to lie behind the poem's criticisms of flatterers who oppress the poor and commit other kinds of injustice, *Poems*, p. xiii. To produce a specific parliamentary context for this poem is impossible. The comments are generic, and as the notes make clear, the criticisms can be paralleled in a variety of poems from the later fourteenth and early fifteenth centuries. The milieu from which this poem originates is not, however, one that is parliamentary. Although the tenor of the remarks against flatterers, the oppression of the poor, and the need for priests to defend Holy Church is similar to the regular parliamentary petitions and debates, this poem is steeped in proverbial and wisdom sentiment. There are numerous parallels to the axiomatic good sense of many of the lines from wisdom literature, common proverbs, and from the bible. The poem combines 'contemptus mundi' tropes with sententiae about the proper governance of the tongue. Throughout, there is a conflation of the spiritual and the worldly. The poem is an example of the poet's construction of the voice of common sense to shore up political and ecclesiastical stability. See further, Introduction, pp. 42–4, 55–60. Close parallels to this poem can be seen in the *Vernon* lyrics, especially 'Prouerbes of Diuerse Profetes and of Poetes and of oþur Seyntes', Furnivall, *Vernon Poems* II.522–53, 'Luytel Caton', Furnivall, *Vernon Poems* II.553–62, 'Who says the sooth, he shall be shent', Furnivall, *Vernon Poems* II.683–6, and 'Try to Say the Best, Control Your Tongue', Furnivall, *Vernon Poems* II.723–5.

4. Lerne say wele, say litel, or say noȝt

As þe see doþ ebbe and flowe,
So fareþ þe world hyder and þedere;
Aȝen þe wynd they sayle and rowe
To gadre worldys goodis togedere.
At þe last, it goþ Y wot not whyder,   5
As ende of web out of slay;
And hemself stoden so slydere –
How it is wiþ hym Y kan not say.

Sum man dar not be þef for drede;
His trouþe is vice and no virtue.   10
In heuene he nys not worþi mede
Þat cloþes trouþe in falshed hewe.
Maugre his teeþ, he is trewe
Stoken in presoun as best fro stray.
Here wikked wille groweþ newe;   15
Þey thenke more þan þey say.

Men may not staunche a comoun noys,
Noþer for loue ne for awe.

1–2] **see doþ ebbe and flowe**: the comparison of the tenure of worldly prosperity to the ebb and flow of the sea is proverbial; the many examples cited in Whiting, *Proverbs*, pp. 244–5, G.330 include: 'Yt faryt be all thys warldly good/As be and ebbe and be a flood', *Ipotis* 31, 193–4 and 'This werldely gude/That ebbes and flowes here als the flode', *Barlam and Josaphat*, 235, 695–6.

4] **Aȝen the wynd**, another proverbial image, see Whiting, *Proverbs*, p. 647, W.332: citing Lydgate, *Troy Book*, III.7086–9, 'But like as he that gynneth for to saille/Ageyn the wynde whan the mast doth rive/Right so it were but in veyn to strive/Ageyn the fate' and *Piers of Fulham*, 13.302–4, 'Men rehercyn in there saw/Hard it is to stryve with wynde or wawe/Whether it do ebbe or flow'.

5–6] Cf. Job 7:6, 'My days have passed more swiftly than the web is cut by the weaver, and are consumed without any hope.'

7] **stoden slydere**, cf. 24/92.

12] **cloþes trouþe**, cf. Poem 13/30. The deception of the false speaker is a conventional trope: see, e.g., Panton and Donaldson, *Destruction of Troy*, 9.253, 'Ne the ffalshed he faynit under faire wordes'. For further variations see Whiting, *Proverbs*, p. 172, F.49.

13] **trewe**. The syntax is confusing here, but 'trewe' must be understood in an adverbial, rather than adjectival, sense: the deceiver is rightly thrown into prison.

17] **comoun noys**. There is no explicit political reference here; the sentiment is a

After men lyue is comoun voys:
In wrongwys dede, or ry3t lawe.   20
Who doþ hem pyne, who doþ hem pawe,
Eche on telle oþer, child and may.
Tho that to vertues drawe,
Hem thar not recche what [...] say.

Tak fro þi foo, and 3eue þi frende;   25
Tak not fro thy frend to 3eue þi foo:
Þy frend wole holde þe vnhende;
Þow haddest on enemy, þan hast þu two.
Man, be war er þu do so;
[fol. 102a] To greue the he wol assay,   30
When þyn enemys wexen mo,
Litel worchipe of þe [...] say.

Oo prouerbe loke 3e preue,
3e þat wole to resoun bende:
Look what ney3ebore most may greue,   35
By al way make hym þi frende.
Þan wole þyn enemys fro þe wende,
Here owen þou3t wol hem afflay.

commonplace on the difficulty of stopping wagging tongues; cf. 'And who may stoppen
every wikked tonge/Or sown of belles whil that thei ben ronge', Chaucer, *Troilus and
Criseyde*, II.804–5 and Hoccleve, *Regement*, 3494–95, 'The pacience of Iob men may nat
hyde,/The common voys wole algate it by-wreye'.

24]   The line appears to lack a word before 'say'. Kail, *Poems*, supplied 'men'; this reproduces
the formula seen in lines 40, 72, 128, 136 and 160.

25–32]   Cf. Ecclesiasticus 6:1, 'Instead of a friend become not an enemy to thy neighbour:
for an evil man shall inherit reproach and shame, so shall every sinner that is envious
and double tongued.'

29]   man be war, cf. the title and refrain of Poem 14.

32]   The line appears to lack a word before 'say'. Kail, *Poems*, did not supply a correction.
It is possible that 'þey' has been omitted; cf. lines 16, 80 and 184.

33–5]   prouerbe, a reference to Wisdom literature, see Ecclesiasticus 39:1–3, 'The wise
men will seek out the wisdom of all the ancients, and will be occupied in the prophets.
He will keep the sayings of renowned men, and will enter withal into the subtilties of
parables. He will search out the hidden meanings of proverbs, and will be conversant
in the secrets of parables.' For the sentiments of the stanza as a whole, cf. Ecclesiasticus
28:2, 'Forgive thy neighbour if he hath hurt thee: and then shall thy sins be forgiven to
thee when thou prayest' and Zupitza, 'Proverbis of Wysdom', 244:23, 'Lete thy neyghburgh
thy frendshep fele'.

Be out of daunger of the fende,
And recche neuere what men say.   40

To synge or preche generale,
Werkys of vices for to blame,
Summe tak to hem speciale,
And say, 'Felow þu dost vs blame'
Þere he accuseþ his owen name.   45
All þat hym se, knowe it may;
He can not hele his owen shame,
And so all folk wole say.

3if men speke of Goddis wille,
To preyse werkys of virtue,   50
A good man wole holde hym stille,
And lete as he hem neuere knewe,
And noþer chaunge hyde ne hewe;
For vaynglory wolde hem betray.
Who is fals, and who is trewe,   55
After þey lyue all folk wole say.

Thou3 a man holynes preche,
He sheteþ no3t, but bent his bowe,
But he lyue as he teche,
He nys not trusty for to trowe.   60
For suche seed he doþ sowe

42-4] **blame**. As with Poem 3/52, the repetition of identical rhyme words may be
dittography, see note to the line. It is possible that the scribe has substituted 'blame'
for 'lame' in the sense of slander, accuse falsely, cf. Poem 3/5.

47] Cf. Poem 6/60. The sentiments of the line are proverbial, see Whiting, *Proverbs*, A.130,
p. 10: Gower, *Confessio*, II.579–80, 'For who so wol an other blame/He secheth ofte his
oghne schame'.

51] Cf. Ecclesiasticus 21:31, 'The talebearer shall defile his own soul, and shall be hated
by all: and he that shall abide with him shall be hateful: the silent and wise man shall
be honoured.'

58] **bent his bowe**. Whiting lists this as a proverb, *Proverbs*, p. 55 B.481.

60] **lyue as he teche**, cf. Chaucer's Parson, 'That first he wroghte, and afterward he taughte',
General Prologue, A.497 and Schmidt, *Piers Parallel Text*, C.5.141–2, 'That 3e prechen to
þe peple, preue hit 3owsylue;/Lyue 3e as 3e lereth vs, we shal leue 3ow þe bettere'. The
lines are also in A and B, but the C text is closest to the verbal texture of Digby.

61-3] Cf. Matthew 13:1–8 and note to lines 129–32.

In stones, in thornes, and in clay,
The same he shal repe and mowe;
So he is worthy folk wole say.

A lord of hym self haþ no wyt: 65
He knoweþ wele but no wo;
Of pore men he mot haue hit:
Knowelechyng of frend and fo.
He is wys that can do so,
And wel twynnen hem o tway.   70
In sykernes may he go,
And recche neuere what men say.

Gloseres maken mony lesynges;
Al to sone men hem leues,
Boþe to lordys and to kynges,   75
Þat boþe partye ofte greues.
Wolde lordis seche repreue,
Glosers shuld not go so gay,
Ne not so hardy for to meue
Suche wordes as they say.   80

Thou3 prestes prechyng hem avyse,
Or mynstrallis synge in song now,
A glosere wole a lord askuse:
'Sire, þey synge or preche of gow!'
Þe lord vnderstondes not how   85

70]   **tway**, cf. 'twey' Poem 24/303. In both instances, the spelling is used to secure rhyme. Elsewhere the form is 'two' Poem 1/90 and 7/33.

74-6]   **leues ... greues**. Kail, *Poems*, emended to 'leue' and 'greue', possibly on grounds of grammatical concordance, or to secure a more perfectly matched rhyme scheme.

78]   **glosers ... gay**, cf. the description of the flatterer, Poem 2/1–2, and 'The Bisson Leads the Blynde', Robbins, *Historical Poems*, pp. 127–30/9, 'Now gloserys full gayly þey go'.

81-2]   The conjunction of priests with minstrels as sources of authority is unusual, though the Prologue of Trigg, *Wynnere and Wastoure* laments the disappearance of sage 'makers of myrthes' (l. 20) whose places in front of lords has been taken by juvenile japers incapable of 'wyse wordes' and 'witt' (ll. 22–5).

84]   **gow**: the word is obscure. It may be related to *MED* 'giue-goue' (*n*.), 'a plaything, toy, gewgaw'; *fig*. something trivial or worthless', a word which may derive from OF 'gogue' a joke, game & goguer to jest, make merry.

Þe fals glosere hym betray;
Wolde he make þo wordis avowe,
He wolde auyse hym eft to say.

Many can stomble at a stre
Þ[at] nyl not snapere at a style,   90
And graunte purpos 'nay and ȝee',
Þouȝ his þouȝt be þens a myle.
Whan falshed lawheþ, he forgeþ gyle;
Half in malice is his play.
Wiþ wisdom, who so voydeþ that wyle,   95
He is [fol. 102b] wys all folk wole say.

Thouȝ men in erþe trouþe hyde,
On halle roof he wole be sayn;
In botme of see he nyl not byde,
But shewe in market on the playn.   100
And þouȝ trouþe a while be slayn,
And doluen depe vnder clay,
ȝut he wole ryse to lyue agayn,
And al the sothe he wole say.

Many callen conscience fleschly willis,   105
And nelen non oþere counseil craue,
But soule of reson is gostly skillis,
Þat conscience shal hem deme or saue.

89-90] þat the MS reads 'þey'. I have emended in order to bring the line closer to the
    idiom of contemporary axioms which suggest that one may trip over a small object even
    though there is no problem in negotiating an object which is large, see Whiting, *Proverbs*,
    'straw', p. 559, S.823. Whiting cites examples from Fitzjames, *Sermon*, 'Stomblynge atte a
    straawe/And lepynge over a blocke'; *Colyn Blowbol*, 105/307, 'And yet they wille stombile
    at a straw' and John Heywood, *Works*, p. 78, 'Ye stumbled at a strawe, and lept over a
    blocke'.

97-104] The indestructibility of Truth is commonplace, see Whiting, *Proverbs*, p. 611, who
    lists variations under the following heads: T.508: 'Truth may not fail'; T.509, 'Truth must
    stand' and T.513, 'Truth shall surmount'. Close in temper to the remarks of the Digby
    poet is *Mum and the Sothsegger*, 171-92, especially 'Trouthe is so tough and loeth forto
    teere ... For though men brenne the borough there the burne loiggeth,/Or elles hewe
    of the heede there he a hows had,/Or do hym al the disease that men deuise cunne,/Yit
    wole he quyke agayne and quite alle his foes,/And treede ouer the tares that ouer his
    toppe groued,/And al wicked wede into waste tourne', ll. 184-92.

Fleschely wille is fendes knaue,
Out of reson, out of stray;   110
As they disserue, þey shal haue,
For so doþ þe gospel say.

Falshed wolde trouþes tunge teyȝe
For trewe wordis þat he haþ spoken.
God biddeþ vengeaunce hiȝe   115
And helpe trouþe be wel wroken.
For trouþe lippes ar faste stoken,
And false mede haþ þe kay.
Whan vengeaunce haþ look broken,
Þan trouþe shal al þe soþ say   120

Sumtyme men halwed the holyday;
Now holiday is turned to glotonye.
Sumtyme men vsed honest play;
And now it is turned to vilonye,
And paramour is turned to lecherye.   125
Sumtyme was loue of good fay,
And shameles haunted so comounly,
Vnneþe þey recche what men say.

Summe men sowe here seed in skornes,
Ofte on oþere mennys londes;   130
Summe on stones, summe on thornes,
Summe on hiȝe way, summe on sondes.
He þat wel vnderstondes,
Amende while he mende may;

109]   **fendes knaue.** The same phrase is used at Poem 1/55 and 17/142; cf. being in thrall
   to devils Poem 20/182 and 24/338.
111–12]   A reference to 2 Timothy 4:14, 'the Lord will reward him according to his
   works'.
113]   Cf. Poem 13/100.
117]   **lippes … stoken,** cf. Poem 3/1.
121–8]   The stanza is based on the familiar topoi of reversals characteristic of 'abuses of the
   age' poems. For examples see Robbins, *Historical Poems* nos 49, 57 and 63. Especially close
   to the diction of Digby is Poem 55, lines 11–12, 'Wyth is trechery, & loue is lecherye;/&
   pley turnyt to vylanye, & holyday to glotonye'.
127]   Cf. Poem 14/84.
129–32]   Cf. the parable of the sower, Matthew 13:1–8.

Make hym clene, and wasche his hondes,   135
And recche neuere what men say.

Thou3 holy chirche shulde fawtes mende,
Summe put hem of for mede;
And summe wiþ maystri3e hem defende,
That holy chirche stant of hem drede.   140
Þo þat rechelesly sowe here sede,
Here lond of vertues ligge ful lay.
Þe holy chirche þe corn shulde wede;
For cowardis þey dar not say.

Gloseres that wiþ lordis bene,   145
Þey thryue faste þou3 þey come late,
For þey wole a lord to wene
Þat he is byloued ther men hym hate,
And wiþ his frendis make debate,
Of pore puple pyke here pray.   150
Of all degre of eche astate,
After þey lyue all folk wole say.

Fro Goddis sy3t, who may stele
Word or werk, þe lest þou3t?

141-4]   The parable of the sower is interleaved with the later parable told by Matthew in
the same gospel chapter; the sower whose field is contaminated by the cockle sown by
the enemy, Matthew 13:22-30. Cf. also verse 38, 'And the field, is the world. And the good
seed are the children of the kingdom. And the cockle are the children of the wicked one.'
The image of separating the cockle from the corn is used in variety of Middle English
texts to describe the intrusion of heretics into the true belief of the Church, e.g. *The
Man of Lawe*, II.1182-3, 'sowen som difficulte,/Or springen cokkel in our clene corn',
Gower, *Confessio*, II.1881-3, and *Right as a Rammes Horn*, Lydgate, *Poems II,* 'Eretikes
han lost here frowardenesse/Wedid the cokle from the pure corn', ll. 53-4. The pointing
of the Digby verse, rather than targeting the heretics, as is more customary, places the
responsibility of weeding the cockle from the church's clean corn firmly in the hands of
the clergy. The suggestion here is less of heresy, than clerical indulgence of sin because
of cowardice in dealing with offenders, see further, Introduction, pp. 33-4.

145-9]   Cf. Ecclesiasticus 28:11, 'For a passionate man kindleth strife, and a sinful man will
trouble his friends, and bring in debate in the midst of them that are at peace'.

150]   **pore ... pray**, cf. the very similar formulation at Poem 8/14 and the sentiment appears
also 8/68 and 21/58.

153-62]   Cf. Ecclesiasticus 17:16-19, 'And all their works are as the sun in the sight of God:
and his eyes are continually upon their ways. Their covenants were not hid by their
iniquity, and all their iniquities are in the sight of God.'

Þe comoun voys nyl not hele,   155
[fol. 103a] But loue or hate as werk is wrou3t;
For soþnes neuere hernes sou3t.
Who secheþ wel, he may assay.
The good lyuere neuere rou3t
Of his werkis what men say.   160

Of all degree, of eche astate
After desert þe name haþ prys.
Þat lord his owen worship doþ hate,
Þat 3eueþ anoþer his offys –
For in astate grace lys –   165
And wilfully wast it away.
Who is fool, who is wys,
After þey lyue all folk wole say.

A glosere is gredy ay to craue.
3eue hym no thing, þou3 he bede.   170
A lord þat wole his worschip saue,
Lerne not at a glosere to don his dede.
3eue to vertuous men þat haue need,
Þat to God wole for þe pray.
Þe pore mannys erande God doþ spede;   175
God wil not here what glosere wole say.

Alle þe þou3tes ben but wast
Wiþoute contemplacioun;
Fro heritage of heuene is borne o hast.
Shrifte wiþoute contricioun,   180

155] **comoun voys**, cf. Poem 4/17/19 and note. The collocation 'comoun' plus 'voys' or 'noys' is found only in Poem 4, and appears to be used without pejorative political associations. See also note to Poem 4/207.

157] **neuere hernes sou3t** is proverbial, cf. Poem 3/5 and 12/74; see Whiting, *Proverbs*, p. 612, T.512 who cites *Romaunt* C6712 'For sothfastnesse wole none hidyngis' and Caxton, *Golden Legend*, 39–41, 'For as St Jherom sayth, "trouth seketh no corners"'.

175] Cf. Job 34:28, 'So that they caused the cry of the needy to come to him, and he heard the voice of the poor.' There is a closer paraphrase of this Poem 12/109.

177] **Nota** is written in the margin next to this line.

180] The line is identical to Poem 18/35 and the sentiments of this stanza similar in temper to 18/33–40.

And werkys wiþoute discrecioun;
Þat ʒifte pleseþ not God to pay,
Ne preyer wiþoute deuocioun:
God nyl not here what þey say.

Sum tyme, and a worschip felle   185
To a lord in batayle by Goddis grace,
ʒif a glosere wolde telle
Among folk byfore his face,
Þe lorde wolde bidde hym voyde þe place:
'Þu corayest fauel and stelest his hay.'   190
Of alle degree, of eche [space],
After þey lyue all folk wole say.

A cheuenteyn may fyʒte o day,
Þe victorye wiþ hym st[o]nde.
For synne, God mon tak it away   195
And put his swerde in enemys h[o]nde.
Vertues make free vices make bonde
Today is quyk, tomorwe is fay.

181]   Cf. Poem 18/33.
183]   Cf. Poem 18/37.
190]   **corayest fauel**, to curry (i.e. groom Favel the horse) is a proverbial idiom to suggest
       flattery, see Zupitza, 'Proverbis of Wysdom', 246:91–2, 'Who so wyll in court dwell/Nedis
       most he cory favelle' and Hoccleve, *Regement*, 5280–5, 'But he hyde/Þe trouth and can
       currey fauel, he nat þe nere is/His lordes grace; and vntrouth ful fer is/ffrom him, þat
       worthy corage hath honoured;/Grace of his lorde by fauel is deuoured.'
191]   **space**. MS reads 'astate', but the rhyme scheme requires a word ending in *ace. It
       appears that the scribe has written a line which conforms to earlier formulae, see Poem
       4/151/161. I have emended to 'space' in the sense of 'assigned position, office'; see *MED*
       'space' (*n.*); 12b.
194/196]   **stonde ... honde** MS reads 'stande' and 'hande', which disrupts the rhyme. I have
       emended in line with the correct copying of 'stonde' and 'honde' in rhyme position. Cf.
       Poem 18/81 and 83.
198–9]   The transitoriness of the world and the unpredictability of prosperity are frequent
       refrains in the Digby poems, cf. Poem 3/121. The axiom of these lines can be paralleled
       elsewhere, e.g. Zupitza, 'Proverbis of Wysdom', 246:115–16, 'We shall dye I nott, how
       son:/To day a man, to morow non'; Gower, *In Praise of Peace*, 292, 'That now is up,
       tomorowe is under grave', and 'Each Man ought himself to know', Furnivall, *Vernon
       Poems* II.672–5/25–6. 'Knowe þi lyf; hit may not last,/But as a blast blouh out þi
       breth'. For further examples see Whiting, *Proverbs*, T.351, p.599. The ultimate source is

Þat knew hym self, he wolde wonde
Any good of him self wolde say.   200

What a glosere here or see,
Þou3 it shulde to shame falle,
He knoweþ in chambre preuytee
Telleþ his felow in þe halle,
And felow to fellow, tyl þey knowe alle,   205
Fro toun to toun in all contray.
The glosere, þe comoun voyce hit calle,
For non shulde knowe who first dede say.

A good man doþ a lord gret ese
Þat is a trewe officiere,   210
Þat wel can serue a lord to plese;
Passe not þe boundes of his powere,
In preuyte, vnwetand he may come nere.
Be handles and stele no þyng away,
Be blynd of ey3e, and deef of here,   215
Be dombe of mouth, and no þyng say.

I wolde such a statute were,
And þere vpon set a payne:
What soget [fol. 103b] wolde make his souereyn swere
Þat he tolde in counseil layne.   220
Ofte glosere makeþ lordis fayne,
Passe þe boundes of here play.

---

1 Maccabees 2:62–3, 'And fear not the words of a sinful man, for his glory is dung, and worms: Today he is lifted up, and tomorrow he shall not be found, because he is returned into his earth; and his thought is come to nothing.'

199] Cf. note to 1/8.

201–8] The unstoppable spreading of slander; the originator remaining obscured, is a criticism seen in other lyric poems, e.g. 'Who says the sooth, he shall be shent', Furnivall, *Vernon Poems* II.683–6/25–36.

213] **vnwetand**, the Northern form of the present participle; not needed for rhyme.

217] **I ... statute**: a rare moment of singular voice in the poems; there is an abrupt shift from generic tropes about counsel and gossip to a plea for parliament to impose a statutory penalty on any subject who persuades the king to break the confidential bounds of counsel. The lines attest to the growing importance of parliament in regulating the behaviour of the monarch.

Al þat trouþe haþ herd and sayne
All tymes nys not soþ to say.

When al þe world is þurgh souȝt,   225
In his best tyme is worst to trest.
Þis world is a fayre nouȝt,
A fals leman þat chaunge lest.
His last ende is had ywist,
When deþ haþ þy lyues kay.   230
'Litel while he mon be myst' –
So þe executours wol say.

They rekene his richesse, what it amountes,
Ete and drynke, synge 'Hay ȝol hayl!'
Þe while þe fendis his synnes countes,   235
And bryng to hym þe countertayl;
Wiþ hard paynes hym assaile,
Wiþ berkande fendis brouȝte to bay.

223–4]   The need to keep guard of one's tongue is a commonplace, Whiting, *Proverbs*, p. 504, S.76: see 'Try to Say the Best, Control Your Tongue', Furnivall, *Vernon Poems* II.723–5/35 'Euure þou kepe þi tonge clos'. Zupitza, 'Proverbis of Wysdom', 245:60, 'Say not all that thou kanne' and *Proverbs of Good Counsel*, 'Wysdom stondyth not all by speche'. The ultimate source for the sentiment is probably biblical, see Ecclesiasticus 22:6, 'A tale out of time is like music in mourning: but the stripes and instruction of wisdom are never out of time', and Ecclesiasticus 1:30, 'A good understanding will hide his words for a time, and the lips of many shall declare his wisdom'.

227–8]   **fayre nouȝt ... fals leman**, cf. Poem 3/121 and note to 3/146.

232–4]   **executours**, the uselessness of worldly wealth at the time of death, and the fraudulence of executours is a trope; it is given extended treatment in *Mum and the Sothsegger*, 1697–720. Executours feature in Mede's entourage in Schmidt, *Piers Parallel Text*, C.II.189, and cf. Wastour's advice to Wynnere not to hoard his wealth 'thi sone and thi sektours ichone slees othere, ... A dale aftir thi daye dose the no mare/Þan a lighte lanterne late appone nyghte', Trigg, *Wynnere and Wastoure*, 303–6; 'Tarry not till To-morrow', Furnivall, *Vernon Poems* II.725–7, warns of the fraudulence of executours in lines 37–48 with a refrain, 'Trust nouȝt on hem after to-Morn' (l. 48).

235–6]   **counts ... countertayl**: these witty lines contrast the counting of riches with the accounting of sin. The image of the tally stick is used again to discuss the reckoning of sin Poem 22/47 and 24/393, and cf. Poem 1/29 and 35.

237]   **paynes** puns on the senses of punishment; *MED* 'peine' (*n.*); 1a; and financial penalty; 1b.

238]   **berkande** Northern form of the present participle; not required for rhyme.

What helpeþ his riches or wys counsaile?
Hym self his owen tale shal say.   240

God made oo lawe for eche astate,
Riche and pore in al degre.
Do no wrong, ne debate,
But as þou wolde men dede by þe.
For God hym self þis wrot he,   245
Betok to Moyses in his lay;
Be Goddis childre in charyte,
As God doþ in the gospell say.

240]   **tale** puns on the sense of tally stick; *MED* 'taille' (*n*.); 3c; and narrative, or pleas;
        MED 'tale' (*n*.); 4c. See Alford, *Glossary,* pp. 150–2 for both words.
241–5]   These lines appear to refer to the summary of the commandments given to Moses
        in Romans 13:8–10, 'Owe no man any thing, but to love one another. For he that loveth
        his neighbour, hath fulfilled the law … Love therefore is the fulfilling of the law.'
244]   Cf. Luke 6:31, 'And as you would that men should do to you, do you also to them
        in like manner.'
247]   Cf. 1 Corinthians 16:14, 'Let all your things be done in charity'.

Poem 5. Wyt and Wille

The refrain of the poem draws on the axiomatic opposition between the faculties of reason and will: rational behaviour and self-indulgent wilfulness. This loose framework allows for a collection of warnings on the dangers of wicked counsel, the eternal consequences of sinful behaviour, and the threat posed to a kingdom when selfish motives dominate. The narrative voice weaves in and out of addressing those in a position of authority over others. The axioms, however, have a wider valency. The address to governors shows the need for self-government. Like the warnings of mortality in the last stanzas of the poem, ruling oneself is relevant to all – both for the health of their souls – and for the good of the realm. Cf. Hoccleve, *Regement*, 4831–2, 'By wise conseil settith your hy estat/In swhiche an ordre as ye lyue may'.

5. Wyt and Wille

Man, be war of wikkid counsaile:
He wol the lede in wayes slidre,
In day of batayle he wol þe faile,
And make þi goode men to shidre.
Riȝt as hay þey mon widre,   5
As blades of gres his seed doþ spille.
Gostly blynd goþ, and not neuere whidre,
Þat leueþ wit and worchiþ by wille.

1-4] The opening uses one of the poet's frequent 'be war' formulae (see also Poem 1/1, 4/29, 9/79, Poem 14, 18/81, 19/33) to advise against the dangers of bad counsel. Warnings against wicked counsel are common: Poem 2/73, 3/82, 7/21, 21/15 and 24/406. The closest in temper to Poem 4 is 24/405, 'wykked counsel scholde be refusyd'. For references to other widespread usage of this topos see note to Poem 1/2. The poet constructs a mini-allegory in lines 1-4: 'wikkid counsaile' is personified as a bad leader, one whose guidance will result in being stranded on slippery paths, and far from offering protection, causes loyal followers to break rank on the day of battle (shidre). The image of dispersed allegiance resonates with the reiterated concern in the sequence as a whole for political unity. In a few lines, the poet has compacted moral wisdom with political relevance for the times in which he is writing.

5-6] **riȝt as hay ... blades of gres** conflates two images: the withering of grass to hay as a metaphor for human mortality, and the spilling of the seeds a metaphor for the dispersal of the battle troops. The conflation spells out that lack of unity is deadly. The lines draw on biblical reference: Psalms 89:6, 'In the morning man shall grow up like grass, in the morning he shall flourish and pass away: in the evening he shall fall, grow dry, and wither; cf. Psalms 102:15, Ecclesiasticus 14:18 and Isaias 37:27, 'The inhabitants of them were weak of hand, they trembled, and were confounded: they became like the grass of the field, and the herb of the pasture, and like the grass of the housetops, which withered before it was ripe.' The same metaphor is found in closely contemporary Middle English texts, Gower, *Confessio*, VIII.2436-7, 'That which was whilom grene gras/Is welked hey at time now' and 'Complaynt of Criste', Furnivall, *Political, Religious and Love Poems*, pp. 190-224/191-2, 'Furst A man growys As A gras,/And afftyr-warde welkythe as floure or hay'.

8] **wit ... wille**: the opposition is commonplace, both in devotional lyrics and in more overtly political literature, Whiting, *Proverbs*, p. 642, W.268, lists variations: see 'Will and Wit', Brown, *English Lyrics XIII*, p. 65/1-2, 'Hwenne so wil wit oferstieth/Thenne is wil and wit forlore'; 'Always Try to Say the Best', Brown, *Religious Lyrics XIV*, p. 191-3/20, 'Let noȝt thi wille passe thi witt'; *Proverbs of Good Counsel* 69/39, 'Lett never thi wyll thi wytt ouer-lede'; 'This world is variable', Robbins, *Historical Poems*, 148-9/7, 'Wyll ys tak for reson' and Hocccleve, *Regement*, 3995-7, 'And wit restreyne his wil can & aswage/In tyme due, and in conuenable,/And thus tho two ioynt ben ful profitable'.

Whoso wist what tresoure
He haþ þat worcheþ by wit,   10
Þe fader of heuene is gouernoure,
Þe holigost þe sone wiþ hit.
In oo Godhede alle þre are knyt;
Non departe fro oþer nylle.
In eche mannys herte, alle þre þey syt,   15
Þat makeþ wit lord aboue his wille.

Who so wyste what wille harmes,
Þat willefully fro wyt wendes,
Fro þe fader of heuene his soule he charmes,
Fro grace of þe holygost hym blendes.   20
Fro angels pere, soget to fendes,
Þat nyl not mende, but ay don ylle.
Gostely and bodily, hymself he shendes
Þat leueþ wyt and worcheþ by wille.

9–16]   **tresoure,** one of many occasions where earthly concepts of wealth are re-registered
to suggest spiritual reward. Underpinning the stanza are the verses from Christ's Sermon
on the Mount, Matthew 6:19–21, 'Lay not up for yourselves treasures upon earth, where
moth and rust doth corrupt, and where thieves break through and steal: But lay up for
yourselves treasures in heaven, where neither moth nor rust doth corrupt, and where
thieves do not break through nor steal: For where your treasure is, there will be your
heart also.' Cf. Luke 12:34. The stanza likens behaving according to wit to the Trinity
which sits in man's heart. There is a mini-allegory on good rule. God is 'gouernoure',
but it is significant that all are 'knyt' and do not wish to separate from the other. This
contrasts to the men who break rank in the opening stanza and the 'debate' of line 25.
'Knyt' is an important word in the sequence to suggest harmonious incorporation. Man
is 'knyt' to God's law Poem 10/85; man's love should be 'knytte' to God's Poem 17/135
and in the extended body politic image of Poem 15, the neck is said to 'knyt' the head
and the body. The neck symbolises justice through which comes 'all wordis of wyt'
(Poem 15/18).

17–24]   Cf. Wisdom 3:11, 'For he that rejecteth wisdom, and discipline, is unhappy: and
their hope is vain, and their labours without fruit, and their works unprofitable.'

20]   **blendes,** cf. Poem 13/82 where the same eastern vowel is used to facilitate rhyme.
Elsewhere the form is 'blynde' Poem 3/77, 9/26, 10/13 and 17/134.

21]   The image of turning from an angel's peer to a fiend's subject continues the figurative
diction which conflates worldly and spiritual governance. Similar imagery is used at
Poem 1/55, 4/109, 17/142/165 and 20/182.

In kyngdom, what make debate?   25
Riche and pore both anoy3ed,
3ong counseil, and preuey hate,
And syngulere profit ys aspi3ed;
Hi3e and lowe men aby3ed,
Echon wayte oþer for to kille.   30
Þat kyngdom mot nede be stri3ed,
Þat leueþ wit and worcheþ by wille.

That leueþ trouþe and falshed vse,
And [fol. 104a] lyue not after Goddis sawe,
Suche folk God doþ despuse,   35
Rebell and ryse a3en his lawe.
Þo puple that stondes of God non awe,
But robbe and reue, coffres to fylle,
Þe swerd of vengeaunce on hem is drawe,
Þat leueþ wit and worcheþ by wille.   40

25]   Cf. very similar line in Poem 14/89. **debate**: the perils of internal division in the
     kingdom are a frequent warning in the sequence Poem 4/149, 12/33, 15/125 and 21/91. The
     poet provides a spiritual counterpart to this in warning against making debate with God
     Poem 10/67, 11/39, 17/106 and 20/80.
27]   The dangers of young counsel are a standard topos, cf. note to Poem 1/5. **preuey
     hate** stands diametrically opposed to the poet's concern for corporate public harmony.
     Elsewhere the phrase is associated with tyranny Poem 1/3 and homage paid out of fear
     Poem 1/99.
28]   **syngulere profit**: see note to Poem 1/4.
29]   **aby3ed**, either in the sense of 'to pay back, take revenge for (a wrong)' *MED* 'abien'
     (*v.*); 1c, or to incur someone's anger; 3b.
30]   **oþer for to kille**. This may comment on the baronial unrest which so unsettled the
     kingdom in the later years of Richard II's reign and which plagued also the reign of
     Henry IV. There were plots against the life of Henry V at the start of his reign, see
     Introduction, pp. 6–10. Equally the line might refer to more localised disputes between
     landowners, of which the Rolls of Parliament for these years are full. The line is charac-
     teristic of the poet's open-ended topicality, one which fuses a moral standpoint with
     cultural resonance. Cf. notes to Poem 3/113.
33–40] God's vengeance on those who desert truth in favour of falsehood is seen also
     in Poem 13/81–8, and on those who will not hold his law, 9/105–12. Cf. also notes to
     Poem 3/8.
35]   **despuse**. Elsewhere the form is 'despi/y/se' Poem 6/26, 10/132, 22/70 and 24/289. The
     western spelling has been used to secure rhyme.

That ouer puple han gouernaunce,
Loke how Goddis lawe ȝe vse;
Whom ȝe refuse, and whiche auaunce,
For Goddis loue, or ȝoure owen seruyce,
Whiche is þe charge, ȝow auyse.   45
Let eche man serue his charge in skylle;
And ȝoure werkis preue ȝow wyse,
Let wit be lord aboue thy wylle.

Be not to crowele in þy wele;
Þu nost how sone þou myȝt haue lesse.   50
Be not to sykere of þyne hele,
Þu not how sone falle in sykenesse.
Deþ claymeþ eche man for hesse,
And sodeyn deþ no dayes s[ki]lle.
Siþ no man is in sykernesse,   55
Be redy euere at Goddis wille.

And on þy strengþe be not to bold,
Ne skorne no pore, ne feble of elde;
For lyue long, ȝe mon be old,
In feblenes to hoke and helde,   60
In cowardys ȝoure corage kelde;

41]   Identical to Poem 1/10.

47]   The line is identical to Poem 13/164 and the sentiments close to 1/79 and 1/125. The converse is seen at Poem 2/34.

49–56]   A characteristic warning from the poet not to trust in health and prosperity as no one knows the time of one's death. Cf. notes to Poem 4/198–9.

53]   **hesse**, elsewhere 'hi/y/s' is the form of the masculine possessive pronoun; the unusual spelling secures the rhyme scheme.

54]   **s[ki]lle**. MS reads 'selle', which does not fit the rhyme scheme and the sense is obscure. I have emended to 'skille' from *MED* 'skillen' (*v.*), 1: 'to distinguish, make difference between or separate'. Lines 53–4 thus mean, 'death claims each man for his own, and sudden death may not differentiate between days'. The sentiment is proverbial. Whiting, *Proverbs*, p. 121, lists numerous examples, see D.96. Close in tenor to these lines is *The Clerk's Tale*, E.124–6, 'And al so certein as we knowe echoon/That we shul deye, as uncerteyn we alle/Been of that day whan deeth shal on us falle'.

57]   **strengþe**, cf. Psalms 48:7 which warns of the misery of those who that trust in their own strength, and glory in the multitude of their riches.

60]   **hoke and helde**: a distinctive alliterative formula which means to bend and stoop. The image of physical decrepitude contrasts strongly with the bold mistrust in one's own strength and contempt for the weakness of others.

But ʒe had help, ʒe shuld spille.
Ʒe þat heuene blisse wole welde,
Let wit be lord aboue ʒoure wille.

God haþ lent ʒow discrecioun,   65
Boþe of wele and of woo;
Werkis of deuocioun,
Vyces, vertues, frend, and foo.
Siþ ʒe can part hem wel o two,
Let vyces on ʒow brynge no bille.   70
Þe weye of grace, and ʒe wol go,
Let wyt be lord aboue ʒoure wille.

65] **discrecioun**. The ability to distinguish right from wrong is seen as an important virtue
in the sequence, see Poem 4/181, 18/22/33/166 and 23/76. It is a virtue as important to
individuals as it is to rulers.

70] **bille**, in the legal sense of a written petition or complaint, see Alford, Glossary,
p. 16.

Poem 6. To lyf bodyly is perylous

This poem is a parody of tropes from 'lerne to dye' poems which warned human beings to think of their death, and to take stock of their life. There was a rich tradition of such devotional writing. Hoccleve's *Lerne to Dye* (*Minor Poems*, pp. 178–212) for example, is based on the second book of Henry Suso's very popular *Horologium Sapientiae*, '*De scientia utilissima homini mortali que est scire mori*'. 'Lerne to dye' poems urge human beings to consider their sins at once instead of delaying repentance until death. There are examples of such poems within the Digby sequence; this poem is followed by a conventional rehearsal of warnings of worldly transitoriness, the need for repentance of sin, and warnings of the suddenness of death. Parts of Poems 1, 9, 14, 21 and 22 also fall into this tradition of writing. Many of the ironic statements in this poem reverse axioms found in these other poems. The refrain, with its insistence on the body, reverses the conventional focus on matters of the spirit, and there are subtle shifts of sense within the use of the rhyme word. Kail (*Poems*, p. xiv), assigned a date of some time between 1404 and 1408 for this poem, on what grounds remains unclear.

6. To lyf bodyly is perylous

Lerne bodyly to lyue!
Þy seruaunt non hyre þu pay,
Pore ne riche, no ӡiftes ӡeue,
But take and gedre al þat þu may.
Þouӡ it come wiþ wrong, say not nay,   5
But falsely loke þu swere and liӡe;
Þe pore man is the riches pray,
Lerne þus to lyue bodilye.

There market beteres gadre in þrong,
Loke þat company þu lede.   10
Stalworþly mayntene wrong,
So may þu wynne moche mede.
To reue fro pore take non hede;
Do as þu þouӡt neuere to dye.

2]   The injunction not to pay the servant's wages runs counter to the concern throughout
the sequence to look after the poorly paid, and flatly contradicts the sentiment expressed
in Poem 2/40, that the true servant deserves his reward.

3]   **ӡeue**, possibly a scribal miscopying. While the poems use both 'ӡeue' and 'ӡyue', the
choice of form is normally determined by matching spelling of rhyme words, as in Poem
14/49/51 where 'lyue' rhymes with the form 'ӡyue'.

3-7]   The command to give nothing either to rich or poor contradicts the frequent criticism
of those who practise extortion against the poor, e.g. Poem 1/145, 4/67/150, 8/14. In
Poem 10 Christ admonishes man for making war against Him by hoarding worldly
goods to keep them from the poor who ought to be his brothers. Elsewhere there are
exhortations to give to the poor, e.g. Poem 21/4/38 and in Poem 7/65-6.

6]   **swere and liӡe**. The condemnation of such practice is seen in the next Poem 7/86.

8]   The refrain neatly reverses the terms of line 1 and the emphasis on living rather
than dying parodies the refrain of conventional learn to die lyrics, as used in the next
poem.

9]   **market beteres**: an obscure phrase, but one which makes sense if 'betere' be understood
figuratively in the sense of one who 'beats, or pounds the streets', as in OED 'beater' 1.a:
Barclay, *Shyp of Folys*, 116, 'Of night watchers and beters of the stretes'. This would give
the sense, 'where those who beat a trail to markets gather in a crowd'. The line suggests
over-attraction to the secular delights of the market place.

10]   **company**: could be understood as a trade group *MED* 'cumpaignie' (*n.*); 1, but the
stanza's suggestion of wrongful extortion, together with the preceding word 'þrong'
suggests that it may also carry a more threatening (and hence, punning) sense of
'multitude'; see *MED* 'cumpaignie' (*n.*); 2b.

14]   A reversal of the standard formulae in more conventional poems e.g. 'Death, the

Say noþer pater noster ne crede;   15
Lyue þu in ese bodyly.

Rechelesly þe gouerne:
Day and ny3t, walke late
At cokes hostry and tauerne.
Þou3 þu no man oþere hate,   20
Go not ere þu make debate.
To lewed, lettred, and clergye,
Do no reueraunce to non astate;
Þan men wole drede þe bodylye.

Tho þat þe good wolde teche,   25
Rebuke hem and foule despise;
Byd hem go to þe chirche and preche,
Folowe [fol. 104b] fooles, and fle fro wyse.
3eue no doom in ri3t assyse,
Fle fro trouþe, and þu hym spyse.   30
Loke þu be proudest in alle gyse –
Þan men wole preyse þe bodylye.

Soul's Friend', in Brown, *Religious Lyrics XV*, pp. 256–8/61–2 'Thynk þat þou art ded alway/qwyllis þat þou dwellis here'. Cf. Poem 22/57–8.

15]   **pater noster ne crede**. The Lord's Prayer and the Apostle's Creed were two of the three elementary texts that all Christians were supposed to know (the other being the Ave Maria). The Council of Beziers in 1246 ordered that children who attained the age of seven be taught these three texts. The narrator of Digby, then, orders spurning fundamental Christian understanding.

17]   **gouerne**, a statement at odds with the concerns throughout the sequence for careful government both of the self and of the realm, cf. Poem 5/11 and note to Poem 5/9–16.

21]   **debate**: at odds with the injunctions elsewhere in the sequence to avoid debate, cf. note to Poem 5/25.

24]   **bodylye**. The sense here shifts; men will fear the physical power of the sinner.

28]   Opposite to the normative admonishment to flee folly and seek wisdom, e.g. Poem 4/167, 7/11, 8/76, 10/20, 16/71, 18/79. The line is a reversal of Poem 1/167, 'Folowe fooles and fle fro wyse'.

29]   **assyse**, cf. the opposite sentiments at Poem 1/164, 3/13/25 and 9/65–7.

30]   **spyse**, the unusual spelling of 'spies' (which, grammatically, ought to be 'spiest') used to secure the rhyme.

32]   **bodylye**: here in the sense of bodily appearance. Lines 30–2 praise a lying gallant of the kind that is excoriated in Poem 2.

Loke þu haue sorwe sad
Whan þu seest folk haue welfare;
Loke þu be mery and glad   35
Whan þu wost folk haue sorwe and care.
Fede non hungry, ne cloþe no bare,
Lete herberweles þerout ly;
Visite no syke, and presoners spare;
Loue þy seluen þus bodyly.   40

3if þy man be a good serua[nd]
Þat þe were loþ for to go,
Stele þyn owen good fro his hand;
Bere on hym he stal it so.
Bryng hym in preson tho,   45
Longe there for to lye,
Til he be fayn, for sorwe and wo,
To swere to serue þe bodylye.

And 3if þu haue a damysele,
Þat serueþ þe wel of trewe lynage,   50
Fonde to make here wombe to swelle;
Make no fors of maryage.

33-6] A reversal of Romans 12:15, 'Rejoice with them that rejoice and weep with them
that weep'.

37-40] The lines are a reversal of the seven works of mercy, see Holmstedt, *Speculum
Christiani*, p. 40/5-7 '1. I visette the seke. 2. I 3eue drynke the thursty. 3. I fede the
hungry. 4. I bye the presoner oute of thraldom. 5. I couer the nakede. 6. I herbere the
pore man housles. 7. I bery the ded body.' Cf. Poem 1/149-50, 7/65-6, 9/123-7, 17/33-6,
19/89 and 22/66. The seven works are based on Matthew 25:35-44, where in a description
of the Last Judgement, the king states that the blessed who shall inherit the kingdom
are those who have fed the hungry, given drink to the thirsty, clothed the naked and
visited the sick and those in prison.

40] **loue þy seluen**, a concept akin to the practice of singular profit which is so alien to
the poet's vision of corporate harmony; see note to Poem 1/4.

41] **seruand**. The MS reads 'seruaunt'. This is the spelling at Poem 6/2, 9/130, 15/77/78,
20/36 and 21/148; at Poem 2/40 and 15/80 it is 'seruant'. None of these is in rhyme
position. In order to rhyme with 'hand' the poem needs 'seruand', a form chiefly found
in the North, the North East and North West Midlands and the West Midlands. Since
there are numerous examples of varying dialect forms in order to facilitate rhyme, I
have emended.

49-56] The stanza sketches a scenario more frequently found in secular lyrics where a
maid is seduced and finds herself abandoned and with child, e.g. 'The Serving Maid's
Holiday' in Brown, *Secular Lyrics*, pp. 24-5.

And ȝif she grucche wiþ þe to rage,
And always fro the wole wrye,
Bete here, and ȝeue here non oþer wage,   55
And lyue in lustes bodylye.

Thus make þe byknowe:
After þy dede resceyue thy name,
So shal þyn horne ofte blowe,
And hunte after his owen shame.   60
Ȝe þouȝ þu be of feble fame,
Bere good visage, þy nouȝt aspye;
Make þerof but iape and game
In fleschly lustis bodylye.

At masse, at matins, rule ȝow so: 65
Leue dewe deuocioun ȝow byhynde.
Speke no good of frend ne foo;
Lete non skorneles fro ȝow wende;
Loke no man by thy frende,
Lete no man thryue, but do hem nye,   70
Kepe hem pore, and to þe bende –
Þan wole þey drede þe bodylye.

58]   The same line is seen verbatim at Poem 2/20 and 14/7. See note to Poem 2/20.

59–60]   Declaring one's own shame is proverbial, see note to Poem 4/47. The poet combines two proverbs here, to have one's horn blown also means to blow one's cover, to be discovered, e.g. *The Legend of Good Women*, 1383 and Audelay, *Poems*, 13/77–8, 'For here cursid covetyse/Here horne is e-blawe'.

62]   nouȝt, see *MED* 'nought' (*n.*); a: 'evil, an evil act; worthless or evil conduct'. **aspye**, in the sense of 'search out'; *MED* 'aspien' (*v.*); 2a.

66]   Opposite to the sentiment expressed at 18/117, 'But loke deuocion growe ay newe' and cf. Poem 10/130 where Christ advises man that 'deuyne seruyse' is man's 'duwe dette'.

68]   **skornles**. The line personifies a man without scorn as the addressee's constant companion. Cf. 'shameles' Poem 4/127 and 14/84.

69]   Opposite to the sentiment expressed at Poem 18/131.

Poem 7. Man, knowe thy self, and lerne to dye

This is a more conventional (compared with the preceding) poem in the 'ars moriendi' tradition. Poems 1, 17 and 22 are written in the same vein. Numerous sermons, tracts and lyrics survive which exhort humankind to reflect on the vileness of human conception and birth, the brevity of life, and the inescapability of brutal death. The bleak warnings are delivered in no uncertain terms in order to galvanise humankind into repentance for their sins and to try to live a better life. The sources for these texts were chiefly the Latin prose works *Meditationes piisimae de cognitione humanae conditionis* (attributed to St Bernard), and Pope Innocent III, *De miseria condiciones humanae*. There is a vernacular version of the latter in the Vernon Manuscript, 'The Sayings of St Bernard', Furnivall, *Vernon Poems* II.511–12, and in MS Digby 86, Furnivall, *Vernon Poems* II.757–61. While seemingly timeless, the exhortation to go to auricular confession (line 53) and the curiously anodyne lines on heresy (ll. 79–80) would have particular resonance in the second decade of the fifteenth century; see further, Introduction, pp. 19–25 and notes to Poem 9.

7. Man, knowe thy self, and lerne to dye

Mannys soule is sotyl and queynt,
Shal neuere ende þou3 he dede gynne.
The flesch is fals, frele, and feynt –
Þe world alone wolde wynne –
Is wormes mete, and sek of synne.   5
He nys neuere filt of glotonye,
His cloþyng is a dedly skynne.
Man, knowe þy self and lerne to dye.

Lerne to dye and go to skole,
Siþ þu fro deþ may not fle.   10
Lete not þy werkys preue þe fool
When deþ wole assaile þe.
Sende warnestor to þy soule to be;
Þy vices fro þy vertues tri3e.
3e sette 3oure soule in kynges gre   15
Þat lerneþ wisely for to di3e.

1–2] Contrasts the immortality of the soul with the mortality of the body.

5] **wormes mete.** Several scriptural sources from penitential and wisdom literature remind that the sinful body will be food to worms: Job 17:14, 'If I have said to rottenness: Thou art my father; to worms, my mother and my sister', lines which are paraphrased in Poem 24/267–71; Ecclesiasticus 7:19, 'Humble thy spirit very much: for the vengeance on the flesh of the ungodly is fire and worms'; and 10:13, 'For when a man shall die, he shall inherit serpents, and beasts, and worms'; Isaias 14:11, 'Thy pride is brought down to hell, thy carcass is fallen down: under thee shall the moth be strewed, and worms shall be thy covering', and 1 Machabees 2:62 'And fear not the words of a sinful man, for his glory is dung, and worms'. Cf. 'The Sayings of St Bernard', Furnivall, *Vernon Poems* II.758/1–2, 'Seint bernard seiþ in his bok/Þat man is werm and wermes hok' (cf. II.511/1–2); 'Each Man ought himself to know', Furnivall, *Vernon Poems* II.673/65, 'Þi fleschly foode þe wermes wol fye'; and Edden, *Maidstone's Psalms*, ll. 174–5, 'Þenke þi coruptible cors/Is nou3te but wormes mete, iwis'.

5] **sek of synne**, cf. Poem 22/7–8.

8] The refrain also of Poem 1 and the title of Poem 22.

11] **werkys ... fool**, a formula seen also at Poem 2/34, 9/173, 13/164 and 14/63.

13] **warnestor**, a characteristically abrupt slip into a mini-personification allegory. The sense is that, when death assails, humankind should send for military defence or provision which, in the next line, takes the form of separating vice from virtue.

Eche man in certayn is to dye;
At domesday stonde in drede,
Þere al þe worldis tresorye
May not bye [fol. 105a] thy lyf for mede.   20
No wys counseil þat dede þe lede,
Ne glosere wiþ his flaterye:
Non may helpe oþer at nede,
Forthy man, wysely lerne to dye.

What may thy richesse þe auayle   25
Whan þu art to deþe dryue?
Thy wynd is layd, þu mayst not sayle,
Þou3 þu lete out bonet and ryue.
Loke to vertues, þu þe 3yue,
Er tombe be held to þe li3e: 30

17–18]   Cf. 'Each Man ought himself to know', Furnivall, *Vernon Poems* II.673/61–2 'Knowe þi-self þat þou schalt dye/But what tyme, þou nost neuer whenne' and 'ffor certes þou mai3t not longe endure' (II.674/74).

18]   Identical to Poem 24/388.

20–2]   Characteristically the poet infuses the 'de contemptu mundi' sentiments with political concerns about the proper distribution of money, wise counsel and the problems of flattery. **mede**, cf. Poem 24/200 on the inability of humankind to prolong their life, for 'mede'.

23]   nede, cf. Poem 24/196.

25–8]   May be influenced by Revelation 18:17, 'For in one hour are so great riches come to nought, and every shipmaster, and all that sail into the lake, and mariners, and as many as work in the sea, stood far off.' The nautical image suggests the uselessness of human possessions and the absolute limits of human agency in face of the inevitability of death and God's judgement. The ship is marooned for lack of wind, and no human endeavour, such as letting out the sails, can make any difference.

28]   **ryue**, from of *MED* 'rif' (*n.*) in the sense of reef sail. The spelling form facilitates rhyme. The stanza may be compared to 'Think on Yesterday' where the narrator urges the addressee to take account of their life as the end of life fast approaches and 'vr bodies in erþe be þrast/Vr Careyns chouched vnder clay' (Furnivall, *Vernon Poems* II.677/69–70).

29]   3yue, in the sense of giving alms.

30]   The grammar and sense of this line are difficult. **'be held to þe'** may have the sense 'reserved for you'; see *MED* 'holden' (*v.*); 1.11b to ~ **til**, reserve (sth.) for (sb.). As a verb li3e is used only intransitively elsewhere in the sequence (Poem 1/149, 20/86), and it is difficult to conjugate the verb with the rest of the words in the line. It is possible that 'li3e' is an adjective meaning 'weary', referring to 'þe'; see *MED* 'lei(e)' (*adj.*); b '*fig.*'; c '?weary'. It is also possible that the line is corrupt. 'Beld' or 'teld' yield easier sense with

For he þat gostly wel doþ lyue,
He lerneþ wysely for to di3e.

Two skilles Y wole telle
Why eche man shuld repreue oþeres synne.
And he wyst hym self shuld go to helle,   35
Counseyle no mo to come þerynne.
Þe mo brondes, þe hattere brynne,
Incresyng of his maladye.
Here nys no charite, 3ut shal he wynne
To lasse his pyne after he dye.   40

And 3if he wiste to heuene to go,
His soule be saued in sikirnes,
He shulde counseile all folk do so;
Saue here soulis and do not mys,
Nou3t for here profyt, but al for his;   45
His owen ioye for to hy3e.
Þe mo soules, þe more blis;
Þenke hereon and lerne to dye.

reference to **tombe**. The final word might have been 'hi3e', referring back to the tomb
– or perhaps 'fi3e' formed to suit the rhyme scheme but with the sense of 'doomed to
death' from 'feie'; see *MED* 'fei(e)' (*adj.*); 1a.

31–2] The poet takes advantage of the metrical form to create a neat near chiasmus to
underscore the paradoxical importance of learning how to die if one is to be able to
live spiritually.

33–40] A very witty stanza which knowingly comments on its spiritually empty
pragmatism. The justification for rebuking sin in others is taken to ensure that hell is
a less densely populated place.

37] Sounds proverbial, but I have been unable to find analogues. **hattere**, the Northern
form, not needed for rhyme, is evidence of the mixed dialect of the poems.

39] **nys no charite** playfully acknowledges that the reproof of sin on such grounds is not
exactly 'holy love' but at least, if the sinner go to hell, the torment will be slightly less
scorching.

41–8] A mirror image of the previous stanza; here the motive for counselling people to
avoid sin and save their souls, is that the more souls there are in heaven, the more bliss
there is to go round.

45] **here profyt**, rather as the reference to 'charite' in the previous stanza, is playful. It is
a rare, and ironic, instance of the narrator encouraging singular profit.

Thy wikked werkis in þy ȝowthe,
Seke hem wel tyll þu hem fynde,   50
And al þy tyme riȝt til nowþe
Loke þat fardel þu vnbynde,
And shewe it wel wiþ shrift wynde.
No fende spot vppon the spyȝe,
And haue repentaunce in mynde.   55
On þis manere lerne to dyȝe.

While man doþ synne in werkis wylde,
Al þat tyme he nys but ded.
He nys not counted as fool, ne childe,
But as a man can good and qued.   60
For his soule, he telyeþ no bred;
Here landes of vertue laye don lyȝe.
Do comaundementis þat God bed;
Þan lernest þu wysely to dyȝe.

49–50] Cf. Poem 24/144 and 24/150.

50–1] **wel ... al** ... The lines enjoin a thoroughness of confession which is in keeping with the advice in confession manuals to tell it 'all' and for the confessor to find out all the sin, see note to Poem 9/44.

52] **fardel**. A similar image is used Poem 24/391, where the narrator will stand at the day of doom with no good deed to show except a 'fardel of synnes gadred in store'.

53] **shrift wynde**. The emphasis on oral confession anticipates the fervent admonishments in Poem 9 to make confession to the parish priest. While there may be nothing intentionally topical in this line, the mention of oral confession positions the poem very much as a defence of traditional doctrine. Cf. 'St Bernard on Man's three Foes', Furnivall, *Vernon Poems* II.513/26–7, 'Whon deþ draweþ his kene knyf/I rede þat þou þe shryue'.

56–60] Lines which sternly warn the sinner that there can be no excuses for indulging in sinful behaviour. He will not be excused on the grounds of being foolish or a child, but will be judged as a man who knows how to distinguish good from evil, cf. Poem 5/65 and note.

61] **telyeþ**, in the sense of 'produce crops for', *MED* 'tillen' (v.); 1.2b. The Eastern vowel evidence of the mixed dialect forms of the poems. **bred** cannot literally be 'tilled'. The word is used in the figurative sense of 'food for the spirit or soul' *MED* 'bred' (n.); 1.5a. It also fulfils the rhyme scheme. The line may be compared to *Ancrene Wisse* (Cambridge, Corpus Christi College, MS 402), 42/11, 'Heo [silence] itilet bringeð forð sawles eche fode'.

62] Very similar to the sentiment in 'The Mirror of the Periods of Man's Life', in Furnivall, *Hymns to the Virgin and Christ*, 'To reepe myn heruest, whidir mai y winde?/Mi londis of vertues liggen al lay', p. 70/375–6.

Pore, nedy, and gredy þat noȝt ne haue,   65
In Goddis name, ȝeue þat asken ouȝt.
Pore, nedy, and not gredy þat noȝt ne craue,
Ȝeue hem þouȝ þey ne aske nouȝt.
And nedeles, gredy þyn almes souȝt,
Ȝeue hem no þyng þouȝ þey crye.   70
Þere nys no nede: ȝifte haþ no mede [bouȝt].
Suche almesdede mon neuere dye.

What argument may beter preue
Why men ben bent to don omys?
Not but defaute of byleue –   75
I trowe þey wene no God þer nys,
Ne helle pyne, ne heuene blys,
Paradis, ne purgatorie.
Or elles anoþer heresy þere is:
As a best wiþoute soule to die.   80

Man of his own nouȝten haue;
Al is Goddis, and he it lent.

65–72]   An ironic reversal of this exhortation to give only to the deserving poor, irrespective
of whether they ask for it is seen in Poem 14/109, 'Take fro þe nedy, to þe nedeles dele'.

71]   **bouȝt**: not in the MS. Although the MS line produces a pithy chiasmus, which may
have distracted the scribe, the rhyme scheme is incomplete and I have supplied 'bouȝt',
which fits both the sense and the metrical demands of the stanza.

72]   **dye**. In order for the line to make sense 'dye' must refer back to the first, and virtuous,
act of giving described in lines 66–8. The other possibility is that the scribe has written
'dye' because of attraction to the refrain of each stanza. 'thrye' makes easier sense of
the stanza as a form of 'thriven'; *MED* (*v.*); 1a: 'to prosper, flourish', and produces the
sense for lines 71–2 that such wrong almsgiving will never prosper. *MED* attests a form
of this verb without concluding /v/, see *Rawlinson proverbs* p. 122: 'Beter latte to thri
[L vigere] than neuer', S. B. Meech, 'A Collection of Proverbs in Rawlinson MS D.328',
MP 38 (1940). Since it is possible to produce a reading from the MS as it stands, I have
not emended the text, but note the possibility of scribal error.

73–80]   In keeping with the other two mentions of heresy or heretics (Poem 1/126 and
8/81–8) there is nothing in these lines to suggest that the Church might be under attack
from Wycliffite ideas. Rather, the stanza suggests a fundamental ignorance, or refusal
to believe in basic tenets of Christianity: the existence of God; the torments of hell;
heavenly bliss; paradise and purgatory. All Christian cosmology is summarily dismissed,
along with belief in the existence of the soul. For further discussion, see Introduction,
pp. 19–21.

82]   Cf. Poem 1/27 and 1/34.

Þerof God wole rekenyng craue:
How þou it wan, held, and spent.
Þy leste þou3t, and what it ment;   85
Trouþe and [fol. 105b] lesyng þu dede li3e.
And 3et þy soule is Goddis rente;
To quyte þat wel, lerne to di3e.

Whanne þu dest þyn almesdede,
Crie God mercie it is so lite.   90
To counte þy richesse þu my3t haue drede,
In partye of payment so litel quyte.
þou3 þu do mys, God nyl not flyte,
Ne þrete þe ones ne twy3e.
Body and soule he can smyte;   95
Man, drede God, so lerne to dy3e.

Man synne not in ouerhope.
Þu wynnest not Goddis mercie wiþ fi3t.
Hit wolde brynge þe into wanhope;
To wene no mercy, þu haue ne my3t.   100
Goddis mercy is medled wiþ his ry3t,
And fro ry3t God nyl not ply3e.

83]   **God ... rekenyng**, cf. Poem 1/29 and 1/35.

84–5]   Similar imagery of giving account for one's deeds is used at Poem 1/31, 8/7, 10/198 and 10/208.

87]   Identical to 1/39.

89–96]   A further twist on the imagery of accounting applied to humankind's soul. The lines warn that one cannot put one's trust in the giving of alms as a way of securing salvation. Instead one should ask God's forgiveness that the alms offered have been insignificant compared to the riches amassed. Far from being complacent about almsgiving, the narrator warns that God will not dispute with humankind even though they sin, nor will He threaten them once or twice; all such behaviour is unnecessary, implies the narrator, since God has the power to smite both body and soul. The playfulness of earlier stanzas is quite lost sight of here.

94]   **twy3e**, a form of 'twice' used to secure the rhyme. The word is not used elsewhere.

97–9]   **ouerhope ... wanhope**. The narrator warns of the chief sins against the holy spirit: presumption and despair. Line 97 is identical to Poem 1/129 and line 99 to Poem 1/131. The same idea is also expressed, though not verbatim, Poem 20/201–3.

101]   Cf. Edden, *Maidstone's Psalms*, 'How þour3e þi mercy and þi my3t/Two kyndes beþ togider kny3t' (ll. 435–6).

After þe dede, þe doom is dyȝt –
Man knowe þis wile er þu dyȝe.

Eche dedly synne is a dedly knyf –   105
Why loue men þanne so ofte to synne?
Eche vertue is a plastre of lyf –
[ȝe] haþ fre wille, lese or wynne.
To salue ȝoure sores now begynne,
Þe holigost ȝoure grace gyȝe,   110
Siþ body and soule mon parte o twynne;
To saue þy soule lerne to dyȝe.

Truste not al to oþere men
In almesdede ne preyere.
For state of soule can no man kenne,   115
For þey ben alle in Goddis daungere.
In helle pyne, or blisse clere,
Repentaunce mot mercy byȝe.
While þy dede is in þy powere,
Be þyn awen frend er þu dyȝe.   120

103]   Apart from a change to a second person pronoun the line is identical to Poem 19/103, and the same formula reappears at 1/155, 2/22, 13/8 and 24/243.

105]   Identical to Poem 21/127, cf. Edden, *Maidstone's Psalms*, 'For synne is sharpe as knyf or sword' (l. 811).

108]   **3e**. MS reads 'He', which interrupts the sequence; there is no clear antecedent. Since the rest of the stanza addresses a second person, I have emended to 'ȝe'.

109]   The same image is used at Poem 9/178.

113–20]   A fierce warning that, although it is within God's power to determine whether a soul receives the torments of hell or heavenly bliss, humankind must do their utmost to repent while they still have the power to act (l. 119). While no man can know his spiritual destiny, one must be a friend to oneself before death and not put one's trust in almsgiving, nor – significantly – the prayers of others after one has died. There may be an oblique criticism of chantry chapels here; the practice of offering masses and prayers for the souls of the dead encouraged simony, competed with the pastoral care of the parish priest in his own parish, and encouraged spiritual laxity, see *General Prologue* A.510–11 and Schmidt, *Piers Parallel Text*, C.5.45–50. The stern enjoinder to strict penitence is in keeping with the ardent penitential tone of the whole sequence.

Poem 8. A good makynge of iour delaye

Kail subtitled this poem 'Against the Clergy' and dated it to 1408–9 because of criticisms of the clergy in the seventh and eighth parliaments of Henry IV, *Poems*, p. xiv. This assignment of date is confusing, given that the seventh parliament was in October 1407 and the eighth in January 1410. Kail's references are, in fact, to the March 1406 parliament in which the commons did complain against non-resident curates, their unwillingness to distribute their goods to the poor, and the wrongful exaction of tithes, see *PROME*, March 1406: Item 114. The same complaints, however, had already been voiced in the parliaments of January 1401 and September 1402. In March 1410 the commons complained again in protractedly vociferous terms that there were men of Holy Church who neglected their benefices in order to reside with the nobility, or at the universities, with the result that they controlled the riches of the realm, and that priests held several benefices, but disregarded any duty of pastoral care towards their parishioners *PROME*, 1410:Item 70. In the April 1414 parliament, the commons presented a petition complaining that clergy exacted exorbitant fines from poor people in the proving of wills *PROME* Item 14, and that spiritual men were despoiling hospitals, *PROME* Item 15. Given the repetition of the grievances against the clergy, it is hard to assign the composition of Poem 8 to one specific parliament. It is more likely that the tenor of the comments is informed by cumulative knowledge of recent parliamentary discourse. As so often, however, the timely complaints presented by the petitions of the commons echo generic criticism in satire and complaint literature: see notes.

As a whole, this poem has much in common with the moral exhortations of the Poems 1, 7, 14 and 22 and their warnings to repent before it is too late, hence the play in this poem on the refrain of a day's delay, to which one might compare 'Tarry not till To-morrow', Furnivall, *Vernon Poems*, II.725–7/8, 'mak no tarijing til to-Morn'. The criticisms of the clergy produce, not so much a poem against the clergy, as Kail describes, but a poem which reminds the clergy of their responsibility ('charge' l. 17) to Christian folk; all of whom stand in terror of doomsday, come death when it may.

8. A good makyng of iour delaye

Man, haue hit in þy þou3t
Of what matere þu maked is;
God made the of nou3t,
Al þat þu hast, þu wost is his.
Wheþer hast þu serued pyne or blisse,   5
Seche þy werkis and assaye
Þy getyng, þy holdyng, þy spendyng mysse;
Fro blisse wolde make iour delaye.

To þy bed whan þu shalt go,
Þenk what þu hast don sen morn: 10
Wheþer serued blisse or wo,
Or Goddis name in ydel sworn,
Or ellys fals witnesse born,
Letted pore men of here pray,
In þy defaut here goodis lorn;   15
Þu shalt answere here iour delay.

1–4] Cf. Poem 22/1–5 which also opens with a exhortation to think of the matter at one's beginning, but while Poem 22 dwells on the vileness of the human body, Poem 8 urges its reader to reflect on the nothingness out of which s/he is made (cf. Genesis 2:7), and that all that they have belongs to God.

3] **made … nou3t**, a statement repeated at Poem 10/15, 20/177 and 22/17, and close in tenor to 7/81.

4] Cf. the same sentiment at Poem 1/27/34, 3/132, and 7/82.

6] **seche … assaye**. The same collocation is used at Poem 4/158, but in the context of seeking truth. The sentiment is similar to Poem 7/49–50.

7] The line is identical to Poem 1/31.

8] It is difficult to connect the refrain syntactically to the preceding lines; the subject of 'wolde make' is obscure unless it be the 'werkis' of (l. 6) which include the various ways of acquiring wealth in line 8.

9–10] Cf. 'Think on Yesterday', Furnivall, *Vernon Poems*, II.677/64–8, '… we wolde take good hede/And, in vr hertes a-countes cast,/Day bi day, wiþouten drede,/Toward vr ende we draweþ ful fast.'

12] Cf. Exodus 20:7, 'Thou shalt not take the name of the Lord thy God in vain: for the Lord will not hold him guiltless that shall take the name of the Lord his God in vain.'

14] **pore pray**. A similar collocation is used at Poem 4/150 and 6/7, though in these latter instances the criticism is directed at the nobility. Line 14 chimes with parliamentary complaints that the clergy appropriated money that ought properly have belonged to the poor.

Who takeþ cure, he bereþ charge
By Goddis lawe þe folk to preche.
Þey make conscience large,
Take tyþe and nyl not teche.   20
Crist his postles tauȝt in speche
Fro worldis worschip to wende away,
Gostly and bodyly þe soules to leche,
And bad hem make no iour delay.

17] **charge**. Responsibility is a key concern of these poems, cf. Poem 5/46 and 9/171; the latter a plea to clerics who have cure of souls to administer the sacrament of penance.

18] **Goddis lawe ... preche**. Lollard texts ground criticisms of the contemporary church by appeal to God's law, and the primacy of preaching over all other clerical duties is frequently stressed, e.g. Matthew, *Works of Wyclif,* pp. 56–7, 111/9ff., 188/1; Arnold, *Wyclif,* III.130/16ff., 145/9, 202–3, and Swinburne, *Lanterne,* p. 55/10ff. The Digby poet is clearly no Lollard, however, and it is possible that this remark is one of many in which appeals for church reform are couched in diction used more commonly from a dissident position in order to outflank and bypass heretical discussion. See further, Introduction, pp. 34–7.

19] **conscience large**. The implication is that clerics do not administer the sacrament of penance properly; an ample conscience sits uncomfortably with the enjoinder to 'seche þy werkis' (l. 6) and to think each night on the deeds of the day (ll. 9–10). Cf. the importance of conscience in the spiritual destiny of the soul, Poem 1/137–40, 4/108 and 17/143.

20] **nota** is marked in the margin adjacent to this line. The criticism of priests' exacting tithes without instructing their parishioners is a complaint voiced by the commons in parliament (see headnote), but it is also generic, see Chaucer, *General Prologue,* A.486–90; Peacock, *Myrc's Instructions,* p. 111/356ff., 'I holde hyt but an ydul þynge/To speke myche of teythynge,/For þaȝ a preste be but a fonne,/Aske hys teyþynge wel he conne.' More overtly radical texts make the same point, e.g. *Mum and the Sothsegger,* 613–7. There is no suggestion of the Wycliffite claim that parishioners have the right to withhold tithes from sinful priests, e.g. Matthew, *Works of Wyclif,* 132/14–25. Church law made the payment of tithes obligatory, see Brandeis, *Jacob's Well,* 'ye schul tythe truly, for to kepe you sekerly out of the artycle of cursyng', p. 37/5–6. The position of the Digby poet is that clerics ought not to abuse the payment of tithes by failing their parishioners by being slack in their responsibilities towards them.

21–3] **nota** is marked in the margin next to line 22. The lines draw on Christ's commandments to his apostles: Mark 6:7–8, 'And he called the twelve; and began to send them two and two, and gave them power over unclean spirits. And he commanded them that they should take nothing for the way, but a staff only: no scrip, no bread, nor money in their purse.' Cf. Luke 9:1–3, 'Then calling together the twelve apostles, he gave them power and authority over all devils, and to cure diseases. And he sent them to preach the kingdom of God, and to heal the sick. And he said to them: Take nothing for your journey; neither staff, nor scrip, nor bread, nor money; neither have two coats.'

23] **leche**, cf. ll. 21/22 where the importance of correction of souls is stressed.

Worldis good nes not holichirche,   25
Richesse and worschep Y ȝow forbede,
Þe folk is cherche, in hem ȝe worche,
Here noo oþer to don þy dede.
Þat doþ þe dede is worþy mede;
Þu mayst not serue two lordis to pay,   30
Þat on he serueþ in loue and drede,
Þat oþere he serueþ wiþ iour delay.

Who ressayueþ benefys for richesse and ese,
To haue his lyuyng in sykernes,
Raþere þan serue God to plese,   35
He ressayueþ hit omys.

25] A sharp reminder against abuse of temporality, cf. note to lines 57–64.

27] The pithy assonance of this line asserts that the primary function of the institutional church is the spiritual care of its parishioners, cf. note to Poem 23/1–4.

28] The opposition between a true shepherd and a hireling is repeated, Poem 9/164. The source is John 10:11–13, 'I am the good shepherd. The good shepherd giveth his life for his sheep. But the hireling, and he that is not the shepherd, whose own the sheep are not, seeth the wolf coming, and leaveth the sheep, and flieth: and the wolf catcheth, and scattereth the sheep: And the hireling flieth, because he is a hireling: and he hath no care for the sheep.' The complaint about hired clergy is seen also in Chaucer, *General Prologue*, 'He sette nat his benefice to hyre/And leet his sheep encombred in the myre', A.507–8.

29] Reiterated Poem 9/165 and see note to Poem 2/40.

30–2] From Matthew 6:24, 'No man can serve two masters. For either he will hate the one, and love the other: or he will sustain the one, and despise the other. You cannot serve God and mammon', cf. Luke 16:13. The poet alters the biblical text to suggest that clerics are in awe to worldly goods but are negligent in their service to God.

33] **benefys**. The criticism may be inflected by parliamentary petitions in the first two decades of the fifteenth century (see headnote), but the criticism is also generic, see Chaucer, *General Prologue*, cf. note to line 28; Schmidt, *Piers Parallel Text*, C.3.33, 'bygge ȝow benefices pluralite to haue'; Gower, *Confessio*, Prol.314–18, 'The strong coffre hath al devoured/Under the keye of avarice/The tresor of the benefice,/Wherof the povere schulden clothe/And ete and drinke and house bothe'; Hoccleve, *Regement*, 1408–9, 'Fful many men knowe I, þat gane and gape/After som fat & riche benefice', and *Of the Leaven of the Pharisees*, Matthew, *Works of Wyclif*, p. 22, 'where ben þo prestis þat maken hem so bisy aboute grete benefices, wordly worschipis and stynkynge muk or drit of worldeli richesse' and Furnivall, *Handlyng Synne*, 10982–5, 'ȝe shul auaunce;/To gode men ȝyueþ ȝoure benefyces/Þat kun hem kepe fro wykked vyces;/Þan make ȝe gode presentëment'. See also Poem 9/161–2 and 14/25–30.

For ri3t [fol. 106a] as Iudas dede kys
Ihesus, and after hym betray,
So þey gyle þe soules fro blisse;
Of Goddis seruyce make iour delay.   40

Many seyn 'God is so wys,
Endeles ful of all mercy;
God nyl not, þou3 Y be nys,
Lese me þurgh myn owen foly,
So dere God mankynde dede bye.   45
What greueþ God þou3 Y go gay?'
Þat synnen in ouerhope, in helle mon ly3e;
Þereof mon be non iour delay.

Many wole say þat leue vneuene,
'And it were soþ þat clerkis telle,   50
Fewe folkes shulde come in heuene
So fele as shulde renne hedlyng to helle'.
Hit were hard þere to dwelle,
Wiþ helle houndes stonde to bay:
'Synne mon be punisched' as saiþ þe gospelle;   55
Þerof mon be no iour delay.

37–8] Luke 22:47 tells of Judas's betrayal of Christ in the Garden of Gethsemane with a kiss.

41–8] The poet ventriloquises the foolish theological reasoning of complacent souls; namely that God redeemed humankind at such a cost that He will not want them damned simply as a result of their own folly. Frivolous living will not grieve God. Speaking in the admonitory voice, the narrator condemns this folly with phraseology that recalls Poem 7/97–9 – see notes thereon and cf. Poem 22/29.

49–56] The stanza is organised around a strategy similar to that in the previous. The poet ventriloquises the misunderstanding of theological discussions of salvation. To claim that fewer souls will go to heaven than the hordes that run headlong to hell grossly oversimplifies a complex theological debate. The narrator's stance response is to spell out the misery of living in hell.

54] Cf. Poem 2/76 and 4/238.

55] **Synne mon be punisched**. Although the poet sources this statement to the Gospel, I have been unable to find an equivalent verse. The writer may have had in mind either John 20:23, 'Whose sins you shall forgive, they are forgiven them; and whose sins you shall retain, they are retained', or Romans 6:23, 'For the wages of sin is death'.

That ouere puple haue astate,
Colege, or eny oþer degre,
Mayntene no debate
For synguler profyt of temperalte: 60
3oure rule is groundid in charyte,
As li3t of lanterne to lede þe way;
To gouerene þe puple in vnyte
God bad hem make no iour delay.

Beter is litel ry3twys [to wynne],   65
Þereof among þe pore to dele,
Þan ouer moche geten wiþ synne;

57]   Cf. similar formula Poem 1/10 and 5/41.

57-64]   The poet's concern with corporate unity is here extended to include the role of clerics in fostering concord. **synguler profyt** is a key term in the sequence and actively opposed to the common good, see note to Poem 1/4. In this stanza the church's concern with temporal possession is seen to threaten common welfare. The comments may be influenced by parliamentary petitions, see headnote, but criticisms of the temporalities of the Church are also generic, *How the offices of curates*, Matthew, *Works of Wyclif*, p. 155, 'be absent fro his cure; þat his souereyn schal not dore correcte him for drede of his temperaltees & wraþþe of lordis; & þus lordis ben made schildis of synne for a litel money'; Schmidt, *Piers Parallel Text*, B.20.127–8, '[Symonye] … preched to the peple, and prelates thei hem maden/To holden with Antecrist, hir temporaltees to save', and Gower, *Confessio*, II.3490–2, 'To day is venym schad/In holi cherche of temporal,/Which medleth with the spirital'. Cf. also Poem 10/135, 16/67 and 18/11.

59]   **debate**, cf. note to Poem 6/21.

61]   **rule … groundid** is a collocation of terms that would not look out of place in a Wycliffite text: e.g. 'rule' *Pierce the Ploughman's Crede*, 291, 376–7, 466; Matthew, *Works of Wyclif*, p. 301/2/4; and 'grounded', Matthew, *Works of Wyclif*, p. 268/8, 301/27; *Jack Upland*, 15, 264, 282, 287. The echo is part of the writer's attempt to appropriate the terms of debate used by dissidents and make them serve the voice of orthodox reform, see Introduction, pp. 34–7.

62]   **li3t of lanterne**. This phrase – or lantern of light – is often used to describe the ideal clergy, e.g. *Mum and the Sothsegger*, 1749; Gower, *Vox*, III.1070–80. It forms the title of the Wycliffite tract *The Lanterne of Li3t*. The phrase reappears Poem 21/153–6 where the phrase is glossed with reference to Matthew 5:14–15 and Luke 8:17, verses which might be the source of the Middle English phrase. See also Poem 23/7–8.

63]   Identical to Poem 1/21 and 3/130.

64-72]   The narrator argues that it is better to win a little righteousness by dealing with the poor than sinfully acquiring surplus by wrongfully stealing from the goods of the poor. This comment is close in tenor to parliamentary petitions of the early fifteenth century. Cf. the same criticism but slightly differently worded Poem 21/58.

65]   **to wynne**. MS reads 'wonne', which does not fit the rhyme scheme. I have emended to secure the rhyme, and also to match the infinitive form of 'dele'.

Wiþouten desert take pore mennys wele,
And helpe not þe soule to hele,
But crye in pyne weylaway.   70
Þe soules þe curatours wole apele
To answere of here iour delay.

Why ressayue ȝe worschipe þat ȝe haue –
For ȝoure vertues or for ȝoure vys?
And ȝe ful worschip saue,   75
In word and werk, ȝe mot be wys.
Þis worldly wysdom is gostly nys
Whan werk acordeþ not wiþ wordis ȝe say;
Heuene blys and þis worldis delys,
Þat on wil make iour delay.   80

Thow may not knowe a cristen man:
Þouȝ þu here hym say his crede,
Þe ten comaudementis tan.
[Þat] speke and do not þe dede,
Ne serue God in loue and drede,   85
Is heretyk out of fay.

71] **apele** has legal force, see Alford, *Glossary*, p. 7, and may be influenced by the petitions against the clergy in successive parliaments.

77] Almost identical to Poem 1/45.

78–80] The syntax of these lines is loosely paratactic. The narrator appears to argue that when there is a discrepancy between deeds and word, and heavenly bliss is opposed to worldly delights, the one (the worldly delights) will cause a day's delay.

81–8] The stanza argues that ability to say the creed and the ten commandments is not proof that a man is a good Christian believer. The stanza continues the concern that speech and deeds match up.

83] **tan** in Poem 9/81 and 24/227 is a past participle meaning 'taken', a sense which does not fit here. The most plausible explanation is that it is a Northern spelling of 'ton' in the sense of 'announce noisily, or declaim', see *MED* 'tonen' (v.); b. The Northern spelling secures the rhyme.

84] **Þat**. MS reads 'And' which makes the syntax very difficult. I have emended to produce continuity of sense in lines 84–6: the person that speaks but without matching their words to action, and does not serve God in love and fear, is a heretic out of the true belief of the Church.

86] **heretyk out of fay**. Another puzzling reference to heresy. The ability to recite the creed and the ten commandments without matching that performance with actions is not a conventional definition. Once again, the silence over contemporary heresy is deafening. Cf. note to Poem 7/73–80.

After ȝoure werkis ressauye þy mede;
Þerof mon be no iour delay.

Thouȝ worldis richesse on þe falle,
And wolde gon bytwen God and þe,   90
Suffre not þy soule be þralle;
Þenk God bouȝt it to make þe fre.
Þouȝ þy mayster a tyraunt be,
Fro Goddis lawe wolde say nay,
Do as Poule bad þe: 95
Abyde, and suffre wiþ iour delay.

Man, þu wost wel þu shalt dyȝe;
What deþ, ne where, þu nost whenne.
And synnes wolde þy soule nyȝe,
Ay more and more rerage we renne,   100
And sodeyn deþ nyl no man kenne.
I rede we drede domesday;
Be euene wiþ world, we ȝe gon henne;
For þere schal be no iour delay.

87]   Cf. Poem 9/151, and Psalms 27:4, 'Give them according to their works, and according to the wickedness of their inventions. According to the works of their hands give thou to them: render to them their reward.'

89–96]   The stanza contains delicate play on the value of riches and bondage and freedom. If a person happen to be prosperous, the value of that worldly wealth is to enslave his soul. God, however, bought (through His redemption) the soul to make it free.

95–6]   The poet may have in mind either Romans 8:17, 'if we suffer with him, that we may be also glorified with him' or 2 Timothy 3:12, 'And all that will live godly in Christ Jesus, shall suffer persecution'.

97–8]   Cf. note to Poem 7/17–18 and cf. 'Each Man ought himself to know', Furnivall, *Vernon Poems*, II.673/61–70 and 'Make Amends for thy Sins', II.728/25–8.

100]   **rerage**. Similar accounting imagery in relation to the accumulation of sin is seen at Poem 9/103 and 11/111.

Poem 9. With God of loue and pes ȝe trete

Kail dated this poem to the year 1410 because he saw it to contain allusions to the parliament of that year. He connects the reference to Easter at the opening of the poem to the adjournment of the parliament until after Easter (*Poems*, p. xiv), see *PROME*, Item 13. This was not the only parliament, however, with an explicit connection to Easter: the opening words of the first parliament of Henry V's reign also refer to Easter – in this instance, one just passed, *PROME*, 1413: Item 1. More significantly, Kail's identification of the poem's opening line with Easter is mistaken: Lent is the tide indicated, see note to line 1.

Kail also traced parallels between many of the topics discussed in the poem and the business of the 1410 assembly: the reference to coin-clipping (ll. 49–50) to complaints of the circulation of bad coin; cheating the cloth measure (ll. 52–5) to the commons petition about regulating the length and width of cloth; the proper conduct of law (ll. 57–68) to criticisms of the malpractice of legal officers, and exhortation of clergy to discharge their pastoral duties (ll. 153–76) to the commons' repetition of their complaint about non-residence and other abuses of the clergy (see *PROME*, 1410: Items 48, 49, 68, 69, 70 and 72). Kail concluded that 'the connection of the ninth poem with the above-quoted parliamentary transactions is evident' (*Poems*, p. xv). It is certainly the case that many of the specific comments in this poem map more closely onto this meeting of parliament than of any other between 1401 and 1419. But this need not mean that the poem was necessarily written in that year. The abuses raised in this parliament were not new, nor was this the last time that such views were voiced. Further, the criticisms are commonplaces of pastoral instruction literature (see notes to individual lines).

There are also lines in the poem that, if one were to seek a topical context, point to years later than 1410. The repetition of 'pes' and 'trete' chimes almost uncannily with the passing of the Statute of Truces in the 1414 Leicester parliament (cf. notes to Poem 13/121–8). Might parliamentary discourse here have prompted the poet's re-registration of this pervasive topic into a spiritual key? The reference to 'riȝt querel' (l. 139) might easily be taken as a reference to Henry V's deliberations about the invasion of France, and 'chastise the rebell in charite' (l. 140) is a tantalising line given the Oldcastle revolt in 1413 and the Cambridge plot in 1415. It appears more pointed than the reference to rebellion in Poem 5/36, but once again, given the almost continuous history of risings and revolts in individual counties, the

Welsh and Scottish Marches, and incursions into English waters in the first two decades of the fifteenth century, to attempt to find a definitive context, localised to a particular topical event, still risks effacement of the particular social temper of these poems (see further, Introduction, pp. 43, 55–60).

What emerges very strongly from this poem, however, is its orthodox defence of the sacrament of confession. The diction is more distinctive than a call for penitence because one is foul and doomed to die. There is an insistence, not just on oral confession, but the presence of the priest is ostentatiously repeated (ll. 34, 42, 83, 95, 186). The criticisms of neglectful clerics in the poem are part of an attempt to reform the Church from within. Because the role of the priest is vital in enduring that Christian folk properly repent, then priests must perform their duties properly. The sentiments of the poem as a whole bear close comparison with 'Love Holy Church and its Priests', Furnivall, *Vernon Poems*, II.721–3, especially lines 33–64 where priests are enjoined to discharge their duties honourably and the necessity of priests for confession is stressed, 'of alle bales he may beete/Vnder god in Trinite;/ Þenne Schrift & hosul is ful swete,/And hit trewely holden be' (ll. 53–6).

9. With God of loue and pes ȝe trete

[fol. 106b] This holy tyme make ȝow clene;
Burnysche bryȝt ȝoure soules blake!
Fro ȝow to God, let þe prest be mene
To do penaunce and synnes forsake,
Wiþ almes dede amendes make.   5
And repentaunce may grace gete,
In goode werkis wysely wake,
And wiþ God of pes Y rede ȝe trete.

Wiþ soulis briȝt in God ȝe glade,
As shynyng angels out of synne,   10
In worschip of hym þat ȝow made.

1] **holy tyme ... clene** may refer to Easter as Kail claimed, though the obligation for each
parishioner to make confession to their parish priest specifies *before* Easter. *Speculum
Sacerdotale* explains that there are four lenten seasons in the year; three are optional,
but not the 'one *afore* Paske, the whiche is comen to *alle men*' (my emphasis), Weatherly,
p. 74/24–5. References to Easter are more secure in Poem 11/1–2, 12/4 and 23/25–32.

3] **prest be mene**. The importance of the priest as an essential mediator between sinners
and God is stressed in this poem, cf. notes to lines 34, 42, 83, 95 and 186.

3–7] The lines correspond closely to the orthodox formulation of the sacrament of penance,
e.g. 'Penaunce is a nedeful thyng vnto a synner þat desireþ for to recouere heleþ of
his soule. And in doyng of penaunce there be thre thynges to be considerid, scilicet,
compunccion of herte, confession of mowthe, and satisfaccion by dede', Weatherly,
Speculum Sacerdotale, p. 63/6–10.

7] The line is identical to Poem 20/209 and cf. 21/159.

8] **trete**. The refrain of this poem is also seen at Poem 3/152, with a similar formula at
3/16. The meaning of 'trete' is not straightforward. One sense is to plead, or to entreat,
MED 'treten' (v.); 6a, but not entirely separable from this is the sense of 'to negotiate,
especially terms of peace', 1a.a. This is particularly evident in line 17. I have not been able
to find a comparable use of 'trete' in these senses in a penitential, or broadly spiritual,
context. The closest I have found is Hoccleve, *The Epistle of Grace Dieu*, 50–3, 'Forr if
þat deth the sudeynly assaile,/beleue it weel, he spariþ no persone;/With him to trete,
it may no thing avayle'. The only other collocations of 'trete' and 'truce' are found in
secular texts, Hanna and Lawton, *The Siege of Jerusalem*, 410–500, 501–600, 1101–200,
and Panton and Donaldson, *Destruction of Troy*, 11237 and 11399. One explanation for
the Digby poet's distinctive usage is that he has blended penitential and parliamentary
discourses. There is especially abundant use of the word 'truce' in the parliament roll of
January 1410, referring both to internal and external threats; and especially dense usage
once again in the April 1414 parliament in which the Statute of Truces was passed.

9–11] These lines suggest an Easter context, with the soul now cleansed. Cf. close analogue
Poem 11/73–6.

To knowe ȝoure seluen now bygynne;
To stryue wiþ God we may not wynne;
Boþe body and soule he can bete.
Ihesus is broþer of oure kynne,   15
Forþy wiþ God of [pes] ȝe trete.

Ofte han we treted wiþ God o trewe,
And sayde no more synne we wolde,
And euery ȝeere we breke it newe,
Þre dayes no trewes wiþ hym nele holde.   20
Synne to bay, many a folde,
On soules, helle houndes slete.
Er ȝe come þere, ȝonge and olde,
Wiþ God of pes Y rede ȝe trete.

Trete while ȝe haue ȝoure hele,   25
For sodeyn deþ [ȝe] stomblen as blynde.
Þe grettere lordschipe of worldis wele,
Þe more in þraldom hit doþ hem bynde.

12]   Cf. note to Poem 1/8.

15]   Sentiments which can be paralleled in a number of confession manuals, e.g. Furnivall,
      Handlyng Synne, 11340–4, 'Syn Ihesu Cryst toke flesshe and blode,/And was cloþed yn
      oure man-hede,/And wyst oure wykkednes & oure nede,/To man behoueþ vs to telle
      oure trespas,/Syn he knew alle þat yn man was'.

16]   **pes** omitted in MS. I have followed Kail's emendation.

17–20] The importance of not falling back into sin is stressed in *Speculum Sacerdotale*
      where true penance is said to be sorrow, thinking on one's misdeeds, making confession
      'and no more to be in wille for to falle ther-to a-ȝeyn', Weatherly, p. 65/17–19. The lines
      in Digby are distinctive, however, framing this as a broken truce with God.

21]   **synne to bay** is obscure. Elsewhere 'bay' is a noun Poem 2/76, 4/238, 8/54. Here it may
      be the infinitive of *MED* 'baien' (v.); 1a: 'to bark; ~ at (sb.)' with the sense that the many
      hell hounds attack souls to bark at sin.

25–32] Standard confession manual material: cf. 'Therefore sone whiles that thou art
      in helþe and art fre, haue compunccion, make confession with satisfaccion folowyng,
      and abide noȝt tyme of dyinge', Weatherly, *Speculum Sacerdotale*, p. 64/29–31 and 'the
      doctoure Austyn schewiþ in his scriptures how þat it is ful perelous and gretely to be
      drede by manye resouns of taryinge in penaunce to be don and of late penaunce, for
      he seiþ: … "there may falle to hym a sodeyn deþ"' p. 64/6–12.

26]   **ȝe**. Not in MS, but the verb requires a plural antecedent which cannot be 'sodeyn
      deþ'.

27–8] Cf. Weatherly, *Speculum Sacerdotale*, p. 68/12–13, 'What profetteþ it a man for to yeue
      to God his goodis and yeve hym-self to the deuel?' cf. notes to Poem 8/89–96.

Man, þynke þy lyf is but a wynde,
When þat is blowen, þu art forȝete.   30
Holde couenaunt to God, and be kynde;
Forþy wiþ God of pes ȝe trete.

Ʒe mot hit shewe wiþ herte sorwe
To a prest, and weel ȝow shryue;
Noȝt turne aȝen þerto tomorwe,   35
But þenke be good al thy lyue.
Wiþ Goddis sonde look ȝe not stryue,
Ne derne mornyng counterfete,
Rekne wysely all þy wittes fyue
Wiþ God of pes when ȝe do trete.   40

The synnes þat wolde þy soule apayre,
To a prest shewe þe cas,
Loke þat þu not paynte hit fayre,

29]   **but a wynde**: the fragile transience of human life is an ever frequent trope of penitential lyrics, e.g. 'St Bernard on Man's three Foes', Furnivall, *Vernon Poems* II.512/19–36; 'Each Man ought himself to know', II.672–3/25–39/61–4 and 'Mercy passes all Things', II.661/109–12.

31]   **couenaunt** has the legal sense of a legally binding agreement between two parties, see Alford, *Glossary*, p. 39 and cf. Holmstedt, *Speculum Christiani*, p. 102/16–17 'Augustinus: Confession of al synnes es begynnynge of gude werkes and makeȝ trewe conaunte wyth god'. **kynde** in the sense of 'faithful and true', *MED* 'kinde' (*adj.*); 6b. The sinner who fails to take the sacrament of confession seriously in Furnivall, *Handlyng Synne* is said to be 'Goddes treytour, and ryȝt vyleyn' (11557).

33–6]   Cf. Weatherly, *Speculum Sacerdotale*, p. 69/31–3, 'And they þat makeþ confession of here synnes and wol noȝt forsake hem, they auȝt gretely to be a-dredde' and p. 71/14–16, 'And therfore there schuld none be asoylid but he þat dewly and with alle his herte absteyneþ hym fro alle his synnes and behoteþ for to leue hem fro that tyme forþeward'.

39]   **rekne**. Accounting diction is frequent in penitential lyrics, e.g. 'Think on Yesterday' Furnivall, *Vernon Poems* II.676/66. 'And in vr hertes a-countes cast'. **wittes fyue** Brandeis, *Jacob's Well* calls the five senses the water gates, or entries to the body, which must be stopped to prevent the entry of the slime of sin: 'to se, to here, to swelewe, to smelle, to fele', p. 217/4–5. The speaker of 'Ay, Mercy, God', Furnivall, *Vernon Poems* II.697/41–2, calls for mercy 'þat I haue mis-spent/Mi wittes fyue! þerfore I wepe' and in Holmstedt, *Speculum Christiani* the third measure listed to cleanse humankind from sin 'es besynes to kepe thi fyue wyttes fro al wickede thynges' (p. 108/1–2).

41–3]   Standard confession material: cf. 'But doþ not as many men doþ, scilicet, for to make ȝoure synnes whit and to gyldyn hem vnder excusatorie wordes and colours.' Weatherly, *Speculum Sacerdotale*, p. 65/5–7, and Furnivall, *Handlyng Synne*, 11759–63, 'Þy synne

But shewe it forþ riȝt ful as it was.

Þat shame is mede for þy trespas,   45

For synne þat wolde þy soule þrete,

Aske mercy, and seche grace

Wiþ God of pes when ȝe trete.

That clippen money, þey haue þe curs

Foure tymes in þe ȝere;   50

Here waȝtes þat þey waye þe wors,

Ȝerde, or elne, fer or nere;

Wheþer þey selle good chep or dere,

But þey þe fulle mesure mete,

Hit semeþ in skornyng þat it were   55

Wiþ God of pes whan ȝe trete.

---

naked shalt þou make,/And opunly, hyt forsake,/hyle hem nat with feyre wurde,/Þat semeþ to gadyr þy synnes to hurde:/yn tyfed wurdys þat slyked are'.

44] **ful as it was**. The need for total and complete confession is often stressed in the manuals, e.g. Weatherly, *Speculum Sacerdotale*, p. 66/10–11, 'kepe no-thyng vnschewid' and Furnivall, *Handlyng Synne*, 11819–22, 'No poynt þou shalt with-holde,/For, alle holy, hyt oweþ to be tolde;/And, þat shal y shewe þe/On two maners; þy shryfte al hole shal be'.

49] **clippen money … curs**. Brandeis, *Jacobs Well* contains a compendium of the articles of the sentence of excommunication. It includes 'alle false monye-makerys & false clypperys and wasscherys of monye', p. 62/17–18 and the similar list in Peacock, *Myrc's Instructions* covers 'all þat falsen þe kinges money or clippen it' p. 22/710. Coveitise admits to this sin in Schmidt, *Piers Parallel Text*, B.V.238–9, 'I lerned among Lumbardes a lesson, and of Jewes –/To weye pens with a peis, and pare the hevyeste'. The sentence of excommunication was read out four times a year.

51] **waȝtes … waye**. The use of false weights and measures is often listed among the sins of covetousness, see Brandeis, *Jacob's Well*, p. 133/28–31. Holmstedt, *Speculum Christiani* lists 'fals mesure' among contraventions of the 7th commandment, 'thou shalt not steal', p. 30/7. Peacock, *Myrc's Instructions* includes those 'þat falsen or vse false measures … or false ellen yerdes' in categories for which one might be excommunicated under the great sentence of curse, p. 22/711–13. Biblical injunctions against false measure include: Wisdom 11:21, 'thou hast ordered all things in measure, and number, and weight', and Leviticus 19:35, 'Do not any unjust thing in judgement, in rule, in weight, or in measure'.

52–3] False measure of cloth is commonly listed among the sins of covetousness, see Schmidt, *Piers Parallel Text*, B.V.205–10, 'Thanne drough I me among drapiers, my Donet to lerne,/To drawe the liser along – the lenger it semed;/Among the riche rayes I rendred a lesson–/To broche hem with a pak-nedle, and playte hem togideres,/And putte hem in a pressour and pyned hem therinne/Til ten yerdes or twelve tolled out thrittene.' Coveitise's wife is guilty of the same offence, B.V.211–14.

Auyse 3ow þat leden lawe,
For drede of lordschipe, or for mede,
Holde no pore men in awe,
To storble here ry3t, or lette here nede.   60
Hit bryngeþ þe soule in grete drede
A3ens Goddis lawe to plete:
Þe rolles ari3t Y red 3e rede,
[fol. 107a] Wiþ God of pes when 3e trete.

That haldeþ questes or assise,   65
Þat takeþ or 3eueþ fee or hire,
Lette not lawe fro ri3t gyse,
Ne mayntene wrongis as master and sire.
Þey may be ferd for helle fire
To [m]ete here ney3bores at here mete;   70
Þat lyf shal not euere more dure –
Forþy wiþ God of pes 3e trete.

3e þat comeþ to Goddis bord,
Resceyueþ hym in clene lyf;
Holde non olde synnes in hord,   75
For þanne begynneþ a newe stryf;
For he to God haþ drawen his knyf

57–68]   The perversion of the law is listed under the sins of covetousness, Brandeis, *Jacob's Well*, 131/10–29 and perjury and false judgement under the contraventions of the 7th commandment in Holmstedt, *Speculum Christiani*, p. 30/8–9.

63]   **rolles ari3t**. The perversions of justice listed in Brandeis, *Jacob's Well* include the making of false letters, records and acts, p. 131/20–3.

65]   **haldeþ**. The Northern form is not used for rhyme here and is evidence of the mixed dialect of the poems.

70]   **mete**. MS reads 'ete' and while one might well imagine that the torments of hell will come to those who practise cannibalism, this surely cannot have been the intended sense here. I have emended to 'mete' in the sense of entertain at a meal. Those who destroy law through accepting the bribe of hospitality are criticised in *Richard the Redeless*, III.312–14, 'For mayntenance many day well more is the reuthe!/Hath yhad mo men at mete and at melis/Than ony cristen kynge that ye knewe euere'. Once a case was accepted to be heard in court, the jury was assembled to hear the pleading. If any of the jurors were spoken to, or treated to food and drink by either party, the verdict could be quashed.

71]   A commonplace of penitential lyrics, e.g. 'Each Man ought himself to know' Furnivall, *Vernon Poems* II.675/73–4 'Knowe þi flesch, þat wole rote; ffor certes, þou mai3t not longe endure'. In this poem 'endure' rhymes with 'Empyre', 'syre' 'myre' 'enspire', and 'huire'.

73–7]   Cf. Weatherly, *Speculum Sacerdotale*, p. 66/30–2, 'He must also beware that he come

Þat þenkeþ in skorne þere wolde hym ete.
Here be war, man and wyf:
Horde no synne when ȝe trete!   80

Man, ȝif þu haue tan a fal,
Ryse vp, and no more slyde!
O prest þy shrifte to schewe it al,
But hyde no synne in hord bysyde;
In venyale synne longe to byde   85
Makeþ dedly synnes to growe grete.
Wiþ ȝoure werkis ȝe mot chyde;
Wiþ God of pes when ȝe trete.

Seuene syþes on þe day
Men seyn the riȝtwis man doþ falle.   90
Þanne he þat falleþ in synnes alway,
How shulde he rekene þo synnes alle,
But he wrot hem grette and smalle?
Summe at shrifte he schulde forȝete;

no̧t to receyve his God til the tyme that he be clene schryven with a good sorowe that
he is no̧t worþi ne dare no̧t ȝit reseyve him', a point also made in Furnivall, *Handlyng
Synne*, 10835-8, 'Ȝyf þou wylt haue þe sacrament,/Þe behoueþ ȝyue weyl bettyr entent,/And
recorde euery dede/with sorow of herte, and with drede', and in Holmstedt, *Speculum
Christiani*, 'Who that desyreȝ to take the sacramente or Cristes body … he muste go to
hym wyth … true contricion of synnes, wyth wyl to do no more euyl, and wyth stedfaste
purpos of perseuerance in gud werkes' (p. 176-8/36-4), 'a man that, knowynge his gilte,
himselfe gylty in synne, wil abstene hym-selfe fro the auter' (p. 180/3-4).

81-2] Cf. 'St Bernard on Man's three Foes', Furnivall, *Vernon Poems* II.514/49-50, 'Mon, I
rede þat þou be wys,/And ȝif þou falle, sone arys'.

83] On the need to make a full confession see note to line 44 above and cf. Weatherly,
Speculum Sacerdotale, p. 69/14-16, 'And some ben schewynge the lasse and holdeþ
behynde that þat is more and worse'.

89-90] **seuene syþes**. The same biblical verse (Proverbs 24:16, 'For a just man shall fall
seven times and shall rise again: but the wicked shall fall down into evil') is quoted in
Furnivall, *Handlyng Synne* when the writer discusses the second part of shrift, 'Salamon
to vs seyþ and kalleþ,/Seuene tymes on a day þe ryȝtwys man falleþ;/As ofte þan behoueþ
þe ryse' (11405-7).

93] **but he wrot hem**, cf. Furnivall, *Handlyng Synne*, 11769-72, 'Þou mayst nat þy synnes
wryte,/Yn shryfte þe so to quyte,/Ȝyf þou mayste speke, and haste space,/To fynde a
preste yn any place'.

94-5] **forȝete … oftere calle**, cf. Furnivall, *Handlyng Synne*, 'Synne þat þou yn shryfte
forȝat,/Þou art holde to telle hyt þy prest' (10854-5) and 'Þe ofter þat þou shewest þy

He shulde þe prest þe oftere calle,   95
Wiþ God of pes when ƷE go trete.

Foure acountes þu shalt Ʒelde:
God made þe lyk to his ymage;
How þu it wan; how þu it helde,
How þu it spendid in wast outrage.   100
Forfete not heuene þyn heritage,
Among seyntes þy soule sete.
Rekene, er þu renne in rerage,
And wiþ God of pes Ʒe trete.

Holy writ biddeþ God sende vengeaunce   105
To kyngdom þat nele not holde his lawe.
Wraþþe, and stryf, and alle greuaunce
Among prynces and pore men þrawe
Þat nele not leue Goddis sawe,
Ne counte his gynnyng at o clete.   110
To werkis of wysdom by tyme Ʒe drawe,
And wiþ God of pes Ʒe trete.

Whoso leued þat God were trewe,
Þan wolde þey do þat God hem bede,

blame,/Þe more me þenkeþ þou hast of shame;/Þe shame þat þou hast yn þy shewyng,/hyt
ys forƷyuenes, to gode endyng' (11425–8) and the importance of 'ofte shryuyng' (11485).
97–101]   Furnivall, *Handlyng Synne* makes a similar argument: 'God hymself of mageste,/
Vnto hys lykenes he formed þe ... Sorowe oghte þan þyn herte bynde,/Þat þou art to
hym so vnkynde;/Þou dysonourest hym yn þat outrage,/And reuylyst hys feyre ymage'
(11535–46), and 'St Bernard on Man's three Foes', Furnivall, *Vernon Poems* II.520/169–74,
'ffiht faste for þyn owne riht/And get þe heuene-blisse briht,/While þou hast tyme þer-to;/
Þin owne heritage hit is,/And þerof schaltou neuer mis/But Ʒif þou hit fordo'.
99–100]   Cf. Poem 1/31 and 8/7 and notes thereto.
103]   Cf. note to Poem 1/29 and 1/35.
105–6]   God's vengeance on lawless and sinful kingdoms is a recurring theme: cf. Poem
3/8 4/115/119, 12/148, 13/84 and 14/87 and see biblical references listed in note to 3/105–12.
Here, the poet may have in mind Ecclesiasticus 5:8, 'Delay not to be converted to the
Lord, and defer it not from day to day. For his wrath shall come on a sudden, and in
the time of vengeance he will destroy thee'.
108]   **þrawe** (strife, conflict), a striking use of a Northern form for rhyme. At Poem 14/78
'thro' is the form, again in rhyme position.
110]   **clete.** *MED* lists the sense of something worthless, or not giving a damn for something
under 'clet' (*n.*); 3b; a word which means 'lump' or a 'small portion'.

Þat mende no mysse, but synne ay newe,   115
Hem lakkeþ all þe poyntes of þe crede.
Serue God for helle drede,
Lest þy soule falle in chete,
And loue God for heuene mede;
Wiþ loue and drede wiþ God ȝe trete.   120

Þouȝ þu take ordre or religeoun,
[fol. 107b] Wiþoute charite þu seruest no mede.
ȝeue drynke to þursty þat han and mown,
Cloþe þe naked, and hungry fede,
Vysite þe pore and syk þat nede,   125
And giltles presoneres loos ȝe lete,
And burye þe dede is charite dede;
Wiþ þes werkis wiþ God ȝe trete.

Þere þu hast borwed, quyte þy dette,
And to þy seruaunt þat reson is.   130

116]   **lakkeþ all þe poyntes of þe crede** may be a generalised comment that the unrepentant sinner flouts Christian doctrine, or it may be a more targeted reference to the priest's duties in attending to a person on their death bed; confession is followed by receipt of the Eucharist, unction and 'also the seke muste be examynede in the artycle of the feyth conteynede in the Credo', Holmstedt, *Speculum Christiani*, p. 206/22–4.

118]   **chete**: a legal term meaning the reversion of property or goods back to the lord or landlord, cf. Schmidt, *Piers Parallel Text,* where at B.4.175 the King accuses Meed of impeding the law 'Thorugh youre lawe, as I leve, I lese manye chetes'. Cf. Alford, *Glossary,* pp. 52–3.

121]   **ordre or religeoun**: become a priest or a monk.

122]   **withoute charite**, cf. 1 Corinthians 13:3, 'And if I should distribute all my goods to feed the poor, and if I should deliver my body to be burned, and have not charity, it profiteth me nothing'. The stanza is reminiscent of Holy Church's indictment of those priests who may stay strictly within God's law, but who lack charity, Schmidt, *Piers Parallel Text,* B.1.190–4 'Manye chapeleyns arn chaste, ac charite is aweye:/Are none hardere than hii whan hii ben avaunced;/Unkynde to hire kyn and to alle Cristene,/Chewen hire charite and chiden after moore, –/Swich chastite withouten charite worth cheyned in helle'.

123–7]   A compressed account of the seven works of mercy, see note to Poem 6/37–40, 19/89 and 22/66. Holmstedt, *Speculum Christiani,* p. 174/4–7 urges parish priests to perform these works to act as examples to their parishioners.

129–33]   These lines are strikingly similar to kinds of robbery listed by the author of *Jacob's Well* under the sin of covetousness: 'whan þou art a fals dettoure, þou borowyst mych & noȝt qwytest. & þou þat wyth-holdyst þi seruauntys hyre, þou art a raueynour be goddys lawe, þat wyth-holdyst þise dettys', Brandeis, p. 129/14–17. The author of the *Speculum Christiani* lists under the sins of Britain which cry out for God's vengeance

Loke what degre God haþ þe sette,
Quyte hym þy dette, þy soule is his,
And resceyue þy dette, heuene blis.
Þere, thar þe noþer swynke ne swete,
And ordeyne þe wele and amende þy mys,   135
Þus wiþ God of pes 3e trete.

Caste þe not to couetys,
3e þat ry3twys werryours be,
But loke where ri3t querel lys,
Chastise þe rebell in charite.   140
Þere God is frend, his foomen fle,
3e thar not counte hem at o pete.
God doþ batayle, and not 3e;
Forthy wiþ God of pes 3e trete.

And 3e in batayle haue maystrie,   145
And fortune serue, and God 3ow spede,
Thank God þe victorie,
And holde it not 3oure owen dede.
Serue God in loue and drede,
And be not proud of 3oure by3ete.   150
After 3oure werkis wayte aftur 3oure mede,
And so wiþ God of pes 3e trete.

'fals wyth-holdynge of wages or dew dettes of seruantes or of eny other' (Holmstedt, p. 220/7–8).

139] ri3t querel. There may be no precise topical reference here but the diction is very similar to that used in Poem 13/113–20; diction which unmistakeably points to the legitimacy of the English claim to the French crown, see notes thereon.

140] rebell may have no topical referent; or could allude to a figure such as Sir John Oldcastle who organised a rebellion in 1413 and then subsequently escaped capture; see further, Introduction, pp. 7–10.

142] pete: this is an obscure word. Kail *Poems,* glossed it as a fibre of peat. More likely, however, though unattested in *MED*, is that the word means 'fart' from Middle French 'pete' see Barclay, *Egloges* IV, sig.Ciij, 'Though all their connynge scantly be worthe a pet' cited in OED.

143] The line is identical to Poem 13/111 in a context which explicitly makes reference to making war against France to recover the French crown.

147] Possibly 'for' has been omitted before 'victorie'.

149] The same formula is used in Poem 1/41/64 etc. and 8/85 and 18/106.

151] Cf. Poem 8/87.

3if a clerk haue, þurgh hap,
Cure of soules, or bischopriche,
He hat not bischop – he hat a by shap;   155
Make oþere after his werkis like,
To kepe his shep fro helle tike,
In folde go amonge hem blete,
Saf and sounde brynge hem ylyk
Bytwen God and hem to trete.   160

Benefice of holychirche first was graunted
For prestis holy lyf to lede;
Dryue out synne, suffre non be haunted,

153–60]   This is one of the most ingenious stanzas in the whole sequence. It takes the form
  of a witty turn on the pastoral trope that can be traced back to the words of Christ to
  Peter, 'feed my sheep' (John 21:17), and the trope of the 'good shepherd' (John 10:11), cf.
  note to Poem 8/28. The imagery is taken up in many pastoral manuals, e.g. Furnivall,
  Handlyng Synne, '… yche shepard 3yueþ no gode kepe,/Þat betecheþ þe wulfe hys shepe;/
  At þe last acounte shal he mysfalle,/whan he shal answere for hem alle;/And þe lorde
  shal þe shephard hate,/Þat wasteþ hys store …' (10883–8) and 'As þe gode shepard kepyþ
  hys shepe,/So shalle þe prest, hys parysshenes, kepe;/Þere shepe gone wrong besyde þe
  paþ,/Þe shepard cryeþ for drede of skaþe;/And 3yf þey wyl nat at hys crye/Turne a3en to
  here pasture nye,/Þan setteþ he on hys hounde,/And bayteþ hem a wel gode stounde,/And
  bryngeþ hem to her pasture weyll'. (10895–903).
155]   **bischop … by shap**. Kail, *Poems*, printed 'byshap' but there is clearly a space in the
  MS between 'by' and 'shap'. The sense of both of these words is far from certain, but
  MED does record the sense 'of association between persons: in (someone's) company
  or presence, with (sb.)' for 'bi' (*prep.*). **shap** may have the sense 'something created, a
  creature'; see *MED* 'shap(e)' (*n.*); 3a. If these identifications are secure, then the sense
  of the line is that if any cleric happen to have pastoral cure of souls, or to become a
  bishop, his true name is not 'bishop', but 'creature alongside'. In order to set an example
  to others a bishop needs to go into the sheepfold among his flock, bleating alongside
  them to protect them. The sound play between **schop** and **schap** would appear to pun on
  the verb 'shapen'; see *MED* 1b: to give a 'specific shape, form, fashion', 'give (sb.) shape';
  and 1c *ppl.* 'shapen', 'formed in a certain way; having a particular natural form, shape,
  construction, or character; arranged in a certain pattern'.
157]   **helle tike**: the hound of hell. A very similar image is used in 'How Men Ought to Obey
  Prelates', Matthew, *Works of Wyclif*, p. 32, 'shepe vnkept among þe wolues of helle'.
160]   **bytwen God and hem** stresses the role of priest as intermediary. It is the priest who
  has the care to clean the fleeces of his flock.
161]   **benefice … first was graunted**. The plea for a return to first principles would not
  look out of place in a Lollard tract (though obviously not the defence of benefices). But
  it is an example of the writer calling for the reform of the priesthood from within the
  institutionalised church. See also note to Poem 8/33.

Here non oþer to do his dede;
Þe werkman is worþy his mede,   165
In felde, in toun, and in strete.
Teche vnwys, helpe hem þat nede,
Byfore God for hem to trete.

In wordis, þey sayn þey wil do wel;
Take cure of soules as worthi clerkis,   170
And resceyue þe charge euery del
To wasche synful soules serkis;
Þey preue hemself fooles in werkis,
Wiþ holy water nele no parischen wete.
Caste away antecrist merkis!   175
Goþ wiþ God of pes to trete!

164]   Apart from the personal pronoun the line is identical to Poem 8/28, see note thereon
    for the conventional opposition between a true shepherd and a hireling.
165]   Cf. Poem 8/29 and note to Poem 2/40.
167]   **teche vnwys**. The importance of priests teaching the unlearned is stressed in Peacock,
    Myrc's Instructions, 'thy paresche Ʒerne teche' (l. 70). What, and how, they must teach
    ranges from the care of pregnant women, baptism, the duties of godparents, behaviour
    in church, the ability to say the paternoster and Creed and Hail Mary (ll. 404–535), and
    matters of church doctrine, e.g. 'Teche hem þenne wyth gode entent,/To be-leue on that
    sacrament' (ll. 244–5).
171]   **charge**: see note to Poem 8/17.
172–3]   **wasche ... serkis**. A conventional image of the priest's penitential duties to his
    parishioners, cf. Brandeis, *Jacob's Well*, p. 185/27–31, 'Ʒif þi scherte be vsyd al þe Ʒere
    vnwasschyn, be þe Ʒerys ende it is ryƷt foul. Þi lauendere may noƷt, þanne, wasschen
    it als whyƷt als clene as Ʒif it be wasschyn euery woke onys'. **serkis** is a Northern form
    but used in Digby for the rhyme on 'werkis'.
174]   A reference both to the sacrament of penance which continues the image of shirt-
    washing, and also harks back to the duty of the parish priest to baptise his parishioners,
    see Peacock, *Myrc's Instructions*, ll. 536–674.
175]   The stern imperatives of the narrative voice are an index of the urgency of church
    reform. The reference to **antecrist merkis** sails close into characteristically Lollard
    waters, given the tendency in Wycliffite texs to figure their opponents as Antichrist
    (e.g. Hudson, *Lollard Preacher*, E1226, E1656, and E1917), and to create an opposition
    between the true congregation of saved souls and Antichrist's institutionalised church
    on earth. The Pope is regularly referred to as 'antichrist', e.g. 'De Papa', Matthew,
    Works of Wyclif, p. 462/4/7, p. 463/26/30. It is tempting to see an appropriation of diction
    characteristically used in dissident contexts to urge orthodox reform (see further,
    Introduction, pp. 34–7).

Now sumwhat Y haue ȝow sayd
What is salue to ȝoure [sore].
To sauȝten wiþ God, holde ȝow payed,
And arraye ȝow wel þerfore   180
To resceyue God, ȝoure soules store,
His body in forme of brede o whete,
And kepe hym so ȝe nede no more
Eft of pes wiþ hym to trete.

Whan þu hast told al þy greuaunce,   185
Þan do as þe prest þe tauȝte,
Holde wel þy penaunce;
Repentaunce, [fol. 108a] forȝete þat nouȝt.
Whan ȝe wiþ loue God han lauȝt,
Neuere fro ȝow hym ȝe lete,   190
God brynge ȝow to his angels sauȝt,
Þere neuere nys nede o pes to trete.

177]   **Y haue ȝow sayd**. The tone here resembles that of a pastoral manual.
178]   **sore**. MS reads 'store' in anticipation of line 181. I have followed Kail's emendation. The same diction is used at Poem 7/109.
180–1]   **arraye ... resceyue**. The poem as a whole reads rather like a Lenten preparation for the receipt of the sacrament at Easter. Cf. the stress in Peacock, *Myrc's Instructions*, that the parishioners must be shriven before they receive communion on Easter Day, ll. 234–41, and in Weatherly, *Speculum Sacerdotale*, p. 66/30–2.
182]   **forme**. The precise nature of the sacrament is discussed more fully in Poem 23.
185]   **al**: a final stress on the completeness of confession; see note to line 44.
186]   **prest**: a final reminder of the importance of the role of the priest.
187–8]   Cf. notes to lines 17–20 and 33–6.
189]   **lauȝte**: *pa.ppl.* form of 'lacchen' in *MED* sense 4a 'to obtain'. There is a fine dissonance with **lete** which underscores the importance of not letting God go once he has been received.
190]   **sauȝt**. Preceded by the possessive **angels**, the word has the sense of 'rest', but lurking also in the line are the senses of 'reconciliation', 'peace' and even 'atonement'; see *MED* 'saught(e)' (*n.*); a.

Poem 10. A good steryng to heuenward

Kail dated this poem to 1411 (*Poems*, p. xvi). No explanation is given, but the implication is that this is where it should be placed in the chronological sequence. I think it is impossible to assign a date for this poem. It is an example of a popular kind of religious lyric in the 'complaint of Christ' tradition where the crucified Christ enumerates the sufferings accumulated in dying to redeem humans who, nevertheless, persist in their sinful ways. Poems 17 and 19 are written in a similar mode. The origins of these poems were the speeches of God in Lamentations 1:12, 'O all ye that pass by the way, attend, and see if there be any sorrow like to my sorrow', Micah 6:3, 'O my people, what have I done to thee, or in what have I molested thee? answer thou me,' and Isaiah 5:4, 'What is there that I ought to do more to my vineyard, that I have not done to it?' These biblical texts formed part of the Easter liturgy. An especially important source of inspiration for Poem 10 are the *Improperia*, or Good Friday reproaches, which comprise a series of ingenious antitheses. A number of English translations survive, see Woolf, *Religious Lyric*, pp. 36–8. Their structure and tone are important influences on the poet's singular version of this tradition, lines 65–8, 107–12. As such, this poem provides a continuation of the preoccupations of Poem 9 and acts as a Good Friday precursor to the evident Easter of Poem 11. The biblical texts cited above also provided an authority and structure for a complaint of Christ at the Last Judgement. God's Judgement and vengeance pervade the poem. What is singular in Digby's treatment of this type of lyric is the social inflection of the accusations, especially lines 99–106 and 127–40. The urgent reform of the clergy, especially their abuse of temporalities, is here put into the mouth of God.

The rhyme scheme of this poem is especially demanding, and calls for some word-coinage to fulfil its demands. But as a whole, this is a vigorously adroit piece of writing which still has the power to 'strike such terror in a fainting soul'.

10. A good steryng to heuenward

Many man is loþ to here
Repref of vices and werkis ylle;
For pride, hem þenkeþ hem Goddis pere
Þat welde þis worldis wele at wylle;
At a sarmon wil bid a frere   5
Make it short, or ellys be stylle.
Hym þat is loþ good to lere –
He shal, wheþer he wole, or nylle.
We fareþ as knaue þat takeþ his hyre byfore,
Serue his mayster wel þe worse þerfore.   10
Richesse and hele makeþ men vnkynde,
Þat Goddis seruyce is out of mynde,
For graceles, and gostly blynde,
Þe flesch distroyeþ soules store.

God seiþ, 'Man, Y made þe of nouȝt,   15
And put the in to paradys,

1–4]   In contrast to most other examples of this genre, the poem begins in the third person
with an axiomatic complaint that humankind is unwilling to hear reproof of sin, and
on account of pride think themselves equal to God. The need for repentance and the
acknowledgement of sin, the backbone of Poem 9, are thus the frame for this complaint.

3–4]   Cf. 'What More Could Christ Have Done', Brown, *Religious Lyrics XV*, p. 163/9–11,
'Wyth these grete gyftis þu cowdyst not be content,/Butt by grete presumpsioun Assentyst
to þe serpent;/by-cause þu woldyst be lyke god omnipotent'.

5]   Intriguingly, the only reference to friars in the poem. There is no suggestion that they
are corrupt, and this may be another example of the poet's conspicuously deafening
silence on matters that might be identified with dissidence.

11]   **vnkynde**: an important word in the poem. 'kynde' combines several senses in the
poem: ingratitude, disloyalty and unnaturalness. It is a keyword of complaint lyrics,
see note to line 61.

15]   Cf. Poem 8/3, 20/177 and 22/17. God's making of humankind out of nothing, yet
rewarding them with paradise and redemption, is an opposition seen often in religious
lyrics, e.g. 'How to Live Perfectly', Horstmann, *Vernon Poems* I.228/251–2, 'Whon þou
weor nouȝt, þen formed he þe,/Whon þou weore lore, þen fond he þe'. The source is
Genesis 2:7–8, 'And the Lord God formed man of the slime of the earth: and breathed
into his face the breath of life, and man became a living soul. And the Lord God had
planted a paradise of pleasure from the beginning wherein he placed man whom he
had formed.'

Of erþely þynges þat Y wrouʒt
To neme þat neded to þyn eys.
I lent þe fre wil and þouʒt,
Warnyng of foly to be wys;   20
At þe tre of wysdom foly þu souʒt,
And ʒaf for an appyl þe most of prys.
Þe same mouþ þat þe appyl gnewe,
In þat mouþ þe holy croys grewe,
Wheron Y dyed for ʒoure gylt.   25
Þurgh þe herte, and þurgh þe mylt;
I hadde þe poynt – and ʒe, þe hylt!
ʒoure heritage Y bouʒt ʒow newe.

17–18]   Cf. 'The Castle of Love', Horstmann, *Vernon Poems* I.359/182–3, 'God ʒaf him so muche miht/To welden al þis worldes winne', and 'Why Art Thou, Man, Unkind?', Brown, *Religious Lyrics XV*, p. 160/41–8, 'Whane I made þe to my lykenesse,/I made þe lorde Above all þynge,/And gave to þe all plentousnesse/Of fisshes þat arn in þe see swymmyng;/And ouer all bestes þat are crepynge/On erthe I made þe lorde to be,/And ouer all fovles in þe eyre fleynge/. Quid ultra debui facere?' The source is Genesis 1:26, 'let him have dominion over the fishes of the sea, and the fowls of the air, and the beasts, and the whole earth, and every creeping creature that moveth upon the earth'.

19]   Cf. Poem 17/151 and 'Why Art Thou, Man, Unkind?', Brown, *Religious Lyrics XV*, p. 161/81–5, 'I gave þe Reasoun and eyene clere,/To teche þe flee from all evyll;/And also erys þu hast to here,/And in þy sovle I sette fre vill./And now I hange on caluery hill'.

20]   Genesis 2:16–17, 'And he commanded him, saying: Of every tree of paradise thou shalt eat: But of the tree of knowledge of good and evil, thou shalt not eat. For in what day soever thou shalt eat of it, thou shalt die the death.'

23–4]   An ingenious turn on legends of the holy cross that describe how the seeds of the apple fell into the ground and formed the tree which became Christ's cross. The poet conflates the cross and Christ here, which together with the repetition of 'mouþ', creates a graphic image of redemptive suffering where the second Adam redeems the penalty of the first. **gnewe**, the rarer strong form of the preterite, completes the rhyme.

25]   Cf. Poem 17/116.

26]   **mylt**. The piercing of Christ's spleen is not a standard feature of crucifixion lyrics; but here it is chosen for the rhyme.

27]   An ingenious and pointed antithesis that imaginatively converts the lance which pieced Christ's side into a sword in order to show Christ's suffering at the hands of an indifferent human being.

28]   Cf. Poem 22/20.

3e þou3te 3e had not ynow:
Euere lastyng lyf, and euere more rest.   30
3e braken my byddyng; 3e benden a bow;
3e boten an appyl þat þirled my brest.
Wiþ water for synne, þe world Y slow,
Saue seuene, and Noe, þat was my gest.
My loue to man, it was so tow,   35
Hit lasted forþ, and nolde not brest.
For mannys loue, I come fro blisse to pyne;
Man was so pore he had not to fyne.
3oure gyltes greued God so sare,
3oure gyltes on my bak Y bare,   40
Þat God my fader nolde me not spare
Tyl He had 3euen my lyf for þyne.

My puple, where greued Y 3ow, or þyne,
But ladde 3ow þurgh þe see so rede,

29–30]   The selfishness of humankind is suggested here by greediness. Not content with
everlasting life, humankind (unnaturally) wanted more. The grasping nature of humans,
in contrast to Christ's generosity, is an important theme of the poem and modulates
into the imperative to take care of the poor on this earth, lines 203–5.

32]   One of the most powerfully imaginative lines in the whole sequence. Once again, the
poet conflates Adam's eating the apple with Christ's pain on the cross. The primal bite
is overlaid with the image of the lance which pierces Christ's side, here figured as **brest**
in order to secure the rhyme.

33–4]   Genesis 6:17, 'Behold I will bring the waters of a great flood upon the earth, to
destroy all flesh, wherein is the breath of life, under heaven. All things that are in the
earth shall be consumed.' **seuene** the number is exact: Noah was saved along with his
wife, their three sons and their wives, Genesis 7:13, 'In the selfsame day Noe, and Sem,
and Cham, and Japheth his sons: his wife, and the three wives of his sons with them,
went into the ark'.

35]   **tow**: the spelling of 'tough' (a word not used elsewhere) suggests a concern for
eye-rhyme.

37]   **blisse … pyne**: a formula reversed Poem 19/26 and 19/50.

38]   **fyne**. The rhyme produces an unusually intransitive form of the verb, but, theologically,
the choice is exact. The financial metaphor of humankind being unable to pay the
fine commutes into the theological point that humans are in debt to God on account
of original sin, and the only person able to pay that penalty is Christ, who, with his
supererogatory offering, pays more than he owes.

39–40]   Cf. Poem 11/103. **gyltes**. Given the financial metaphor, there may be a pun here
on 'guilt' *MED* (*n.*); 1; and 'gilt plate'; *MED* (*n.*); 3. **sare**. The Northern form is used to
secure rhyme; elsewhere in rhyme position the form is 'sore', see Poem 12/114, 19/11/73,
20/106, 21/33 and 24/387.

With Aaron and Moyses myn owen hyne,   45
And alle ʒoure enemys Y drowned to dede?
For ʒe shuld kepe lawe myne,
In wildernes Y made ʒoure stede,
To ʒow Y planted myn owen vyne,
And fourty ʒeer fed ʒow wiþ angels brede.   50
Wiþ loue Y dede ʒow my lawe to teche,
Bycom a man to be ʒoure soule leche;
Wiþ a spere, ʒe shed myne herte blod.
Þe pore, ʒe harme, and do no good;
ʒeue I chastyse, ʒe calle me wood,   55
And but ʒe mende, Y wol take wreche.

Man, hast þu ouʒt in mynde
Þe pyne Y suffred wiþ þe Iewes felle,
ʒoure soules of derknes to vnbynde?
[fol. 108b] I suffred deþ and heryed helle.   60
Answere me, man, was þu kynde?

43-50]   This account of God's protection of humankind, which is met only by ingratitude
and hostility, can be paralleled in other religious lyrics, e.g. 'A Dialogue Between Natura
Hominis and Bonitas Dei', Brown, *Religious Lyrics XV*, p. 165/25-9, 'Man, þo rede see I
partud in too,/owte of egypte qwen I browghte þe;/I was þy frynde, þu was my foo,/þu
in deserte haste for-sake me;/With awngels methe þer I fedde'. See also Gray, *Religious
Lyrics*, p. 28/4-14. The biblical sources are: Exodus 13:18, 'But he led them about by the
way of the desert, which is by the Red Sea: and the children of Israel went up armed out
of the land of Egypt'; Exodus 16:35, 'And the children of Israel ate manna forty years,
till they came to a habitable land: with this meat were they fed, until they reached the
borders of the land of Chanaan'. The knitting together of these episodes is seen in God's
rebuke to the Israelites, Jeremiah 2:6-7, 'And they have not said: Where is the Lord, that
made us come up out of the land of Egypt? that led us through the desert, through a
land uninhabited and unpassable, through a land of drought, and the image of death,
through a land wherein no man walked, nor any man dwelt?'

49]   **vyne**. Jeremiah 2:21, 'Yet I planted thee a chosen vineyard, all true seed: how then art
thou turned unto me into that which is good for nothing, O strange vineyard?'

57-70]   A stanza which is very close in temper to complaint lyrics and the *Improperia*.
See Gray, *Religious Lyrics*, pp. 26-31, Brown, *Religious Lyrics XIV*, p. 88/3 and p. 94/3 and
especially 'Why Art Thou, Man, Unkind?', Brown, *Religious Lyrics XV*, pp. 159-62.

61]   **kynde**. Many lyrics accuse humankind of ingratitude, ungraciousness, disloyalty and
unnaturalness, e.g. 'Vnkinde man, take hede of mee', Brown, *Religious Lyrics XV*, p. 158/1;
'Why art þu mane, vnkynde to me?', *Religious Lyrics XV*, p. 159/6; 'O man unkynde',
Gray, *Religious Lyrics*, p. 25/26b)/1.

Miȝt Y do more, canst þu me telle?
A betere frend, and þu can fynde,
Leue me, and go wiþ hym dwelle.
I do þe wele; why dost me woo?   65
I am þy frend; þu art my foo.
Þere Y ȝeue pes, þu makest debate,
Þere Y loue, þu dost hate,
And stekest me wiþoute þe ȝate;
My worldys goodis þu holdest me fro.   70

Man, þu dost as a thef
Þat ha[s]t holycherche gre;
Whan men wold take h[y]m wiþ repref,
Þat to chirche he wole fle.
So doþ man þat is in gref,   75
Or in syknes, þan calleþ he me.
And ȝut, man, þu art me so lef,
Wiþ mercy and ruþe Y bowe to þe.
Ȝif Y byd þe my lawe to fulfille,
Þu hauntest þy synne and wonest þeryn stille.   80

62]   **Miȝt Y do more** is an accusation found in a number of lyrics; its source Isaiah 4:5:
e.g., 'Popule meus quid feci tibi', Brown, *Religious Lyrics XIV*, p. 88/3, 'wat miht i mor ha
don for þe',; 'Christ pleads with His swete Leman', Brown, *Religious Lyrics XIV*, p. 94/3;
'What myght I do þe more' and 'A luytel tretys of Loue', Furnivall, *Vernon Poems* II.462/9
'What miht I more don þen þis?' See also Poem 19/15.

63]   **frend**. The spurning of God's friendship is a characteristic trope, see Woolf, *Religious
Lyric,* pp. 216–17, e.g. 'A Dialogue Between Natura Hominis and Bonitas Dei', Brown,
Religious Lyrics XV, p. 164/12, 'qwy flese þu, man? I am þi frynde' and p. 167/81–4, 'So
sykur a frende was newur borne,/to do so mycul for luf of me./ffor any oþur frenschyp,
I had bene lorne,/had þi passioun, lorde, ne be'. Cf. Poem 17/167.

66]   Cf. 'A Dialogue Between Natura Hominis and Bonitas Dei', Brown, *Religious Lyrics
XV*, p. 165/27 'I was þy frynde, þu was my foo'.

69–70]   The inhospitality of humankind in response to God's generosity is a trope seen in
other lyrics, e.g. Gray, *Religious Lyrics*, p. 39/6–9, 'Undo, my lef, my dowve dere!/Undo!
Wy stond y stekyn out here?/Ik am thi make!'

71–80]   The poet compares the repentant sinner who turns to God in time of trouble to a
thief who calls for grace by seeking the sanctuary of the church. But despite God's love
for sinful humankind, such that he grants him mercy, humans persist in sinning. *Mirk's
Festial* Sermon for Good Friday tells of, in this instance, not a thief, but a murderer who
seeks the sanctuary of the church when he sees the Good Friday procession, 'when he
saw all cristen men and woymen draw to chirch, forto worschip hor God, he þoȝt þat
Crist deyd þat day on þe cros for all mankynd, and put hym holy yn Godis mercy, and

Þu hatest all þat loue my name,
Þu wost þu seruest so gret blame.
How darst þu byd me, for shame,
To bowe to þe, or worche þy wille?

Man, þu to my lawe art knyt,   85
Why ha[l]dest þu were agaynes me –
My worldis goodis in hord to pyt
Fro pore þat þy breþeren be?
Art þu not warned by holy writ
I made, and bouȝte hem, as dere as þe?   90
Hit is wanhope goþ byfore ȝoure wit.
Þat ȝe hyde, ful bryȝt Y se,
For þe pyne Y dede for ȝow dryȝe,
Ȝeue þyn herte wiþ teres of þyn eyȝe,

ȝede to þe chyrch wyth oþyr men, to here and se Godys seruyce', Erbe, *Mirk's Festial*,
p. 123. The murderer is subsequently forgiven.

72] **hast**. MS reads 'hat', which makes little sense in conjunction with **gre**, 'favour or
protection', and a second-person verb is needed. The scribe could have accidentally
omitted medial 's'.

73] **hym**. MS reads 'hem', but a singular pronoun is clearly needed and I have emended.

81] **name**: possibly a reference to the popular devotion to the holy name of Jesus, see Woolf,
Religious Lyric, pp. 172–8. She quotes a devotion from John of Grimestone's preaching
book in which every line begins anaphorically with the word 'Ihesu', p. 178.

86] **haldest**: medial 'l' is omitted in the MS. I have followed Kail's emendation.

87–90] The biblical warning is probably the parable of the rich man told by Luke 12:18–21,
'And he said: This will I do: I will pull down my barns, and will build greater; and into
them will I gather all things that are grown to me, and my goods. And I will say to
my soul: Soul, thou hast much goods laid up for many years take thy rest; eat, drink,
make good cheer. But God said to him: Thou fool, this night do they require thy soul
of thee: and whose shall those things be which thou hast provided? So is he that layeth
up treasure for himself, and is not rich towards God.'

87] **pyt**: the spelling is used to secure the rhyme. If this has the sense of 'put', it is the
only example of the verb in rhyme position and elsewhere 'put' is the usual form, e.g.
Poem 3/25, 4/138/196. It is likely that it is a form of 'picchen', in the sense of 'thrust'.
No infinitive form of the verb is listed in *MED* 'picchen' (v.), though the past participle
'ipeȝt' is recorded.

90] Cf. Proverbs 22:2, 'The rich and poor have met one another: the Lord is the maker
of them both.'

94] Characteristic diction in complaint lyrics, cf. 'Homo vide quid pro te patior', Brown,
Religious Lyrics XIV, p. 88/7–10, 'Al þis i drey for loue of man,/But werse me dot, þat he
ne can/To me turnen onis is eyȝe,/þan al þe peine þat i dryȝe'.

Repente sore for þy trespas,   95
So ly3tly my3t þu come to gras,
To heuene to þat worþy plas,
To by3e to þe on rode gan dy3e.

Man, how darst þu my lawe preche
And telle þe articles of þe fay?   100
My wit word wiþ þy mouþ teche
And in þy werkis þu seyst hit nay?
Wiþ theues, and wiþ spouse breche,
Þu delest and rennest ny3t and day;
In pyne, þu sechest þyn owen wreche,   105
Thow temptest me to be wrappeful ay.
I mad þe wys, and fayre angels pere,
Þu makest þe fool, and foul fendis fere.
Þy ly3tnes þu spendest in harlotrye;
Þy strengþe, in wrappe and tyrauntrye,   110
Þy fayrenesse, in pryde and lecherye;
Þu settest at nou3t Y bou3t so dere.

To greue me, men þenke it game
To breke þe lawe þat Y þe bed.

95] **trespas**: both sin, and more specifically wrong doing, violation of God's **lawe** (l. 85),
see Alford, *Glossary*, p. 158.

96] **gras**. The same form is used Poem 17/148 to preserve eye-rhyme, elsewhere, both
medially, and in rhyme position, the form is 'grace', e.g. Poem 4/186, 9/47, 10/129/170,
12/49/61.

98] This line is corrupt. **by3e** is seen elsewhere (Poem 7/118 and 13/67), but it is possible
that there has been scribal attraction to **dy3e** which, while it produces a powerful internal
rhyme, makes little sense. While **by3e** is supplied with an indirect object, there is no
object in the line. It is hard to see what the original line might have been.

99–106] The switch in address here is startling. God suddenly rebukes hypocritical clergy.
They are accused of the kinds of sins that are treated in pastoral manuals and there is
no explicit topical political pointing, but I have not found another example of a lyric
influenced by the *Improperia* which abruptly turns the guns on the clergy. See further,
Introduction, pp. 39–40.

107–12] While antitheses form the basis of the *Improperia* and many complaint lyrics, the
oppositions here are reminiscent of the 'abuses of the age' topos seen in Poem 4/121–8 but
there is a close analgue in 'Mercy passes all Things', Furnivall, *Vernon Poems* II.662/133–
42, 'Now harlotrye for murþe is holde,/And vertues tornen in-to vice,/And Symonye
haþ chirches solde,/And lawe is waxen Couetyse;/Vr feiþ is frele to flecche & folde,/ffor
treuþe is put to luytel prise;/Vre God is glotenye and golde,/Dronkenes, Lecherye and
dyse:/Lo heer vr lyf and vre delyce,/Vr loue, vr lust and vre lykyng.'

In despyt, forswere [my] name,   115
By woundis Y had in handis and hed.
I do þe worschipe; þu dost me shame;
I ȝaf þe lyf; þu ȝaf me ded;
Mirre and galle to drynke wiþ grame,
I ȝeue þe my body in fourme of bred.   120
Ȝe fare wiþ me as gest his yn doth borwe –
Resceyue today, and put me out to [fol. 109a] morwe.
Agayn to synne whan ȝe go,
Shamely ȝe put me ȝow fro.
And ȝe desyre I be ȝoure foo.   125
Ȝe gete but wreche and dowble sorwe.

And ȝe defoule my holy place,
Þat turneþ þe chirche out of his gyse.
Holy chirche is spirytuall grace,
Þe duwe dette, deuyne seruyse.   130
Þey calle me as he þat no God was,
Þat cure of soules don despise;
Fro hem Y wole turne my face,
And calle hem as fooles, out casten fro wyse.
Þat sellen soules for temperal getyng,   135

115] **my** omitted in MS. **name**, cf. note to line 81.
116] **handis and hed**. The number of Christ's wounds varied: the five wounds referred to
the nails in each hand and foot, and the gash in Christ's side from the spear. But the
total could reach seven if Christ's circumcision were included, and, as here, the wounds
caused by the crown of thorns on Christ's head. The formula in Digby is also, however,
inflected through the demands of the rhyme.
116–20] The antitheses here are very close to those complaint lyrics informed by the
Improperia, 'Of the ston ich dronk to thee;/And you wyth galle drincst to me.' and 'Ich
yaf the croune of kynedom;/And thou yyfst a croune of thorn' (Gray, *Religious Lyrics*,
p. 29/28–9/32–3); cf. Poem 17/131.
121–2] Cf. note to lines 69–70.
127–40] As with lines 99–106, the charges against human lawlessness and ingratitude
suddenly turn to the sins of the clergy. The verse is as forthright as it is possible to be
against those who despise **cure of soules** (cf. Poem 9/153–60/169–76). Damnation will
be theirs.
133] **turne my face**, cf. Ecclesiasticus 18:24, 'Remember the wrath that shall be at the last
day, and the time of repaying when he shall turn away his face'.
135] **temperal getyng**, cf. Poem 8/60 and note to 8/57–64.

Þey maken skourges to here owe betyng.
Here good dayes ben wastyng,
And þey to helle hastyng,
To be wiþ fendes chastyng,
Fulfille on hem my thretyng.   140

My swerd is fyre þat brynneþ bry3t,
Shal shede þe ri3t fro þe wrong.
I brenne sheldis and swerdis in fy3t,
As whirlewynd Y skatre þe fals þrong.
No kyng shal be saued by his my3t,   145
Ne þe geaunt, be he neuere so strong.
Þat Y am God, 3e shal knowe ry3t;
Nes non bot I, endeles long.
3e may not serue two lordis to plese,
Fede fatte shep in greceles lese.   150
Þat plesen me, 3e holde hem nys;
Þat gyleþ þe world, 3e holde hem wys.
3e may not wynne wiþ 3oure delys
Here, and in heuene, boþe 3oure ese.

136]   skourges. The scourging of Christ before His crucifixion is here re-registered to create an image of the clergy bringing eternal punishment on their own heads.

141-8]   There is no exact scriptural source for this terrifying picture of God's vengeance on false priests, but the tenor of the verse is very similar to Hebrews 10:26-30, 'For if we sin wilfully after having the knowledge of the truth, there is now left no sacrifice for sins, But a certain dreadful expectation of judgement, and the rage of a fire which shall consume the adversaries. A man making void the law of Moses, dieth without any mercy under two or three witnesses: How much more, do you think he deserveth worse punishments, who hath trodden under foot the Son of God, and hath esteemed the blood of the testament unclean, by which he was sanctified, and hath offered an affront to the Spirit of grace? For we know him that hath said: Vengeance belongeth to me, and I will repay. And again: The Lord shall judge his people.'

145-7]   'Each Man ought himself to know', Furnivall, *Vernon Poems* II.674/85-96 warns mankind to think on Christ's sacrifice and remember that all worldly honour comes to nought, and given that even Arthur and Hector are dead, one should make amends for sin.

149]   Cf. note to Poem 8/30-2.

150]   Draws on Christ's injunction to 'feed my sheep', John 21:17, cf. note to Poem 8/28 and 9/153-60, but is somewhat dense. The implication appears to be that the clergy feed fat sheep (i.e. themselves) while allowing their flock to graze in grassless pasture.

153-4]   Cf. 'St Bernard on Man's three Foes', Furnivall, *Vernon Poems* II.521/199-200, 'Heore paradys þei hedden hyr,/And now þei liggen in helle-fyr'. Cf. Poem 1/123 and 8/79-80.

In this world to folk ful fele,   155
Goddis wordis þis myȝt be:
"Man, þu serued me not in þi wele,
Why shulde Y knowe þi pouerte?
Þu loued me not in þi hele,
In syknes why shulde Y rewe þe?   160
Fro my comaundement þu dede stele,
Of hem þu serued, fong þy fee".
Ȝet o God, þe fader of blysse,
Þe holy gost salueþ soule syknesse.
Þouȝ we agylte þe Godhed,   165
Mercy moueþ þe manhed,
For loue of his breþered;
Ȝeue mercy to mekenesse.

Ȝif man ligge long in synne,
And wilfully fleeþ fro grace,   170
To sharpe my wreche Y wole bygynne,
Take vengeaunce for his trespas.
His enemys, I wole leten hem ynne,
As bestes in forestes, ȝow to chas.
For drede, ȝe shal nowhere wynne,   175

155–60]   This rebuke is found in other complaint lyrics, e.g. 'Mercy passes all Things', Furnivall, *Vernon Poems* II.660/52–8, 'What hast þou suffred for my sake?/Me hungred, þou woldest not me fede,/Ne neuer my furst ne woldestou slake;/Won I of herborwe hedde gret nede,/Þou woldest not to þin hous me take;/Þou seȝe me among todes blake/fful longe in harde prison lyng.' The source is the account of the Last Judgement, Matthew 25:42–3, 'For I was hungry, and you gave me not to eat: I was thirsty, and you gave me not to drink. I was a stranger, and you took me not in: naked, and you covered me not: sick and in prison, and you did not visit me.' These lines are quoted in the entry for Good Friday in Weatherly, *Speculum Sacerdotale*, p. 113/4–25. The Digby poet is drawing on traditional materials in yoking the Good Friday *Improperia* with the reproaches at Judgement Day. See also note to Poem 1/149.

162]   Cf. Poem 19/24.

163–8]   Temporarily the narrator usurps the narrative voice from God, but God resumes narration at the start of the next stanza.

166]   Cf. Poem 19/108.

167]   **breþered**: a very unusual form of 'brotherhood' which looks to have been coined for the purposes of rhyme. It is not a form recorded in *MED* and elsewhere in the sequence the form is 'breþeren' Poem 10/88, 17/80, 18/185, 23/21 and 'brethern' 24/270. None of these is in rhyme position.

But fynde my wraþþe byfore here face.
I saued Moyses in þe rede see,
Ionas in whales wombe dayes þre,
Þre children in þe fyre so rede,
Dauyd slow Golyas to dede.   180
Do ȝe þe lawe þat Y hem bede,
And ȝe shal haue þe same degre.

[fol. 109b] Man, I can do þe erþe to shake,
Wiþ flood and drowtes, distroye ȝoure wele.
I chastise erþe, ȝe sample take;   185
I may sle, ȝeue lyf, and hele,
Fyre and thonder fro heuene make;
Nes non fro my strokes may stele;
At domesday, do ȝow alle quake,
Whan ȝoure owen werkis wole ȝow apele.   190
Þanne knaue, beggere, pore broþelyng
May apere wiþ pape, and wiþ kyng.
Þere shal non reuerence haue,
Ne mercy þouȝ þey wolde craue.
Here dedis shal hem deme or saue,   195
Þan alle to me shal ȝelde rekenyng.

Man, þe worldis good is myn:
How þu it spende, tak good hede;
Hit is myn, and not þyn.

177–80]   References to Moses crossing the Red Sea in Exodus 14:15–31; Jonah living for three days and nights in the belly of the whale before being spewed up alive, as told in the Book of Jonah 2:1; the saving of Sidrach, Misach and Abednago from the fiery furnace, Daniel 3:93; and David's slaying of the giant Goliath, Ecclesiasticus 47:5.

183–96]   The terrifying vengeance of God can be paralleled in other complaint lyrics, e.g. 'A Dialogue Between Natura Hominis and Bonitas Dei', Brown, *Religious Lyrics XV*, p. 166/57–64, 'Man, þe erthe I can do qwake,/for al þis word is in my hande;/ Vengans also I may take,/qwere me luste, one watur or lande./Be synus, tokunus & spekynge to,/my luf al-way þu myghte a-spye;/And for þu shulduste take hede þer-to,/ I lefte my myghte and toke mercy'. The Digby poem is more relentless in its threat of punishment and judgement than lyrics which hold out the promise of mercy if humankind repent.

198]   Cf. line 208 and Poem 1/31 and 8/7.

199]   Cf. Poem 19/36.

No more þan þu hast of nede,   200
Not to fostre þe as a swyn,
Þy foule flesche in fylþe to fede,
And leue þe pore in hunger and pyn,
And fynde hem noþer foode ne wede.
And pore folk in þy defaute dyӡe,   205
Wiþ Diues in pyne þu shalt lyӡe.
For þu shuld ӡeue God dede þe sende,
Tak kep how þu it spende,
For þat leueþ þe byhende,
Þow, man, rekene or þe abyӡe.   210

200]   Seems deficient, and it is possible that the imperative 'Tak' or a similar verb has
been omitted from the start of the line.

204-5]   The poet returns to the account of the Last Judgement from Matthew, see note
to lines 155–60.

206]   **Dives** refers to the story of Dives and Lazarus as told by Luke 16:19–25. The import
of the poet's reference is seen in the following verses (22–5), 'And it came to pass, that
the beggar died, and was carried by the angels into Abraham's bosom. And the rich man
also died: and he was buried in hell. And lifting up his eyes when he was in torments,
he saw Abraham afar off, and Lazarus in his bosom: And he cried, and said: Father
Abraham, have mercy on me, and send Lazarus, that he may dip the tip of his finger
in water, to cool my tongue: for I am tormented in this flame. And Abraham said to
him: Son, remember that thou didst receive good things in thy lifetime, and likewise
Lazareth evil things, but now he is comforted; and thou art tormented.'

209]   **byhende**, see note to Poem 17/49.

210]   **rekene**, cf. notes to Poem 1/29/35.

Poem 11. God & man ben made atte on

After the stern calls to penance and God's rebukes in Poems 9 and 10, the Digby poet turns from Lent to Easter. Kail, *Poems,* dated this poem to 1412, but, although the lyric invokes no specific contemporary time-frame, it forms a spiritual and liturgical companion piece to the 1413 Easter Poem 12. Starting with the liturgical 'alleluya', the poet marks Easter day as a time of celebration and thanksgiving for God's victory over his enemies. The refrain of the poem stresses reconciliation and harmony through structuring the first half of the poem around five 'saw3tenyngs' (reconciliations, cf. Poem 9/179) and with the repeated rhyme 'on'. Thanksgiving modulates quickly into stern moralising: while the joy of redemption is celebrated, from line 65, God's voice takes over the narrative and transforms the poem into a complaint of Christ lyric which reprises Poem 10. Throughout, the writing is sprightly and vigorous with crisp use of antithesis and assonance to assert victory from apparent defeat, and the obligation to observe God's sacrifice with proper devotion and love.

11. God & man ben made atte on

Glade in God þis solempne fest,
Now Alleluya is vnloken!
Þenkeþ how God, lest and mest,
On oure enemys haþ vs wroken,
Þat hadde vs in cheynes stoken,   5
Wrappid in synnes many on.
Þe fendis are flowen; þe cheynes are broken;
And God and man are wel at on.

First, whan God wiþ man was wroþ,
Þat Adam forfeted for his vys,   10

1]   **solempne fest**, cf. Weatherly, *Speculum Sacerdotale*, which observes that 'the solempnyte
of Paske … is syngulerly to be worschippid ouer alle the festes of the yere. And þerfore
if is callyd þe solempnyte of solempnytees, for in it oure saueoure rose fro deþ and by
his resurreccion he ʒaue to vs a certeyne hope of oure aʒeyn rysynge' (p. 117/9–13).

2]   **Alleluya … vnloken**. During Lent, the Alleluya was not sung at the Mass. Its return
at the Easter Mass signalled the joy of Christ's resurrection. See Introduction, pp. 31–2
for the political significance of the liturgy.

3]   **mest** is used for rhyme, Poem 24/10/12. Elsewhere (12 instances) the form is 'most'
and seen in rhyme position Poem 23/87. The variation shows the poet raiding dialect
diversity to secure rhyme.

4]   **oure enemys … wroken**. The crucifixion is presented in the familiar terms of a battle
won; enemies (the devils defeated) and with Christ as a triumphant hero, see further,
Woolf, *Religious Lyric*, pp. 52–4. The triumphalism is not without secular suggestion,
especially when read in conjunction with lines 82 and 84 and the discussion of enemies
of the realm in Poem 12/26/29, 13/123/138 and 156.

5]   **stoken**: the conventional form of the past participle of 'stiken' is '(ge)stikede'. The poet
converts to a strong verb formation in order to secure rhyme.

7]   The use of isocolon and assonance stiffens the texture of the line and creates a sense
of affirmative victory.

8]   **at on**. The refrain stresses unity and harmony which is appropriate for Easter time, cf.
Holmstedt, *Speculum Christiani*, on the effects of receiving the sacrament at Easter, 'it
ioyneʒ more stronge the menbres to the hede, that es gude cristen men to Criste', p. 182/15–
17. The refrain anticipates the combining of spiritual and political corporateness in Poems
12 and 13. There is a greater density of rhyming on the same word in this poem than
elsewhere in the sequence, and the rime riche of 'on/on' (see also lines 62/64 and 78/80)
may be part of the concern to stress wholeness (see further, Introduction, pp. 42–50).

9–16] The whole stanza is infused with legal vocabulary to assert the rightfulness of the
redemption and God's entitlement to ransom the souls of sinners, cf. Schmidt, *Piers
Parallel Text*, B.Passus 18.380–404.

10]   **forfeted**: to overstep the bounds, transgress or offend, Alford, *Glossary*, p. 62.

Man to angels was so loþ,
Þey dreuen hym out of paradys.
To amende here foly, God so wys,
Wiþ fals Iewes, let hym slon.
Here raunsom was his blod o prys;   15
So was God and man at on.

And ȝit a ferly more byfelle,
Þat God dede þurgh his grete myȝt –
Þe soules he loued, he fet fro helle,
To paradys among his angels bryȝt.   20
Hem þouȝte þat was a wonder syȝt,
Among here frendes brynge here foon:
Al on wrong, God made riȝt;
So made God angels and man at on.

The þridde sawȝtenyng mowe ȝe proue: 25
When posteles stryuen for hiȝe degre,
God spak to hem a word of loue,
And seyde, 'Pes wiþ ȝow be,
Elles ȝe may not folwe me,

12]   **dreuen**: an example of the dialect diversity of the sequence. Elsewhere the form is 'dryue(þ)' Poem 3/120, 7/26, 23/29.

13]   **amende**: to make satisfaction for the sins of others and/or to correct, reform, Alford, *Glossary*, p. 5. As in Langland's usage of the word, the two senses are difficult to distinguish. The sense of reparation, or compensation in an unequal bargain, is also relevant.

14]   **fals** carries a sense of deceit or criminality, Alford, *Glossary*, p. 54. **slon**, possibly 'be', has been omitted before this unusual form of the past participle.

15]   **raunsom**: the redemption of souls through the payment of Christ's blood, Alford, *Glossary*, p. 126. Cf. Schmidt, *Piers Parallel Text*, B.18.353 and Furnivall, *Handlyng Synne*, 5294, 'My blode y ȝaf for hys raunsun'.

17]   **ferly**. The stanza invokes vocabulary more familiar from romance contexts to stress the extraordinary reparation of the Redemption; see also **wonder** line 21 and cf. the reregistration of romance diction in Schmidt, *Piers Parallel Text*, B.Prol.4–6.

19]   **fet**: to recover what is rightfully one's own, Alford, *Glossary*, p. 56.

22–3]   **frendes ... foon ... wrong ... riȝt**. The use of alliteration and isocolon highlights the antitheses; the crispness of the line forms a sharp contrast to the antithetical reproaches of Poem 10.

26–30]   A confection of biblical texts lies behind these remarks: the competition for supremacy among the disciples is drawn from Luke's account of the last Supper: 'And there was also a strife among them, which of them should seem to be the greater' (Luke 22:24). Both Luke and John record that when Jesus appeared to his disciples on

But ȝe will in my gates gon.'   30
So God bond man in charite;
Byddis man and man be wel at on.

The ferþe sawȝtenyng God vs tauȝte
Þat best may kepe eche in state:
Let body and soule togydre be sauȝte,   35
Kepe God [fol. 110a] wiþyn ȝoure ynnere ȝate.
For who so loueþ þere God doþ hate,
Is bersell to his owen flon;
We ben vnkynde wiþ God debate,
For euere he profreþ to ben at on.   40

The fyfte sawȝtnyng: synne refuse!
Let eche man haue þat shulde ben his.
On mannys syde, repentaunce doþ arise,
And on Goddys syde mercy is.
Þay treteþ of pynes, and of blis;   45
Repentaunce makeþ wepyng mon,

the evening of his resurrection, he stood in their midst 'and saith unto them, Peace be
with you' (Luke 24:36; John 20:19). Jesus addresses the same words to Thomas eight days
later (John 20:26). Line 29 recalls Jesus's words to his disciples in front of the multitude,
Mark 8:34–5, 'And calling the multitude together with his disciples, he said to them: If
any man will follow me, let him deny himself, and take up his cross, and follow me.
For whosoever will save his life, shall lose it: and whosoever shall lose his life for my
sake and the gospel, shall save it' (cf. Matthew 16:24).

30] **gates**: in the sense here, not of gates to a kingdom, but 'way' or 'mode of behaviour';
see *MED* 'gate' (*n.*); 2.5a.

31–2] **bond** puns on the two senses of 'binden': 'to join'; *MED* 'binden' 3a; and 6a: 'to
impose', or 8: 'to pledge allegiance'. Cf. 1 John 4:12, 'If we love one another, God abideth
in us, and his charity is perfected in us'. The sentiment anticipates the topical inflection
of the Easter significance of poem 12.

34] Cf. line 64.

36] **ynnere ȝate**, cf. lines 65–70 and Poem 17/110 and note to Poem 10/69, where there is
a similar blend of devotional and secular household imagery.

38] **bersell ... flon**: a variation on the proverb that one's arrow returns to hit the shooter,
see Whiting, *Proverbs*, p. 14 A.182 and Barclay, *Ship of Fooles*, 213, 'his owne dartis
retourne to him agayne', quoted Whiting, *Proverbs*, p. 117, D.22.

39] **vnkynde**, cf. Poem 9/31 and 10/61. **wiþ God debate** cf. Poem 10/67.

40] **profreþ**, cf. Poem 17/15.

42] The line is identical to Poem 14/59 and very close to 1/116 and 14/66.

42–7] Cf. Wisdom 11:24, 'But thou hast mercy upon all, because thou canst do all things,
and overlookest the sins of men for the sake of repentance.'

When repentaunce and mercy kys,
Þan is God and man at on.

Thow made not þy self, God dede þe make;
Put soule of resoun in flesche so frele.   50
God can leue, God can take,
Richesse, strengþ, fayrnesse, and hele.
He is victorye in batayles fele;
Can sle soule, blod, and bon.
Nes non fro his strokes may stele;   55
Glade in God, ȝe ben at on!

God ȝaf erþe to mankynde,
And heuene to hem þat wole be wys.
Þat holden his lawe, haue hym in mynde;
And helle to hem þat wole be nys.   60
In oure fre wille, þe choys it lys,
Heuene or helle, to haue that on:
In heuene, and ȝe wole haue delys,
Let body and soule be wel at on.

God may say, 'Fernȝere, folk were fayn   65
To resceyue me ymydde here brest;

47] The line is almost identical to Poem 24/63.

51–5] Cf. note to Poem 1/95.

56] The poet's injunction forms the first line of the next poem.

57–60] An ingenious spin on the spiritual topography of earth, heaven and hell. Taking as his starting point Genesis 1:26, 'And he said: Let us make man to our image and likeness: and let him have dominion over the fishes of the sea, and the fowls of the air, and the beasts, and the whole earth, and every creeping creature that moveth upon the earth,' the poet extends the geographical reference to explain that heaven will be the domain of the wise and hell the final resting place of those fools who disdain both God and his law.

61–2] Similar reminders that humankind has free will and can choose whether to follow a path that leads to redemption or to damnation are seen at Poem 3/167, 7/108, 10/19 and 17/151.

62] **on**. It is possible that this is a scribal error for 'won' in the sense of dwelling, cf. line 94, but since the poet unusually rhymes on slightly different senses of the same word in this poem, I have not emended.

65–70] The narrative moves into God's voice and the tenor is close to complaint lyric.

66] **resceyue me ymydde her brest**. The Eucharistic image of receiving the sacrament is conflated with letting God into one's heart.

On morwe, þey put me out aȝayn –
In my palays, þey made þe fendis nest.
To lityl whyle Y was here gest;
My loue, Y loste; Y make my mon'.   70
Let God now lengere wiþ ȝow rest;
Now God and man is wel at on.

Folk þat were fendis fere,
Sulpid in synne derk as nyȝt;
Now are þey fayre angels pere,   75
As shynyng sune in Goddis syȝt.
Ȝe haue resceyued ȝoure God of myȝt;
Ayþer in oþer ȝoure wille is on.
Ȝoure hertys were heuy; þey may be liȝt:
Glade in God – ȝe ben at on!   80

68] **palays ... gest**. Instead of admitting God into their lives, homes and hearts, humankind has spurned Him. The narrator urges his readers to take the occasion of receiving God's body at Easter to make Him a permanent visitor and ensure a lasting reconciliation.

70] **Y make my mon** is informed by the *Improperia* of the previous lyric, cf. notes to Poem 10/69–70 and 155–9. Woolf lists several lyrics which employ the trope of Christ returning from battle only to be shut out of doors by his lover, the soul, *Religious Lyric*, pp. 50–2. They draw on a tradition of religious lyrics which have their source in Song of Solomon 5:2, 'I sleep, and my heart watcheth; the voice of my beloved knocking: Open to me, my sister, my love, my dove, my undefiled: for my head is full of dew, and my locks of the drops of the nights', and Revelation 3:20, 'Behold, I stand at the gate, and knock. If any man shall hear my voice, and open to me the door, I will come in to him, and will sup with him, and he with me.' See fuller discussion of the fusion of biblical and household tropes, Introduction, pp. 53–5.

72–5] Refers to Christ's harrowing of hell and the redemption. The souls are figured as having been transformed from being the companions, **fere**, of devils (cf. Poem 20/182) polluted with sin, to the peers of angels like the shining sun. See also Poem 10/107–8.

77] **resceyued**: the receipt of the sacrament of the Eucharist.

78] Penitential handbooks observe how the receipt of the sacrament restores concord and unity to the community. Communicants are advised that they must settle any discord between themselves and another before they take communion, e.g. Weatherly, *Speculum Sacerdotale*, p. 122/28–30, 'ȝif that we be in discorde with eny man, we moste first be reconsilyd with hem, for ellis we take dome to vs'. Cf. Matthew 5:23–4, 'If therefore thou offer thy gift at the altar, and there thou remember that thy brother hath any thing against thee; Leave there thy offering before the altar, and go first to be reconciled to thy brother: and then coming thou shalt offer thy gift'.

Man, and 3e holde my lawe,
All þyn enemys shal þe drede;
And þou stonde of me non awe,
Þyn enemys outeray þe in dede.
For þere as I my frendis lede,   85
Þey shul not sporne at stok ne ston;
In all here werkis, þey shal wel spede,
3if God and man be wel at on.

Myn enemys Y shal reue here sy3t;
3eue syknes, and drede, pouert and wo.   90
My frendis, Y 3eue sy3t and my3t,
Richesse, strengþe, ouer here foo.
Hem thar not drede where þey go;
Here wele and worschip in euery won.
Siþ 3e be syker, kepe 3ow so,   95
Now God and 3e are [fol. 110b] wel at on.

Man, Y aske no þyng of þyn,
For loue my loued in helle Y sou3t;
3eue me þy loue; þy soule is myn,

81]   The importance of holding God's law reprises line 59 and is stressed again at line 114.

81-96] God's support for those who hold allegiance to Him, and his vengeance against
those who spurn him, revisits God's threats and promises in Poem 10/169–96, see notes
thereon.

82]   **enemys**. While there is not explicit comment, these remarks are pertinent both to
spiritual enemies and enemies of the political realm.

93]   **drede where þey go**, cf. the same sentiments at Poem 3/108/157–9 and 9/141.

97-104]   Christ's appeal to humankind to return His love and to think on the suffering
He underwent in order to win it is part of a long tradition of religious lyric writing
with Christ figured as the wounded lover imploring and reproaching his beloved to
reciprocate his love (Woolf, *Religious Lyric*, pp. 58–66). Examples are in Gray, *Religious
Lyrics*, nos 42, 43 and 45. The wordplay of this stanza, is reminiscent of the rhetorical
strategies of the *Ancrene Wisse* '3ef þi luue nis nawt to 3eouene, ah wult þet me bugge
hire – buggen hire? Oþer wiþ luue, oþer wiþ sumwheat elles, me suleþ wel luue & swa
me ah to sulle luue & for na þing elles. 3ef þin is swa to sullen, ich habbe iboht hire wiþ
luue ouer alle oþre', Shepherd, p. 25/13–18. In Digby, anaphora and polyptoton create a
rhetorical bond between God's **loue**, the soul's **loue** and the **loued**. See further analysis
of the poet's word craft, Introduction, pp. 63–4.

97]   **þyn**. The sense of this is that God demands nothing that belongs to humankind since
the soul belongs to Him **myn** (l. 99).

99]   Much of the rhetorical power of this stanza depends on the skilful manipulation of

Or ȝeue it hym þat haþ it derrere bouȝt.   100
Suffre pyne for þe, me nedid nouȝt,
In hed, in hand, in foot, ne ton.
Ȝoure gyltis Y bare in herte and þouȝt;
I made my fadir and ȝow at on.

Sum of my kyndenes ȝe myȝte me quyte;   105
Do [þe] wordis of my comandement:
My name, my py[n]e, take not in despite;
Rule wel þy selue in good atent;
Thow nost how sone be after sent,
To ȝelde rekenyng of Goddis lon.   110
The rolles of rerage þe fendis han brent;
For God and man is wel at on.

pronouns. The patterning dissolves a clear sense of **me, þy** and **myn**, and the blurring of clear subject boundaries and possession delicately articulates the state of God and man being **at on**.

100]   **haþ** is the MS reading which Kail, *Poems,* omitted in his emendation of the line. He does not explain why, and as the line stands as written, I have not altered it. **derrere** God speaks here with taunting irony. Who has redeemed humankind at a greater price than God?

102]   A more conventional listing of Christ's wounds (cf. note to Poem 10/116). The asyndeton intensifies the suffering with its monosyllabic catalogue.

105]   **kyndenes,** cf. notes to Poem 9/31 and 10/61. **quyte** has the sense of to repay a debt or to make amends, Alford, *Glossary,* p. 125. Underlying this line is a challenge to man's 'unkyndenes' or 'ungratefulness' in the sense of reciprocating kindness with contempt, Alford, *Glossary,* pp. 73–4.

106]   **þe wordis.** The MS reads 'þre' but I think that this is a mistake for **þe**. It is not clear to what *three* words might refer.

107]   God invokes the words of the commandment: 'Thou shalt not take the name of the Lord thy God in vain' (Exodus 20:7). **pyne** the MS reads 'pyle' which could refer to Christ's skin, but it would be an oblique use of synecdoche to refer to Christ's passion, and it seems more likely that it is a copying error.

110–11]   **rekenyng.** This is the most extended use of the fusion of spiritual and secular accounting, cf. note to Poem 1/29 and 35. **lon** has a legal sense of loan or debt (Alford, *Glossary,* p. 90), and **rerage** previously used at Poem 8/100 and 9/103, has the sense of unpaid debt or the balance due on a debt, Alford, *Glossary,* p. 10. While the devils have burned the **rolles** or documents which create a legal sense of what humankind owes God, the reckoning of God's loan isn't entirely cancelled out. It is no longer within the devil's jurisdiction; it lies within God's. God's act of love and kindness has cancelled the debt of original sin, but it is still incumbent on human beings to reciprocate God's act of kindness by observing his law, ruling themselves in good estate, and reciprocating the act of love performed in the passion on the cross.

And þu me loued, þou wolde me leue,
And do my lawe, and holde it trewe.
How myȝtest þou me more repreue   115
Þan leue my lawe and tak[e] newe?
Þy vyces wole make þy soule to rewe,
In derkenes, neuere sonne shon;
Vertues shyne bryȝt of hewe,
Holde Goddis lawe; ȝe ben at on!   120

113–14]   The love-longing of lines 97–104 and the legalistic obligations of lines 105–12 are
brought together in this final stanza. The argument is that if humankind did love God,
they would believe in him and observe His law. There can be no greater reproof to God
than to abandon His law and take another. The comments reprise Poem 10/85–6/114. The
final stanza knits up the key concerns of this lyric: joy at Easter reconciliation; the need
to be obedient to God's law and to requite his suffering for humankind if the transfor-
mation of darkness into light accomplished by Christ's resurrection (lines 118–19) is to
be replicated in the fate of every individual soul.

Poem 12. God kepe oure kyng and saue the croune

Kail, *Poems,* transposed the two clauses of the title in the manuscript; the correct reading is here restored. The poem is also edited by Robbins, *Historical Poems,* pp. 45–9. He gives a modern title, 'God Save King Henry V (1413)' but also prints the correct order of the title in the MS. Kail dated the poem to 1413. While the poem does indeed take its impetus from the coronation of Henry V in 1413, it may also refer to events as late as 1414. For detailed discussion of the dating of this lyric, see Introduction, pp. 6, 10, 15–16. As a whole, Poem 12 is not triumphalist. While it endorses the new reign and expresses confidence in the new King, the Easter theme of concord and harmony is used to warn against the dangers of internal dissension. The emphasis on wholeness symbolised by the poet's exegesis of the crown does not efface the anxiety about past and future factionalism. Anxiety is also clearly present in the lines which warn about the predatory wiles of England's external enemies. Here as elsewhere, the poet advocates proper regard for the parliamentary commons, and for their voice and for their needs to be heeded. As in Poem 15, mutual interdependence between the king, his subjects and all estates is emphasised. The last stanzas of the poem call for a return to the glory days of England, but it is a call dogged by diction of 'werre … among vs', 'fi3t … among oure self', 'shent', 'lorn', and 'skorn'.

12. God kepe oure kyng and saue the croune

Glade in God, call hom ȝoure herte!
In ioye and blisse, ȝoure merþe encres,
And kepe Goddis lawe in querte.
Þes holy tyme, lete sorwe ases;
Among oure self, God sende vs pes.   5
Þerto, eche man be boun
To letten fooles of here res;
Stonde wiþ þe kyng, mayntene þe croun.

What doþ a kynges crowne signyfye
Whan stones and floures on sercle is bent?   10

1] **Glade in God** reprises the first line of Poem 11 and alludes to the receipt of the sacrament of the Eucharist.

2] **ioye ... blisse ... merþe**. Scattergood, *Politics and Poetry*, notes that Henry V's accession was greeted with enthusiasm by most contemporary poets, pp. 126-7, see especially 'Balade to Henry V at Kennington', Hoccleve, *Minor Poems*, IV.1-8.

4] **sorwe ases** fuses spiritual and political connotations: the end of Lent, penitence and God's passion are mapped on to the end of the troubles of Henry IV's reign.

5] **Among oure self**. The anxiety about internal dissension can be gauged from the repetition of this phrase at lines 33, 129 and 146.

7] **fooles ... res**. Scattergood, *Politics and Poetry*, p. 128, suggests that this line might refer to the small-scale conspiracies in the earlier part of Henry V's reign; in 1413, shortly after his accession, a conspiracy organised by a John Wightlock, once a groom in the household of Richard II, was discovered. He and his accomplices attempted to excite revolt against Henry, as they had done against his father, by spreading the rumour that Richard II was still alive and would return to claim his throne. If the poem were written in 1414, but with an eye cast back to the hopes expressed at Henry's coronation, then the rebellion organised by John Oldcastle is also a likely target of the remarks. A precise topical reference is entirely plausible, but the narrator speaks in his characteristic axiomatic voice. Warnings against fools and folly are rife throughout the sequence, e.g. Poem 1/46/ 58/153, 3/39, 7/11, 13/79, and Poem 16, which is written in 'the follies' tradition.

9-24] The extended analogy of the crown, with the stones interpreted to signify a realm working in unity and concord bears comparison with *Richard the Redeless*, I.120-35. Here, too, the allegory of the properties of the crown is placed within a coronation context. Gower interprets the king's crown as a symbol of its moral excellence, *Confessio*, VII.1751-82. See Introduction, pp. 45-7, for analysis of the political significance of the image of the stones set in a circle as a model of the incorporated estates of the realm (lines 9-16).

10] **is**: grammatically incorrect as there are plural antecedent nouns, but there is no evidence of scribal corruption.

Lordis, comouns, and clergye
To ben all at on assent.
To kepe þat crowne, take good tent
In wode, in feld, in dale, and downe:
Þe leste lyge man wiþ body and rent –   15
He is a parcel of þe crowne.

What signyfyeþ þe stones aboute?
Richesse, strengþe, and gret bounte;
Oure townes, and castels, þe reme wiþoute –
Þey are oure stones of gret pouste: 20
In pes, þey kepe all þis contre,
Holynes, contemplacioun.
God let hem neuer skaterid be,
And saue þe kyng, and kepe þe crowne.

11]   The narrator invokes the conservative three estates model to produce an image of
political harmony, but the extended body politic analogy of Poem 15 shows awareness that
the demographic stratification of community is rather more complicated and nuanced.

12]   **at on assent**, cf. Poem 13/2. There may be influence of parliamentary discourse here: in
the 1410 Parliament, the speaker, Thomas Chaucer, remarked that all the estates of the
realm had come for the common good and profit of the king and the realm and 'with one
assent and one accord to bring about unity and union', *PROME*, January 1410: Item 10.

14]   The polysyndeton helps to secure the rhyme, but also attests to the scrupulous
universality of protecting the crown in every part of the realm.

15]   **leste lyge man**: one of many examples of the poet's concern for the more vulnerable
members of the political community; cf. Ecclesiasticus 32:1–3, 'Have they made thee ruler?
be not lifted up: be among them as one of them … that thou mayst rejoice for them, and
receive a crown as an ornament of grace and get the honour of the contribution.'

16]   **parcel** has a precise legal sense, that of an allotted share or portion, Alford, *Glossary*,
p. 109; diction which asserts both the political importance of the commons and the
corporateness of the community. The least powerful are not to be patronised but to be
partners in maintaining the crown.

17–24]   These lines extend the image of the crown by describing the precious stones as
powerful buttresses against war, whether internal or external is not made clear.

18]   Cf. similar formulation Poem 11/52/92.

19]   **reme wiþoute**: throughout the realm. The poet compares the durability of the precious
stones of the crown to the fortifications provided by towns and castles.

20]   **pouste** occurs also in rhyme position Poem 23/31 and 92. As here, the poet rhymes
only on the final 'e'.

22]   Prompted by the mention of **pes** (21) the poet swerves abruptly from considering
military defence to religious qualities vital for a harmonious realm.

23]   Cf. *Richard the Redeless*, I. 95 and *Mum and the Sothsegger*, 'Hovgh the coroune moste be
kept fro couetous peuple,/Al hoole in his hande and at his heeste eke,/That euery knotte of
the coroune close with other,/And not departid for prayer ne profit of grete' (ll. 1–4).

Byȝonde þe see, and we had nouȝt,   25
But all oure enemys so neyȝe vs w[o]re,
Þouȝ all here gold were hider brouȝt,
I wolde set hit at lytel store.
Oure enemys wolde coke þerfore,
Wiþ ordynaunce, and habergeoun,   30
Wynne þat, and wel more:
Oure landes, oure lyues, þe reme, þe crowne.

Ȝif we among oure self debate,
Þan endeþ floure of chyualrie:
Alle oþere londis þat doþ vs hate,   35
Oure feblenes wole aspye.
On euery syde, þey [fol. 111a] wole in hye;
Þe stalworþe cast þe feble adoun,
Ȝif þey wiþ myȝt haue maystrye,

26]   **wore.** MS reads 'were' (l. 26). This could be understood in the sense of 'to mount an attack' *MED* 'weren' (*v.*); 1.4a, but it ruins the rhyme scheme. I have emended to **wore** in the sense of 'trouble, disturb' *MED* 'woren' (*v.*); 1b.

27]   Truces secured through monetary settlements, this stanza argues, will not dispel external foes; they will return to win even more territory and even the crown. See further Poem 13/137–44 and note to 13/128–36, where hostility towards truces is stated more clearly.

33]   **debate.** The anxiety over internal division and the importance of avoiding debate is seen also Poem 3/113–20, 5/25, 15/125 and 21/91. See also note to line 85, and Introduction, pp. 44–5.

34]   **floure of chyualrie**, the only use of this phrase in Digby. In Chaucer the phrase is used of individual knights: Theseus, Arcite, Averargus and (ironically) Sir Thopas. In Lydgate's *Troy Book* it refers to individual Greeks. While in Digby, it could refer to Henry V, there appears to a more widespread application to the English nobility. Cf. 'Truth is Ever Best', Furnivall, *Vernon Poems* II.700/41–4, 'Wolde we rule us al wiþ trouþe,/And mak him hollych vr gouernour,/We schulde keuere out of synne & slouþe,/And of Chiualrye bere þe flour'.

35]   **alle oþere londis … hate.** England was under threat from a number of enemies. As William Stourton, the speaker in Henry V's first parliament makes clear, these included the Scots, the Welsh, and the Irish (see *PROME*, 1413: Items 9 and 10). The situation with France was also perilous; as a result of the civil war that had broken out (see note to line 85), the fate of Calais hung in the balance, and it was unclear whether John of Burgundy would seek Henry V as an ally or as an opponent.

39]   **myȝt … maystrye.** The bishop of Winchester, chancellor of England who opened Henry's first parliament, singled out three matters in particular on which the king wished to have parliamentary advice: the proper and effective support of his high royal estate, good governance and the upholding of laws within the realm and the 'nurturing of his

Fro þe riȝt heire wolde take þe crowne.   40

ȝif sercle, and floures, and riche stones
Were eche a pece fro oþer flet,
Were þe crowne broken ones,
Hit were ful hard aȝen to knet.
Auyse ȝow, er ȝe suffre þat fit;   45
Amende ȝe, þat mende mown.
ȝe þat ben wysest, cast ȝoure wyt:
Stonde wiþ þe kyng to kepe þe crowne!

To kepe þe crowne, God graunte ȝow grace,
And let it neuere be tobroken,   50
For word of wynd, lityl trespase;
Non harm nys don, þouȝ word be spoken.
Let wysdom be vnloken,
Apert and preuyly to rowne,

foreign allies and *also the resisting of his enemies outside the kingdom*' (my emphasis), *PROME*, 1413: Item 2.

40]   riȝt heire could refer both to the persistent anxieties about the legitimacy of Lancastrian rule following Richard II's deposition, and also (and more likely here given the context) to Henry V's rightful claim to the crown of France. See note to Poem 13/113–20.

41–5]   Cf. note to line 23.

42–4]   flet … knet. These Eastern rhymes are seen again Poem 20/25/27. As in the present lyric, the remaining rhymes use the 'i' spelling. Elsewhere the poet uses the form 'knyt' in rhyme position Poem 1/59, 5/13, 10/85, 15/18.

45–7]   May show influence of parliamentary discourse. The bishop of Winchester took as the biblical text for his opening sermon Ecclesiasticus 37:20, 'Consultation precedes every action'. The Rolls continue: 'in support of this he most wisely and discreetly cited many good and noble authorities and noteworthy remarks; and he especially reiterated that your said lord the king wishes to have their good advice and counsel so that good and sufficient ordinance might be made …', *PROME*, 1413: Item 2. He goes on to single out the three priorities quoted in note to line 39 above.

49–64]   Kail saw these lines to refer to the conspiracies against Henry's life at the start of the realm in which the duke of Albany was a key player, *Poems*, pp. xvi–xvii. Robbins reprises these comments, *Historical Poems*, pp. 270–1. This is possible, but equally the remarks might be influenced by generic Wisdom literature, e.g. Wisdom 1:11, 'keep yourselves, therefore from murmuring, which profiteth nothing and refrain your tongue from detraction, for an obscure speech shall not go for nought', and Ecclesiasticus 28:13, 'a tongue that beareth witness bringeth death', and 28:15, 'the whisperer and the double-tongued is accursed: for he hath troubled many that were at peace'. Cf. *The Crowned King*, 85–92.

For non euyll wille no man be wroken,   55
But stonde wiþ riȝt, mayntene þe crowne.

A man myȝte be forborn
Fer fro a kynges place,
Wolde make a kyng to be forsworn
To lette þe lawe – it most not passe,   60
And make hym wene þat he grace,
And holy in condicioun,
And mayntene hym in his trespace,
While he pykeþ þe stones out of þe crowne.

A kyngdom must be gouerned by riȝt: 65
To chastyse false þat ar aspyed.
Falsed and trouþe togydre wole fiȝt,
Til oon þat oþer haþ distroyd.

55–6] Either a generic remark warning against reprisals, or a reference to Henry's attempt
to heal the legacy of strife brought about by factionalism in the previous reign by
restoring the earldom of Northumberland to Henry Percy. Richard of York, the son of
Edmund Langley, who had plotted against Henry IV, was made earl of Cambridge, see
Scattergood, *Politics and Poetry*, p. 128.

57–64] Robbins interprets this stanza to refer to the 40 days reprise granted to Oldcastle
in the hope that his condemnation might not come about. Oldcastle would make Henry
think that he were in a state of grace and was holy in his religious condition and that
Henry should defend his opinions in sin, *Historical Poems*, p. 270. For discussion of
possible references to Oldcastle in the sequence, see Introduction, pp. 7–10.

57–8] Robbins reads: 'a man might be removed far away from a king's residence', *Historical
Poems*, p. 270. **forborn** could be understood in the sense of 'to become separated from
[companions]' *MED* 'forberen' (*v.*); 4a; a reading which is suggestive of the relationship
between Henry V and Oldcastle, see Introduction, p. 10.

59] **forsworn**: to lie under oath, to commit perjury, Alford, *Glossary*, p. 62.

60] **lette**: to impede or obstruct justice, Alford, *Glossary*, p. 87. The line is very similar
to Poem 16/53.

61] **grace** ought to be preceded by a noun and preposition, such as 'were/stonde in'. **grace**
may have the sense of God's grace, *MED* 'grace' (*n.*); 1a, or the power to show mercy,
Alford, *Glossary*, p. 66.

63] **mayntene**. Throughout the poem this has the sense of upholding the law, but here is
used in the sense of aiding and abetting a wrongdoer, and upholding a wrong cause,
Alford, *Glossary*, p. 95. **trespace**: violation, or transgression of the law, Alford, *Glossary*,
p. 158.

64] **pykeþ** positions the 'man' as a thief, Alford, *Glossary*, p. 115.

65] Cf. Poem 3/138.

Til trouþe be fro treson tried,
Shal neuere be pes in regyoun;   70
In all kyngdomes þat man haþ gyed,
To þe place of vertues God geueþ þe crowne.

Thou3 falsed trouþe defame,
Trouþe secheþ non hernes to shewe his speche;
Trouþe of his craft, þenkeþ no shame –   75
He is bold alle folk his craft to teche.
And euere by trouþe stondes wreche,
For wreche is Goddis champioun.
Or wreche smyte, God be leche,
And saue þe kyng and kepe þe crowne.   80

Loke of þyng þat 3e bygynne:
Caste before how it wole ende:
Gostly, bodyly, what mowe 3e wynne,
Eche man destroy3e his best frend.
So dede Flaundres, how dede it wende,   85
Of noblay, þey han lore þe sown.
Pray we God his bowe of wraþþe vnbende,
And saue þe kyng and kepe þe crowne.

65–80] The axiomatic statements are similar to those voiced in Poem 3/1–16, 4/97–104/113–
20. See notes to Poem 4/97–104 for contemporary parallels and analogues.

69] Cf. Poem 14/61. **trouþe** in the sense of justice, Alford, *Glossary*, p. 159, **treson** is deceit
or treachery, Alford, *Glossary*, p. 156 and **tried** to judge a cause or question, Alford,
Glossary, pp. 160–1.

72] A line which justifies the position of the present monarch, but also insists on the need
of the king to possess moral virtue; cf. *The Crowned King*, 79–80.

73–80] Cf. Poem 3/7–8.

73] An annotator has written 'veritas' next to this line in the MS. Cf. Poem 3/2/83–4.

74] Identical to Poem 3/5, 4/157. **shewe** has the legal sense of laying a complaint, Alford,
Glossary, p. 143.

75] **shame** in the sense of defamation, Alford, *Glossary*, p. 68; cf. Poem 3/83.

77–80] Cf. Poem 4/113–20.

81–2] A proverbial idiom; cf. Chaucer, *The Canon's Yeoman's Tale*, G.1414: 'Ye been as boold
as is Bayard the blynde/,That blondreth forth and peril casteth noon'; Lydgate, *Troy Book*,
5.3506, 'For blind Baiard cast pereil of no þing/Til he stumble myddes of þe lake', and
Chaucer, *The Romaunt of the Rose*, 5620, 'He cast nought what shal hym bitide'.

84–5] For discussion of these lines, see Introduction, pp. 10–12.

87] Cf. Poem 1/69/81.

God ȝeueþ his doom to alle kynges þat be,
As a God in erþe, a kyng haþ myȝt.   90
Holy writ byd, 'blissed be he
In alle tymes þat demeþ ryȝt'.
Men do in derk, God seeþ in lyȝt:
Synne, morþere, derne tresoun
Not may be hyd fro Goddis syȝt.   95
To ryȝtwys iuge God ȝeueþ þe crowne.

That [fol. 111b] lord loueþ lityl hym selue
Þat ȝeueþ his blisse for sorwe and woo:
For þe loue of ten or twelue,
Make alle folk his foo,   100
And lese þe loue of God also.
For fawte of perfeccyone,
Þouȝ he had no vauntage but of þo,
He myȝte were a symple crowne.

Eche a kyng haþ Goddis powere   105
Of lyf and leme to saue and spille.
He muste make God his partenere
And do not his owen wille.
For God resceyueþ eche pore mannys bille,
And of here playnt God hereþ þe sowne,   110

89–90] **God in erþe**: a reference to the commonplace idea of the king as the 'vicarus dei'. Cf. Poem 13/47–8.

91–2] Cf. Matthew 5:6, 'Blessed are they that hunger and thirst after justice: for they shall have their fill'.

93] Cf. Poem 19/101.

95] Cf. Poem 4/153 and 14/71.

99] Cf. Poem 1/11 and note thereon.

102] **perfeccyone**: in the sense of completeness, a state of being complete, *MED* 'perfeccioun' (*n.*); 2a.

103–4] These lines are obscure, chiefly because it is unclear what the antecedent of þo (l. 103) could be. If **þo** were a scribal error for 'ro' in the sense of 'peace', 'quiet'; *MED* 'ro' (*n.*); 4; the sense might be: even if the king had no position from which some benefit can be acquired (*MED* 'avauntage' (*n.*); 2a: 'benefit') except that of peace, he might wear a sound/healthy crown (*MED* 'simple' (*adj.*); 1b: 'sound/healthy').

105–6] Cf. Poem 3/139–40.

106] **lyf and leme**, cf. Poem 13/17.

107] **partenere**: a co-ruler *MED* 'partenere' (*n.*); 2a.

109–10] **playnt**: to lodge a formal complaint, Alford, *Glossary*, p. 117. Cf. Poem 4/175

Sette 3oure [domes] in euene skille:
Counseile þe kyng to kepe þe crowne.

The fadir þe wanton child wole kenne;
Chastyse wiþ 3erde, and bete hit sore,
So after þe fadyr þe 3erde wole brenne   115
When child is wys, and takeþ to lore.
We han ben Goddis 3erde 3ore:
Chastysed kyngdom, castell and towne:
Twyggis of oure 3erde we haue forlore.
God saue þe kyng and kepe þe crowne!   120

Englische men dede maystry3es make,
Þurgh all þe world, here word it sprong;
Cristne and heþen þey mad to quake,
Tok and slowen kynges strong.

and note thereon. Cf. *The Crowned King*, 'The playnt of the pouere peple put thou not behynde' (l. 65).

111]   **skille**: sound judgement *MED* 'skil' (*n*.); 2b. There is a direct object missing from this line. Given that 13/71 reads 'Sette 3oure domes in euene skille', I have emended the MS reading to conform to this statement.

113–20]   The stanza plays on Proverbs 13:24, 'He that spareth the rod hateth his son: but he that loveth him correcteth him betimes'.

117]   **3erde**, cf. Poem 1/81–4.

119–20]   **3erde** puns on the sense of 'country/region' *MED* 'yerd' (*n*.); 1.2a; and 'a stick used for punishment' *MED* 'yerd' (*n*.); 2.1b.b. The poet suggests that God has punished the realm for its sinfulness with the loss of territory. The most likely reference is to lands in France.

121–2]   **Englische … maystry3es**. The English or England are mentioned specifically only here and in Poem 13/27. Poem 13 clearly has the military successes of Edward III in mind. These lines in Poem 12 are less direct, but a contrast between the previous conquest of territories in France and the threat of future civil dissension fits the temper both of this poem and the following. Cf. 'The Song on the Death of Edward III', Robbins, *Historical Poems*, p. 103/17–24. 'Sum tyme an Englische schip we had,/Nobel it was, and heih of tour;/Þorw al Cristendam hit was drad;/and stif wolde stand in vch a stour,/And best dorst byde a scharp schour/And oþer stormes, smale and grete;/Now is þat schip, þat bar þe flour,/Selden se3e and sone for3ete'.

123]   Refers to crusades. As kings, neither Richard II nor Henry IV went on crusades, although Henry IV's desire to do so is well documented.

124]   Cf. 'The Song on the Death of Edward III', Robbins, *Historical Poems*, p. 104/44–7, 'Þei tok and slou3 hem with heore honde,/Þe power of ffraunce, boþ smal & grete;/And brouþt þe king hider to bynde her bonde'. Robbins interprets these lines as a reference to the capture of John of France in 1356 at Poitiers. He was held in England until the Treaty of Bretigny in 1360.

God let neuere werre be vs among,   125
To lese þat blo of gret renowne;
Ne neuere oure riȝt be turned to wrong.
God saue þe kyng and kepe þe crowne!

Among oure self, ȝif fiȝt be raysed,
Þan stroye we oure awen nest.   130
Þat haþ victor wole be euel payed,
So many good men ben lest.
Ȝit is beter bowe þan b[re]st;
Eche man is bounden to resoun:
Ȝe þat ben wysest, take þe best: 135
Conseile þe kyng, mayntene þe crowne.

A comons myȝt sone be shent
Wiþouten kyng or gouernour.

125] Cf. note to line 5. The anxiety over civil war stems not just from the memories of factionalism but also the situation in France after the murder of the duke of Orléans, see note to line 85.

129–31] **raysed … payed.** The rhyme is imperfect unless the poet rhymes only on the inflectional ending 'ed'. 'raysed' is not seen elsewhere in the sequence. At Poem 9/179 'payed' rhymes with 'sayd'. There remains the possibility that 'payed' ought to have been 'playsed' – a form of the past participle of 'plesen'.

131] **victor.** The form of the noun usually ends in 'i' or 'ie' and it is possible there is scribal omission here.

132] If the reference is to the factionalism that plagued Henry IV's reign, and indeed, Richard's, then there were several members of the nobility who lost their lives: in the 1400 Cirencester rising, the earls of Salisbury and Kent were beheaded by the mob, and the earl of Huntingdon was executed at Plesshy. Henry Hotspur was killed in the battle of Shrewsbury 1403 and Thomas Percy was executed. Archbishop Scrope was executed after the rising in 1405 and the earl of Northumberland was killed in the battle of Bramham Moor in 1408. In Richard's reign the most prominent deaths among the nobility were the execution of the earl of Arundel in 1397 and the probable murder of the earl of Gloucester in the same year.

132] **lest:** an unusual spelling of the *pa.ppl.* of 'losen'.

133] **brest.** MS reads 'berst', but **brest** is necessary to secure the rhyme. I have followed Kail's emendation. The comment is proverbial; see Gower, *Confessio*, I.1248, 'So is he … that selve of whom men speke? Which wol noght bowe er that he breke'; Zupitza, 'Proverbis of Wysdom', 245:58, 'Bettyr is to bowe þen brest', and Chaucer, *Troilus and Criseyde*, 1.257, 'The yerde is bet that bowen wole and wynde/Than that that brest'; Roos, *La Belle Dame*, 491–2, 'For wers it is to breke þan bowe, certeyn,/And better bowe, than falle to sodenly'.

135–36] Cf. Poem 1/60 and note, and *The Crowned King*, 'Thi peres in parlement pull hem to-geders,/Worche after wysdom, and worshipe will folowe' (ll. 77–8).

And a kyng wiþoute rent
Myȝt liȝtly trussen his tresour.   140
For comons mayntene lordis honour,
Holy chirche, and religyoun:
For comouns is þe fayrest flour
Þat euere God sette on erþely crowne.

God lete þis kyngdom neuere be lorn   145
Among oure self in no distance;
Oþer kyngdomes lauȝhe vs not to skorn,
And sey, for synne God send vengeance.
God ȝeue vs space of repe[n]tance,
Good lyf, and deuocioun.   150
And God kepe in þy gouernance
Oure comely kyng, and saue þe crowne.

139–40] The mutual interdependence of king and commons reprises the sentiments of
Poem 3/99–104, especially line 102. The poems stress the need for parliamentary subsidy
from the commons, but also the need for the king to safeguard the interests of the
commons. The poet returns to this issue Poem 13/49–56.

143–4] Cf. Poem 3/99 and Poem 15/73–80 and *The Crowned King*, 'And yit the most
preciouse plente that apparaill passeth,/Thi pouere peple with here ploughe pike oute of
the erthe,/And they yeve her goodes to gouerne hem euen./And yit the peple ben well
apaid to please the allone' (ll. 71–4).

145–6] Cf. Hoccleve, *Regement*, 5216–50.

147–8] The sentiment, and most of the diction of these lines are reprised in Poem 16/63–4,
which suggests that in Poem 12 the poet is anxious lest the scornful laughter visited on
the French as a result of their civil war be turned on England should the realm suffer the
same fate.

149] The Easter celebration of the opening of the poem here gives way to the call for
repentance more characteristic of the earlier Lenten sequence of lyrics. **repentance**: the
scribe omits the first 'n'. I have followed Kail's emendation.

152] **comely kyng**: the phrase is used to describe Henry IV, *Mum and the Sothsegger*, 143
(partly to fulfil the demands of alliteration), but, given the date of the Digby sequence,
and Henry's disfigurement by leprosy, the phrase must refer to Henry V. 'The Agincourt
Carol' describes Henry as 'þat knyȝt comely', Robbins, *Historical Poems*, p. 91/13. Audelay,
in his recollection of Henry V writes that he is 'Semele to see' Robbins, *Historical Poems*,
p. 108/2.

Poem 13. Dede is worchyng

Kail dated this poem to 1414 because of parallels with the business of the second parliament of Henry V's reign, held in April at Leicester. Kail discerned two parts to the poem, and formally marked the division into Parts One and Two at line 104. There is a switch of address at this point in the poem but there is no formal rubrication in the manuscript to mark the existence of two parts (Kail, *Poems*, pp. xvii–xx). Kail may well have been right to have seen this poem to have emerged from the concerns of the 1414 parliament, and certainly right to see the poem to have been influenced by parliamentary discourse. As notes to individual lines below indicate, however, the issues broached in the poem had been at the forefront of parliamentary business for a number of years. The problem of public order in Henry IV's reign had reached acute proportions in some areas of the kingdom, prompting complaints in the parliaments of 1410, 1411 and 1413. It is clear that even before his accession, Henry V was deeply concerned to address the issue of public order and to try to restore peace and unity within the realm. In the first parliament of his reign, May 1413, the Commons complained at Henry IV's failure to carry out his repeated promises to restore law and order and petitioned the new king to suppress disorder throughout the kingdom. The first two years of Henry's reign saw an energetic programme of law enforcement, and this was particularly dense in 1414, with legislative measures in parliament and a vigorous reform of judicial proceedings. The court of the king's bench had remained in Westminster during Henry IV's reign. Under Henry V, the court travelled to the parliament in Leicester in 1414 and held sessions in Leicestershire, Staffordshire and Shropshire. Special commissions were also sent to Yorkshire, Devon, Nottinghamshire, Derbyshire and Wales (Powell, 'Restoration', p. 56). The poem stresses the importance to the realm of honest and legal parliamentary assemblies, but also registers anxiety about the legitimacy of its workings, especially in its treatment of the commons. Once again, this suggests that the poet had knowledge of the business of parliamentary assemblies in the latter years of Henry IV's reign and the early meetings of Henry V's. The poem reprises many of the issues and tropes of Poems 3 and 4.

The last third of the poem turns its attention war against France. The poet asserts the right of Henry V to the French crown. He expresses hostility towards truces and treatises and urges the king to reclaim his rightful inheritance with the sword. It is likely that the antipathy towards treaties arises from the 1412 Treaty of

Bourges and the subsequent French violation of its terms (see notes to lines 121–8). Preparations for war were begun in 1414, and the poet's remarks seem to draw on this knowledge. The encomium on knighthood, lines 145–52, is a spur to Henry's military ambitions, and it may also be an oblique attack on Sir John Oldcastle in a vein similar to Hoccleve's 'Remonstrance against Sir John Oldcastle', *Minor Poems*, II.145–52.

13. Dede is worchyng

Whanne alle a kyngdom gadrid ysse
In Goddis lawe by on assent,
For to amende þat was mysse,
[112a] Þerfore is ordayned a parlement.
Trouþe wiþ glad chere þeder went,   5
And falsed stondis ay in drede,

Title] The ambiguous **dede** may refer to Thomas Beaufort's opening sermon which requested
financial aid for Henry's military campaign at the November parliament, 1414. He took
as his theme Galatians 6:10, 'Therefore, whilst we have time, let us work good to all
men, but especially to those who are of the household of the faith', *PROME*: Item 2. See
further discussion, Nuttall, *Lancastrian Kingship*, pp. 127–30.

1]   ysse: the only example of this form of the 3rd singular present 'is' in the whole sequence.
The form is clearly confected in order to secure eye-rhyme with **mysse** (l. 3), but elsewhere
there is inconsistent concern to achieve this effect for 'mys' or 'mysse', see Poem 14/57–9,
17/178–80, 19/28–30, 23/1–3 and 24/342–4 and further, Introduction, p. 71.

2]   See note to Poem 12/12.

3]   The line is identical to 14/57.

4]   ordayned has the sense of decreed, see Alford, *Glossary*, p. 106. **parlement** is envisaged
here as parliament sitting as a court of law, Alford, *Glossary*, p. 110. The remarks in the
stanza echo addresses in a number of parliaments in the second decade of the fifteenth
century. In the November parliament of 1411, Thomas Beaufort stated that parliament
had been summoned for the good governance of the realm, the due execution of the
laws within the realm, and the proper defence of the country, *PROME*, November 1411:
Item 2, a plea echoed by the bishop of Winchester in Henry V's first parliament, May
1413, see note to Poem 12/39. At the same parliament, the speaker for the commons,
William Stourton, 'recalled how it was desired by the king, with the advice of the lords
and commons there present, that good governance might be done, such as would be
upheld and preserved in time to come; and he recounted how the said commons had
requested good governance on many occasions, and their request had been granted. But
our lord the king was well aware of how this was subsequently fulfilled and carried out.
And for this reason the said speaker prayed in the name of the said commons that since
God had endowed him with great sense, and with many other bounties and virtues, that
henceforth he might practise and maintain good governance', *PROME*, 1413: Item 8. In
the April 1414 parliament, Henry Beaufort took as his theme, 'He prepared his heart to
seek the law' (1 Esdras 7:10) and told the assembly that the king had always committed
himself to living and existing under the commendable precepts and governance of the
most holy law of God. He spoke of the importance of keeping God's laws, without which
a kingdom could not be in a state of well-being, *PROME*, April 1414: Item 1.

5–8]   While the poet may be drawing on precise parliamentary discourse for commentary
in this poem, the universality of his remarks is seen by the moves into allegorical and
moral discourse, here with the introduction of the abstractions 'Trouþe' and 'falsed';
cf. Poem 3/1–8 and 4/113–20. The use of abstraction sets up a parliamentary ideal.

For ferd of ryȝtwis iugement,
For to be demed after his dede.

In doom of parlement ofte is fauour,
Þat afterward it harmeþ grete;   10
Make oþere bold take þerof sauour,
To mayntene falsed for beȝete.
Slouþe vntyme eft mon swete,
When it is hot and gloweþ as glede;
Stonde wiþ trouþe, and smyte an hete,   15
Þat God þonke ȝow for ȝoure dede.

Lawe ȝeueþ kyng lyf and leme,
To hasty slauȝt, and sodeyn fed.

8]   Close variants on this line are at Poem 1/155, 2/22, 7/103, 19/103 and 24/243.

9]   **fauour** has the sense of bias and partiality, *MED* 'favour' (*n.*); 4, and is singled out as a perversion of law both in Digby: Poem 1/156, 13/22 and 15/46 and elsewhere, e.g. Gower, *Confessio*, VII.2787, 'The Sampnites to him broghte/A somme of gold, and him besoghte/ To don hem favour in the lawe', and VII.2844, '... every man the lawe dradde,/For ther was non which favour hadde'; Lydgate, *Troy Book*, 4.164, 'Mediacioun Of [b]rocage, roted vp-on mede,/Ay vnder-meynt with fauour or falshede'. A commons petition in the January parliament of 1410 asked for the lords of the council and the king's justices 'to acquit themselves well and loyally in their advice and deeds, for the good of the king and of the realm in all points, without showing favour, fear, partiality or affinity to any kind of person' *PROME*, January 1410: Item 14. In May 1413 Henry V is reported to have invited the commons to appeal against injustice, 'And because our said lord the king wishes that fair and impartial justice shall be done to all his lieges, poor men as well as rich, if anyone should or should wish to complain of any wrong or crime done him, he should hand in his petition between now and next Friday [19 May]', *PROME*, 1413: Item 2.

13–16]   The gist of these lines is that when sloth is unseasonably hot with sweat, one must strike (seize the opportunity) to stand with truth. There are several obscurities; see following notes.

13]   **vntyme** as an adverb appears only in this example from Digby in *MED* 'untime' (*adj.*); b and is glossed uncertainly as 'soon' or 'unseasonably'. From the context, it appears to have sense of 'unseasonably' and suggests 'out of character'. Sloth and sweating might be seen to be opposite characteristics.

15]   **an hete** is also problematic. Is this 'in heat' *MED* 'hete' (*n.*); 1 or in 'reproof, rebuke' *MED* 'hete' (*n.*); 2c, or is it an Eastern spelling of the imperative 'hitten' (*v.*) 'to strike'? What emerges from this dark proverbialism is that the truth of parliament must be upheld through the ruthless reforming of wilful self-interest. For contemporary variations on the proverb 'strike while the iron is hot', see Chaucer, *Troilus and Criseyde*, 2.1275–6, *The Tale of Melibee*, VII.1036; Hoccleve, *Regement*, 2015–16 and Lydgate, *Troy Book*, 1.6110–12.

17]   **lyf and leme**: a formula used in oaths, charges and judgments, Alford, *Glossary*, p. 88; cf. note to Poem 12/106. The Eastern spelling secures rhyme (but see note to line 19);

Lawe ȝeueþ no grace to [ȝ]eme
Morþere, ne treson, ne forcast ded.   20
To ȝeue þere mercy God forbed,
Þat fauour myȝt destroye a þede.
God in his lawe ȝaf Moyses red,
Wiþoute he damneþ þe dede.

In alle kyngdomes here lawe is wryten: 25
For mede ne drede þey chaunge it nouȝt;

there are no other examples of limb in the singular. The plural spelling is always 'lymes'
see Poem 15/39 etc. and 19/76.

17–24]   The stanza urges ruthless treatment of those who commit murder or treason, or who
plot death. The tenor of the remarks may be influenced by the king's stated resolutions
in parliament to stamp out such criminal behaviour from his realm, see note to line 4.
If the poem were written as late as the end of 1414, then the stringency of the remarks,
and the use of the word **fauour** (l. 22), might be a reaction to the proclamation of a
general pardon in the December parliament of that year. The clampdown on disorder
had resulted in a flood of indictments, and the king's bench struggled to deal with the
cases. The remedy was to issue a general pardon in return for a generous tax subsidy.
The terms of the pardon included even treason, murder and rape among pardonable
offences (see *PROME*, November 1414: Item 23, and for discussion, Powell, 'Restoration',
p. 67). An alternative (or co-existent) prompt for these remarks might be the early
conspiracies against Henry V's life, see note to Poem 12/7 and the Oldcastle rebellion. It
is also possible that the comments are generic rather than markedly topical; cf. Gower's
comments on Saul's sparing of Agag: 'For in the handes of a king/The deth and lif is
al o thing/After the lawes of justice/To slen it is a deadly vice/Bot if the man the deth
deserve,/And if a king the lif preserve/Of him which oghte forto dye/He suieth noght
thensaumplerie/Which in the bible is evident', *Confessio*, VII.3851–9.

19]   **ȝeme**. MS reads 'heme', and while this word is recorded as a noun meaning 'household
servant' in *MED*, this can hardly fit the sense here. If it is a confected form of the third
person plural pronoun, then the antecedents are unclear. There is no verb 'hemen'
recorded in *MED*, and it is likely that there is scribal corruption. I have emended to give
the sense of 'to tolerate', *MED* 'yemen' (*v.*); g, although *MED* 'quemen' (*v.*); 2d: 'absolve
of former offences' may also be possible.

23–4]   Cf. Deuteronomy 24:16, 'The fathers shall not be put to death for the children, nor
the children for the fathers, but every one shall die for his own sin'.

25–32]   Complaints about corruption in the law are endemic in Middle English political
poetry, e.g. *Richard the Redeless*, III.305–10; *Mum and the Sothsegger*, 1187–95, 1490–7;
Schmidt, *Piers Parallel Text*, B.3.154–62; Gower, *Confessio*, VII.2695–701; *Mirour*, 24601–12;
'The Twelve Abuses', Robbins, *Historical Poems*, p. 143/2; 'England May Sing Alas',
p. 145/1–2, and Hoccleve, *Regement*, 2780–835. Hoccleve's lines are especially close to
the temper of the comments in Digby. In both, the remarks in the stanza may be
entirely generic, or may be influenced by complaints about abuses in the legal system
in successive parliaments.

26]   **chaunge it nouȝt**. A commons petition in the January 1410 parliament appealed for

In Engeland, as all men wyten,
Lawe as best is solde and bouȝt;
Eche ȝeer, newe lawe is wrouȝt,
And [falsed cloþed] in trouþe wede.   30
Fernȝer was lawe, now nes it nouȝt;
We ben newefangyl, vnstable in dede.

To stonde wiþ comons in here ryȝt
Is hyȝest poynt of charite;
To quyte þat dede no man myȝt,   35
Saue onely God in trynyte.
Þouȝ þe comons vnkonnyng be,

'the common laws, statutes, and good ordinances made and used, and not repealed ... should be kept and put into execution in accordance with true law and reason', *PROME*: Item 18. In the November 1411 Parliament, the commons petitioned for the statute of assizes to be maintained: 'that the same statute should be firmly kept and maintained. Let this statute be kept and maintained, notwithstanding any statute and ordinance made to the contrary', *PROME*: Item 34.

28] **solde and bouȝt**, cf. Poem 1/156 and Hoccleve, *Regiment*, 2710–16, 'Cristen men, ȝelde oughten iust iugement/ffrely, for vnleful is it to selle/Thogh it be leful and conuenient,/A wyse man for rewarde his reed to telle./A iuges purs, with golde noght shulde swelle;/If one iustice he shape his dome to bilde,/His iugementes he ȝiftles must ȝilde'. A commons petition in Henry V's first parliament complained of such corruption in a petition 'concerning the punishment of corrupt jurors': 'triers of arraignment have received from one party or the other various sums of gold and silver or other goods to affirm or deny the said arraignments, and thus to try the witnesses and the title of the action wholly on behalf of the party from whom they have thus received the said goods: having little or no consideration for anything except the value of what they receive, or what they have been promised that they will receive, thereby hindering greatly the execution of the common law throughout all the kingdom of England and causing the ultimate destruction and ruin of your poor lieges, who bring their actions by recourse to the common law, and have nothing with which to satisfy the wicked greed of the aforesaid jurors, who ought by law to receive nothing for thus serving at the trial', *PROME*, May 1413: Item 31.

30] **falsed cloþed**. MS reads 'cloþe falsed'. A past tense is clearly required and I have emended. The line echoes Poem 4/12.

32] **newefangyl**. Before the November parliament of 1411, Henry IV apparently declared that he would have no 'novelleries' at the assembly, Jacob, *Fifteenth Century*, p. 112.

33–43] As in Poem 3/99 and 12/143, see notes, the poet is concerned to champion the role of the commons in working towards the good of the realm. **ryȝt** has legal force, Alford, *Glossary*, p. 137, and the stanza as a whole upholds the right of the commons, even if they are acknowledged to be **vnkonnyng** (l. 37). That God alone can reward those who stand with the commons recalls Poem 12/109. Once again these lines may show knowledge of the business of the first and second parliaments of Henry V's reign. Although the ten statutes enacted as a result of the 1413 parliament were all based on petitions submitted

God ȝeueþ ȝow neuere þe lasse mede;
Þat mede askeþ so heyȝ degre,
Nes non bot God may quyte þat dede.   40

ȝet o wysdom mot ȝe lere:
Most profyt, and heyest honour,
ȝoure tenauntes playntes ȝe mot here,
For þey kepen all ȝoure tresour,
ȝe are holden to ben here socour,   45
Non wiþ wrong oþer mysbede.
Forþy God made ȝow gouernour,
In Goddis ryȝt to deme þe dede.

Lordis þat han castels and toures,
Alle folk stonden of ȝow awe.   50
Þe puple is Goddis and noȝt ȝoures:
Þey paye ȝoure rente to gouerne lawe.
Let no man here ryȝt wiþdrawe,
Body ne catell hem mysbede.
Who doþ so, God sayþ in sawe   55
He shal haue heuene for þat dede.

by the commons, six of these statutes were significantly emended from their original wording by the king and his legal advisors. The commons complained about it in the following parliament: since they were 'as much assenters as petitioners', the king should not of his own accord alter the wording of petitions once it had been agreed that they would be enacted as statutes. The king replied, slightly evasively, that he would not in future enact anything contrary to what they had requested, at the same time reminding them that it was his right to grant or reject any of their petitions as he saw fit, *PROME* April 1414, Introduction.

38]   **ȝow** refers not to the previous antecedent, the commons, but to the addressee of the poem, which vacillates between the nobility, the king, and the realm in general. To stand with the commons earns a reward very different from the 'fauour' castigated in the previous stanzas. As a work of holy love, only God is in a position to reward that action.

41-8]   Cf. notes to Poem 12/109–10/143–4. Compare Schmidt, *Piers Parallel Text*, B.6.38–40, 'Loke ye tene no tenaunt but Truthe wole assente./And though ye mowe amercy hem, lat mercy be taxour/And mekenesse thi maister, maugree Medes chekes'.

51]   Identical to Poem 1/19 and similar to 3/131.

52]   **rente** suggests grants from the commons at parliament.

55-6]   The most likely biblical source for these remarks is Matthew 5:6, 'Blessed are they that hunger and thirst after justice: for they shall have their fill'. Cf. note to Poem 12/91–2.

Þe lord þat wole haue good loos,
Stonde fast in trouþe, waxe not faynt:
Let trouþe gon out of cloos,
Þat alle folk may here his playnt.   60
Let treson be shamely ataynt,
Graunte hem no mercy, ne take no mede;
For mede wiþ poyson sotyly is maynt,
Mercy my3t cherische hem in here dede.

3if a man wolde þe ouertylt,   65
Caste þy deþ for to kille,
Let not anoþer by3e his gylt
Þat [fol. 112b] neuere in dede dede þe ylle.
Dampne no man for non euyll wille,
To do þe gylteles blod to blede;   70
Sette 3oure domes in euene skille,
In drede of God 3e deme 3oure dede.

Who skorneþ hem þat telleþ hem wit
Is rebell to God þat repreueþ reson;

57-64]   Cf. Poem 3/25-32 and Hoccleve, *Regement*, 2542-55, 'A kyng, me thinkeþ, for þe
seuerte/Of his good loos, by-houeþ it enquere/Of hem þat han his estate in cheerte,/
What fame þat his poore peple him bere;/He of iustice is bounden hem to were/And to
diffende; and if þat þei be greued,/By him their mot be holpen and releued … /ffor þat
he peple haþ in gouernance,/He clept is kyng: if his men peple oppresse,/Witinge hym,
and noght rekke of the duresse,/He may, be rygth, be clept no gouernour,/But of his
peple a wilful destroyour.'

59-60]   Cf. Poem 4/113-20 and 'Truth Ever is Best', Furnivall, *Vernon Poems* II.700/31-40,
'ffor Godes loue wis þou so among,/Þat trouþe be meyntened for þe best … /Hose medleþ
wiþ þe lawe:/Let neuer falshed a3eynes vnkuynde/ffordon trouþe ne soþ sawe./ffor falshed
euermore schal stonde awe/On trouþe þau3 he be neuer so prest./ffor godes loue let neuer
gold þe drawe/A3eynes trouþe þat euer is best.'

60]   **playnt**, cf. note to Poem 12/109-10.

61]   **ataynt**: convicted for perjury, or for giving a false verdict, Alford, *Glossary*, p. 11.

65-8]   Either generic advice, or injunctions not to spare the lives of those who conspired
against the king at the start of his reign, see note to Poem 12/7/49-64.

71]   Cf. note to Poem 12/111.

72-6]   Reprises the concerns – and diction – of Poem 1/56-60, 4/73-80 and 5/33-6. The
syntax of these lines is difficult. Clearly the gist is that those who scorn wisdom and
rebuke justice are rebels against God and bring false accusations against God's counsel.
The grammatical relation of the relative **þat** clauses is problematic. In line 75 the referent
for the first **þat** is unclear, as is the antecedent for **hit** and how the line connects with

Þat loueþ hym most þat hateþ hit,   75
Aȝenst Goddis counseill cast a cheson.
To worschipe hym þere wit is geson,
For fawte of grace vertue ben gyde.
To chastyse fooles is ay in seson,
To worschip or shame after þe dede.   80

Syngulerte is sotyle þefte:
Þay calle hit custom trouþe to blende,
Whan trouþe wole reherce þat efte,
Þan God wil vengeance wiþ trouþe sende,
Shamely falsed to shende,   85
Drede and stryf among hem shede
To preue who is Goddis frend;
Comons be witnesse of here dede.

Putte fro court þat chericheþ vys,
Þat place of vertues wolde shende;   90

line 76. The balanced antitheses of line 75 introduce confusion and either the poet has been defeated by the demands of the stanza form, or the scribe has scrambled the sense.

76] **cheson,** *MED* 'chesoun' (*n.*); 2b, lists the sense of make an accusation against, although this line from Digby is not cited there is a quotation from Robert Mannyng's *Chronicle*, Part II, p. 172, 'Som chesons þei cast, & som for him said; Bot here now at þe last what dome was on him laid'.

79] Cf. the moralistic comments of Poem 1/167 and 6/28.

81–8] The legal diction of this stanza creates a scenario of Falsehood being tried in a court of law. When Truth presents his accusations, God will send vengeance to destroy Falsehood and his followers in order to prove who are God's friends. In a characteristic move of support for the importance of the commons, they are presented here as witness of the action. The generic statements may harbour contemporary resonance with the concerns of the parliaments of 1410–14 to stamp out riot, corruption and perversion of the law.

81] Cf. note to Poem 1/4.

82] **custom,** a common usage having the force or validity of law, Alford, *Glossary,* p. 42. **blende** the Eastern dialect form secures rhyme, as it does when the same verb is used Poem 5/20. As an adjective, and always in rhyme position, the form is 'blynd(e)' Poem 3/77, 4/215, 5/7, 9/26, 10/13, 15/110, 17/134, 23/39.

83] **reherce**: to recite aloud a list of charges or accusations, Alford, *Glossary,* p. 130.

84] **Shamely,** cf. note to Poem 12/75.

87] **preue**: 'to prove an accusation against'; *MED* 'preven' (*v.*); 7a.

88] **witnesse**: one who witnesses, and hence attests to the validity of an action, cf. Alford, *Glossary,* p. 168.

Nedeles delys and nedeles gys,
Þe wastours out of worschip spende.
Wiþ wit and vysement all amende,
Lete werk be witnes ȝe can ȝoure crede,
Wiþ corage and hardynes ȝoure reme defende,   95
In Goddis querell ȝe do ȝoure dede.

A trewe man reccheþ neuere a dell,
Þouȝ all þe world his werkis aspyȝed,
And falsed, for he doþ not well,
He wolde trouþes tonge were tyȝed;   100
For he shulde not telle who hym nyȝed,
Þerfore þe fals þe false fede,
Til trouþe in preson be faste alyȝede,
And dampne trouþe for falsed dede.

Whanne ȝe han made pes wiþynne,   105
All ȝoure reme in vnyte,
Vtteremore ȝe mot bygynne,
Strengþe ȝoure marche, and kepe þe see.
Ofte haue ȝe made ȝoure fomen fle,
Here hatest blod o brod to sprede,   110

89–96] These lines resonate with the parliamentary demand for 'bone governance',
Harriss, 'Parliament', pp. 141–4 and see note to line 4, above.

100]   Reprises the diction of Poem 4/113.

102–4] The vignette of Truth's languishing in prison on account of being convicted
of Falsehood's crimes provides a check on the optimism of lines 81–8 and Poem
12/73–80.

105–12] From 1406 to 1414 there were repeated petitions from the commons in parliament
for the secure defence of Calais, the sea and the Welsh and Scottish marches. The
repetition of the demands is an index of the scale of the problems.

106] The importance of governing the realm in unity reprises Poem 1/13/21, 3/130 and
8/63.

109–12] These lines anticipate lines 113–20 which are an unambiguous call to arms
against France. Contemporary chroniclers stress that the series of victories won since
the reign of Edward III showed that England had received clear signs of divine
approbation in the long struggle for justice against France. Since England's cause was
a just one, the war fought by Henry V was a just war, and his victories were signs
of God's justice, Taylor and Roskell, *Gesta Henrici Quinti*, pp. 123–5 and *St Alban's
Chronicle*, p. 121.

God doþ batayle and not 3e,
Þou3 3e fau3t, God doþ þe dede.

To Fraunce kyng Edward had queryle:
Hit was his kynde heritage,
And 3e han þe same style,   115
Wiþ armes of þe selue parage.
And 3it 3oure querell dede neuere aswage
Þat God haþ shewed in 3oure manhede;
On see, or land, on eche vyage,
In dent of swerd God demed 3oure dede.   120

Stuffe 3oure castels in eche coost,
Warnestor and folk þeder sende,
So mow 3e abate 3oure enemys bost,
But not in trete in wast to spende.
Wheþer 3e assayle or defende,   125
On see, on land, God 3ow spede:
Wiþ word of wynd mad neuere [fol. 113a] werre ende,
But dent of swerd endid þe dede.

And 3e þenke werre to holde,
Do after hem is most wys,   130

111–12]   Line 111 is identical to Poem 9/143 (cf. also 3/111), and the comments recall 9/145–52.

113–20]   **kynde heritage** asserts a natural right to the French crown. Edward III's claim to the French throne rested on the rights of his mother Isabel, French wife of Edward II. The French sought to refute this claim on the basis of Salic law, which allegedly barred the succession of females to the throne, Jacob, *Fifteenth Century*, p. 137. See Introduction, pp. 14–15, for further discussion of this stanza.

113]   **queryle**: a confected form of the noun to secure rhyme with **style** (l. 115). Elsewhere the form is 'querel(l)' Poem 3/87, 9/139, 13/96, 13/117, 21/116/123.

118]   **manhede**, cf. Hoccleve, *Regement*, 3963–6, 'O worthi Prince! I truste in 3our manhode,/ Medlid wiþ prudence and discrecioun/That 3e shal make many a kny3tly rode,/And þe pride of our foos thristen adoun'.

120]   **dent of swerd**, cf. lines 128 and 159–60, and the chroniclers' appeals for 'a Heavenly arbitrament carried out by the sword', Taylor and Roskell, *Gesta Henrici Quinti*, p. 123.

121–8]   Here, and in lines 137–44, the hostility towards resolving dispute via treaty appears to pick up on recent negotiations. The details of these are discussed in the Introduction, pp. 11–12.

129–36]   This is reminiscent of the moral instruction to follow wisdom in Poem 1/57–64, but here transposed into a military context.

Corage of ȝong and wit of olde
Can telle where þe vauntage lys.
In dede of armes wonnen prys,
Whan gloser and flaterer on tapetis trede,
For wynnyng þey counseled to cowardys,   135
Man wan neuere worschip by here dede.

Als ofte as ȝe trete,
Ȝoure enemys ordynaunce þey diȝt,
While ȝe trete, ay þey gete;
Ȝe trete ȝoure self out of ȝoure riȝt.   140
Þere lakkeþ conscience of knyȝt,
Lete falsed growe tyl he sede;
Ordre of knyȝt was made to fyȝt,
In Goddis riȝt to ende þe dede.

Ordre of knyȝt hardest is: 145
On see, on lond, on sholde, or depe.
He passeþ relegous ywis,
Þouȝ þey preye and faste wepe.
Ofte wiþ ful wombe relegous slepe,
Whan knyȝtes han hunger and moche in drede;   150
Þe beter in clene lyf þey auȝt hem kepe,
As Goddis knyȝt to don here dede.

On of two ȝe mot chese:
On lond, or see, or shippes bord.
Wiþ fiȝt ȝe wynne, wiþ trete ȝe lese;   155
Ȝoure enemys han þat eure in hord.
Þat þey wynne wiþ word:
Ȝoure townes and castels in lengþe and brede,
And þat ȝe wynne, ȝe wynne wiþ sword;
Þerfore wiþ swerd do ȝoure dede.   160

135] **wynnyng** may refer to the financial settlements made with France in November 1412;
    See Introduction, pp. 11–12.
141–2] The same diction is used Poem 1/62.

God ȝeue ȝow grace þis reme to ȝeme,
To cherische þe goode and chastyse þe nys.
And also serue God to queme,
Þat ȝoure werkis preue ȝow wys.
And in ȝow þe helpe it lys,   165
Þe puple in Goddis lawe to hede.
Do so now, ȝe wynne ȝow prys,
And heuene blisse for ȝoure dede. Amen.

161–8] The final stanza of the poem is addressed to Henry V in terms which resemble strikingly the words of the speaker, William Stourton, at the first parliament of his reign. See note to line 4 above.

Poem 14. Man be warre er the be woo

Kail, *Poems*, dated this poem to 1418 on the grounds that it appeared to contain veiled allusions to the death of Oldcastle, who was hanged at the end of 1417. He comments that some of the advice seems to censure the folly of a nobleman who was a confidant and counsellor of the king (ll. 9–12) and that line 45 might contain a reference to the manner of Oldcastle's death. Kail also saw in lines 81–8 allusions to a petition to the king from the University of Oxford in 1418 in which they asked for simony to be punished effectually and that care should be taken to prevent unworthy persons from intruding into sacerdotal office. Kail, rather vaguely, takes the criticisms of false measure and weight (ll. 65–8) to refer to complaints of the commons 'somewhat later' (*Poems*, pp. xx–xxi). As the notes to individual lines below make clear, I think it is impossible to assign a specific date to the poem on the evidence of individual lines. See Introduction, pp. 7–10, for further discussion of dating references. The poem returns to the moralistic discourse of the earlier poems in the sequence, especially Poems 1–7. It may be the case that a more sober exhortation to all persons in the realm balances the assertive militarism of the previous poem and also sounds a more moralistic note after the cautious optimism of celebrating the beginning of the reign of Henry V. The temper of the poem is very close to wisdom lyrics and complaint/abuses of the age poetry. While precise reference to particular events or persons is difficult to determine, the generically sage advice offered to each man chimes harmoniously with the use of a public voice concerned to offer timeless counsel to a morally stable political community. A close parallel to the fusion of the moralistic and the political can be seen in the Vernon lyric which has a refrain very similar to that of this poem, 'A warnyng to be ware' (Furnivall, *Vernon Poems* II.719–21). In contrast to Digby, the Vernon poem refers unambiguously to events: the riots of 1381 and the Earthquake Council of 1382, but the tenor of the poem is that of generalised moral comment.

14. Man be warre er the be woo

The herrere degre, þe more wys;
Þe gretter worschip, þe noblere fame:
Þe herrere degre, þe more nys;
Þe gretter foly, þe more blame.
After foly folweþ þe shame,   5
Repreued of frendis, and scorned of fo;
After þy dede ressayue þy name;
Eche man be war er he be wo.

3if þou be kyngis chaunceller,
Kepe þe crowne hool in stat;   10
3if þou be kyngis counselere,
Loke no stones þerof abate.
3if oþer wolde make þe kyng þe hate,
Or falsed ouer trouþe go,
Tak þy leue, and kisse þe 3ate;   15
Eche man be war er hym be wo.

On a mowntayne a sete may not be hyd,
Ne lordis werkis in no degre;

1–4] The balanced antitheses, sustained across two lines, sharply make the point that to a person of high rank, great fame and wisdom brings in its train the risk of even greater folly and shame. Cf. Poem 6/57–60, 18/61, and 'Prouerbes of Diuerse Profetes and of Poetes and of oþur Seyntes', Furnivall, *Vernon Poems* II.548/393–4, 'Þe herre of stat þat þou be/Þe more meke haue þou be'.

6] The generic advice anticipates the 'follies tradition' vein of Poem 16, see especially line 74.

7] Identical to Poem 2/20 and 6/58. Cf. Lydgate's 'Advice to the Several Estates I', Robbins, *Historical Poems*, p. 232/11, 'Knyght, lete thy dedes worshyp determyne'.

8] The refrain picks up on the first line of Poem 1; and cf. 4/29.

10–12] Cf. Poem 12/49–64 and notes thereon. The lines form an injunction to the chief officers of the king to defend the crown.

12] Cf. Poem 12/64.

13–14] **þe kyng þe hate**. The line suggests concern over conspiracies against the king's life, cf. note to Poem 12/7 and 'Truth Ever is Best', Furnivall, *Vernon Poems* II.700/49–56, 'Trouþe was sum tyme here a lord;/ ... And made hem lordes to lyue in rest:/Þer dorste no falshede with hem be sene,/So loued þei trouþe, þat euer is best'.

17] From Matthew 5:14, 'You are the light of the world. A city seated on a mountain cannot be hid,' and cf. note to line 71.

A lordis werkis wiþ comouns is kyd:
Þat he doþ most in preuete,   20
Gouernour of kyngdom or cyte,
After þey lyue, men deme so.
For eche a werk God [fol. 113b] ȝeueþ a fe;
Eche man be war er hym be wo.

A symple prest wole synge his masse,   25
Whule his lyuyng is but smal;
As summe encrese, serue God þe lasse,
Wiþ benefices ten myȝte lyue wiþal,
And fynde þere noþer houshold ne halle,
Ne serue þe parische but take hem fro.   30
Er God suche rekenyng calle,
Be tyme be war er þey be wo.

Man, do resoun þouȝ þou be riche,
Ouer cite or town hast gouernaunce,
Loue al crafty folk yliche,   35
Mayntene no party in distaunce,

19]   Elsewhere in the sequence there are warnings that humankind cannot conceal their
deeds from God. The suggestion here that the nobility cannot conceal their actions from
the commons is of a piece with the concern throughout the poems to hold the political
importance of the commons in high regard, cf. Poem 13/88 and note thereon.

21-4]   Cf. 'Prouerbes of Diuerse Profetes and of Poetes and of oþur Seyntes', Furnivall, *Vernon
Poems* II.526/67-8, 'Vse þe to do priueliche/As þou wolt do to-fore men openliche'.

22]   A common sentiment in the sequence, see Poem 1/155, 2/22, 4/56/152/168/192.

23]   Cf. Poem 9/151.

25-32]   The criticism of worldly clergy is characteristic of 'abuse of the age' poetry. While
there may be particular topical criticisms, as ever in this sequence, criticism of the church
is kept generalised, see further on this, Introduction, p. 38, and notes to Poem 9/161. A
line in 'The World Upside Down', Robbins, *Historical Poems*, p. 151/12, 'Prestus in litille
han there suffisaunce' encapsulates the tenor of this stanza in Digby.

31]   Cf. note to Poem 1/129 and 135.

32]   þey. This is the only occasion in the poem where the generic third person masculine
pronoun, referring back to 'eche man' is not used. The use of **þey** may suggest a distancing
on the part of the narrator from the worldliness of the clergy.

33-40]   The remarks in this stanza are characteristic of 'abuses of the age poetry' and
reprise comments elsewhere in the sequence.

36]   Cf. Poem 1/13 and 'The Bisson Leads the Blynde', Robbins, *Historical Poems*, p. 130/75,
'Among ȝou make no dystaunce'.

Sette mendis for trespas in euene balaunce,
For a penyworth of harm tak not two,
Rule wel mesure and sustenaunce,
Eche man be war er hym be wo.   40

Þe wyseman his sone forbed
Masouncraft, and all clymbyng,
And shipman craft for perile of dede,
And preuey in counseil be ney3 no kyng.
For his mysrulyng þou my3t hyng,   45
Þat shep my3te grese vnder þy to,
To fli3e to hy3e treste not þy wyng;
Eche man be war er hym be wo.

Þou3 þy kyng be fre to 3yue,
Be þou not gredy to craue,   50
Make oþere folk þe worse to lyue,
For synguler profyt þou wolde haue.
Er drede and repref þy berd shaue,
Asese of couetys and say 'hoo!'
The man þat wole his worship saue,   55
Be tyme be war er him be woo.

37] Cf. Poem 1/164, 3/13, 12/111, 13/71 and 'The World Upside Down', Robbins, *Historical Poems*, p. 151/27, 'Law so parfit þat woll chaunge for no hire'.

39] Standard advice to rulers material, pithily summarised by Lydgate in, 'Advice to the Several Estates II', Robbins, *Historical Poems*, p. 233/23–5, 'spende nat yovr ryches en prodygalte./a meane es mesvre attaynyng nat to vyce/wythyn the boundys of lyberalte'.

41] **wyseman ... son**, a reference to Wisdom literature, which often takes the form of a wise father teaching his son, e.g. 'Luytel Caton', Furnivall, *Vernon Poems* II.554/7–8, 'How þe wyse man tauhte his sone/Þat was of tendere age'. I have been unable to trace the precise comments which follow in Digby in wisdom texts.

45] **hyng**. *MED* does record this form of 'hongen', suggesting influence from Old Norse. with ME change of 'eng' to 'ing'. Elsewhere in Digby, the 'hong' form is used, see Poem 3/165 and 16/83. The spelling here secures rhyme.

46] **grese**. *MED* records this as a form of 'grasen' (*v.*), 'to graze'. Whiting, *Proverbs*, lists this as a proverb, p. 514, S.224.

52] See note to Poem 1/4.

53] **berd shaue**: a proverbial idiom meaning 'to get the better of', cf. Hoccleve, *Regement*, 4338–40, 'Ful slily he disceyuyd þis meyne,/His sonnes and his doughtres boþ, I mene;/ Hir berdes shaued he right smothe & clene'.

For to amende þat was mys,
Þerfore is ordeyned eche iustice.
Lat eche man haue þat shulde ben his,
And turne not lawe for couetyse,   60
Ne contryue tresons þere trouþ lys,
In tyrauntrie to robbe and slo;
Er ȝoure werkis preue ȝow nys,
Eche man be war er hym be wo.

ȝif ȝe wole haue pes of ȝong and old,   65
Let eche man haue þat is ryȝt;
Let comon lawe his cours hold,
Euene mesure, mett, and wyȝt.
Man, þouȝ þou be moche of myȝt,
Mende fawtes er þou make mo;   70
For þat ȝe hid, God seeþ in syȝt;
Eche man be war er hym be wo.

Eche lord knoweþ his astate:
Lyue on þat God hym lent;

57–8] These lines reprise the opening two lines of Poem 13, see notes thereon. Here **iustice** replaces parliament as the source of correction of abuse.

59] Identical to Poem 11/42, and cf. 1/116. The same idea is repeated at Poem 14/66, 18/180. Cf. 'Luytel Caton', Furnivall, *Vernon Poems* II.561/105–6, 'Oþer mennes þing with wrongle/ Coueyte hit nouȝt in herte'.

60–1] Cf. Poem 13/57–64 and 'Truth Ever is Best', Furnivall, *Vernon Poems* II.700/34–6, 'Hose medleþ wiþ þe lawe:/Let neuer falshed aȝeynes vnkuynde/ffordon trouþe ne soþ sawe'.

65–72] This stanza returns to sentiments expressed Poem 1/1–8.

66] See note to line 59.

67] Cf. Poem 3/40 and 18/63.

68] Cf. Poem 1/61, 3/13 and see notes to Poem 9/51–4. **wyȝt** *MED* does record this form of 'weght' (*n*.); 1, suggesting influence from Old Norse. The spelling here secures rhyme. In Poem 9/51, the form is 'waȝtes' in the middle of the line.

69–72] Cf. Poem 19/53.

71] Cf. Poem 1/95/103. The line is a partial re-working of Poem 12/93.

73] Cf. Poem 16/107.

73–8] The moral tenor of these remarks can be paralleled elsewhere, e.g. 'Fy on a faint Friend', Furnivall, *Vernon Poems* II.687/33–6, 'ȝif þou wolt not ben frendles,/Lern to kepe þat þou hast;/Loke þou be not penyles,/Ne spend þou nouȝt þi good in wast', but line 77 suggests inflection from parliamentary discourse. There had been significant disputes over taxation during the reign of Henry IV. A row had erupted in 1407

Þat borweþ moche he geteþ hate,   75
Spende waste passyng his rent.
For suche, a kyngdom haþ ben shent;
Stryf wiþ comons, threp and thro;
To brynge þat in amendement,
Eche man be war er hym be wo.   80

Whanne holichirche suffreþ symonye,
And is [fol. 114a] wiþ hym enchaunted,
And lawe of land suffreþ vsurye,
Vnkyndely synne, and shameles haunted,
And vicious folk auaunsed and dawnted,   85
And vertues flemed fro eche a wro:

when the king's council tried to tell the commons how much tax they were to grant, and in 1410 Prince Henry threatened to withdraw unless adequate supply was voted, Harriss, 'Parliament', p. 143. A commons petition in the 1410 parliament argued that 'the common people, both because of the scarcity of corn and because of the deaths of animals, cannot afford to pay taxes or tallages', *PROME*: Item 70. In the first parliament of Henry V, regular taxation was demanded as the price of good governance, and the commons did, 'for the great love and affection, for the good of the realm, and for good governance in future, grant the wool subsidy for four years and a whole lay subsidy, allocated to the defence of the realm and sea'. (See *PROME*, 1413: Item 17 and Harriss, 'Parliament', p. 144). Harriss notes further that, at the same time, by disclaiming any obligation to grant further taxes for the maintenance of garrisons, they underlined the principle that direct taxation was extraordinary and should be confined to open war. In the first parliament of 1414 the commons were advised that 'the king had no intention of asking them for a tenth and a fifteenth in this parliament in the hope that he will find them more willing and amenable to him and his needs in time to come' (*PROME*, April 1414: Item 1).

74]   **lent**, cf. Poem 1/37, 7/82. Parliamentary demands for the king to live 'of his owne' (cf. *Mum and the Sothsegger*, 1630–69) are inflected with the moral tenor of penitential lyrics which remind that all possessions are merely on loan to humankind from God.

81–8]   A further 'abuses of the age' stanza which lists generalised corruption. 'The Twelve Abuses', Robbins, *Historical Poems*, pp. 143–4 and 'Abuses of the Age II', Robbins, *Historical Poems*, pp. 144–5, contain many parallel statements listed in notes to individual lines which follow.

81]   'Virtus Ecclesia Clerus Demon Simonia. cessat. calcatur. errat. regnat. dominatur', Robbins, *Historical Poems*, pp. 144/17–8; 'Symony is aboue, & awey is trwloue', Robbins, *Historical Poems*, pp. 144/23.

83]   'Ʒeft is Domesman, … Lordes ben owtyn lawe', Robbins, *Historical Poems*, pp. 144/9–10.

84]   Cf. Poem 4/127.

86]   'Vertues & good lyuinge is cleped hypocrisie', Robbins, *Historical Poems*, pp. 144/1.

In þat kyngdom God haþ vengeaunce graunted;
Eche man be war er hym be wo.

In a kyngdom what makeþ stryf?
No man standes of oþer awe,   90
Vnkyndely synne, and tyrauntes lyf,
Vsurye, symonye, and letter of lawe,
And holy chirche rebell to Goddis sawe;
To kepe his comaundement þey say no.
Fro þat kyngdom God his loue wil drawe;   95
Eche man be war er hym be wo.

3if eny folk forgeþ gyles,
Wiþ falsed þy deþ to cast,
Pulle vp þe stakes and breke þe styles,
Let hem no more styke so faste.   100
And whan 3e be þe perile paste,
Kepe 30w wel fro deþes flo,
Fro costage, and be no more agaste;
Eche man be war er hym be wo.

þe flesch haþ many frele frendis: 105
Richesse, strengþe, fayrenesse, and hele.

87] 'and here-fore ueniaunce god wol take/on us, but 3if we amende', Robbins, *Historical Poems*, pp. 145/24–5 and 'A warnyng to be ware', Furnivall, *Vernon Poems* II.719/10, '... god wol vengeaunce on vs stele'.

89] The line is almost identical to Poem 5/25, and the stanzas of both poems share similar concerns. See also Poem 3/153–60.

93–4] Revisits Poem 5/33–40, and cf. Poem 3/106.

97–8] Reprises the diction of Poem 13/65–6. It is hard to determine whether the comments are generalised axiom (cf. Poem 4/93), or allude to conspiracies against the king's life, see notes to Poem 12/7 and 13/16–24.

99] **Pulle vp þe stakes**, 'to abandon a position', drawn from the image of pulling out the stakes of guy ropes on a tent, see *MED* 'stake' (*n*.); 2f. Cf. Lydgate, *Troy Book*, 15523. **styles** 'the rungs of a ladder' see *MED* 'stele' (*n*.); 1d. *MED* records the form 'stile'. The word is not used elsewhere in Digby, but the spelling here facilitates rhyme.

105–12] The warnings about following bodily desires recall Poems 1–7 and anticipate Poems 17, 19 and 22.

105] Cf. Poem 7/3.

106] Identical to Poem 11/52. Cf. Poem 1/53 and, for the sentiments more broadly, lines 1/49–56. Also Poem 10/11 and Poem 18/171/173.

Whan it is mysvsed, þe soule it schendis;
Richesse, rauenere of worldis wele.
Take fro þe nedy, to þe nedeles dele,
And wylde recheles as a roo.   110
Er ȝoure synnes ȝoure soules apele,
Eche man be war er hym be woo.

109]   **nedy ... nedeles**. The criticism and the wordplay recall Poem 7/65–72.
110]   A verb may be missing from this line – perhaps 'lyue' before **wylde**. The syntax of
lines 109–10 does not make sense as the MS stands.
111]   Cf. Poem 8/71 and 10/190 and notes.

Poem 15. The descryuyng of mannes membres

The basis of this poem is the traditional trope of the 'body politic' which derives from Corinthians 12:12–14, 'For as the body is one, and hath many members; and all members of the body, whereas they are many yet are one body, so also is Christ. For in one Spirit we were all baptised into one body, whether Jews or Gentiles, whether bond or free; and in one Spirit we have all been made to drink. For the body also is not one member, but many. If the foot should say, because I am not the hand, I am not of the body; is it therefore not of the body?' The trope is used in a range of Middle English writing, e.g. Andrew and Waldron, *Pearl Poems*, ll. 457–67; Gower, *Vox*, VI.497–8; Hoccleve, *Regement*, 3928–34; *Richard the Redeless*, II.62–6, *Mum and the Sothsegger*, 1472–4. The closest in temper to Digby is Lydgate's equally extensive analogy, *Fall of Princes*, 806–917. What is distinctive about use of this trope in Digby is the manner in which the poet cross-fertilises this political trope with a debate between the various parts of the body which is reminiscent of debates between the body and the soul. Suddenly, at line 86, the poem erupts into a cacophony of warring dialogue, which is eventually tamed and framed by the poet's moralisation at lines 121–36 after the mouth determines to behave in accordance with 'mesure'. A similar treatment of the relationship between the mouth and other members of the body is seen in the discussion of temperance in Nelson Francis, *Vices and Virtues*, p. 106. The extended analogy and subsequent dramatisation in Digby create a model of a unified political realm in which debate has been resolved and the value of every component has been realised. Only then, as the final stanzas of the poem make clear, can the kingdom tackle the threat of external enemies. For further discussion, see Introduction, pp. 47–50. While there is nothing conclusive to date this poem (perhaps the reason for Kail's omitting to discuss it in his introduction), its concerns are clearly relevant to the early years of Henry V's reign, and to the energetic programme to establish law and order and to settle the quarrel with France.

15. The descryuyng of mannes membres

Whereof is mad al mankynde?
Of seuene þynges, and it be souȝt:
Erþe, and water, fyre, and wynde;
Þerof is þe body wrouȝt.
Þe soule of þre: þat haþ þe mynde,   5
Of lyf of felyng, and of þouȝt.
Þe soule fro þe body vnb[y]nde,
Whan on of þese lakkeþ ouȝt.

The heued Y likne to a kyng –
For he is lord souereyn of al;   10
Haþ foure to his gouernyng:
Mouþ, and nose, and eyen wiþal,
Eryn fayre to his heryng.
To serue, þe brayn is pryncypal,
Chef of counseil, ymagenyng   15
To caste before, er after, fal.

1–8] The opening stanza establishes that the body is composed of the four elements, cf. Weatherly, *Speculum Sacerdotale*, p. 231/36, 'the body is i-made of iiii. elamentis'. The wholeness of the body and soul is mapped onto the harmonious composition of the world. In *Piers*, the commonality of the four elements is stressed, 'Ac to bugge water, ne wynd, ne wit, ne fer the ferthe,/Thise foure the Fader of Hevene made to this foold in commune:/Thise ben Truthes tresores trewe folk to helpe' (Schmidt, *Piers Parallel Text*, B.7.52–4).

7] **vnbynde**. The MS reads 'vnbende'. I have emended in order to restore rhyme.

8] In his opening sermon to the 1407 parliament, the archbishop of Canterbury took as his theme, 'Honour the king' (1 Peter 2:17). He went on to say that 'in time of need, each of the members of a man's body should, for its own part, support and succour the head, which is the member of each of them, so in similar fashion, should each liege honour, support and succour his king in time of need', *PROME* October 1407: Items 2 and 3. Gower states, 'the king and his people are like the head and the body. Where the head is infirm, the body is infirm. Where a virtuous king does not rule, the people are unsound and lack good morals' (*Vox*, IV.83–6).

9] Cf. Lydgate, *Fall of Princes*, 841–4, 'Mihti pryncis for ther hih renoun,/As most worthi shal ocupie the hed,/With wit, memorie and eyen of resoun/To keepe ther membris fro myscheeff & dreede'.

11–12] Only four of the five senses are listed; touch is omitted.

14–16] The function of the brain, in a mini-household allegory, is likened to the primary need for counsel. **chef of conseil**, cf. Poem 20/36, where the soul is described as chief servant of the household of the body.

16] Cf. similar proverb at Poem 12/82.

I lykne þe nekke, moche of myȝt,
Þat body and heued togydre knyt
To a iustice þat demeþ ryȝt,
For þurgh it comeþ all wordis of wyt.   20
ȝif a man take ordre of knyȝt,
Þe coler in þe nekke het;
And feloun forfete in þefte or fyȝt,
Þe iugement in þe nekke set.

Now I lykne mannys brest   25
[To] presthod in good degre;
Most in perile, lest in rest,
For besynesse in spiritualte.
In penaunce, and in preyer, prest,
Meke of spirit in pouerte;   30
[fol. 114b] Holde hospytal to Goddis gest,
And fede þe pore in charyte.

Þe shuldres and þe bakebon
I likne to lordis of [londes].

19]   **demeþ ryȝt**, cf. the importance of right judgement and justice in Poem 18/178. In Poem 12/92 this quality is required of the king. Lydgate likens prudent judges to sight, *Fall of Princes*, 855–7.

22]   **het**: to touch in the neck, see *MED* 'hitten' (*v.*); 1f.

23–4]   The poet plays ingeniously on the contrast between a knight's neck being touched with a symbol of prestige and a criminal's neck (**feloun**, Alford, *Glossary*, p. 57) being graced with the hangman's rope.

23]   **forfete**: past participle of 'forfeten', to overstep the bounds, transgress or offend, Alford, *Glossary*, p. 62.

26]   **to**. MS reads 'In' which must be a error, possibly scribal attraction to 'in' in the next line. In every other instance in this poem where the poet 'likens' a body part to a group of people the preposition 'to' follows the verb.

26]   A corrective to the prioritisation of the trials of knighthood in Poem 13/145–52. Lydgate likens the Church to the soul, *Fall of Princes*, 876–82.

27]   **besynesse**. The Eastern vowel, not needed here for rhyme, provides evidence of the mixed spelling of the poems.

31]   The image of offering hospitality to God's guest contrasts strongly with God's reproaches to humankind for denying Him refuge and shelter, Poem 10/121 and 11/69.

31–2]   Cf. Poem 17/33–40, where the injunction to perform the seven works of mercy includes feeding the poor and offering them shelter.

33]   **londes**. The MS reads 'þe lond'. I have emended to the plural in order to restore the rhyme. Cf. line 62.

Þe armes to knyȝtes to fende fro fon,   35
Þe squyers I likne to þe hondes,
Þe fyngres to ȝemen þat byfore gon,
Wiþ bent bowes and bryȝt brondes.
While all þys lymes arn wel at on,
Þe body in good plyt it stondes.   40

Mannys rybbes Y likne now,
Flesch and skyn in body hydes,
To men of lawe is to alow,
Þat kepes in loue boþe sydes;
Rybbes to resoun, þouȝ þey bow,   45
So lawe doþ ofte in fauour bydes;
Tyl ground be souȝt þere lawe doþ grow,
E[r]de in charite þat no man chydes.

I likne þe thies, flesch and bon,
Þat beren þe body quantite,   50

35] **armes**. The comparison allows for a pun on the human arm, *MED* 'arm' (*n*.); 1a,
weapons, *MED* 'armes' (*n. pl*); 1a and the insignia of a knight, 3a. Lydgate also likens
the arms to 'cheualrie', *Fall of Princes*, 851, to whom he entrusts the defence of the realm
from foreign attack, and the succour of the Church, 848–54.

36–38–40] **hondes ... brondes ... stondes**. The flexibility of dialect in furnishing rhyme is
evidenced by the poet's rhyming **handes** with **wandes** and **standes** lines 58, 60 and 64.

38] The sudden density of alliteration may have been chosen to suggest martial vigour. **at
on** reprises the refrain of Poem 11.

42] **hydes**. The plural is used for rhyme, not strictly for sense.

44] **loue boþe sydes**: to maintain concord between both sides involved in a dispute,
cf. Alford, *Glossary*, p. 91.

45–8] The syntax is dense owing to the constraints of the stanza form. I take the sense to
be that the ribs are likened to justice even though they bend, just as law does because
it often resides in partiality (a state of affairs that will persist) until ground is sought
where justice grows, and land in charity that no man disputes.

46] **fauour**, cf. note to Poem 13/9.

48] **Erde**. MS reads 'Ende', which produces obscurity. The emendation, cf. *MED* 'erd' (*n*.);
1.2, land, or country, provides a parallel to **ground** in the preceding line.

49] **thies**. In *Richard the Redeless*, the thighs of the body politic are the king's subjects who
have been so weakened by lawless retainers that the body is unable to stand, II.60–6.

49–56] Merchants are often the butt of estates satire and criticism (for instance their
exclusion from the main body of the pardon sent to Piers in Schmidt, *Piers Parallel
Text*, B.7.18–38), see further, Strohm, *Social Chaucer*, pp. 3–10; bearing this in mind, their
worth to the good of the commonwealth is here, perhaps, distinctive. The importance of
merchants in maintaining **burgh, toun, and cyte** recalls the concern for the defences of

To marchaundes in perile ride and gon,
Bryngen wynnyng, gold, and fee,
Make hiȝe houses of lym and ston,
Mayntene burgh, toun, and cyte;
Welþe and worschip in here won, 55
And good houshold of gret plente.

Mannys leggis likne Y may
To all craftes þat worche wiþ handes;
For al þe body beren þay,
As a tre þat bereþ wandes. 60
Þe feet to lykne Y wole assay
To alle trewe tylyers of landes;
þe plough, and all þat dygge in clay,
Alle þe world on hem standes.

The toes of þe mennys feet 65
Þo Y likne to trewe hyne

the realm, Poem 12/19 and 13/158. See also Hoccleve, *Regement*, 2374–6, 'Now if it happe, as it haþ happed ofte,/A kyng in nede borwe of his marchantis,/Greet wisdom were it trete faire and softe'.

51] Lydgate includes merchants in what he calls the 'agregate off peeplis and degrees', knit together in perfect peace, grouping them with mayors, provosts, burgesses and artisans, *Fall of Princes*, 862–8.

56–7] leggis ... handes. The ironic wordplay of legs and hands actually serves to scupper the analogy. On rhyme here, cf. notes to lines 38–40.

58] handes. In the body politic image in Hoccleve, *Regement*, if a king fall, he must defend himself with his hand (3934). Cf. Schmidt, *Piers Parallel Text*, B.7.60–3, 'Alle libbyng laborers that lyven with her hondes,/That treweliche taken and treweliche wynnen,/And lyven in love and in lawe, for hir lowe herte/Haveth the same absolucion that sent was to Piers'.

61–4] In 1373 Thomas Brinton preached a sermon in London which likened the feet of the body politic as the farmers and labourers who support the whole body firmly, Brinton, *Sermons*, Part III, Sermon 28. Cf. Lydgate, *Fall of Princes*, 891–6, 'Laboreris, as ye han herd deuised,/Shal this bodi bern up and susteene/As feet and leggis, which may not be despised;/For trewe labour is iustli auctorised,/And ner the plouh vpholden be trauaile,/Off kynges, pryncis farweel al gouernaile'. Cf. also *The Crowned King*, 71–2, 'And yit the most precious plente that apparaill passeth,/Thi pouere peple with here ploughe pike oute of the erthe'.

63] dygge in clay, cf. the Sermon for Septuagesima Sunday which exalts the 'grobbyng about þe erthe' 'of þe comyne peple', their 'erynge, and dungynge, and sowynge, and harwynge', Cigman, *Lollard Sermons*, p. 86/206–14.

Þat trauayle boþe in drye and weet,
In þurst, in hungere, and in pyne,
In het, in cold, in snow, and slet.
Many hiȝe none er þey dyne,   70
And wiþ good mete selde met,
But after howsel þey drynke no wyn.

Toes helpeþ man fro fal to ryse;
He may not stonde þat haþ no toon,
Lepe, ne renne, ne ryde in syse,   75
Wrastle, ne fyȝte, ne put þe ston.
Ȝif seruaunt þe maystere refuse,
Þe seruaunt lyuyng sone were gon;
And maystres, þouȝ þey ben wyse,
Wiþout seruant lyue not alon.   80

I likne þe wombe, and þat wiþynne,
To botemeles purs þat moche doþ take,
To couetous, no wyket pynne,
To glotoun, þe garner wyd open make.
Þe wombe preyed þe mouþ to blynne,   85
'þou etest and drynkest þat Y ake!'
'To slepe', quod þe eyȝe, 'we may not wynne;
Þe wrecched wombe so doþ vs wake!'

66–9]   The description recalls the vignette of the ploughman in *Pierce the Ploughman's Crede*, 421–32.

69]   The characteristic use of polysyndeton for emphasis stresses the importance of the labourers' work.

70–1]   A vivid contrast to Gower's vignette of the lazy, drunken ploughman, *Vox*, IX.561–70, 572, 582ff. and 648.

73–4]   Lydgate remarks that as a statue, 'withoute feet or leggis may nat vaile/To stonde vpright', so a prince cannot prosper without subjects, *Fall of Princes*, 827–33.

77–80]   While the stanza stresses the importance of labourers to the body politic, the last four lines assert the mutual interdependence of servant and master. Cf. Schmidt, *Piers Parallel Text*, B.16.190–2, 'So thre bilongeth for a lord that lordshipe cleymeth;/Might and a mene his owene myghte to knowe,/Of hymself and of his seruaunt, and what suffreth hem bothe'.

80–120]   The story of the dispute between the limbs and the stomach is told by John of Salisbury, *Policraticus*, VI.24. The *Livres des bonnes meurs*, written between 1405 and 1410 by the French friar Jacques Le Grand, achieved wide popularity in the fifteenth century. It describes the moral and controlled prince as a 'stomake whiche dystrybuteth the mete

'We dulle of heryng!' quod þe ere,
'We dase for dronken!' quod þe eyȝe,   90
'I wende but o mone þere were,
And me þouȝte two y seyȝe!'
Quod þe handis, 'Fro mouþ may we not vs were!'
Quod [fol. 115a] þe mouþ, 'Y drank while Y myȝte drye!'
'Allas!' quod þe feet, 'all we bere,   95
And ȝoure bargayn dere abye!'

The handes and feet þe mouþ gan preye,
'Let vs thre dayes reste;
Wiþ alle þyn oþere lymes pleye,
Wiþ felaschip, frend, and geste.'   100
Þe mouþ in anger he dede saye,
'Þes þre dayes do ȝour best;
Al þat tyme, nyȝt ne daye,
No mete ne drynk come in my brest'.

Thre dayes the mouþ dede faste   105
Tyl wombe calde þe mouþ vnkynde.
'Vn[b]ynde thyn handes; are þey faste?
Stere, and lete þe mylle grynde!'
Quod þe eren, 'Oure heryng is at þe laste'.
Quod eyen, 'We dase and waxe blynd'.   110

that it receyueth to all the members and reteyneth no thynge to hym selfe but only the
nouryssynge' (Caxton's translation quoted in Jacob, *Fifteenth Century*, p. 306).

91–2]   A proverbial reference, cf. 'Satan and his Priests', Matthew, *Works of Wyclif*, p. 267,
'Þei demen of o mone or candel to be two, for þei ben vndisposid to deme & knowe þe
treuþe bicause of here dronkenesse'. See also Appendix to Introduction, p. 78.

91–3]   the rime riche on 'were' is created from two different verbs: the past tense of the verb
'to be', and the verb 'were' meaning 'to defend oneself against', *MED* 'weren' (v.); 1.2b.

96]   **bargayn**: an agreement between two parties setting how much each gives and takes, or
what each performs and receives; a compact or business deal, Alford, *Glossary*, p. 13.

105–7]   rime riche with 'faste' as a verb meaning to abstain from food, and 'faste' as an
adjective meaning bound tight.

106]   **vnkynde**. A number of senses are possible here: 'not in accord with the regular course
of nature'; see *MED* 'vnkinde' (*adj.*); 1a; 'injurious to health', 1c and 'ungenerous', 5b.

107]   **vnbynde**. MS reads 'unkynde'; a scribal repetition of the last word of the previous
line. Emendation to this verb restores sense of a kind. How does a mouth have hands?

108]   **mylle grynde**. The proverbial image of grinding and milling is seen also in John
Ball's letter of 1381, see Dobson, *The Peasants' Revolt*, p. 381.

Quod handes and feet, 'Oure strengþe is paste'.
Quod brayn and herte, 'Vs wantes mynde'.

Quod þe mouþe, '3e playne whyle Y ete,
And while y faste, 3e make gret doel'.
Quod handes and feet, 'Also we gete   115
Þat þou spendest eche a deel;
We may play, swynke, and swete,
While mouþe in mesure makeþ his mele:
For mesure kepeþ kynde hete,
And al þat tyme we fare wele.   120

I likne a kyngdom in good astate
To stalworþe man, my3ty in hele;
While non of his lymes oþer hate,
He is my3ty wiþ anoþer to dele.
3if eche of his lymes wiþ oþer debate,   125
He waxeþ syk, for flesch is frele;
His enemys wayte, erly and late,
In his feblenesse on hym to stele.

118–19]   **mesure.** The importance of mesure to combat gluttony is a standard feature of pastoral literature, e.g. the section in gluttony in Furnivall, *Handlyng Synne*, advises 'Be mesurable yn alle þyng' (p. 210/6526), and 'Be nat to þy self so large,/Ouer mesure þyn herte to charge,/Þat þou ne kast for vylaynye/Ne for þe foule lust of glotonye' (p. 211/6541–4) and Brandeis, *Jacob's Well*, p. 142/1–2, 'Glotonye is, whan þou hast a talent, wyth-outyn temperure & mesure, to mete or drynke'. There may be influence of Ephesians 4:16, 'From whom the whole body, being compacted and fitly joined together, by what every joint supplieth, according to the operation in the measure of every part, maketh increase of the body, unto the edifying of itself in charity'. Cf. Poem 14/39 and 16/35.

119]   **kynde hete**: the natural temperature of the body *MED* 'kinde' (*adj.*); 1b.

121–6]   Cf. Lydgate, *Fall of Princes*, II.869–72, 'And as a bodi which that stant in helthe,/Feelith no greef off no froward humours,/So eueri comoun contynueth in gret welthe,/Which is demened with prudent gouernours'.

121]   **I likne.** The poet steps in to provide an unequivocal moralisation of his analogy, as he does also at line 141.

125]   **debate.** The anxiety about internal debate is a recurrent issue in the sequence: Poem 4/149/243, 5/25, 12/33, 21/91. The settlement of the dispute in the body politic enables the poet to model a harmonious realm.

127–8]   As in the previous poem, a well-ordered kingdom is seen to be necessary to repulse attacks from foreign enemies.

And hed were fro þe body stad,
Noþer partye were set at nouȝt;   130
And body wiþoute armes sprad,
Were armes wiþoute handis ouȝt;
Ne handis, but þey fyngres had,
Wiþoute fingere what were wrouȝt?
Þes lymes makeþ hed ful glad –   135
And al þe body, and it be souȝt.

Ȝif a man hurte þy fynger or too,
But þou make deffens o ferre,
Leg or arm may take þe fro,
To body or hed auntre hym herre.   140
Ensample to kyngdom Y set this so,
And oure frendis be distroyed by werre,
Þan kepe þe wisely fro þy foo,
For wiþ all his myȝt he wole come nerre.

God saue þis man is so deuysed,   145
Hed and body, all lymes in kynde,
But þere as vertues ben despysed,
To preye to God þey waste here wynde.
God leue þat synne may be refused,
And of dedly synnes vs vnbynde,   150
And eche stat in his kynde be vsed;
God, of his mercy haue vs in mynde! Amen.

129–36]   An extended illustration of the need for all parts of the body to be regarded, especially those members that might be dismissed as insignificant.

134]   Cf. the analogy of the Trinity as a hand in Schmidt, *Piers Parallel Text,* B.17.167, 'Namoore than may an hande meve withoute fyngres'.

137–40]   Reprises the sternness of Poem 13/17–24; cf. notes thereon.

140–1]   If there is a topical allusion behind these lines, it is likely to be the civil war in France and the worries about its implications for war on England. The stanza continues the discussion of Poem 13/129–68 and anticipates the subject of Poem 16.

146]   **in kynde:** according to natural constitution, see *MED* 'kinde' (*n.*); 3a, 'proper'; 6a and 12a befitting 'one's rank or station', cf. line 151.

147]   The moral basis of good government is asserted also in Poem 2/39, 12/72 and 13/90.

149]   **synne … refused:** reprises Poem 11/41.

Poem 16. A remembraunce of Lij folyes

Kail dated this poem to 1419 because he took line 62 to refer to the assassination of John the Fearless, duke of Burgundy, by followers of Charles VI's son. As I argue in the Introduction, this reading can be challenged. The poem is not a review of the career of one man; rather, it is an extended example of a Middle English text capitalising on the dissolute reputation of Flanders as a means to counsel good government in England. Flanders is the glaring example of a kingdom gone wrong (see *Poems*, pp. 11–14). It is important that the Digby poem is titled 'A *remembraunce of Lij folyes*' (my emphasis). It is a recollection of foreign civil disorder to sound a note of warning about contemporary conditions in England. A miniature example has already occurred in the sequence, cf. note to Poem 12/85. The word 'folyes' is also important: the poem is an example of the 'catalogue of fools' tradition of writing, see Swain, *Fools and Folly*, ch.2. Invective combines with moralising to hold up the follies of Flanders as a mirror to English rule. The command of the verse form, which in the final four lines of each stanza, moves into 'flytyng' mode, is virtuosic.

16. A remembraunce of Lij folyes

Loke how Flaundres doþ fare wiþ his folyhede!
Durste no man dygge after trouþe wiþ no manere toles;
To wynne [fol. 115b] wrongly wele, wod þey gan wede,
But werkis of wys men were cast vnder stoles,
Glosers counseled lordis for to take mede,   5
To maken hem riche and here lordis pore foles.
Whan þe souereyns were set here sogettis to drede,
Þe glosers skulked away for shame of here sooles.
Falsed shal neuere ben ateynt
Til iuge here eche mannys pleynt,   10
Redresse and make an ende,
Or ellys to mercy bende,
Make hem kyssen and be frende
Þat were fon feynt.

Fyfty folyes ben and two;   15
Alle þo Y wole mynne among:
To triste in trete to his fo
Þat haþ begyled hem ofte and long,

1-8]   The generic tenor of the opening stanza recalls Poem 1/57-72 and 7/11, 14/4-5, and
    cf. 22/72.
2]   **dygge after trouþe**: a new metaphor for a persistent theme in the poems, especially
    Poem 3/1-8 and 4/97-104/113-20. Cf. 'The Bisson Leads the Blynde', Robbins, *Historical
    Poems*, p. 128/34, 'ffor trouthe ys sonkyn vndur þe grounde'.
3]   **wynne wrongly**: condemned also in Poem 1/122, 17/83/91, 19/34/77, 21/37/58. **wede**: MED
    does record this form as an infinitive of 'wadan', though not this example from Digby.
    It has the sense 'to go, proceed', *MED* 'wadan' 1a.
4]   Cf. Poem 2/35-6, 6/28 and 10/134.
5-6]   These lines recall especially Poem 13/134-5 and cf. 4/169-76.
7]   **drede** the subject is **souereyns** who frighten (*MED* 'dreden' 6a) their **sogettis**. It is hard
    to tell whether there is a topical reference here, or whether the scenario is timeless.
8]   Elsewhere, the spelling is uniformly 'soules' and the form here suggests a concern
    with eye rhyme.
9-10]   **ateynt**: diction very close to Poem 13/60-1, and cf. notes thereon.
11]   **make an ende**: bring a legal case to its conclusion, Alford, *Glossary*, p. 50.
13]   Cf. Poem 1/163-4.
15-16]   An explicit reference to a catalogue of follies, though I count only 50 in the poem.
17]   Cf. Poem 13/121-8 (and note), 137-44/155.

And hate hem þat telle hym so,
And wilfully wolle suffre wrong,   20
It is worthy he smerte and be wo,
Þat of his owen skyn wole kerue a thong.
Þat chepen moche and not han to paye,
And wiþ his lord to homly wole playe,
Swere moche and not be trowed,   25
Boste moche and not allowed,
Threte alle men and neuere on bowed,
All are folyes þat Y say.

He is a fool þat werre wole wrake
Þat may not maynten it wiþ mede;   30
And so moche vndertake
Þat wot he wel he may not spede,
And of his ney3ebour his enemy make,
For a straunge mannys dede.

19] Might this be a reference, not to Flanders, but to the silencing of those who counsel against making treaties? – such counsellors would, of course, include the Digby poet.

22] Cf. proverb at Poem 11/38 and notes thereon.

23] Cf. line 96.

24] **homly**, cf. the flatterer in Poem 2 who pleases his lord 'at bed and bord' (l. 25) and is found in 'halle and chambre' (l. 64).

25-7] The catalogue here is similar to the composition of moral axioms known as the *Facetus*, 'Tres sunt stultitiae, quibus insipiens perhibetur: qui tantum loquitur, quod nulla fides adhibetur/qui tantum terret, quod nulla fides adhibetur/qui tantum tribuit, quod mendicare videtur' (quoted Swain, *Fools and Folly*, p. 13 from Carl Schroeder, *Der deutsche Facetus* (Berlin, 1911), p. 24). 'There are three follies by which the fool declares himself: that he talks so much no credence attaches to his word/that he menaces so much that his threats are not respected/that he bestows so much that he appears to beg.'

26] **allowed**: not from 'allouen' but 'louen', *MED* (*v.*); 1f dispraised or belittled. *MED* lists 'on loue' in the sense of declined.

29-30] It is hard to know whether this is a generic folly comment or whether it refers to John the Fearless's failed military enterprises. In April 1413 the Burgundians and Orleanists fought a battle over Paris which resulted in ignominious failure for Burgundy and John being forced to flee (Owen, *Connection*, p. 36). In 1418 (though this is probably too late for the poem) the 2,000 Burgundian forces which John had assembled at Rouen were easily routed by the English (Owen, *Connection*, p. 49).

33-7] If there is a specific reference, the most likely is to John's murder of the duke of Orleans in 1407 which resulted in civil war, cf. Poem 12/84, and Introduction, pp. 10–14.

34] **straunge**. Several senses are possible here: *MED* 'straunge' (*adj.*); 1b: 'barbaric'; 2b: 'outlandish' or 3e: 'unnatural', all of which could point to the **dede**'s being John's act of

And he þat mesure wole forsake,   35
And nedles put hymself in drede,
Of mannys deþ haue no rouþe,
But hate hem þat tellen hym trouþe,
Loue hym þat cherische hym in synne,
And suche games bygynne,   40
Where þat he wot he may not wynne,
But besyen hym in slouþe.

He is a fool þat no good can,
Ne non wole lere but slow in dede;
A gret fool Y holde þat man   45
Þat of his enemys haþ no drede.
Þurgh suche foly Flaundres began,

murder. Scattergood, *Politics and Poetry*, p. 70, suggests that this refers to John's taking up arms against Charles VI on behalf of Henry V, but once again this places the poem as late as 1419.

35]   **mesure**, cf. note to Poem 15/118–19. Job 42:3, 'Who is this that hideth counsel without knowledge? Therefore I have spoken unwisely, and things that above measure exceeded my knowledge', and Wisdom 15:14, 'But all the enemies of thy people that hold them in subjection, are foolish, and unhappy, and proud beyond measure'.

37]   May allude to John of Burgundy, who had originally appeared a sincere mourner for the death of Orleans; as soon as he had made his position secure, however, he made an open avowal of his complicity in the crime (Owen, *Connection*, p. 30).

38]   Cf. note to line 2 and Proverbs 13:16, 'The prudent man doth all things with counsel: but he that is a fool, layeth open his folly', and 18:2, 'A fool receiveth not the words of prudence: unless thou say those things which are in his heart'.

39–40]   The games may refer to the complicated negotiations between England, Burgundy and Orleans between 1411 and 1414 where each party tried to play off the other in forming alliances and counter-alliances. On each side, promises were broken. A full account of these diplomatic and military intrigues is given by Jacob, *Fifteenth Century*, pp. 100–17. See discussion in the Introduction, pp. 11–12. See also Proverbs 10:23, 'A fool worketh mischief as it were for sport: but wisdom is prudence to a man'.

42]   **slouþe**: a rather surprising end to the stanza if the energetic duplicity of John the Fearless be behind the remarks. It is possible the choice is dictated by the stringent demands of the rhyme scheme, or that the oxymoron of being busy in sloth is a scathing comment at the uselessness (and sinfulness) of foolish activities.

45–6]   A proverbial comment, cf. 'Twelve Profits', 21–2, 'These are to enmyes of whilk [tho] comune proverbe tellis, fool ne dred(s) tham noght', cited in Whiting, *Proverbs*, p. 197, F.98.

46]   **enemys** might allude to Burgundy's efforts between 1411 and 1414 to seek alliance with England in order to bolster his position against the Orleanists despite the tradition of hostilities between England and France.

Of after perile þey tok non hede.
Hit is worthy he ete bred of bran
Þat wiþ floure his foo wil fede,   50
And truste al in gloser charmes,
In hyndryng in worschip of armes.
And lette lawe it mot not syt,
And conscience away flyt,
May brynge a lord er þat he wyt   55
Emyddis grete harmes.

Flaundres was þe richest land and meriest to mynne,
Now is it wrappid in wo and moche welþe raft,
For defaute of iustice and singulere to wynne,
Þey were rebell to ryse craft aȝen craft.   60
Here lord had part of þe foly þey were wounden ynne,
Forthy he les his lordshipe and here fraunchise raft,
Here enemys lawhen hem to skorne and seyn, for synne,

48]   Lack of foresight is criticised also at Poem 12/82.
49–50]   A pithy sentence drawn from the familiar distinction between fine bread made
of flour and that of poor quality made of bran, e.g. the statement in *The Wife of Bath's
Tale*, D.478, '... age ... hath me biraft my beautee ... The flour is goon ... The bren, as I
best kan, now moste I selle'. See also 'The Bisson Leads the Blynde', Robbins, *Historical
Poems*, p. 127/4, 'No man may knowe hys frend fro foo', and 'Four Proverbs', Furnivall,
Political, Religious and Love Poems, p. 251/13, 'secundus dixit frend is foo'.
51]   **gloser charmes** recalls the flatterer of Poem 2. Cf. Isaias 32:6, 'For the fool will speak
foolish things, and his heart will work iniquity, to practise hypocrisy'. 'The Bisson Leads
the Blynde', Robbins, *Historical Poems*, p. 127/5, 'Now gyllorys don gode men gye', and
line 9, 'Now gloserys full gayly þey go'.
53]   **lette lawe**, cf. Poem 12/60.
54]   **conscience**: used here in the sense of a legal faculty to determine right from wrong,
see Alford, *Glossary*, p. 34.
57–70]   Cf. 'The Bisson Leads the Blynde', Robbins, *Historical Poems*, p. 130/69–72, 'Take
hede how synne hath chastysed frauns,/Whan he was in hys fayrest kynde,/How þat
flaundrys hath myschauuys/ffor cause þe bysom ledyth þe blynde'.
57]   **richest land**. A great deal of the English concern at affairs in Flanders, stemmed not
only from the long-seated military hostility between England and France, but from the
economic importance of the region. Owen notes that while, politically, Flanders was
French, economically it was English, *Connection*, p. 11.
59]   **singulere**, cf. note to Poem 1/4. 'The Bisson Leads the Blynde', Robbins, *Historical
Poems*, p. 128/19, 'Robberys now rewle ryȝtwysenesse'.
60]   **craft aȝen craft**, cf. note to Poem 3/33.
61–2]   See Introduction, p. 11, for discussion of these lines.
63]   See headnote, and cf. Poem 12/147.

Of here banere of grace God broken haþ þe shaft.
[fol. 116a] When prelat is forbode to preche,   65
No trewe man trouþe dar teche;
Encresyng of temperalte,
Suspende spiritualte,
What land is gouerned in þat degre,
May wayte after wreche.   70

I holde hym a fool þou3 he be wys,
Þat spekeþ among men of name,
Þat at his wysdom set no prys,
But skorne hym and don blame.
And he þat telleþ where peryle lys,   75
And gete no þonk but harm and shame;
And he þat pleyneþ Y holde hym nys,
Þat get no mendys but dowble grame.
By þese poyntes Flaundres was lest,
Now is it out of rule and of rest,   80
Drede is here chef gayte,

64]   God's vengeance against dissolute kingdoms reprises the concerns of Poem 12/87/148 and 13/81–8. The idea recurs at Poem 16/92.

65–6]   **prelat is forbode to preche … trewe man trouþe**: diction that would not look out of place in a Wycliffite text, though here 'prelate' is used without the particular pejorative associations that it gathers in Lollard works, e.g. 'Of Prelates', 'Þat prelatis leuen prechynge of þe gospel ben gostly manquelleris of mennys soulis', Matthew, *Works of Wyclif*, p. 55, and 'prelatis letten & 'forbeden prestis to preche þe gospel', Matthew, *Works of Wyclif*, p. 57, and 'bi þis cause pharisees pursuen trewe prestis', Hudson, *Wycliffite Writings*, p. 80/215–16. The reregistration of Lollard diction in the sequence is discussed in the Introduction, pp. 34–7.

65–70]   As **what land** (l. 69) suggests, these are generic comments about corruption in the clerical estate rather than specific topical references. Cf. 'The Bisson Leads the Blynde', Robbins, *Historical Poems*, p. 128–9/35–8, 'With offycyal nor den no fauour þer ys,/But if ser symony shewe þem syluer rovnde./Þer among spiritualte it ys founde,/ffor pete ys clene out of þer mynde.' Cf. note to Poem 9/161 and 14/25–32/81–2.

70]   **wreche**, cf. Poem 12/78–89.

71–4]   Cf. Proverbs 15:5, 'A fool laugheth at the instruction of his father: but he that regardeth reproofs shall become prudent'. Cf. Poem 6/28.

73–6]   Cf. Poem 2/33–6.

79]   **poyntes** in the sense of 'item in a list' *MED* 'pointe' (*n.*); 1.7a; a sign of the poem's knowing indebtedness to the catalogue of follies tradition. **lest**: the sense is 'lost' and must be a past participle of 'losen' *MED* (*v.*); 2, but this spelling form is not recorded, cf. Poem 12/132.

So eche man on hem bayte,
Þat ȝet þey honge in awayte
Of a newe conquest.

He þat myȝt thryue and nel not thee,   85
Ne his owen harmes knawe,
Apert ne in preuytee,
Serue God for loue ne awe,
Ne gouerne wel his owen degre,
Ne rule hymself in ryȝtwys lawe;   90
Whan wyse men fro hym fle,
Þen God his grace wole fro hem drawe.
Þat moche wynneþ and no thyng wole haue,
But ȝeue it awey to nedeles þat craue,
Aȝens conscience despit,   95
Borwe moche and neuere quyt,
When God for þat gylt smyt,
What glosere can þat wounde saue?

Þat freek may wel be holden a fool
Þat wayueþ wit and worcheþ by wille,   100
And skippe into sclaundre scol,
And scorne hym þat telleþ hym skylle,
And lyue in Lenton as in ȝool,

84]   **newe conquest**. While Burgundy's forces suffered military defeats, Flanders was not conquered as such. It is more likely that the remark is directed towards English readers and the danger of invasion from their foreign enemies. A 'wicked age' Flanders is fashioned as a mirror in which the English should look in order to avoid disaster.

86]   A version of the 'know thyself' tag, see note to Poem 1/8. **knawe**: Northern form is used for rhyme. Elsewhere the form is 'knowe', apart from Poem 24/212, where the Northern form is in the middle of the line and not used for rhyme.

88]   An inversion of the injunction to monarchs, Poem 9/149.

89]   The line is repeated almost verbatim, Poem 21/101. See also the same idea at Poem 12/65.

92]   Cf. line 64 and note thereon.

94]   Cf. Poem 14/109.

96]   Cf. line 23.

100]   Cf. refrain of Poem 5/8, 'þat leueþ wit, and worchiþ by wille.'

102]   **scorne** recalls line 74 and, almost verbatim, Poem 13/73.

103]   **Lenton … ȝool**, i.e. to eat, drink and celebrate in a way appropriate to the Christmas season during the forty days of Lent which were a time of fasting and abstinence.

His flesch in foly to fulfille.
Þouȝ þe dotard deye in dool,   105
Þe ryȝtwys nel not rewe his ylle.
Who so wil not knowe his awen astat,
Ne deliuere chekkys er þat he be mat,
He shal haue worldis wondryng,
And his soule hyndryng,   110
And ay in paynes pondryng;
To mende þanne is to late.

Of all folk vppon fold, Y fynde but foure trewe,
Þat don here deuere dewely, and take no mede:
Syknes is oon, and sorw doþ sewe,   115
Þe thridde hat deþ, and þe fierþe drede.
Þey clayme vs by custom, for þey oure kyn knewe,

105]   **dool**, cf. note to Poem 15/114.

107]   **awen**: the Northern spelling is not needed for rhyme. **astat**, cf. Poem 14/73.

108]   The image of check mate is seen in a number of Middle English texts, e.g. Gray, *Religious Lyrics*, p. 93/11–12, 'Tyll sotell deth knokyd at my gate,/And onavysed he seyd to me, "Chek-mate!"'; Chaucer, *The Book of the Duchess*, 659, 'Fortune seyde "Chek her!".' And "Mat"'; *Troilus and Criseyde*, 2.754, 'I am myn owene womman, wel at ese,/Shal noon housbonde seyn to me "Chek mat".' 'Lament of a Prisoner against Fortune', *Anglia* 32 (1909) pp. 484–90/110, 'When men be meriest, alday deth seith 'chek mate!' In Digby the image depicts a fool who fails to make his own moves at check in chess before he is mated.

110]   **hyndryng**. The line makes sense; the soul is harmed or injured *MED* 'hindren' (*v.*); 1, but, unusually, the close rhyme of the three short lines of the stanza is impaired. Might the participle have originally been 'hondlyng'? See *MED* 'hondlen' (*v.*); 3a 'to act towards with hostility'. This still does not yield perfect rhyme, but is closer than the MS reading. One further possibility is 'sondryng' see *MED* 'asondren' (*v.*); a: 'be deprived (of bliss)'. I have not emended the line as the lack of full rhyme may be the result of the stringency of the verse form finally taxing the poet's powers to the limit.

112]   Cf. Poem 19/28.

113–26]   In an ingenious turn in the poem, the conclusion to the catalogue of follies is a mini-allegory on the inevitability of death and the 'last things'. The poem turns outwards into a generalised morality, with the only true loyal workers figured as sickness, sorrow, death and fear who have legal right to humankind, and in a chilling twist creep into the body and clothe it with death's garments. The final stanza belongs to the tradition of 'memento mori' religious lyrics, and the tradition of writing which urges mankind to think on their end and to reflect on the transitoriness of existence, e.g. Gray, *Religious Lyrics*, pp. 83–95 and Furnivall, *Vernon Poems* II.672–80.

117]   **clayme … custom**: legal diction: to assert a right to a possession, Alford, *Glossary*, p. 28, and cf. Poem 5/53, 24/30/186/218/271, and **custom**, cf. note to Poem 13/82.

And endid wiþ oure aunsetres tyl þey to erþe ȝede.
Þey spare prynce ne pore, old ne newe,
For þey crepe in to his cors and cloþe hem in his wede.   120
Drede bryngeþ man to buxomnes,
Sorwe of herte makeþ synnes les,
Syknes breþe stekenyng,
And bowe to a bekenyng,
And bryngeþ hem to rekenyng   125
Tyl deþ all redresse.

125] **rekenyng**, cf. note to Poem 1/29/35.

Poem 17. Loue that God loueth

With this poem, the sequence moves from moralisation on temporal, worldly affairs to a more devotional meditation. Combining features of the 'complaint of Christ' tradition of religious writing (see headnote to Poem 10), with those of Christ's love-longing for humankind (see note to Poem 11/97–104), the poet forges a powerful lyric which urges the forsaking of worldly possession, and the embracing of God's love. The fierce vengefulness of Poems 10 and 11 is here tempered, especially with the use of the image of Christ's skin as the parchment of a charter, lines 181–4, and Jesus as the herb called 'trewe loue', lines 185–92. As notes to individual lines indicate, this lyric reprises diction and motifs both within the poem itself, and from other poems in the sequence, especially Poems 1, 7, 8, 10 and 11; and in turn, the imagery and lexis reappear in Poems 19 and 22. In order to avoid duplication of material, referencing to these common religious motifs, and parallels with other devotional lyrics, will chiefly be directed back to the annotation of these earlier poems. The voice of the poem moves – often without warning – between that of the third person narrator who enjoins his audience to moral devotion, and the voice of God who cajoles, pleads and begs ungrateful humankind for His love. Although the materials of the poem are conventional, the subtlety of the development of the imagery, together with the deft use of rhetorical patterning, produce a lyric of controlled intensity.

17. Loue that God loueth

That ilke man wole lerne wel
To loue God wiþ al his myȝt
Þat loue in his herte fele.
Þere God doþ loue, loue þou ryȝt;
There God doþ hate euerydele,   5
Hat it boþe day and nyȝt;
ȝeue hym [fol. 116b] noþer mete ne mele,
But flyt hym fere out of ȝoure syȝt.

Many gret causes is
To loue God why men ouȝte: 10
He shop vs lyk ymage his,
And wiþ his deþ fro pyne vs bouȝt,
And ȝut þouȝ we don ofte amys,
For eche a gylt he beteþ vs nouȝt;
And we þenke to amende, he profreþ to kys –   15
Man, of loue, he haþ besouȝt.

ȝif a lord ȝeue fee or rent
For to do a gret office,

1] **wel**. The MS may lack final 'e' on this word, cf. line 33 where the spelling produces complete eye-rhyme for the stanza. 'wele' is found as an adverb in non-rhyme positions, e.g. Poem 1/40 and 9/135.

2–6] The rhetorical force of the stanza stems from crisp use of the antithesis between **loue** and **hate** and extended use of polyptoton: **loue** as an infinitive verb (l. 2), a noun (l. 3), third person verb (l. 4), imperative (l. 4), together with epanados – abrupt repetition for emphasis – of **loue** (l. 4).

7–8] **hym**. The stanza invokes, and inverts, the hospitality image of devotional lyrics (see note to Poem 10/155–60); what God hates is suddenly personified as a person who must be refused hospitality and banished from sight.

10–16] Cf. 'Mercy passes all Things', Frunivall, *Vernon Poems* II.659/41–8, 'I made þe, Mon, ȝif þat þou minne,/Of feture lich myn owne fasoun,/And after crepte In-to þi kinne,/And for þe suffred passioun;/Of þornes kene þen was þe croun/fful scharpe vppon myn hed standyng;/Min herte-blood ran from me doun;/And I for-ȝaf þe alle þing.'

11] God's creation of humankind in his own image recurs at line 78 and 114. See also note to Poem 10/15.

12] Cf. Poem 19/26.

15] **amende**, cf. note to Poem 11/13.

17–24] The stanza exposes how earthly service performed for a lord is essentially selfish,

To serue hym wel is þyn atent;
For thy profyt, but not for his –   20
For he fyndeþ þe þy vaunsement;
Þy loue vppon þe profyt lys:
Suche worldly louers are gostly blent –
Suche loue to God is cold as yse.

3if þou serue God for helle drede,   25
Or loue God for his blisse,
Þat loue is worth no parfyt mede:
Þou [louest] thy profyt and not hisse.
To pyne, ne blis, take non hede;
But loue, God for good he is.   30
Suche loue to God his erande doþ spede,
And pleseþ best to God ywys.

Fleschly man may do wele
Þe seuene werkes of mercy þat God bed:
3eue pore folk mete and mele,   35
Herberwe, drynk, cloþe, and fed
For syngulere profyt eche a dele,
For drede of pyne, and couetys of mede;

done for profit and advancement. It transposes into a devotional key, the condemnation
of singular profit throughout the sequence.

23] **blent**: the past participle of *MED* 'blenden' (*v.*); 1 from OE 'blenden'; the past participle
of *MED* 'blindan', from OE 'blind' (*adj.*) or 'ofblindian' (*v.*), would be 'iblint'. **blent** is used
also in Poem 23/54; in both instances to secure rhyme. In very similar phrases at line
17/134, 10/13 and 23/39, the poet uses the adjectival **blynde** – again to secure rhyme.

25–32] The stanza reprises diction from Poem 1/33–40, but here suggests something more
subtle than serving God out of fear of hell, and in the hope of winning heaven's reward.
In Poem 17 such self-serving love is not worthy of reward; only love for God because he
is good (l. 30). Cf. Poem 9/117/149 and 18/106.

28] **louest**. The MS lacks a verb. Kail, *Poems*, supplied 'sechest'. My choice of **louest**
attempts to continue the wordplay of the stanza which is seen elsewhere. **hisse**, cf. note
on the same rhyme, Poem 1/116.

31] **erande ... spede**. Diction repeated at line 172, and cf. Poem 1/46, 4/175 and 18/112.

33–40] Whereas elsewhere in the sequence humankind is urged to perform the seven
works of mercy (Poem 1/149–52, 6/37–40, 9/123–7 and 19/89, here the poet warns that
such good deeds may have **syngulere profyt** as its motivation (cf. note to Poem 1/4).
One must pay no heed to the threat of punishment or the reward of heaven; one must
love God because God is good.

36] Cf. Poem 1/150.

Loue God ouer all, for good [hele]:
To pyne, ne blisse, take non hede.   40

Ȝif þou sette loue in þat degre
To loue God, for he þe wrouȝt,
Þan make þou hym as he dede þe,
Þan loue for loue euene is brouȝt.
Ȝif þou loue God, for he made þe fre,   45
Þat dyȝed for the, to blisse þe bouȝt,
þan dyȝe þou for hym as he dyȝed for þe;
Ȝut heuene blisse þou quytest hym nouȝt.

Ȝit o thyng þere is byhende,
Man, þat God askeþ of the: 50
Alle worldys delys fro þyn herte wende,
Wiþ alle þyn herte, loue þou me,
Þy swete þouȝtes me sende,
For worldis goodis myn are he.
Loue me gostly þat am þy frende,   55
Þanne al euyl shal fro þe fle.

39] The MS reads 'he is', possibly as a result of memorial attraction to line 30. This destroys a rhyme scheme which is sustained throughout the poem. **hele** is used in rhyme position at line 181.

41–8] The devotional inflection of this stanza is very similar to Poem 11/97–104; see note thereon. Cf. also, 'Love Christ who Loves Thee', Furnivall, *Political, Religious and Love Poems*, p. 255, 'Leorne to loue, as ich loue þe;/On alle my lymes þou mith seo/Hou sore ich quake for colde;/For ich soffre much colde & wo/Loue me wel, and nomo;/To þe i take and holde.'

43] **make**: not from *MED* 'maken' (*v.*); 1, in the sense of 'create' (despite presence of **wrouȝt** in the preceding line), but *MED* 'maken' (*v.*); 2, 'to match'. The poet urges humankind to love God in equal measure, only to argue in the final line that one can never repay God for his love.

44] **euene**: justly, equitably; see Alford, *Glossary*, p. 53 and note to Poem 11/97–104 for analogues. The rhetorical force of the stanza is created by polyptoton on **loue** as a noun and verb and the anaphora and polyptoton of **dyȝed**.

48] Cf. Poem 9/131–6, 13/40 and 11/105 and note thereon.

49] **byhende**: the form is used for rhyme; cf. 10/209. *MED* records no forms of the word in this spelling. The only instance in Digby of the more usual spelling **byhynde** is line 17/171, and this disrupts the eye-rhyme of the stanza, see note.

51] **worldys delys**, cf. Poem 1/58 and 8/79.

54] **he**. The usual form of the third person plural pronoun is 'þay'. Here the poet resorts to a more archaic form in order to secure rhyme.

55] **frende**. See note to Poem 10/63/66.

Þat loue me gostly Y can assay,
For gostly loue in herte Y souȝt.
Do worldly thyng fro þyn herte away,
And haue me principal in þy þouȝt.   60
Be lord, and haue richesse þou may,
Worldis richesse for man was wrouȝt;
Gostly loue – þat is my pray;
But worldly goodis in heuene comeþ nouȝt.

For gold and syluer and precyous stones,   65
Swetnes of floures, erþely bewte,
Þe shrynes wiþ all seyntes bones,
In heuene were foul felþe to se.
Tyl body and soule aȝen arn ones,
Mad parfyt in claryte,   70
Saue God hym self, in heuene wones,
Þe principal mankynde shal be.

'God, how may Y, man, bygynne
Wiþ myn herte to loue þe?'
'Repente, and wylne no more synne,   75
So mowe [w]e [fol. 117a] frendis be.
Good soule sybbe to my kynne,
For Y made it lik to me;
Mankynde Y tok a mayden wiþynne,
So gostly and bodyly breþeren be we'.   80

57]   **assay**: in the legal sense of 'to examine', Alford, *Glossary*, p. 10.

67–8]   **shrynes ... foul felþe**. The designation of shrines and relics as foul filth would not look out of place in a Wycliffite polemic, see Hudson, *Premature Reformation*, pp. 304–6. That such a remark could be made in order to rail against the vanity of worldliness is a sign of the scope for a range of religious expression even after the promulgation of the Lambeth *Constitutions* in 1409; see further discussion of these lines, Introduction, pp. 32–3.

69]   Alludes to the re-uniting of body and soul on Judgement Day.

70]   **claryte**: the radiance of redeemed souls.

75]   Cf. Poem 19/52/74.

76]   **we**. MS reads 'ȝe'. I have followed Kail's emendation to restore sense. **frendis**, cf. line 55 and note.

77, 80]   **kynne ... breþeren**, cf. Poem 9/15, 10/167, 20/11, 22/22 and notes thereon.

79–80]   **mayden**. See also line 130 and Poem 20/58. Cf. Julian of Norwich, *Revelation*, ch. 57, p. 69, 'for in that ilk tyme that God knitted him to our body in the maydens womb he

Who loueþ God, he wil bygynne
For to folwe Goddis lore;
Loke where he dede wrongly wynne,
Make amendis, aȝen restore.
Ȝoure loue fro me ȝe parten o twynne;   85
For worldis worship ryches in store,
Heuene ȝates ȝe steken and pynne,
Þat ȝe shulde saue ȝe haue forlore.

To gete loue þus bygynne,
Wiþ clene herte and swete þouȝt,   90
Wiþ trewe tong, not falsely wynne,
Ne stele ne flatre, ne lyȝe nouȝt.
Do ryȝtwys dede out and ynne,
Loke þy werkys be euene wrouȝt,
Do almes and penaunce, and leue þy synne: 95
Wiþ þese þre loue is bouȝt.

God spekeþ to man and lerneþ lore:
Þe comaundementis and þe crede.
'Ȝeue me þy loue, Y aske no more –
Wiþ al þy herte in loue and drede.   100
And þou nylt ȝeue it me, warne me byfore,
Sette pris to selle it loue, and bede,
I wole ȝeue the myself þerfore.
Where myȝtest þou haue a beter mede?

toke our sensual soule; in which takyng he us al haveyng beclosid in him, he onyd it
to our substance'.

83] **wrongly wynne**: another instance of the poems' preoccupation with unlawful profit,
see especially Poem 21/37 where the diction and sense are very close to lines 83–4,
and also Poem 1/122 and 19/34/77. The same concept, though expressed with different
vocabulary, is repeated at line 91.

87] Diction reprised Poem 21/45.

88] The isocolon stresses the antithesis of sense between saved and lost.

94] **euene**, cf. note to line 44.

97–104] The sentiments of this stanza combine God's address to humans, Poem 9/97–104
and 11/113–20.

98] Identical to Poem 19/90.

99–100] Cf. Poem 11/97–100.

And þou nelt ȝeue, ne selle it me,   105
Aȝens me þou wilt debate,
Þan wil Y gon away fro þe,
And ȝelde to þe hate for hate.
My face wiþ loue shalt þou not se,
But steke þe wiþoute heuene ȝate,   110
Fro alle vertues and charyte,
Wiþ helle houndes in endeles date.

Haue Y þy loue, so may þou quyte,
I mad þe lik ymage to me,
And ȝif þe þenke þat was to lyte,   115
Þanne þenk Y dyed on rode tre.
Þouȝ þou trespas, Y do not smyte,
But byd ȝif þou wilt mendid be;
And þou be lost, whom wiltow wyte
Is it long on me – or þe?'   120

Discrecioun of ȝong and old,
Of alle þynge nouȝt ouȝte;
Of alle þat may be bouȝt and sold,
Loue for loue is euenest bouȝte.
Whan worldis loue doþ fayle and folde,   125
Goddis loue fayleþ nouȝt;
Trewe loue makeþ men be bolde,
Wiþ loue felawship togydre is brouȝt.

106–8]   Cf. Ecclesiasticus 18:24, 'Remember the wrath that shall be at the last day, and the time of repaying when he shall turn away his face.'

108]   Recalls Deuteronomy 32:41, 'If I shall whet my sword as the lightning, and my hand take hold on judgement: I will render vengeance to my enemies, and repay them that hate me.'

110]   The image of shutting mankind out of the gates of heaven inverts the trope of man's inhospitality to God and re-registers the diction of the image used in Poem 10/69–70; cf. Poem 11/36.

113–20]   Cf. notes to Poem 10/43–70.

113]   Cf. note to line 48.

121–2]   The sense is compressed. **Discrecioun** has the sense of 'differentiation', MED 'discrecioun' (n.); 5, and the gist is that to make distinction between young and old is immaterial in all things.

124]   Cf. note to line 48 and Poem 11/97–9.

For loue God com fro heuene toure,
In mayden Mary tok mankynde,   130
For oure swete he drank ful soure,
Where myȝt we trewere loue fynde?
His loue passeþ worldis tresoure,
Ȝaf syȝt in helle to gostly blynde,
And we wole knytte his loue to oure,   135
For soþe, þat knot shal neuere vnbynde.

'Haue Y þy loue, so may þou gete;
Þat loue wole þy soule saue,
Among myn angels haue a sete,
In ioye of heuene as seyntes haue.   140
Ȝif þou nelt, [fol. 117b] Y wol þe þrete,
In helle pyne be fendis knaue;
Wiþ þy conscience þou trete
Wheþer is þe leuere for to haue.

And þou madde in þy mood   145
To werne me þe loue þou has,
I wole caste on þe myn herte blod,
To bere witnesse þou forfetest gras.
And my vengeance þat is so wood,
Wiþ helle houndis in fyre þe chas.   150
Þou hast fre wille, knowest euyll and good:
Chese where wyltow take þy plas.

129] **heuene toure**, cf. 'Christ's Testament', Furnivall, *Vernon Poems* II.638/9, 'ffrom my kindome I com doun'.

130] Recycles line 79.

131] Cf. notes to Poem 10/116–20. See also 'Christ's Testament', Furnivall, *Vernon Poems* II.649/167–8, 'A loue-drynke I asked of þe;/Eysel and galle þou ȝaf to me'.

132] **trewere**, cf. Poem 22/23.

134] Cf. Poem 11/19.

135] Cf. Julian of Norwich, *Revelation*, ch.53, p. 63, 'so to be knitt and onyd to him that therin were kept a substance which myte never, ne shuld be, partid fro him'.

137–40] Cf. Poem 11/20–4.

141] **þrete**, cf. Poem 10/139–40.

142] **fendis knaue**, cf. Poem 1/55, 4/109 and 20/182.

148] **bere witnesse**, cf. note to Poem 13/88.

151] Cf. Poem 11/61–2 and note to Poem 10/19.

And þou of þy loue daungere make,
What may thy loue profyte me?
And þou3 þou woldest me forsake,   155
Out of my lordschipe þou my3t not fle.
Angels bry3t and deueles blake,
In helle and heuene my lordschipes be;
Þere be no mo wayes to take.
Is loue or hate more profyt to þe?   160

3if þy loue to þy flesch doþ bende,
To greue me þou dost bygynne;
3if þou loue þe world þat wole make ende,
Of hym þou shalt more lese þan wynne;
3if þou be suget and loue þe fende,   165
He wole þe hate and 3eue pyne for synne.
Loue me – Y am God þy frende,
And oure loues shal neuere twynne'.

Wheþer trewe loue go or sende,
Hym thar not tary in his dede;   170
When mede haþ leue to stande byh[e]nde,
Þanne trewe loue his erande may spede.
Þou3 trewe loue haue lityl to spende,
Euere he fyndeþ a frend at nede,
Þat fro his foon wole hym fende.   175
Who so is loued hym thar not drede.

156] This line is repeated almost verbatim Poem 19/53.
160] **profyt**. There is particularly dense use of this word in Poem 17, lines 20/22/28/37/154/160, accounting for over half the usage in the sequence as a whole. The lyric works to overturn human notions of profit for advantage and gain, with spiritual connotations of the fate of the human soul, and also, more importantly, how God's love for humankind escapes earthly definitions of profit and reward.
164] **hym**: refers back to **world**. Christ continues the metaphor of winning and losing to argue that the reward for loving the devil and the deadly world will be punishment.
171] **byhende**. MS reads 'byhynde', which spoils the eye-rhyme. I have emended to the form used elsewhere in the sequence; see note to line 49.
172] See note to line 30.
176] The same idea is expressed Poem 3/108.

God sayþ, 'Y haue mercyes to dele,
Þat wole amende, no more do mys.
My mercyes þousandes mo ken fele,
Þan þousandis worldis wikkidnes'.   180
His herte blod wrot oure hele,
And Ihesus body þe parchemyn is.
Wiþ trewe loue he prented oure sele
Þat is heritage of oure blis.

Þere is an herbe þat hatteþ 'trewe loue',   185
And by name it haþ no pere;
Is lykned to Ihesus Y may proue:
His handes and feet þe leues were,
His herte was wiþ a spere þurgh shoue,

178]   Diction reprised at Poem 21/54.

181–4]   These lines draw on the popular comparison between Christ's body and a charter.
Christ's skin is represented as parchment, and his blood the writing of the terms of the
Redemption. The image of the seal proves the validity of the document, and is a visible
sign of the truth of the doctrine of atonement. God is presented as having entered into
a legal covenant with humankind, for which he pays with his body and blood. Woolf,
Religious Lyric, discusses the tradition, pp. 212–14, and, more recently, Steiner, *Culture*,
pp. 49–53 and 61–75. One of the fullest expositions of this trope is 'Christ's Testament',
Furnivall, *Vernon Poems* II.637–57.

181]   **herte blod wrot**, cf. 'Christ's Testament', Furnivall, *Vernon Poems* II.644/85–92, 'Þe
penne þat þe lettre was wiþ writen,/weore scourges þat I was wiþ smiten./How mony
lettres þeron beon,/Red, and þou miht wite and seon:/ffif þousend foure hundred fyfti
and ten/woundus on me, boþe blak and wen./To schewen on alle my loue-dede,/Mi-self
I wole þis chartre rede.'

182]   **parchemyn**, cf. 'Christ's Testament', Furnivall, *Vernon Poems* II.641/51–4, 'Ne mihte I
fynde no parchemyn/ffor to laste wiþ-outen fyn;/Bote, as good loue bad me to do,/Min
oune skin I tok þer-to.'

183]   **sele**, cf. 'Christ's Testament', Furnivall, *Vernon Poems* II.647/135–46, 'Þe seles þat
hit was seled wiþ,/Þei were grauen vp-on a stiþ … with þe spere of stel myn herte þei
stongen/Þorw myn herte and þorw my longen; … Þe selyng-wax was deore abouȝt,/At
myn herte rote hit was souȝt,/And tempred al wiþ vermiloun/Of my rede blod þat ran
doun.' See also Hope's patent in Schmidt, *Piers Parallel Text*, B.17.5–8, '"Nay", he seide, "I
seke hym that hath the seel to kepe –/And that is cros and Cristendom, and Crist theron
to honge./And whan it is asseled so, I woot wel the sothe –/That Luciferis lordschipe
laste shal no lenger."'

184]   **heritage**: inherited right or possession, Alford, *Glossary*, p. 70, cf. 'Christ's Testament',
Furnivall, *Vernon Poems* II.646/117–18 quoted in next note.

185–200]   The image of the herb 'trewe-loue' is also found in 'Christ's Testament', Furnivall,
Vernon Poems II.645/114–26, 'And my loue-dedes haue in Mynde;/ffre to haue, and fre
to holde,/wiþ al þe purtynaunce to wolde,/Myn heritage þat is so fre./ffor homage ne

Mannys loue was hym so dere.   190
What soule is syk, lay þat herbe aboue:
Hit makeþ hool al yfere.

God biddiþ vs do no þynges but two:
In loue and drede to hym bende,
Lede þy soule lustes fro,   195
World and flesch and fro þe fende.
Ihesus herte was cleued so
To lete out trewe loue to his frende.
In that blisse God graunte vs go
Þere trewe loue woneþ wiþouten ende.   200

for feute/No more wol I aske of þe,/But a foure-leued gras ȝeld þou me:/O lef is soþfast schrifte,/Þe toþur is for synne herte-smerte,/Þe þridde is "I wol no more do so",/Þe feorþe is "drede god euermo"; whon þeose four leues to-geder ben set,/A "trewe loue" men clepen hit.'

Poem 18. The declaryng of religioun

Kail dated this poem to 1421, *Poems*, p. xxii, because he thought it referred to complaints made to Henry V that the Benedictine monks had deviated from the rules of their first institution, and that, to reform these monks, the next year, a Provincial Capitulary was made, where among other things articles were passed to regulate clothing, money, accommodation, numbers of horses and contact with women. Having noted these parallels, Kail then provides a caveat, that 'it is not impossible that the author mentions certain abuses which prevailed in his own monastery, and which he thought it necessary to reform' (*Poems*, p. xxii). This latter comment derives from Kail's surmise that the author was 'a priest, most probably an abbot, or a prior', p. ix (cf. Scattergood, *Politics and Poetry*, p. 17).

Kail might have been right. But what is especially noteworthy about this poem is the highest praise for the monastic, contemplative life, coupled with the anxiety that its singularity be stringently observed (see especially lines 1–8). Given that a number of the poems in the sequence as a whole address issues pertinent to the early years of Henry V's reign, it is hard not to see this poem as responding to the new king's ardent desire for the rejuvenation of monastic life. The new foundations of Sheen and Syon were not established until 1415, but as Jeremy Catto observes, 'the elements which contributed to this conception had not been evolved overnight', 'Religious Change', p. 110. The author of the *Gesta Henrici Quinti* dates Henry's desire to found new monasteries between the quelling of Oldcastle's rebellion and the English embassy to Sigismund, the Holy Roman Emperor in July 1414, 'And so, amid the storms and stresses caused by these painful experiences, the mind of the king remained firm and was unshakable; nay, rather, abiding by his former most devout intention to extend the Church and encompass the peace of kingdoms, he first began the foundation of three monasteries' (Taylor and Roskell, *Gesta Henrici Quinti*, p. 13). Walsingham also locates the plan to found these new houses in 1414, *St Albans Chronicle*, p. 82. Allmand notes how 'reinvigoration of the monastic life, with the importance which it attached to prayer and to both spiritual and physical discipline, was another aspect of the religious history of this reign which owed much to the personal intervention and initiative of the king himself', *Henry V*, p. 272. The monastery at Sheen was given the name of the House of Jesus of Bethlehem, and the monks who entered the order were reminded at their service of initiation that they were to live a life of strictness and authority. Their clothes were to be rough and simple, their diet basic, and they should live in silence. The charter emphasises the monastery as a place of prayer, especially prayers for the good of the kingdom, Allmand, *Henry V*, pp. 273–4. To date this poem to a particular year poses problems; but it is by no means improbable that the poet may have been aware of the plans for monastic reform and rejuvenation before Sheen and Syon were placed on an official footing, and that Poem 18 is designed to bolster the king's cause, see further, Introduction, p. 41, and on the speculation that the author of the sequence was himself a Benedictine monk, see pp. 72–5.

18. The declaryng of religioun

Who þat wole knowe condicion
Of parfyt lyf in alle degre,
God is foundour of religion:
Obedyent to charyte.
Swete þou3t in deuocion   5
Is weddid [fol. 118a] to chastite;
In brennyng contemplacion,
Þe hi3est lyf of spiritualte.

The goode lyueres in spiritualte,
Þe worldly lyueres hem doþ hate   10
Wiþ occupacioun of temperalte;
Dryueþ relegeon out at þe 3ate
For besynesse of vanyte,
Vaynglory, and hy3e astate.

2] **parfyt lyf**. That in Poem 13/145–52 the order of knighthood is singled out as the best, and surpassing that of **relegous**, is in indication of the strategic nature of the poet's writing.

3] **God is foundour**. The superlative statement establishes the unimpeachable authority for the foundation of monastic orders. The comment may be flattering approval of Henry V's championing of contemplative life, and/or a usurpation of the diction of the founding of private religions more usually associated with Wycliffite texts where the 'founding' of religious orders (more usually friars than monks) is interrogated with great hostility. The 'founder' in these cases is usually Satan. Cf. note to Poem 8/61.

4–6] **charyte ... chastite**: two of the monastic vows. Poverty is treated in the next stanza.

11] **temperalte**, cf. the warning to the clergy that they should not be caught up in temporal possession, cf. line 152 and Poem 8/60.

12] **out at þe 3ate**: the image suggests the violation of the cloister. Worldly corrupt monks are often figured as being outside the monastery, e.g. Chaucer's Monk as an 'outridere', *General Prologue*, A.166, who doesn't care for the text which likens a monk heedless of rules to a fish out of water, A.179–81, and Schmidt, *Piers Parallel Text*, B.10.293–306, 'Whan fisshes faillen the flood or the fresshe water,/They deyen for droughte, whan thei drie ligge;/Right so religion roileth and sterveþ/That out of convent and cloistre coveiten to libbe' ... Ac now is Religion a rydere, a romere by stretes,/A ledere of lovdayes and a lond buggere,/A prikere on a palfrey fro manere to manere,/An heep of houndes at his ers as he a lord were.' See also B.4.120.

13] **besynesse**, cf. the idealised form of the priesthood in Poem 15/28 which figures them in busyness of 'spiritualte'.

Þat þus chaungen here degre   15
Þey come to heuene neuere or late.

What is religion in mynde?
In clene herte is soule o prys,
Out of þraldom doþ vnbynde
A louer of vertues, a hatere of vys.   20
Eche soule is parfyt clerk of kynde
In hyȝe discrecion and wys;
Of soules men may no fooles fynde,
But assente to þe flesch and make hym nys.

Religeon is champion in batayle,   25
Discomfites hys enemy;
Ȝif temptacions hym assayle,
Þere he hath þe victory.
Religeon is trewe trauayle,
In Goddis seruyce neuere werye;   30

15]   **chaungen here degre**. Throughout the sequence there is an insistence of keeping to one's estate and rank, e.g. Poem 9/131 and 14/73. The monastic preoccupation with temporal possession and high estate imperils their souls.

18]   **clene herte**: a variation on the 6th beatitude, Matthew 5:8, 'Blessed are the clean of heart: for they shall see God'. See also Poem 21/97.

21]   **clerk of kynde**: a spiritual version of the natural order and health called for in the account of the political kingdom, Poem 15/145–52. See note to 15/146 for meanings of 'kynde'.

22]   **discrecion**. The faculty of moral discernment, the ability to tell good from evil, MED 'discrecioun' (n.); 1a, is emphasised in this poem, see also lines 33 and 166, and is invoked elsewhere in injunctions to flee vice and folly and to pursue virtue, Poem 4/181, 5/65, 20/166 and 23/76.

25–8]   The image of the military Christian can be traced back to Paul's exhortation in Ephesians 6:11, 'Put you on the armour of God, that you may be able to stand against the deceits of the devil', and verses 16–17, 'In all things taking the shield of faith, wherewith you may be able to extinguish all the fiery darts of the most wicked one./And take unto you the helmet of salvation, and the sword of the Spirit (which is the word of God).' The Digby verses may also be inflected with the contemporary depiction of Henry V as God's champion, see Poem 13/161–8, and Hoccleve, *Minor Poems*, 4/22, 'Be holy chirches Champioun eek ay' and Poem 5/12–14, 'To holy chirche o verray sustenour/And piler of our feith and, werreyour …'

29]   **trewe trauayle** emphasises the *work* of the contemplative life. The same phrase is used in praise of honest labour which earns its due rewards, Poem 2/38.

Haue mede wiþ martyres he may not fayle
Þat euere is redy for to dyȝe.

Werkys wiþoute discrecion,
Vaynglory in staat is brouȝt;
And shrift wiþoute contricion   35
In skorne þe sacrament þey souȝt;
And preyere wiþoute deuocion –
Þouȝ þey preye, God hereþ hem nouȝt;
Þe lippes turne preyers vp so doun
Þat spekeþ oþer þan herte þouȝt.   40

Cherische no vices in ȝoure warde
To serue God in good atent,

31] **martyres**. Lollard texts often encouraged martyrdom for the sake of reforming the Church and promulgating true belief, e.g. *EWS*, I.625/68–9, Matthew, *Works of Wyclif,* 21/25ff, 452/17 and Arnold, *Wyclif,* III.179/25ff and pp. 184–5. The statement that the truly contemplative will earn heavenly reward with martyrs may represent a wresting of the spiritual high ground from the Wycliffites. The Wycliffite text 'Of Clerk's Possessioners' likens monks to 'anticristis martiris', because instead of being dead to the world, they are alive to it and to its vanities, Matthew, *Works of Wyclif,* p. 123.

33] Cf. note to line 22. The line is identical to Poem 4/181.

35] Cf. the insistence on observing the sacrament of confession truly in Poem 9. The line is a reworking of Poem 4/180.

37–40] Line 37 is identical to Poem 4/183. Private prayers and devotion were a target of Wycliffite polemic: see, for example, 'Of Feyned Contemplative Life', Matthew, *Works of Wyclif,* p. 190, '& siþ men þat fulfillen not goddis lawe ben out of charite ben not acceptid in here preiynge of lippis, for here preiere in lippis is abhomynable, as holy writt seiþ bi salomon (Proverbs 28:9)'. In Digby, the practice of outward devotion is defended, but the poet urges the importance of matching outward performance **lippes** with devotion in **herte** in a way which is seen also in the *Myroure of oure Lady,* a text which painstakingly instructs the nuns of Syon in the proper delivery of singing the hours of the Virgin. There is repeated emphasis on the need for devotion and understanding in heart: 'Ye haue by the rewle of youre professyon, whereby ye are bounde to synge euery day these holy houres of oure lady solmpnly. And this solempnyte asketh both inwarde besynes to have deuocyon *in harte* and also in syngyng and redyng with tongue and in other outwarde obseruance' (Blunt, *Myroure,* p. 23); '[God] taketh more hede of the *harte* then of the voyce. But when bothe accorde in hym then is yt beste. And yf ether shulde fayle, yt is better to lacke the voyce then the harte from hym' (p. 35); 'It profiteth but lytel to syng only with the voyce, or to say only with the mouthe, withoute *entendaunce of the hart*' (p. 40) (emphasis mine).

41–8] **warde**: either a wing or section of a convent, or the convent as a whole, *MED* 'ward(e)' (*n.*); ȝe. These remarks appear to be addressed to an abbot and encourage a

And non wiþ other be to harde
Þat ben professed in ȝoure couent;
Þey myȝte forþenke it afterward.   45
Þay tok þe abyte and wolde repente,
Þey lese of God a gret reward
Whan wille fro religeon is went.

A questyon of ȝow Y craue –
Resoun assoyleþ it by skille: 50
Who may here soules saue
To were an abyte wole or n[y]lle?
Þenk on þy berþe, þenk on þy graue,
Þy fleschely lustes not fulfille.
For helle ne heuene shal no man haue   55
Mawgre his teeþ, aȝeyns his wille.

Thouȝ þou be of gentyl blod,
Þenk all com of Adam and Eue;
Gadre not in propre worldis good,
Þat nes no religeous but worldis reue;   60

policy of weeding out corruption with discretion and respect for the commitment that
a professed member has taken.

48]   **wille** must have a sense akin to determination, resolve or spirit, *MED* 'wil(le)' (*n.*);
5a.b. The stanza suggests that the spiritual determination of members of the convent
must be respected even as their spiritual behaviour is monitored.

49-56]   **assoyleþ** provides a solution to an answer, cf. Schmidt, *Piers Parallel Text*, B.3.237,
'And David assoileth it hymself, as the Sauter telleth'. The sense of the stanza is that
whether or not one wears a habit, if one is concerned to save one's soul, then one must
think on the abjection of birth and death, and abstain from sinful lusts. The last two
lines, however, are obscure: no man shall have heaven or hell, in spite of himself, against
his will/determination/desire? If the possessive 'his' refers to God, then some sense
emerges, but there is no antecedent.

52]   **nylle**. MS reads 'nelle'. Throughout the sequence both 'nel' and 'nyl' forms are used, but
this is the only instance where the Eastern spelling is used at the end of a line, and here it
disrupts the rhyme. I think it is a scribal error for 'nylle' – the form used Poem 10/8.

56-7]   Cf. the proverbs, 'When Adam delf & Eue span, sir, if þou wil spede, Whare was
þan þe pride of man?' and 'Whanne Adam dalfe & Eve spanne, ho was þo a gentleman?'
used in John Ball's sermon, see Dobson, *The Peasants' Revolt*, p. 374.

59]   Cf. Poem 4/4.

60]   **worldis reue** may be seen to claim the reformist agenda from Wycliffites, 'Of Feigned
Contemplative Life', Matthew, *Works of Wyclif*, p. 195 argues that monks are now so busy
about 'worldly occupacioun þat þei semen bettere bailyues or reues þan gostly prestis'.

Þe herre degre, þe mekere of mood.
Tak no vengeance þou3 folk þe areue,
Lat comon lawe stonde as hit stood,
Loke no proud herte þy charyte meue.

Haue non enuye [fol. 118b] day ne ny3t   65
To goode lyuers bet þan 3e,
But auy3e faste wiþ all þy my3t
To lyue beter þan doþ he.
Þan countrefetest þou Goddis kny3t
Þat is enuye in charite;   70
Alle þou3tes in Goddis doom are di3t
And dedes after þat þey be.

Tho þat lyuen in fleschly delys,
Fro þat companye remewe;
Loue here bodyes but not here vys,   75
And cherische hem to good vertue.
And þo þat wil algate be nys,
Loke þou no3t here maneres sewe;
Go to company þat is wys;
Lete fooles drynke þat þey dede brewe!   80

Religeous be war wiþ whom 3e stonde:
Wiþ gentyles, or folk þat worldly is,

61]   Cf. Poem 14/1–4.

63]   Recalls, almost verbatim, Poem 14/67. Monks are urged to take no part in either financial or legal transactions.

69]   **countrefetest**, cf. line 128 and the emulative behaviour of Mary at 20/152. **Goddys kny3t**, cf. note to lines 25–8.

70]   The oxymoron of equating one of the deadly sins with one of the virtues pithily encapsulates the injunction to translate spiritual envy into the emulation of spiritual excellence.

71–2]   Cf. the statement at Poem 7/103 which reappears slightly transposed Poem 19/103.

73–80]   Recalls the moral instruction of Poem 1/49–56, but translates it to a monastic context.

80]   **drynke … brewe**. Variations on this proverb can be seen in 'The Song of the Battle of Lewes', Brown, *English Lyrics XIII*, pp. 131–2/11, 'Let him habbe ase he brew!', *The Seven Sages of Rome*, ed. K. Brunner, EETS 191 (1933; reprint 1988), 65/1360, 'Þou schalt … drinke þat þou hast ibrowe', and Gower, *Confessio*, III.1626: 'Who so wicked Ale breweth,/Fulofte he mot the werse drinke'; cf. II.246.

81–3]   **stonde … honde**, cf. note to Poem 4/194/196.

Þat ȝe grype not hand in honde,
When ȝe take leue, loke not ȝe kys.
Man to man hem thar not wonde,   85
Ne woman to woman no peryle ne is,
But man to woman myȝte breke þe bonde:
In towche is susspecioun of mys.

Suche towches not ȝe byde,
Wolde buffete þe soule and wounde wiþynne;   90
Ȝeue oþere cause þat stonde bysyde
To wene it were a bargayn of synne.
Towches in custom þouȝtis hide,
Þan sclaundre and shame nyll not twynne,
With conscience, sclaundre and shame doþ chide,   95
To shewe opert he wol begynne.

With mekenesse ȝe may heuene gete;
Dispyse non in lowe degre,
Resceyue no worschip, ne hyȝe sete,
Þat pryde go bytwen God and þe;   100
Wolde make to hem self forȝete
For worldis ryches and vanyte.
War for dronkenesse of drynkes grete,
Fro glotry of metes of gret daynte.

81–8]   The precise pitch of these remarks is hard to determine: are they generic advice to observe the vow of chastity, or a portrait of monastic lechery; compare, for instance, the monk in Chaucer's *The Shipman's Tale*, who not only kisses the merchant's wife, but embraces her hard and catches her by the flanks, VII.202–3? Or might these lines be a direct reference to the 1421 Benedictine reforms?

89–96]   The stanza begins lucidly with the warning not to have any physical contact with women; such touch can cause mortal sin, and onlookers may interpret the exchange as a sign of lecherous agreement. Lines 93–6 move into one of the poet's abrupt and characteristically dense mini-allegories. The sense appears to be that touch habitually conceals thought with the result of persistent slander and shame, but then conscience (faculty of moral judgement) chides slander and shame and brings out into the open that which was concealed.

97–104]   Generic advice to embrace humility and avoid gluttony which hints at avoiding the trappings of aristocratic life. Chaucer's monk, with his penchant for roasted swan and the aristocratic luxury, provides a striking counterpoint to monastic ideals.

97]   A reference to the first and second beatitudes, Matthew 5:3–4, 'Blessed are the poor in spirit: for theirs is the kingdom of heaven./Blessed are the meek: for they shall possess the land.' These verse also inform line 157.

To religeon mekely bende   105
To serue God in loue and drede;
To herkne tydynges not ʒe wende,
Ne bokes of vanyte not ʒe rede;
Resceyue no lettere, ne non out sende
But hit be for ʒoure hous nede,   110
Oþer to kyn or certeyn frende,
In goodnes ʒoure erande to spede.

Kepe ʒoure wacche and seruyce dewe,
And rule of habyte clenely ʒeme,
And fille ʒoure hertes wiþ good vertue,   115
And wikked vyces fro ʒow ʒe fleme;
But loke deuocion growe ay newe.
Be suche wiþynne as ʒe outward seme,
Good aungel and wikked boþe ʒou sewe,
And wryten ʒoure dedes þat shal ʒow deme.   120

Wacche not outrage in wast despence,
Fro hard to nyce þy flesch to fede.
Wiþ bischop or shryfte ʒe mowe despence
Fro hard to hardere ʒoure lyf to lede.
Withstonde temptacions, make defence,   125
Þe moo ʒe withstonde þe more mede.
And ʒe wiþ seyntes will haue reuerence,
Þan moste ʒe countrefete here dede.

105-20] These lines stress the importance of avoiding worldly distractions and the strict observance of monastic routine.

106] Cf. almost identical formulations of this line at Poem 1/64, 8/85 and 9/149.

113] An imperative to observe the monastic services at the regular hours.

117] The importance of renewed devotion is stressed even as the poet urges maintenance of strict routine.

119-20] **good aungel ... wikked.** Line 119 is repeated almost verbatim at Poem 22/46, and the image of writing a record of the deeds that will come to judgement is also repeated. See also Poem 24/387-402.

121] **outrage ... wast,** cf. Poem 9/100.

123] Given the sustained defence of the importance of shrift in Poem 9, this is a startling comment. The context of the stanza as a whole, however, suggests that the poet enjoins striving for the highest degree of spiritual excellence through individual struggle rather than reliance on external props such as institutional ritual or church dignitaries.

Kepe [fol. 119a] sylence whyder ʒe byde or go;
Fro wordis of vanyte ʒoure lippes steke.   130
Speke faire to frend and fo,
For fayre speche doþ wraþþe breke.
Þat doþ wrong deme so,
Lete not vengeance þy wraþþe wreke:
Vengeance is Goddis; he demeþ þo   135
In werk and word all þat men speke.

In rule of religeon is ordeyned ʒore:
Byʒe no thyng to selle and wynne,
Marchaunt and religeous – on mot be forbore;
Þey may not wone on herte wiþynne.   140
Ne kepe no iewels, ne propre in store;
Þat nes no religeous, but dedly synne
In fleschly delices, and loue it more
To parte þy loue and God atwynne.

That þenkeþ good þouʒt in sylence,   145
Þey speken to God in specyale.
How mow ʒe lette hem for conscience
Calle hem to werkis generall?
Summe bidden in vertue of obedience,
Contemplatyf in spirituale;   150

129] **sylence**. The importance of living in silence may show awareness of the founding
ideals of Sheen, see headnote, or it may be an injunction to observe pristine monastic
practice.

131] Cf. ironic reversal of this advice, Poem 6/67.

134–5] Romans 12:19, 'Revenge not yourselves, my dearly beloved; but give place unto
wrath, for it is written: Revenge is mine, I will repay, saith the Lord.'

137–40] Cf. note to line 60.

137–8] A statute passed by Pope Benedict XII decreed that monks were not allowed to
receive money, 'Ne victualia ministrentur in pecuniis'. This is quoted in article 9 of the
1421 reforms, Myers, *Documents*, IV.789, but the poet may have had knowledge of the
edict independent of reference to these proposals.

141] See note to line 155.

145–52] A sustained defence of the importance of the contemplative life with its focus on
inner devotion and prayer, and a call for monastic life to be left alone and valued on its
own terms. It is precisely the inner devotional life and ritual of monastic practices that
were attacked by Wycliffite writers, most vigorously in the text 'Of Feyned Contemplative

To religeon they don a gret defence
Þat bryngen hem to werkis temperale.

Hyȝe astate ne gentyl blod
Bryngeþ no man to heuene blisse;
Gret hors, ne iewel, ne browded hood   155
Nes no cause of holynesse,
But pore of spirit and meke of mood.
Ȝeue God þy soule and eche man hisse –
Gret lordschipe, ne myche good
Nes no cause of sykernesse.   160

Tonsure, abyte, ne no wede
Nes no cause of religeon.
Ne wakyng, ne fastyng, ne almesdede,
Ne preyere, ne oreson,
But þe herte þerto take hede   165
Wiþ werkys of discrecion.
Deuocion makeþ soules to spede
Wiþ werkis of contemplacion.

Religeon is most meke
In abyte, of alle vertues floures.   170
Richesse, ne worldis worschipe seke,

Life', which argues that such practices deflect from the truly important work, which is
that of preaching, Matthew, *Works of Wyclif,* pp. 188–9.

151]   **Defence**. offence, something prohibited, *MED* 'defense' (*n.*); 5c.

154–8]   **blisse ... hisse**: for the rhyme, cf. note to Poem 1/116.

155]   The 1421 reforms regulated the number of horses that monks or abbots could own
(Item 2) and also proposed the establishment of a uniform cowl, frock and riding hood
(Item 4), Myers, *Documents,* IV.788, but criticisms both of excessive dress and of the
love of horses were a staple of anti-monastic satire, see note to line 12.

157]   Cf. note to line 97.

159]   Cf. Poem 9/27–8.

161–2]   Cf. Gower, *Vox,* 5.42–50, who remarks that if a monk does not renounce the world,
then whatever his outward appearance, his tonsure and his humble garb are of no use to
him. Nowadays a monk withdraws from the world only in respect of his dress and thinks
that a religious order is sufficient for him in outward appearance alone. The outward
habits of the private religions, more usually the friars than the monks, were a particular
target of Wycliffite polemic, e.g. Matthew, *Works of Wyclif,* pp. 315–16.

166]   Cf. note to lines 33–40.

But offre to God alle honoures.
Richesse and worschipe make soules syke
In vaynglory and sharp shoures,
Make vertues þe waxe, deuocioun þe wyke,   175
To brenne briȝt in heuene boures.

Iustice is religeon in sete
Þat demeþ riȝt in all degre,
And queste is religeon trouþe to trete;
Ȝeueþ eche man þat his shulde be.   180
A child may wiþ his fader plete,
And ȝut kepe his charyte,
And of his kyng blameles gete –
Lawe is so gentyll and so fre.

Þouȝ summe of thy breþeren don a trespas,   185
He wole amende and do no moo;
Parauenture þou art in þe same cas,
Or after myȝt ben in suche two.
Loke not þat þou hym chace,
Ne sclaundre hym not to haue shame and wo;   190
Pray God forȝeue hym of his grace,
And kepe þe wel þou do not so.

173]   Variations on this line are at Poem 1/53, 8/26 and 10/11.
175–6]   A number of Middle English texts develop the figurative potential of the wax and wick of a candle, but none in exactly the way that the Digby poet does here. See Schmidt, *Piers Parallel Text*, B.17.205–31, and Lydgate, *Life of Our Lady*, 6.390, 'The wax betokenyth his manhede,/The weyke his soule.'
176–92]   The concern with even-handed justice in the final two stanzas, and the need for discerning charity in correction, suggests that a convent ought to be able to regulate itself from within.
182–3]   Cf. Proverbs 3:12, 'For whom the Lord loveth, he chastiseth: and as a father in the son he pleaseth himself.'

Poem 19. [untitled in manuscript]

The poem returns to the complaint of Christ tradition of devotional lyrics and reprises many of the tropes of Poem 10 as well as the moral axioms of other poems in the sequence. Just as the political concerns of Poem 16 are followed by the religious lyric in Poem 17, so here the particular focus on monks, with its possible topical inflection, is followed by a more timeless reflection on the ingratitude of humankind in the face of God's Passion and Redemption. The poem steers a middle way between invoking God's vengeance and the promise of His mercy. To avoid duplication of material in the annotation to the poems, where common tropes are used in Poem 19, simple line references will be used to signal earlier use and critical comment thereon.

19.

In my conscience I fynde,
And in my soule I here and see,
To repreue man þat is vnkynde.
Goddis wordis þis may be:
'Man, of resoun, haue in mynde,   5
I made þe lyk ymage to me;
For loue Y hadde to mankynde,
I toke manhed lyk to þe.

Mannys loue Y ȝerned ȝore,
Þat loue was in myn herte souȝt;   10
Mannys loue sat me so sore,
Nas neuere bargayn derrere bouȝt.
Man, is þe laft no loue in store?
What is þe cause þou louest me nouȝt?
Telle me ȝif Y myȝte don more;   15
What is byhynd þat lakkeþ þe ouȝt?

For þy loue Y meked me low,
And dyȝed on þe rode tre.
Answere, man, and be aknowe,
Shewe what þou suffred for me.   20
For suche seed as þou dost sowe,
Þerof shal þyn heruest be;

3] Cf. Poem 10/61.
6–8] Cf. Poem 9/98, 17/11/114 and 20/181.
11] Cf. line 73 and note to Poem 10/39–40.
12] Cf. Poem 11/100.
15] Cf. note to Poem 10/62.
18–19] Cf. Poem 10/98 and 17/116.
20] Cf. Matthew 25:37–40, Jesus reports God's words at the Last Judgement where He asks what humankind has done for Him.
21–3] Cf. Matthew 7:2, 'For with what judgement you judge, you shall be judged: and with what measure you mete, it shall be measured to you again', blended with Matthew 13:37–40, 'Who made answer and said to them: He that soweth the good seed, is the Son of man. And the field, is the world. And the good seed are the children of the kingdom. And the cockle, are the children of the wicked one. And the enemy that sowed them, is the devil. But the harvest is the end of the world. And the reapers are the angels.

In heuene or helle to repe and mowe,
As þou deserued fong þy fee.

Man, to þe Y make my mone: 25
I bouȝt þe fro pyne to blisse;
Melte þyn herte as harde as stone,
Þouȝ it be late, amende þy mysse.
In wraþþe, þouȝ þou be fro me gon,
Turne aȝayn – Y wol þe kysse;   30
To make me frendis of my fon,
Þerfore Y ȝaf my lyf for hysse.

Be war, and loue not worldis good,
To get wiþ wrong and calle it thyn.
Man, haue it in þy mood,   35
Þou shalt rekne, for alle is myn.
Why bouȝte Y þe on the rood?
For þou shulde serue and be myn hyne;
Make not myn argumentis wood,
To caste þe fro blisse to pyne.   40

Man, why turmentest þou me so?
Euere þy synnes don encresce,
And þy vices waxen moo,
And þy vertues wanen lesse.
Thenke good Y be thy foo,   45
Whanne wylt þou of þy synne ses?

Even as cockle therefore is gathered up, and burnt with fire: so shall it be at the end of the world.'

24] Cf. Poem 10/162.

25-6] Cf. line 50 and Poem 10/37/93 and note, and Poem 17/12.

27] Cf. Poem 10/27.

28] Cf. Poem 13/3, 9/115, 17/178 and 20/195.

30] Cf. Poem 17/15.

31] Cf. Poem 10/63/66 and note.

32] hysse. The antecedent ought strictly to be **frendis**, and the pronoun ought to be plural. In Poem 1/116, 17/28, 18/158, 24/30/271, this distinctive spelling form of the possessive adjective secure rhymes, but it is possible here that it is a scribal error for 'lis(se)', *MED* (*n.*); b, alleviation of suffering, relief, respite.

34] Cf. line 77 and notes to Poem 2/18 and 17/83.

36] Cf. Poem 10/196–9.

Haue mercy on þy soule woo,
Or haue mynde on me, and ȝeue me pes.

To suffre deþ Y meked me
Fro pyne to blisse þy soule to wynne;   50
To me so shuldest þou meke þe,
Leue and forbere þy synne.
Fro my lordschipe myȝt þou not fle,
Heuene, ne helle, ne see wiþynne,
But where and whenne my wille be,   55
Þy body and soule to parte o twynne.

Thouȝ Y haue graunted þe grace
To knowe boþe good and ylle,
Wyte þy self in eche a place,
Wheþer þou wylt þy self spille.   60
Þouȝ flesch, and world, and fend chas,
Temptacion profre þe tille,
Þou myȝt forbere and nouȝt trespas;
I lente þe knoweleche and fre wille.

In syknesse and pouerte,   65
Glade þerynne and þanke me all;
Þe more þou hast þerof plente,
Þe nerre þe be Y shall.
[fol. 110a] Þan say, "Lord kepe me neyȝ þe,
At nede, here me when Y call;   70
Take fro me hele and prosperite
Raþere þan lete me fro þe fall".

50]   **pyne ... blisse** refers to the soul, not to the speaker; cf. lines 26 and 40 where the
same formula is used.
52]   Cf. line 74 and Poem 17/75.
53]   Cf. notes to Poem 10/145–56 and 14/69–72.
61]   Kail inserted 'þe' before **chas**, but I think that the line makes sense without the
pronoun; **chas** can be understood intransitively.
62]   **tille**. This is the only instance of the Northern form of the preposition 'to' in the
sequence (but cf. **þertille** 20/44); here used to secure rhyme.
69–72] Cf. Psalms 137:3, 'In what day soever I shall call upon thee, hear me: thou shall
multiply strength in my soul' and Psalms 101:3, 'Turn not away thy face from me: in the
day when I am in trouble, incline thy ear to me. In what day soever I shall call upon
thee, hear me speedily.'

Man, rewe on my paynes sore,
Repente þy synne and mercy craue.
By my woundes swere no more,   75
Dysmembre no lymes þat Y haue.
Þy wrong wynnyng aȝen restore
ȝif þou wilt þy soule saue.
Lete soule be lord and go byfore,
And make þy body þy soule knaue.   80

Man, and þou wist how
So liȝtly my gre to make,
Þou noldest for all þe worldis prow,
For fleschly lustes me forsake.
In þy lyue, besye þe now   85
In goode werkis wysely wake,
In loue [and] drede to me bow,
And fle to me fro synnes blake.

Seuene werkis of mercy kepe hem well,
Þe comaundementis and þe crede;   90
All þy lyue as Y þe telle,
ȝeue me þyn herte in loue and drede.
Whyle body and soule togydre dwelle,
Þou myȝt serue pyne and mede;

74–5]   A reference to the common belief that swearing by God's body dismembers it; a sin associated with gluttony, see Schmidt, *Piers Parallel Text*, B.5.307 and 369–70, '... I have trespased with my tonge, I kan noght telle how ofte/Sworen "Goddes soule and his sydes!" and "So helpe me God and halidome!"' and Chaucer, *The Pardoner's Tale*, 629–60.

77]   Cf. line 34.

80]   **knaue** reprises the imagery of the soul in thrall to worldliness or the devil in Poem 1/55, 4/109, 17/142 and 21/152.

84]   The same trope is used Poem 17/153–6.

86]   Identical to Poem 9/7 and 20/209.

87]   **and**: not in MS but clearly lacking; 'helle drede' is a formula seen elsewhere, e.g. Poem 1/41/144, 9/117 and 17/25, but 'loue' when coupled with 'drede' is always linked with 'and', see Poem 19/92 and 1/101, 8/31/85, 9/149 and 17/100. Line 87 is a near repetition of Poem 17/194.

89]   Cf. Poem 17/33–40 and note thereon and 9/123–7 and note.

90]   Identical to Poem 17/98.

93–6]   The sense is that while the body and soul are joined in life, humankind can choose

When soule is out of flesch and felle,   95
Shal neuere do synne ne almesdede.

Mayntene not wrong to calle it ry3t,
Vengeaunce and mercy ney3ebores ben þo,
As messageres þey ben dy3t –
Mercy to frend, vengeaunce to foo.   100
3oure dede in derk Y se in sy3t;
Þere nys no þou3t hid me fro,
After þy dede þe doom is dy3t;
Vengeaunce and mercy departeþ hem so.

For my doom is [ri3twys];   105
[Ri3twisnesse] longeþ to þe Godhede,
And my sones dom is wys,
For mercy longeþ to þe manhede.
Þe holy gost grace lys –
He 3eueþ lyf, he 3eueþ no dede.   110
Ouercome my wraþþe, and fle fro vys,
And do þe comaundementis þat Y bede!

punishment or reward, but once dead, and the soul is separate from the body, the choice
of earning punishment through sin, or reward through almsgiving, is removed.

95–6] Returns to the admonishment of Poem 7/113–20.

101] Cf. note to Poem 1/95 and 12/93/95.

103] Cf. Poem 2/20 and note and Poem 13/8.

105–9] A slightly untidy Trinitarian analogy, with four parts instead of the customary
three: righteousness is attributed to God; wise judgement to Christ, mercy to Christ,
and grace to the Holy Spirit. The analogy makes perfect incarnational theological sense,
but possibly its quadrapartite structure owes as much to the demands of the verse form
as the deft attribution of Christ with both judgement and mercy.

105–6] ri3twis ... Ri3twisnesse: transposed in the MS. I have emended to restore both
grammatical concord and also the rhyme.

108] Cf. Poem 10/166.

109] Possibly 'To' has been omitted at the beginning of the line.

112] Apart from variation in pronouns, the line is identical to Poem 3/106 and 7/63.

Poem 20. [untitled in manuscript]

This ingenious poem takes the form of an inversion of the 'Complaint of Christ' religious lyric. Instead of Christ rebuking humankind for failing to return His love, and for continuing in a life of sin, here the body makes a formal complaint against Christ to God in which he accuses Jesus of having stolen his soul. The poem re-positions religious, legal and literary tropes with adroitness – and no little wit. Other religious lyrics which draw out the spiritual significance of Christ's sacrifice with a narrator who represents humankind stress either: how Christ redressed the evil of humankind and released them from Satan's unlawful grip, e.g. 'Heried be thou, blisful lord above', Gray, *Religious Lyrics*, p. 2; or present a dialogue between God and human nature in which humankind, despite his awareness of lack of entitlement, begs God for his mercy, e.g. 'A Dialogue Between Natura Hominis and Bonitas Dei', Brown, *Religious Lyrics XV*, pp. 164–8. In this poem the complaint topos is blended with traditional body and soul debate motifs and the gendering of the soul as female and the body as male creates the opportunity for ironising the narrative voice of the body. In a twist on the devotional motif of Christ pursuing the errant soul, the body fashions the soul as a harlot for running after Christ (see note to lines 25–32). The soul's exhortations to the body to give up its worldliness are framed as the scolding rebukes of a shrewish wife.

The tixt of holy writ, men sayn,
Hit sleeþ, but glose be among;
The spirit of vnderstandyng quykeneþ agayn,
And makeþ the lyue endeles long.
A fantasie Y herde sayn,   5
Thereof me lust to make a song:
How mannys flesch to God dede playn
On Ihesu Crist – had don hym wrong.

The flesch his playnt þus doþ bygynne
To God fader in heuene on hy3t: 10
'Ihesu, brother of oure kynne,
Haþ bygyled me wiþ his sley3t;
He haþ parted my soule and me o twynne,

1–4] A paraphrase of 2 Corinthians 3:6, 'Who also hath made us fit ministers of the new testament, not in the letter, but in the spirit. For the letter killeth, but the spirit quickeneth'.

2] **glose**: in the sense of spiritual interpretation *MED* 'glose' (*n.*); 1a. Given that the spiritual instruction of the lyric is described both as a **fantasie** (5) and a **song** (6), it is possible that prefacing the debate that follows with the biblical passage from Corinthians contests Wycliffite insistence on the literal interpretation of scripture, and their condemnation of teaching which is not based on biblical text.

7–8] **playn**: to make a legal complaint or accusation, Alford, *Glossary*, p. 117. Cf. Poem 12/110 and 13/60. **wrong**: a criminal action, Alford, *Glossary*, p. 169. The legal diction transposes the 'complaint of Christ' trope, e.g. Gray, *Religious Lyrics*, p. 45/17–18, 'Wrong is went, the devel is schent,/Christ, thurgh the myght of thee'. Instead of Christ appealing to humankind and accusing them of wrongs, the body appeals to God that Christ has committed a trespass. The diction is also an ironic transposition of Christ's dying, guiltless, to atone for human sin, e.g. Gray, *Religious Lyrics*, p. 34/6–12, 'Swete Jesu Crist what is thine gilte/That thus for me thou arte spilte,/Floure of unlothfulnesse?/I am a thef and thou deyiste,/I am gilti and thou abeyist/Al myn wickidnesse', and Brown *Religious Lyrics XV*, p. 159/3–4, 'Criste one a crosse I sawe hangynge,/That deyede for mane withougte trespas'.

12] **bygyled**: defrauded, *MED* 'bigilen' (*v.*); 1b. **sleight** (*n.*); 2a deceit, guile. The legal diction of deception is more usually deployed in contexts where Satan is accused of having used deceit in gaining possession of human souls, e.g. Schmidt, *Piers Parallel Text*, B.18.334–7, 'For the dede that thei dede, thi deceite it made;/With gile thow hem gete, ageyn alle reson./For in my paleis, Paradis, in persone of an addre,/Falsliche thow fettest there thyng that I lovede', and continuation of the analogy, B.18.338–65.

And raft [here] fro me by his my3t.
Now ry3twys God, let mercy blynne;   15
On Ihesu, þy sone, do me ry3t.

Body and soule þou dede me make,
In vnyte togydre so,
Now haþ Ihesus my soule take,
And þus parted oure loue o two.   20
My soule haþ me forsake;
Sumtyme was frend, now is fo;
Byd me go wolward, fast, and wake;
Alle here ioye is of my woo.

Fro me to þy sone my soule is flet,   25
Ful ofte þy sone in me here sou3te,
Now here loue to hym so faste is knete,
Away fro hym wole sche nou3t.
[fol. 120b] She semes dronken or out of wit,

14] **here**. Not in MS but the object pronoun is clearly needed, cf. line 19. **raft**: to rob, take falsely, Alford, *Glossary*, p. 136. The body accuses Christ of stealing his soul from him in diction more usually applied to Satan's unlawful theft of human souls through deception in the Garden of Eden.

15-16] **ry3twys ... ry3t**. The body appeals to God for justice against Christ. **blynne**: in the sense of 'stop', cf. **slake** line 187. The body makes a perverse appeal for Christ to withhold his mercy because God has been too lenient towards his Son's actions; strict justice now needs to be deployed to rectify the indulgence. The body's statement is one of many ironic appropriations of religious diction in the poem.

17-24] In a reregistration of Christ's fetching the souls from purgatory, the body accuses Christ of separating body and soul counter to God's original creation of unity.

21] **forsake** is more usually found in complaint of Christ lyrics where humankind is accused of forsaking the love of Jesus: a trope which is used earlier in the Digby sequence, Poem 17/155. Cf. Gray, *Religious Lyrics*, p. 47/4-6, 'Forthi I pray the speciali/That thou forsake ill company/That woundes me so sare'.

22] An ironic reversal of devotional lyrics, e.g. Brown, *Religious Lyrics XV*, p. 133/6-7, where the speaker addresses Christ and the blood He shed, 'My soule, my body, I yeue alle to the;/So kynde a frende schal I noon fynde'.

23] **wolward**: wearing penitential clothes.

25-7] **flet ... knete**, cf. note to Poem 12/42/44.

25-32] This stanza reregisters the devotional trope where Christ is figured as a true lover of the soul which behaves like a whore in resisting his love and actively seeks out other amorous company. In the Digby stanza, the soul, in being knit fast to Christ, behaves like a true lover in forsaking worldliness. The body, taking on the conventional language usually spoken by Christ, is figured ironically as the abandoned lover. The trope is

Of myn euelfare she has no þouȝt;   30
Þat sorwe is so in myn herte hit,
I trowe to deþe Y mon be brouȝt.

Sum tyme my soule was mylde,
To my biddyng in hoot and colde;
Synge, or playe, or chambres bylde,   35
Chef seruaunt of myn housholde.
Now Ihesu haþ made here made and wylde,
Fro hym departe neuere she nolde;
She setteþ on hym riȝt as a childe,
Aȝens me she bereþ here bolde.   40

Whan I of here counseil craue,
Of fleschly lustes to haue my wille,
She calleþ me wod and seyþ Y raue;
She will neuere graunte þertille.
She biddeþ me haue mynde of my graue,   45
Rule me in resoun and skille;

discussed by Woolf, *Religious Lyric*, pp. 45–7. It derives from an allegorical reading of Osee 2:20 and Ezechiel 16, in which Israel is figured as an ungrateful bride, who, despite her husband's generosity, has become a harlot. Woolf quotes from a fourteenth-century sermon lyric in which Christ is presented as a cuckold, *Religious Lyric*, p. 47.

30–2] Ironically mirrors the diction of Christ to the wayward soul and its secular counterpart with the ardent male lover spurned by his female beloved.

33–40] Several tropes are here entwined: the soul obedient to Christ as lover; the fickle wife more commonly found in fabliau tradition, see Woolf, *Religious Lyric*, p. 47; and the image of household servant which has been used in earlier poems. See also note to lines 47–8.

40] bereþ bolde: a collocation seen also in *The Romance of William of Palerne*, ed. W. W. Skeat, *EETS ES* 1 (1867; reprint 1996). 1982, 'Caste sche sone how bold ȝhe miȝt hire bere, hire best to excuse', and *A Royal Historie of the Excellent Knight Generides*, ed. F. J. Furnivall, *RC* 85 (1865), 1984, 'He bare him bold'. In Digby the collocation suggests shameless or impudent behaviour.

41] counseil: an ironic inversion of the image of the counsellor who urges following one's wit rather than one's will and fleshly desires, cf. Poem 5.

44] þertille, cf. note to Poem 19/62.

45] mynde of my graue: a paraphrase of the injunction in 'memento mori' lyrics, to think on one's end, cf. Ecclesiasticus 7:40, 'In all thy works remember thy last end, and thou shalt never sin'.

I was mayster, now am Y knaue;
In that stat brynge me she wille.

Wolde Y be proud, she biddeþ be meke,
Wolde Y be gloton, she biddeþ me faste,   50
Þere Y wolde take, she biddes me eke,
Wolde Y be lyther, she biddis be chaste,
ʒif Y fyʒte, she biddes ley forþ my cheke,
Þere Y am slow, she biddis be haste.
Here answere is not to seke,   55
To speke to here my wynde Y waste.

Ihesu com fro heuene blisse
And tok flesch in a mayden fre,
Lowely, and most mekenesse
Hyd vnder flesch, fleschly, oure fraternite;   60
Now wolde take my soule to his
For he suffred pyne and pouerte.
ʒit sumwhat Y myʒte acorde to þis –
But why shulde my soule hate me?

Whan Ihesus and my soule be met,   65
Sone my werkis þey aspiʒe,
Here wit on me fast þey whet,
In shame, and skorne, and vylenye:
"To folwe þy fleschly lustes let,

47]   Cf. note to Poem 19/80.
47-8] Cf. line 36, where the soul is described as chief servant in the household. The extended trope may show influence of St Jerome, *Ad Joviniam*, 'If you give her the management of the whole house, you are reduced to being her servant', quoted in Blamires, *Defamed and Defended*, p. 71.
49-56] Transposes the misogynist image of the chiding wife into a body and soul debate, Proverbs 19:13, 'a wrangling wife is like a roof continually dropping through'; 21:9, 'It is better to sit in a corner of the housetop, than with a brawling woman'; and 21:19, 'It is better to dwell in a wilderness, than with a quarrelsome and passionate woman'.
57-64] Reprises the stanza Poem 17/129-36, but twists the conventional image of Christ's incarnational sacrifice to stress the body's ignorance.
63]   **acorde to þis**. The body can concur in this statement of fact, that is the account of Christ's supererogatory action, but remains oblivious to its spiritual implications. It fails to understand that Jesus's actions require humankind to abstain from fleshly lusts.
64]   The injured question is a superb dramatisation of the body's spiritual blindness.
65-72] A continuation of the dramatisation of the body's lack of understanding. The

Or ellis boþe 3e shal dy3e!"   70
Þus am Y vnder and ouer set,
She spettes on me, and doþ me fy3e.

Wiþ me, my soule he doþ þrete,
And makeþ my soule me to hate,
Wiþ plesande wordis he hoteþ here gete   75
In heuene blisse a quenes astate.
Þan comeþ she hom in wraþþe ful hete,
Bedeþ here lette boþe erly and late,
Casteþ me doun, and doþ me bete,
And tredeþ on me and makeþ debate.   80

Thanne renneþ she a3en as she were wood;
To Ihesu, þy sone, she doþ fly3e.
He fedeþ here wiþ his flesch and blood,
But þanne here þou3tes mownten hy3e:
She biddiþ me water and bred to food,   85

cautionary words of Christ and the soul are figured as despising taunts; once again, diction that is appropriate to the treatment of Christ at his crucifixion is ironically transposed to the wilful body, cf. Brown, *Religious Lyrics XV*, p. 137/19–20, 'And at the last – þat grevyd hym worst –/They spyt in-to his facys' and p. 139/7–8, 'Thair the Iowis spittit in his face/And fals witnes spak fast to put him doun'.

72] **spettes**: the Eastern spelling, not in rhyme position, another indication of the mixed spelling of the poems.

73] The more traditional version of the soul being threatened rather than the body is seen at Poem 9/46.

75] **plesande**: the Northern/Eastern form of the present participle, not needed for rhyme, another indication of the mixed dialect of the poems.

76] The body's failure to understand Christ's promise to the soul of a **quenes astate** in heaven is reminiscent of the dreamer's outburst at the Maiden's spiritual elevation in Andrew and Waldron, *Pearl Poems*, 492, 'Bot a quene! Hit is to dere a date.'

77–80] **comeþ she hom ... maketh debate**. The soul's rebukes to the body are figured as a scolding wife. The physical domestic violence of the body's being beaten, quarrelled with, and trodden upon are a reregistration of fabliau representations of domestic discord between husband and wife, see note to lines 47–56 and 133–6.

83–5] Rather as the dreamer in Andrew and Waldron, *Pearl Poems*, the body takes a literal-minded view of spiritual instruction: the body compares Christ's Eucharistic food for the soul with his own diet of bread and water. He mistakes penitential fare for meagre domestic provision.

As mortkyn forsaken she let me liȝe,
She holdeþ me euyll, and no þyng good,
But a stynkyng carayne in here eyȝe.

Þus my soule my body slees
Wiþ gret anguysche and turment;   90
She telles Ihesu dyȝed for pes,
But fro his skole she is went.
Bytwen vs werre doþ encres,
Here swerd is drawen, here bow is bent,
She sayþ, but fleschly lustes sees,   95
We mon be dede, and boþe be shent.

She acordid wiþ Ihesu and me dede flyte,
And sayde Y shulde be [fol. 121a] maked tame,
And sayde my werkys me adyte,
And bryngen me in wikked fame.   100
Ȝif worldly men me don smyte,
And don me boþe wrong and grame,
She loueþ that don me despyte,
And preyeþ for all þat don me shame.

Hyȝe fader, God of riȝtwisnes,   105
Haue mynde of my sorwe sore,

86–8] **mortkyn … stynkyng carayne**. The body-narrator is seen to be oblivious to the penitential implications of this diction. The foul flesh of the body, doomed to be worms' meat, is a staple of moralistic injunctions in 'learn to die' devotional lyrics, e.g. in Poem 7/5–8 and 22/7–8.

89–90] A twist on the usual body and soul debate lyrics in which the body is seen to kill the soul. Cf. Poem 11/54.

91–2] A witty turn on the trope of the shrewish wife: the soul tells the body that Christ died to make peace, to which the body retorts ruefully, that the soul is far from that school of thought.

94] **swerd … bow is bent**: diction which elsewhere in the sequence is used of God's vengeance, e.g. Poem 1/69/81/84 and 12/87.

97] **acordid**, cf. note to line 63.

99] **adyte**. The legalism of the debate is continued: *MED* 'adighten' (*v.*); 1b lists the sense of 'consign to prison' – in this instance – hell.

102] **wrong**, cf. note to lines 7/8. **grame**: something causing disgrace or humiliation; see *MED* 'grame' (*n.*); 3b.

106] **haue mynde … sorwe sore**. Transposes to the body diction used by Christ in complaint lyrics, e.g. Brown, *Religious Lyrics XV*, p. 168/1–2, 'O man vnkynde/hafe in

And it be founden Ihesu loued mysse,
To me my soule aȝen restore.
A litil playnt nes noȝt þisse –
And alle þat Y haue sayd ȝore,   110
Þat Y and my soule be frendis and kisse,
And loue as we dede here byfore.

For my soule Ihesu suffred wo,
Bounden, and beten wiþ skourges ynowe,
Crowned wiþ thorn – nayled also   115
On croos tyl deþ dede hym bowe;
Wiþ a spere his herte let cleue a two,
Wyde open his loue myȝte out flowe –
So loþ hym was his loue forgo,
He is worþy be loued þat so dede wowe.   120

My soule Y holde holy, [esyd],
For she loueþ Ihesu þat loueþ here wel,
But loue were tendere to loue vsed,

mynde/My paynes smert' and Brown, *Religious Lyrics XIV*, p. 93/1–2, 'Vnkynde man, gif kepe til me/and loke what payne I suffer for þe'.

107]   **founden … mysse**: diction which suggests Jesus be found guilty of a crime (Alford, *Glossary*, p. 59).

108]   **restore**: in the sense of making restitution for something wrongly taken; see *MED* 'restoren' (*v.*); 1a.

111]   Diction conventionally used by Jesus in attempting to woo back the soul, e.g. Poem 17/15 and 19/50 and Brown, *Religious Lyrics XIV*, p. 236/70–1, 'Thys hundreth yere yef thow were me fro;/I take the ful fayne, I clyppe, I kysse'.

117–20]   A conventional devotional trope, e.g. Gray, *Religious Lyric*, p. 46/23–6, 'That herte clefte for treuthe of love,/Therfore in him oon is trewe love;/For love of thee that herte is yove –/Kepe thou that herte and thou art above'. The body acknowledges that Christ is worthy to be loved who wooed in such a manner. Cf. note to Poem 10/29–42 and Gray, *Religious Lyric*, p. 42/10–12, 'And sewte lemman, forget thow noght/That I thi lufe sa dere have boght,/And I aske the noght elles'.

121]   **esyd**. MS reads 'es it', which Kail emended to 'it es'. The line is difficult; the rhyme scheme suggests that the final word ought to have been a past participle, but this follows rather abruptly after the adjective **holy**. Versions of the inexact rhyme scheme of this stanza are seen elsewhere, e.g. Poem 1/97–104, 4/81–8, 5/41–8, 15/145–52, 22/65–72, 24/283–90/403–10. The looseness of the rhyme makes it difficult confidently to emend; the most likely original reading is the past participle from 'esen' – to be free from trouble, unencumbered; see *MED* 'esen' (*v.*); 3a. As a noun **ese** appears Poem 4/209, 6/16, 8/33 and 10/154. At Poem 10/18, the form is **eys**.

Were harder þan ston and styffere þan stel.
On Ihesu she is amerous and ful auysed,   125
What worldly þyng she seeþ or fele,
Al worldly ioye she haþ refused,
And me she loueþ neuere a dele.

I wante my wille and euel fare Y,
Fro worldly merþe put o syde;   130
Fro worldis worschip she doþe me tary,
I may no þou3t fro here hyde.
Þere Y blisse, she doþ wary,
Þere Y speke fayre, she doþ chyde:
She is newe waxen al contrary;   135
Þere Y dwelle she nyl not byde.

She repreueþ me my dagged cloþes,
And longe, pyked, crakowed shon;
Vpbreyde[þ] me my grete oþes,
And sayþ Y breke Goddis bone.   140
Þat me is lef, all she loþes.

132]   Elsewhere in the sequence humankind is unable to hide their thoughts or behaviour from God, Poem 10/92 and 12/95.

133-6]   The antitheses create a picture of the contrary, scolding wife, see Ecclesiasticus 25:29-30, 'A woman's anger, and impudence, and confusion is great. A woman, if she have superiority, is contrary to her husband'. But also recall the antitheses used by Christ in reproving the soul for not returning his love, e.g. Gray, *Religious Lyric*, p. 41/26-8, 'I saved hyr fro betyng, and she hath me bett;/I clothed hyr in grace and hevenly lyght,/This blody surcote she hath on me sett' and p. 42/33-6, 'I crownyd hyr with blysse, and she me with thorne,/I led hyr to chambre, and she me to dye;/I browght hyr to worship, and she me to skorne,/I dyd hyr reverence, and she me velanye'.

137]   **dagged**: the taste for slashing or jagging clothes became fashionable at the end of the fourteenth century and became associated with extravagance and moral dissipation, see *Richard the Redeless*, III.162-9 and *The Parson's Tale*, 412-25.

138]   Long pointed shoes were often used as a sign of decadence or moral depravity, e.g. *Richard the Redeless*, III.232 and *Castle of Perseverance*, 1062: 'Loke þou blowe mekyl bost, with longe Crakows on þi schos'. *The Plowman's Tale* condemns priests for wearing piked shoes, 930.

139]   **Vpbreydeþ**. The MS lacks final 'þ'; I have followed Kail's emendation.

139-40]   Blasphemous oaths were seen as a renewal of the crucifixion, e.g. Brown, *Religious Lyrics XV*, p. 167/91-2, 'With þi grete oþus þat þu swerus ay,/my body þu wonduste euurmore newe'. Cf. Poem 19/74-5 and note.

141-4]   The alternation of reported speech reads like a domestic spat.

I seye, "Oþere men so don!"
She seyþ, "Þey go to helle woþes –
Wole to wende wiþ hem to wone!"

Wiþ Ihesu alway is she: 145
And now she lyþ wiþ hym in cracche,
Now into Egipt wiþ hym doþ fle,
Fro Herowdes lest he hem cacche;
In his moders armes born wol she be,
And sowke wiþ hym as chylde in tacche.   150
She folweþ hym in al degre,
And countrefeteþ to ben his macche.

Wiþ hym doþ drynke and ete,
To lerne of his discressioun;
Wiþ hym sche is skourged and bete,   155
And crucyfyed in his passioun.
She is wiþ hym in helle hete,
Wiþ hym in his resurexioun,
And stye into heuene in his fadres se[t]e;
Þens nolde she neuere come doun'.   160

Now þe playnt is at þe last,
God answerd wiþ mylde soun:
'Flesch', he sayde, 'þou iangelest fast,
Moche dene, and no resoun.
Alle þy wordes þou dost waste,   165
Wille wiþoute discressioun;

145–52] The description of the soul's behaviour follows the pattern of the 'Imitacio Christi',
but here described with a literalism that calls Margery Kempe's version of the devotional
practice to mind.

153] Possibly 'she' has been omitted before **doþ**.

153–60] Continues the 'imitacio Christi' motif, but lines 154–5 are also influenced by
lyrics which urge meditative compassion with Christ by reciting the details of Christ's
suffering at each hour of his ordeal; see e.g. 'The Matins of the Cross', Brown, *Religious
Lyrics XIV*, pp. 39–44.

159] **sete**. MS reads 'see'; I have followed Kail's emendation.

160] A petulantly literal reading of the ascension into heaven which recalls the dreamer's
tone in Andrew and Waldron, *Pearl Poems,* cf. note to lines 83–5.

þyn awen pleynt þe doþ caste,
Þou turnest þy self vp so doun.

[fol. 121b] Thou makest maystershepe in al vys
And [takest] here fro my way;   170
And makest here þral to fleschely delys,
In vanyte to al worldly play.
She [wa]s ashamed, now she is wys,
Sche lyued in vowtrye so many a day,
She haþ chosen þe loue most o prys   175
And cast þe fals loue away'.

God seiþ, 'Man Y made þe of nouȝt,
And kyd þat Y loued þe dere,
And soule of resoun in þe wrouȝt,
Fayre and wys angels pere.   180
Þou hast defouled þe ymage þat Y wrouȝt
In seruage to fendis and fendis fere;
She folwed þy wille in dede and þouȝt,
In alle place, fer and nere.

On Ihesu þou pleynt dost make,   185
Sayde he bigyled þe wiþ sleyȝte,
And biddest me lete mercy slake
And on Ihesu do þe ryȝt.
My sone, for þe, dede deth take,
And kydde þe loue most of myȝt,   190

167–8] God points out that the body has made a legal accusation against himself, *MED* 'casten' (*v.*); 12c.

170] **takest**. Not in MS, but a verb is clearly missing from this line. Kail supplied 'turnest'. My emendation continues the assonance of the surrounding 2nd person verbs which produce a repetition of consonants which might have distracted the scribe.

173] **was**. MS reads 'is' but a past tense is clearly needed.

177–84] Cf. Poem 10/15–21; line 177 is identical to Poem 10/15 and 22/17. Both poems (and Poem 19/5–8), are indebted to lyrics in which God rebukes humankind for failing to use wit and discretion in understanding the significance of Christ's sacrifice, e.g. the poem that Brown entitles 'God Bids Us Use Reason and Evidence', *Religious Lyrics XV*, pp. 187–8.

186] Cf. note to line 12.

Þou3 he loue dede forsake,
How woldest þou þis doom were dy3t?

Flesch, þy synnes mochil is:
Þou art cast in þyn awen caas!
Knowleche, repente, and mende þy mys,   195
And be in wille no more trespas.
I nel deme þe in ry3twisnes,
But medle þerwiþ mercy and grace,
And brynge þy soule to heuene blys
Wiþ loue to se my fayre face.   200

In ouerhope be not to bold,
In synne for to haue mercy;
Let not wanhope in þe be old,
For my grace is euere redy.
Fro helle pynes hoot and cold,   205
I assoyle þe, and out of purgatory;
At þy deth, or body be cold,
To Ihesu, in heuene, þy soule shal fleye'.

In good werkis wysely wake,
Playne not on Ihesu what he sende: 210
Sykenes, pouerte, mekely take,
Richesse and hele, wysely spende,
And helpe all pore for Goddis sake,
Þan God wole lede 3ow, as his frend,
To ioye of heuene þat shal neuere slake.   215
Into þat blisse God graunte vs wende! Amen.

191] **loue forsake**: i.e. Christ abandoned love because the body polluted the soul.
193–4] Cf. note to lines 167–8.
195–200] Reprises God's words to humankind, Poem 10/95–8, 17/75–6 and 19/73–4.
201] Repeats diction of Poem 1/129, 7/97 and 8/47.
204] Cf. Ecclesiasticus 47:24, 'But God will not leave off his mercy, and he will not destroy, nor abolish his own works, neither will he out up by the roots the offspring of his elect: and he will not utterly take away the seed of him that loveth the Lord.'
209] Identical to Poem 19/86.
211] Cf. Poem 19/65–8.
212] Cf. Poem 10/198.
213] Cf. Poem 9/125, 17/35 and 21/38.

Poem 21. A lernyng to good leuynge

The poem takes the form of a paraphrase of Christ's Sermon on the Mount, Matthew 5:1–20. All the beatitudes are enumerated (although the poem reverses numbers 6 and 7) and the poem concludes with Christ's instructions to his disciples. The poem shifts between admonitions that are appropriate to priests, and those which have more universal applicability. Behaviour which earns heavenly reward is contrasted with that which is cursed. Moral exhortations of earlier poems are revisited, especially admonitions to the clergy in Poem 8. The poet has cross-fertilised the anaphoric 'blessed be' narrative structure of Matthew's gospel with the 'cursed be' formulae of Moses's words to the people of Israel in Deuteronomy 27:15–25 and 28:16–19. The contents of the 'curse' verses are not identical to those in Deuteronomy; Moses promises that those who fail to keep God's commandments will be cursed. The Digby poet has taken the biblical structure and transposed it into contrasting the fates of those who do, or do not, observe the beatitudes. The poem shares similarities with 'How to Live Perfectly', Horstmann, *Vernon Poems* I.221–51 which is a translation of the first part of St Edmund's *Speculum*. The section on the beatitudes, lines 643–82, follows an enumeration of the seven deadly sins and each beatitude is matched with a sin as an antidote (the last beatitude is omitted).

21. A lernyng to good leuynge

Pore of spirit blessed be:
Þouȝ he be lord of richesse fele,
He bereþ penaunce and pouerte,
That of his good to pore folk dele.
Of þe kyngdom of heuene a lord is he   5
Þat counseyleþ wel þe soule hele,
And lyueþ in werkis of charyte;
Suche folk to heuene preuyly stele.

Siþ God doþ blisse, and graunteþ blis
Þat don his word and holde it trewe,   10
Þan þat man cursed is
Þat lyueþ contrarious þat vertue;
Þat filleþ his herte wiþ ryches,
Nedeles aueryce, gadryng newe;
For wikkid counseil, helle is his,   15
Þere neuere nes reste, but euere remewe.

Blessid be man þat in herte is mylde;
Buxom to lerne, and lef to teche;
Shal owe þe [fol. 122a] erþe and þeron bylde,
In helpe of mony his rychesse reche;   20
Of shrewes make Goddis childe,
Of gostly woundes be soule leche,
Make tame to God þo þat were wylde,
Of eche good lyuere his werkis preche.

1–5] Matthew 5:3, 'Blessed are the poor in spirit: for theirs is the kingdom of heaven', quoted also Poem 15/30 and 18/157.
4] Cf. Poem 8/65–8 and 15/32.
6] Cf. Poem 8/69.
7–8] Cf. Poem 1/113–14.
10] Cf. Poem 11/114.
17–19] Matthew 5:4, 'Blessed are the meek: for they shall possess the land'.
18] Cf. Poem 4/59.
21–2] Cf. Poem 8/22–4.
23] Cf. Poem 24/109.

Þanne cursed be man in herte ruyde,   25
Þat neuere nel lere, ne vnderstond:
Þou3 he owe erþe, he shal not byde
Til it be out of his hond.
When conscience his werkis chyde,
Þat man shal neuere reioyse lond,   30
Fro alle vertues þat doþ hym hyde,
To alle myscheues he makeþ hym bond.

Blessed be he þat morneþ sore:
His breþere synnes, his awen mysdede;
Repente and wille to do no more,   35
But holde þe hestes þat God bede.
His wrong wynnyng a3en restore,
And helpe pore þat han nede.
He shal be counforted þerfore;
In heuene blisse haue his mede.   40

Than cursed be he haþ ioye of synne,
And euere encreseþ mo and mo;
Boste þerof, delyte þerynne;
3eue men ensample to do so.
Heuene 3ates fro hem they pynne;   45
Of Goddis frendis make Goddis foo,
In helle þey purchas here ynne,
His felaschipe with hym thay go.

26]   Cf. Poem 10/7, 16/44.
28]   The line seems short. It is possible that a past participle has been lost after **be**.
33–9]   Matthew 5:5, 'Blessed are they that mourn: for they shall be comforted'. The poet
   substantially reinterprets this verse, delaying the notion of comfort until line 39, and
   introducing it only as a reward for proper penance. Mourning becomes, not simply grief,
   but repentance for sins, and enables the poet to write on one of the most prominent
   issues in the sequence. 'How to Live Perfectly', Horstmann, *Vernon Poems* I.238/659–60,
   gives a more straightforward reading of mourning as sorrow for which one will receive
   consolation.
35]   Cf. Poem 17/75.
36]   Cf. note to line 10 and Poem 1/22, 3/106 and 19/112.
37]   Apart from a change in pronoun, identical to Poem 19/77.
38]   Cf. Poem 1/94 and 4/173.
45]   Cf. Poem 17/87.
46]   The clauses are reversed line 86.

Blessed euere mote he be
Þat hungren and thursten ry3twisnes: 50
He wolde were wel in al degre,
Þat God and man echon had his.
Gostly hunger[es] and thurstes he,
Þat fayn wolde mende þat is mys;
Ful filled he shal wiþ grete deynte   55
At Goddis feste in heuene blisse.

Than cursed is he þat ful is fylde:
Wiþ wrong take pore mennys thrift;
þat makeþ pore men be spi[l]ed,
For synguler profyt is sotyll theft;   60
Make gulteles folk presoned and kylde,
Of hous and land make wrongwys gyft;
Wiþ hunger and þirst his hous is bylde;
In helle is shewed euell sponnen wyft.

Blessid be þe mercyable: 65
Mercy and mede of God he fonges;

49–50]   Matthew 5:6, 'Blessed are they that hunger and thirst after justice: for they shall have their fill'.

53]   **hunger[es]**. There is no final 's' in the MS, but the syntax demands a third person singular inflection rather than the noun 'hunger'.

54]   Cf. Poem 20/195.

57–64]   Cf. Proverbs 24:1–3, 'Seek not to be like evil men, neither desire to be with them: Because their mind studieth robberies, and their lips speak deceits. By wisdom the house shall be built, and by prudence it shall be strengthened'.

57]   **ful**. Picks up on the 'fill' of Matthew 5:6, see note to lines 49–50.

58–60]   **thrift … theft**. Whether in rhyme position or medially, 'theft' is always spelt thus in the sequence. The rhyme here, and in the stanza as a whole, suggests influence of Eastern dialect.

58]   A recurrent motif in the sequence, e.g. Poem 4/150, 6/13, 8/14/68.

59]   **spi[l]ed**. MS reads 'spi3ed', which destroys both sense and rhyme. I have followed Kail's emendation.

60]   Virtually identical to 13/81, and cf. note to Poem 1/4.

61]   **gultles**: the spelling suggests Western dialect.

63]   The despoiler of the poor builds his house at the expense the thirst and hunger of those whom he defrauds.

64]   The proverb is also used in *The Townley Plays*, 21/435, 'This same is he that slo his brother … Yey, ill spon weft ay comes foule out,' and Gower, *Confessio*, VI.2381.

65]   Matthew 5:7, 'Blessed are the merciful: for they shall obtain mercy'.

In Goddis doom he stondes stable
þat wrekeþ not all his owen wronges.
To pore folk he is profytable
Þat leueþ his good hem amonges;   70
Sorefull and hungry, he fyndeþ hem table;
The sorwefull, he gladeþ to synge songes.

Thanne how of hem han hertis stoute,
Þat reweþ non pore þat han penaunce;
Han nedeles gold noȝt to lene it oute,   75
But to þe borwere gret greuaunce.
But he may quyte, is ȝerne aboute
To presone hym, or make destaunce;
But he be cursed, it is in dowte:
Þat haþ no mercy [fol. 122b] mote haue vengeaunce.   80

Blessed be he þat loueþ pes:
Mekely to Goddis byddyng bende;
He shal be cleped at Goddis dees
Goddis sone, good and hende.
He wolde all werre shulde asses,   85
Of Goddis foon make Goddis frende,
Make soule wiþ ioye to heuene pres,
And sorwe and werre to helle wiþ fende.

Than how of hem þat pes doþ hate:
Wolde ouerall were werre and woo;   90
Eche man wiþ oþer debate,

68]   Cf. Poem 18/134–5.
69]   **profytable**: behaviour contrary to the practice, denounced throughout the sequence,
of working for one's own profit.
71–2]   I.e performs the first and sixth works of mercy.
74–6]   Cf. Proverbs 22:7, 'The rich ruleth over the poor: and the borrower is servant to
him that lendeth'.
79]   **dowte**: a cause or reason for fear; something to be feared, *MED* 'dout(e)' (*n*.); 4.
80]   Cf. Poem 19/98/104.
81–4]   Matthew 5:9, 'Blessed are the peacemakers: for they shall be called children of
God'.
85]   **werre**: in the sense of discord between human beings, not nations.
86]   Cf. note to line 46.
91]   **debate**, cf. Poem 6/21, 8/59, 10/67, 12/33 and notes thereon.

Þat shulde be frend, make hem foo.
For synguler wynnyng to his astate,
Lede his men oþere to sloo;
He shal be blessed neuere or late: 95
His werkis curseþ hym where he go.

The clene of herte blissed be
Þat lyueþ after Goddis lore:
God hym self he shal see
Þere as blisse is euere more.   100
And gouerneþ wel his owen degre,
And doþ þe dede þat he come fore;
Fulfylleþ þe werkis of charyte,
His vertue gadereth mede in store.

The herte þat is fyled in synne,   105
And sulþeþ his soule wiþ spottes of blame:
Goddis curs he doþ wynne,
Þat spyseþ hymself and Goddis name.
His astate he nele not dwelle þerynne;
To serue God hym þenkeþ shame.   110
ʒif God and he departe o twynne,
In helle he may be meked tame.

That is p[er]sued for riʒtwisnes
Is blessid where he go or ryde:
Þe kyngdom of heuene is his.   115
Þat querell to ende, in charite byde,
God wole brynge hym to heuene blis;
And fro his enemys þere wole hym hyde,

93]   Cf. notes to line 60 and 69.
96]   Cf. Deuteronomy 28:16, 'Cursed shalt thou be in the city, cursed in the field' and 28:19,
    'Cursed shalt thou be coming in, and cursed going out'.
97–9]   Matthew 5:8, 'Blessed are the clean of heart: for they shall see God'.
101]   Virtually identical to Poem 16/89.
105–6]   Cf. Poem 11/73–4.
109]   A comment that resonates with the concern throughout the sequence that each person
    live according to their social rank.
113]   **persued**. MS reads 'presued'.
113–14]   Matthew 5:10, 'Blessed are they that suffer persecution for justice' sake: for theirs
    is the kingdom of heaven.'.

And þo þat persue hym with mys,
To helle, þey ben here awen gyde.   120

Thanne are they cursed in here lyf
Þat auaunceþ þe fals and stroyeþ þe trewe:
Mayntene fals querell and stryf,
Riȝtwis men wrongly pursue,
Defowle boþe mayden and wyf   125
Þat shulde be clene in alle vertue.
Eche dedly synne is a dedly knyf;
For he shal repe þat he sewe.

Ȝe shal be blessid erly and late,
By vertue of gospell þat ȝe preche;   130
Ȝe shul be blessid whan folk ȝow hate,
And cursen ȝow for ȝoure speche.
Ȝoure tonge is kaye of heuene ȝate,
Ȝoure word þe way to heuene hem teche,
Folk wiþ ȝow schal debate,   135
For me wiþ lesynges ȝow apeche.

Glade ȝe wiþynne and ioye wiþoute,
Ȝoure mede in heuene moche is;
Drede no tyrauntes sterne and stoute,
May sle þy body and take as his.   140

119] An annotator has written 'Nota' in the margin.

127] Identical to Poem 7/105, and cf. Poem 23/77.

128] Galatians 6:8, 'For what things a man shall sow, those also shall he reap'.

129-32] Matthew 5:11, 'Blessed are ye when they shall revile you, and persecute you, and speak all that is evil against you, untruly, for my sake'.

129-36] The diction of this stanza chimes with Wycliffite defences of poor preachers who are persecuted for preaching the gospel against the **lesynges** (l. 136), of the institutional church. See 'Whi pore prestis han none benefice', Matthew, *Works of Wyclif*, pp. 245–56, 'but þere be ony symple man þat desireþ to lyue wel & teche treuely goddis lawe ... he schal be so pursued & sclaundrid þat he schal be ... emprisoned, disgratid or brent, ȝif anticristis clerkis may for ony gold & cursed lesyngis'. The appropriation of diction might be a deliberate hijacking of Wycliffite polemic in order to enjoin the highest standards of priestly behaviour in the clergy.

137-8] Matthew 5:12, 'Be glad and rejoice, for your reward is very great in heaven. For so they persecuted the prophets that were before you'.

141-2] The syntax is compressed; the poet urges to dread no contemporary tyrant, but to fear only God, for only He has the power of judgement and mercy.

God þe fader of heuene ȝe dowte,
May brynge þe soule to pyne or blis.
[fol. 123a] He schal deme all þe world aboute,
To heuene for goode, to hell for mys.

Of erþe ȝe ben cleped salt: 145
For salt of wisdom soule saues;
Go vp riȝt, and be not halt,
For mayster of seruaunt his seruice craues.
Þyn astate rekene þou shalt:
How þou it gat, how þou it saues;   150
Fewe ben chosen, þouȝ mony ben calt:
Fro Goddis seruyce are worldly knaues.

To lanterne ȝe ben likned riȝt:
In all þe world ȝe shal be kyd,
ȝoure prechyng shal be candel liȝt –   155
Nouȝt vnder worldly buschel hyd;
But on a candelstyke on hiȝt,
Nouȝt vnder a chiste vnder a lyd.
In good werkis shyne ȝe briȝt
And lyue ȝe so, riȝt as ȝe byd.   160

145–6]   Matthew 5:13, 'You are the salt of the earth. But if the salt lose its savour, wherewith shall it be salted? It is good for nothing any more but to be cast out, and to be trodden on by men' The poet paraphrases the significance of this verse by transposing the salt analogy into the trope of master and servant.

150]   Cf. Poem 7/84 and 9/99.

151]   Matthew 22:14, 'For many are called, but few are chosen'. **calt** is used for rhyme. Poem 15/106 has 'calde' where the verb is not in rhyme position.

152]   The line reprises an opposition between being in service to God or serving the world or the devil that is seen in a number of previous poems (e.g. Poem 1/55, 4/109, 10/9, 17/142, 19/80). The syntax is very compressed. Although the line is not short metrically, the presence of a verb, participle adjective, or adverb would link the line to the rest of the stanza more cogently.

153–8]   Matthew 5:14–15, 'You are the light of the world. A city seated on a mountain cannot be hid. Neither do men light a candle and put it under a bushel, but upon a candlestick, that it may shine to all that are in the house.' Cf. Luke 8:16, 'Now no man lighting a candle covereth it with a vessel, or putteth it under a bed; but setteth it upon a candlestick, that they who come in may see the light'.

153]   An annotator has written 'Nota' in the margin. The lantern of light image has already been used Poem 8/62 and cf. 23/7–8.

159–60]   Matthew 5:16, 'So let your light shine before men, that they may see your good works, and glorify your Father who is in heaven'.

Poem 22. Knowe thy self and thy God

The poem is written in the same penitential tradition as Poems 1 and 7, see especially the headnote to Poem 7. In comparison to the earlier poems, this poem appears free of contemporary inflection; the focus is resolutely spiritual. In its contempt for the world and for the flesh, the tone of the poem is particularly harsh and graphic, particularly in the first two stanzas. Many of the tropes and much of the diction have appeared in earlier poems. Where close analogues to this tradition of writing have already been cited in the notes to earlier poems, brief reference to line numbers only will be given in order to avoid duplication of material.

22. Knowe thy self and thy God

Thenke hertely in þy þouȝt
Of what matere þou dede bygynne:
Of fylthy seed þou were wrouȝt,
And wan in at þe wyket of synne.
Foulere fylþe knowe Y nouȝt,   5
Þan þou were fed þy moder wiþynne;
In a sake ful of filþe þou was out brouȝt –
In wrecchednes horyble, and stynkyng skynne.

What þou art, knowe þy self wel:
Þou were conceyued in synne and born wiþ woo;   10
Þy moder and þou on fortune whel,
In perile of deþ parted atwoo.
Of pynes of helle, what soules fele,
And þou in mynde keped þoo,
Hit wolde make þy corage kele   15
Whan þou hadde wil to synne goo.

God made þe of nouȝt – haue in mynde –
Wiþ soule of resoun lyk his ymage;

2] Cf. Poem 8/2.

3–7] A particularly graphic account of the filthiness of human conception, with imagery that can be traced back to St Bernard, cf. note to Poem 7/5, and 'A Comment on the Seven Deadly Sins', Arnold, *Wyclif*, III.125, 'As Seynt Bernarde seies, a mon while he lyves is a seck ful of drytt'; 'St Bernard on Man's three Foes', Furnivall, *Vernon Poems* II.516/81–4, 'Hose schulde riht be-gynne/Þat such a foul stinkynde sek/Haþ such a burþen in his nek/Of serwe and of synne' and 'How to Live Perfectly', Horstmann, *Vernon Poems* I.225/127–32, 'As to þi bodi: foulore hit is/Þan euer was eny donge, I-wis –/Was neuer ȝit dounge so foule/Þat wolde so stinke, rote and moule;/Þou weore in so gret fulþe iget,/Abhominable hit is þerof to speke'.

4] **wyket of synne**: a misogynist euphemism for the vulva.

5] **Foulere fylþe**, i.e. the placenta.

9] Cf. note to Poem 1/8.

10–12] Cf. 'Each Man ought himself to know', Furnivall, *Vernon Poems* II.672/19–21, 'Knowe þou come hider wiþ care;/Þou nost neuer ȝif þou byde til morn;/Hou lihtly þou maiȝt be forlorn'.

15] **kele**. The poet appears to have chosen this form from OE 'celan', see *MED* 'kelen' (*v.*) rather than from OE 'colian' see *MED* 'colen' (*v.*); 1.

17] Cf. Poem 8/3, 10/15 and 20/177.

In heuene wiþ angels aboue þe wynde,
He ordeyned þe endeles heritage.   20
Wiþ more loue he dede þe bynde;
Bycome þy brother in mannys lynage,
He [is] ielous louer and trewest to fynde;
Þy soule is spouse to his maryage.

To God, thy wedlok wiþ loue holde   25
In brennyng contemplacion;
And make nouȝt hym cokewolde
To loue in fornycacion.
On Goddis mercy be not to bolde
To falle in temptacion;   30
Kepe charite hot, let it not colde
For quenchyng of deuocion.

Loue all folk in charyte,
Body and soule in good atent,
[Do] as þou wolde þey dede þe.   35
Þat is Goddis comaundement;
Who breke þo hestes cursed is he,
Til þey come to mendement.
Þou preyest eueremore in all degre,
Til þat þou to synne assent.   40

That þou hast don siþ þou were bore,
All þy lyuyng byþenk þe newe,

18]   Cf. Poem 9/98, 17/11/114, 19/6 and 20/181.
20]   Cf. Poem 9/101, and 10/28.
22-4] Cf. Poem 17/167-8/197-8, 20/113-20 and notes thereon.
23]   [is]. Not in MS.
25-8] Cf. note to Poem 20/25-32.
29]   Cf. Poem 8/43 and 20/21.
32]   Cf. Poem 18/117.
33]   Cf. 1 John 4:7, 'Dearly beloved, let us love one another, for charity is of God'.
35]   **Do**. Not in MS, but the allusion from Luke 6:31 requires it; cf. note to Poem 1/113-16.
37]   Cf. Deuteronomy 27:26, 'Cursed be he that abideth not in the words of this law, and
       fulfilleth them not in work', and cf. headnote to Poem 21.
41-4] Cf. 'Each Man ought himself to know', Furnivall, *Vernon Poems* II.673/38-43, 'Sit
       doun, and tac Countures rounde,/Seþþe furst þiu monnes wit bi-gon/Hou ofte sunne
       þe haþ I-bounde./And for vch a synne lei þou doun on,/Til þou þi synnes haue I-souȝt
       vp sounde;/Counte þi goode dedes euerichon'. Cf. Poem 7/49-56.

Wheþer hast þou more in store
Or of vices or of vertue.
And wheþer hast þou folwed more   45
Good aungel, or wykked, for boþe þe sewe;
Þy countretayle þey wil shewe þe skore,
In helle, or in heuene, [fol. 123b] wreten trewe.

Haue mynde God sente his sone adoun,
Tok mankynde in flesch and felle,   50
And suffred hard passioun,
Dyed on croys, and heryed helle.
Haue mynde of his resurexioun,
Byleue all þis trewe gospelle,
Haue mynde on his assencioun,   55
On God his fader riȝt hond doþ dwelle.

Þenke þou shalt dye and nost whenne;
Þou art incertayn, þerfore drede.
Fro heuene to erþe God shal come þenne,
Deme euel and good after here dede.   60
Þe good to heuene blisse renne,
In endeles lyf to haue here mede;
Þe wikked in helle for to brenne,
In endeles pyne deþ shal hem fede.

The ten comaundementis þou hem kepe,   65
Þe seuen werkis of mercy wel hem vse,

46]   Repeats, almost verbatim, Poem 18/119.
47]   Repeated almost verbatim, Poem 24/393, cf. Poem 4/235–56.
48]   **wreten trewe**, cf. Poem 1/87 and Poem 18/120.
49–64]   The contents and order of the stanzas are very similar to 'Each Man ought himself to know', Furnivall, *Vernon Poems* II.673/49–64. Both poems paraphrase the articles of faith, cf. 'How to Live Perfectly', Horstmann, *Vernon Poems* I.245/913–42.
49–52]   Cf. 'Each Man ought himself to know', Furnivall, *Vernon Poems* II.673/49–53, 'Knowe what god haþ for þe do:/Made þe after his oune liknes;/Seþþe, he com fro heuene also,/And diȝede for þe wiþ gret distres,/ffor þe he soffrede boþe pyne and wo'.
57–8]   Cf. Poem 7/17–18 and note.
60–2]   Cf. Poem 8/87.
65–8]   A resumé of categories of instruction found in popular penitential literature, e.g. 'How to Live Perfectly', Horstmann, *Vernon Poems* I.235/523–32.
66]   Cf. Poem 19/89.

Þe seuene synnes þou bewepe,
Þy fyue wittes þe auyse.
Do penaunce and preye whyle þou schuld slepe,
Þe fend and fals world despise,   70
No fleschly lustes þe vndercrepe,
Fle all foly and folwe þe wise.

72]   Cf. Poem 1/58.

Poem 23. Of the sacrament of the altere

This poem is a paraphrase and expansion of the hymn 'Lauda Sion' which, in 1246, Pope Urban IV asked Thomas Aquinas to write in honour of Christ for the new feast of Corpus Christi. As in Poem 9, the poet forges the materials for his verse from the liturgy of the Church. The stress on corporate communion is of a piece with the consistent concern throughout the sequence of poems for wholeness and incorporation. While the poet paraphrases most of the hymn, there are significant reversals of order and also embellishments which are discussed in notes to individual lines. The poet has used 'Lauda Sion' to pen an emphatic defence of the orthodox view of the sacrament of the Eucharist. The additions to his source make it crystal clear that the poem is an attempt to assert true belief and to make the point very forcibly that the miracle of transubstantiation cannot be apprehended by human bodily faculties, but must be accepted by faith. As in Poem 9, the importance of the priest in performing the sacrament is highlighted; priests are not mentioned in 'Lauda Sion'. The poem insists on the necessity of both the doctrine, and the clergy, of the institutional church. See Introduction for further detailed discussion of this poem.

23. Of the sacrament of the altere

I wole be mendid ȝif Y say mys:
Holychirche nes noþer tre ne stones;
Þe hous of preyers God nempned þys –
Boþe goode men and wikked ressayueþ at ones.
Þere as gadryng of goode men ys,   5
Is holychyrche of flesch and bones;
Prestes are lanterne hem to wysse
Þe wise weyes to heuene wones.

Holychirche, heryȝe þy saueour!
Þynk þy hurd God on hiȝt   10
Wiþ song, and ympnes, tyde, and houre;
Reioys in hym day and nyȝt,
For he is more þan any honour,
For his honour passeþ oure myȝt,
For we ben his, and he is oure;   15
All þouȝtes ben to hym dyȝt.

A specyall tyme of heryeng here:
Lyueliche quyk bred is put forþ þis day,
Whyche in þe table of þe holy sopere,

1–8] See Introduction, pp. 25–6, for discussion of these lines.

3] **hous of preyers**. Matthew 21:13, 'My house shall be called the house of prayer' cf. Mark 11:17 and Luke 19:46.

4–6] The gathering of good men again chimes rather closely with Wycliffite diction, see Introduction, p. 26, but it is clear from the poem as a whole that the attempt is to figure a morally sound congregation.

7] **lanterne**, cf. Poem 8/62 and 21/153. There is no counterpart to the importance of priests in 'Lauda Sion'.

9–11] Paraphrases 'Lauda Sion', ll. 1–3, 'Lauda Sion Salvatorem,/lauda ducem et pastorem,/in hymnis et canticis'. The addition of **tyde and houre** is probably needed to fulfil the demands of the stanza form, but it is an addition which stresses church liturgy.

12–14] Paraphrases 'Lauda Sion', ll. 4–6, 'Quantum potes, tantum aude:/quia maior omni laude,/nec laudare sufficis'.

15–16] No equivalent in 'Lauda Sion'. Line 16 reprises the diction of Poem 18/71.

17] 'Lauda Sion', l. 7, 'Laudis thema specialis'. **tyme** is a form of 'theme', see *MED* 'teme' (*n.*); 2a; unless the poet – or scribe – has introduced the notion of a specific time, i.e. Easter, instead, *MED* 'time' (*n.*); 2.5a, cf. Poem 12/4.

Wiþouten doute, was ʒouen oure fay.   20
To þe company of twelfe breþeren þere were,
By here ful heryenge ioyed þay,
Wel sowned in here ere,
Wiþ ioly herte fayre song to say.

A day is mad of solempnyte: 25
Of þis table first ordynaunce is worschipful tolde;
In þis newe kynges table now knowe we
Newe estren endeþ þe olde;
Newe thyng dryueþ old þyng fro his degre,
Out of mynde, þe lasse of tolde;   30
So soþfast sunne, by hys pouste,
Dryueþ awey shadewe and striʒeþ colde.

As liʒt liʒteneþ nyʒt fro derknes of kynde,
So dede crist at þe holy sopere;

18-21] Paraphrases 'Lauda Sion', ll. 8-12, 'panis vivus et vitalis/hodie proponitur./Quem in sacrae mensa cenae,/turbae fratrum duodenae/datum non ambigitur'.

20] ʒouen oure fay, i.e. the account of the breaking of bread at the Last Supper, constitutes the true belief of the sacrament of the Eucharist. The change from the faithful belief of the disciples to the present tense communal **oure fay** may indicate the poet's desire to set forth an orthodox account of the sacrament which has very present relevance.

22-4] The poet ascribes the praise and song to the twelve disciples, whereas in 'Lauda Sion' the invitation to praise is jussive and directed to all, 'Sit laus plena, sit sonora,/sit iucunda, sit decora/mentis iubilatio' (ll. 13-15).

24] Matthew 26:30, 'And a hymn being said, they went out unto mount Olivet', cf. Mark, 14:23.

25-6] Paraphrases 'Lauda Sion', ll. 16-18, 'Dies enim solemnis agitur,/in qua mensae prima recolitur/huius institutio'.

25] solempnyte, cf. note to Poem 11/1.

27-29] Paraphrases 'Lauda Sion', ll. 19-21, 'In hac mensa novi Regis,/novum Pascha novae legis,/phase vetus terminat'. The **newe kynges table** is a direct translation of the Latin, but given the juxtaposition of Easter and coronation in Poem 12/1-8 the expansion of the hymn may harbour topical resonance. The deletion of reference to old and new laws and the substitution of a new Easter and new **thyng** may refer to the coronation of a new king, i.e. Henry V.

30] No equivalent in 'Lauda Sion'.

31-2] Paraphrases 'Lauda Sion', ll. 22-4, 'Vetustatem novitas,/umbram fugat veritas,/ noctem lux eliminat'. **soþfast sunne** equates to 'veritas', and while both the English and the Latin clearly refer to Christ, the stanza may refer also to the coronation of Henry V, see Introduction, pp. 15-18.

33] No equivalent in 'Lauda Sion'; the poet elaborates the dark and light imagery (and

Bad hertely do so of hym mynde,   35
By holy ordynaunce tauȝte vs to lere,
Halwe bred and wyn by hys word and wynd;
To an ost of helþe to cristen men here,
Fro shadwe of deþ [fro] gostly blynd,
To liȝt of lyf to shynen clere.   40

Lore is ȝouen to cristen men:
Into flesch passeþ þe bred,
As holychirche doþ vs kenne;
Þe wyn to blod þat is so red.
Þou seest not fleschly þou takest þenne,   45
Þy byleue of herte makeþ þe fast fro ded;
Wiþouten ordre of þynges to renne,
By tokene and word þat he bede.

at lines 39–40) which stresses the spiritual rejuvenation of Easter and the sacrament of the Eucharist.

34–40] Paraphrases 'Lauda Sion', ll. 25–30, 'Quod in coena Christus gessit,/faciendum hoc expressit/in sui memoriam/Docti sacris institutis,/panem, vinum in salutis/consecramus hostiam.' The poet attributes the salvific quality of the Eucharist more explicitly to Christ, cf. Luke 22:19–20, 'And taking bread, he gave thanks, and brake; and gave to them, saying: This is my body, which is given for you. Do this for a commemoration of me. In like manner the chalice also, after he had supped, saying: This is the chalice, the new testament in my blood, which shall be shed for you.'

39]   **fro**. MS reads 'to', which ruins the sense of moving from the shadow of death and spiritual darkness to the light of eternal life. Possibly the scribe was attracted to the double incidence of 'to' in line 40. I have substituted **fro**, which restores sense and also the balanced opposition between line 39 and line 40.

41–8] Paraphrases 'Lauda Sion', ll. 31–6, 'Dogma datur christianis,/quod in carnem transit panis,/et vinum in sanguinem./Quod non capis, quod non vides,/animosa firmat fides,/ praeter rerum ordinem'.

43]   **holychirche**. The line expands on the hymn, possibly to complete the stanza form, but it also serves to stress that the doctrine of transubstantiation has the authority of the institutional Church.

46]   **byleue of herte**. Paraphrases 'fides' (faith) but there is an especially dense use of **byleue** in Poem 23; see also lines 50/56/71/114/116/118/120 which represents an addition to the Latin hymn. Possibly to combat Wycliffite interpretations of the sacrament, the poet is at pains to emphasise true Church doctrine (see further, Introduction, pp. 28–30).

47–8]   A rather clumsy rendition of 'praeter rerum ordinem' (beyond the order of things). But the sense is that true belief preserves humankind from death, allows them to go beyond trust in natural phenomena, and to adhere to Christ's ordinance.

48]   **þat he bede**. Christ's words and actions are invoked to bolster the authority of the verse.

Wiþouten help of ordre of þyngis
Þe bok of oure byleue is lent,   50
Vnder dyuerce spices only tokenynges,
Þou3 þe spices fro hym be went;
Not durked ne hyd, but ri3t shynynges,
Þou3 fleschly sy3t fro hym be blent;
Þe soule haþ ioye and mery synges   55
When good byleue seeþ þe sacrament.

Þe blod is drynk, þe flesch is mete;
Ys gostly fode, þe soules delys;
Neuere þe lattere, of Crist to trete –
He dwelleþ vnder ayþer spys.   60
Þe ressayuour cou[ ]teþ not þat þey ete,
Ne brekeþ it not, but hool it lys;

49–56] Paraphrases 'Lauda Sion', ll. 37–9, 'Sub diversis speciebus,/signis tantum, et non rebus,/latent res eximiae'.

49] An addition, either for metrical reasons – picking up from line 47 – or an emphasis on the miracle of transubstantiation; each species of bread and wine is annihilated and becomes instead Christ's body and his blood.

50] **lent**: in the sense of 'granted', see *MED* 'lenen' (*v.*); 3.1a. **bok of oure byleue** is added to the source and once again stresses institutional authority for the doctrine about to be expounded.

51–2] I.e. under each species only signs though the species have been annihilated. The repetition of **spices** is presumably an attempt to encapsulate the paradox that only the signs of the bread and wine remain and have become Christ's body. The Latin 'et non rebus' is much clearer.

53–4] Expands on the hymn. While the image of the **ri3t shynynges** affirms the miracle of the bread and wine becoming Christ's body, the **hym** of line 52, the plural form is potentially confusing. The poet is attempting to explain that although human sight cannot apprehend Christ's body, it is certainly, and triumphantly, present. See also Introduction, pp. 28–30.

55–6] Expands the hymn; see note to lines 46 and 50.

57–64] Paraphrases 'Lauda Sion', ll. 40–8, 'Caro cibus, sanguis potus:/manet tamen Christus/totus sub utraque specie/A sumente non concisus,/non confractus, non divisus:/integer accipitur./Sumit unus, sumunt mille:/quantum isti, tantum ille:/nec sumptus consumitur'.

58] Expands the hymn and emphasises the importance of the soul rather than bodily apprehension of the substances on the altar.

61] **couteþ**. MS reads 'counteþ', but as the verb paraphrases the past participle 'concisus' (cut, or sever), I have emended to restore sense. For the form 'couten' see *MED* 'cutten' (*v.*); 1.

Þou3 a thowsand take at o sete,
Alone, on takeþ as moche o prys.

While obley in yrnes or boyst ys stoken,   65
Hit nys but bred and sengyl bake;
Whanne þe prest to hit Goddis wordis hath spoken,
Crystys quyk body vndir bred o cake.
Þou3 it a þousand peces seme broken,
Nes parted ne wasted, but al holl take.   70
In byleue of holychirche, who wyl hym 3oken,
A3en þis non argument may make.

That ressayueþ children, man, and wyf
Not al yliche deuocioun:
Summe taken it in synne and stryf   75
As bestes wiþouten discrecioun;
þe wikkid resceueþ a dedly knyf,
And his endeles dampnacioun;
Þe good resceyueþ endeles lyf,
To body and soule saluacioun.   80

65–72] There is no equivalent to this stanza in the hymn, though lines 69–70 restate 'Lauda Sion' ll. 43–5. The addition emphasises the sacramental role of the priest in confecting Christ's body when he speaks '**Goddis wordis**', i.e. the restatement of Christ's words at the Last Supper in the liturgy. 'Lauda Sion' does not mention the role of the priest at all.

71–2] Cf. note to lines 46, 50 and 55–6. **3oken** makes adherence to true doctrine rather forcibly. **A3en þis non argument** completes the stanza but, given there is no counterpart to this in 'Lauda Sion', is surely a clear sign of the direction of the poem's remarks; to defend true doctrine and the authority of the institutional Church against dissenters.

73–80] Paraphrases 'Lauda Sion', ll. 49–53, 'Sumunt boni, sumunt mali:/sorte tamen inaequali,/vitae vel interitus./Mors est malis, vita bonis:/vide paris sumptionis/quam sit dispar exitus'.

75–7] Expands on the simple mention of the wicked in the hymn and recalls the advice in penitential literature that communicants must have made confession of their sins and settled any dispute between themselves and others before they receive the Eucharist, cf. note to Poem 11/78.

76–8] Cf. Weatherly, *Speculum Sacerdotale*, p. 123/12–15, 'He þat resceueþ þe body of God vnreuerently, *scilicet*, beynge in dedly synne, or in purpos to synne dedely, he resceyueþ his dome; *scilicet*, he doþ þat that schall make hym be dampnyd'. The source is 1 Corinthians 11:29, 'For he that eateth and drinketh unworthily, eateth and drinketh judgement to himself, not discerning the body of the Lord'.

77] **dedely knyf**, cf. Poem 7/105, 21/127.

When þou to chirche gost
To resceyue God, wisely go;
[...] Suppose þe prest haue but on ost,
Breke it and parte to twenty and mo,
As moche is þe leste cost   85
As in þe grettest pece of þo.
Deme all yliche, lest and most,
Quaue not, ne drede, not to sen hit so.

Þou3 þe prest þe sacrament clyue
In a þowsand peces and þre,   90
þe state, ne stature, ne my3t doþ myue,
Ne leseþ, ne lasseþ, of his pouste.
Þy fleschly sy3t þou shalt not lyue,
But tokene of brekyng makeþ he,

81–96] Paraphrases 'Lauda Sion', ll. 54–61, 'Fracto demum sacramento,/ne vacilles, sed memento/tantum esse sub fragmento,/quantum toto tegitur./Nulla rei fit scissura:/signi tantum fit fractura,/qua nec status, nec statura/signati minuitur'.

81–3] The addition of the church and the priest is another assertion of institutional authority.

82] **wisely**, cf. note to lines 76–8.

83] The MS starts the line with 'I', which makes nonsense of the exhortations. I interpret **suppose** as an imperative in the sense of think/believe parallel to **deme** (l. 87).

84–7] Expands 'Lauda Sion' ll. 54–7. 'fragmento' (part) and 'totus' (whole) become **twenty and mo** and the poet introduces **moche, lest** and **grettest** to emphasise that Christ's body remains whole in every part.

85] **cost**: a natural trait or property, an attribute, MED 'cost' (n.); 1.2a.

88] An addition to the Latin, presumably a reassurance that while the host is broken, God's body remains intact.

89–90] An expansion of 'Lauda Sion', l. 54, 'fracto ... Sacramento'.

91–6] Paraphrases 'Lauda Sion', ll. 58–61, 'Nulla rei fit scissura:/signi tantum fit fractura,/ qua nec status, nec statura/signati minuitur'.

91] **state** and **stature** pick up on 'status' and 'statura'. **my3t** is added. **myue** in the sense of 'change, alter', MED 'meven' (v.); 1d.b. This spelling form is not listed in MED and is used for rhyme.

92] Equivalent to 'nec ... minuitur' (is not diminished).

93–6] While the Latin hymn states that only the sign, and not the thing, substance, is broken, the poet expands to reiterate that this miracle cannot be apprehended by bodily sight. Bodily sight cannot prove the sacrament; explanation comes through spiritual belief. Cf. note to line 46.

For fleschly s[y3t] no sacrement kan preue;   95
In gostly bylyue shal saued be.

In old lawe 3e wyten how
At estren þey eten a lamb al ded;
Is ouer put in newe lawe now,
At estre we eten quyk bred.   100
In old lawe, for mannys prow,
God þe comaundementis bed;
And oure newe lawe we don allow,
And kepen boþe by Goddis red.

Lete þy mercy passe ry3t,   105
And for3eue vs oure mysdede;
þy face wiþ loue to seen in sy3t,
In lond of lyf þou vs lede,
Among þy seyntes in heuene on hy3t.
[fol. 124b] At þat feste of lif God vs fede,   110
Soþfast bred, God of my3t,
Ihesus herde, þou vs hede.

95] **sy3t**. MS reads 'skyn' which, either in the sense of 'skin' or 'light', is a peculiar
      observation. It is possible that the scribe started to write **sy3t**, but was attracted to
      the previous **kyn** sequence in **brekyng**. In lines 45–6, 554–6 and 113–20, bodily sight is
      consistently contrasted to belief. The emendation reproduces the observation of line 93.
96] **saved** means explained, *MED* 'saven' (*v.*); 12.
97–102] There is no precise equivalent to these lines in 'Lauda Sion'. The poet has expanded
      on the reference to 'Agnus Paschae', line 68 of the hymn (see notes to lines 121–8), to
      assert the importance of observing both the Old and the New Testaments.
98] God's instructions to Moses on the preparation and eating of the lamb on the
      fourteenth day of the first month are in Exodus 12:1–10.
100] **quyk bred** contrasts neatly with the dead lamb of line 98.
102] Christ's commandment at the Last Supper, see note to lines 34–40.
104–12] Paraphrases 'Lauda Sion', ll. 70–9, 'Bone pastor, panis vere,/Iesu, nostri miserere:/
      Tu nos pasce, nos tuere,/Tu nos bona fac videre/in terra viventium./Tu qui cuncta scis
      et vales,/qui nos pascis hic mortales:/tuos ibi commensales/coheredes et sodales/fac
      sanctorum civium'.
104–5] Loosely renders 'Iesu, nostri miserere'.
106–7] Renders 'Lauda Sion', ll. 73–4.
109–10] Renders 'Lauda Sion', ll. 77–9, though the poet reverses the order of the clauses.
      'Lauda Sion' ends with the image of the community of saints, and the poet translates
      the three nouns which suggest companionship into **feste of lif**.

In sy3t and in felyng, þou semest bred,
In byleue, flesch, blod, and bon;
In sy3t and felyng þou semest ded,   115
In byleue, lyf to speke and gon.
In sy3t and felyng noþer hond ne hed,
In byleue, boþe God and man;
In sy3t and felyng, in litil sted,
In byleue, grettere þyng nes nan.   120

Whan Abraham of Ysaac his offryng made,
For a figure he lykned is,
To angels bred oure fadres hadde,
þat God fed hem in wyldernes.
Afterward God hem bade   125
A paske lomb rosted and eteþ þes.
In stede of þat, oure soules to glade,
We resceyue oure housell, God o blisse.

111–12]   Ends with the first line of the stanza of the hymn and reverses 'panis vere' and
'bone pastor'. **God of my3t** is added.

113–20]   There is no equivalent to this stanza in 'Lauda Sion'. The poet has added a verse of
an almost liturgical quality which reasserts that the miracle of the Eucharist cannot be
apprehended through bodily senses; Christ's present body in the bread can be understood
by faith alone. See note to line 46.

118–20]   **man ... nan.** The unrounded form of both these words may represent scribal
interference as they spoil the rhyme. In the sequence as a whole, there are no instances
of 'mon' for man, but abundant examples of 'non'.

121–8]   Returns to 'Lauda Sion', ll. 66–9, 'In figuris praesignatur,/cum Isaac immolatur,/
agnus Paschae deputatur/datur manna patribus'. By choosing to return to the issue of
signs and typology, the poet stresses once again the presence of Christ's body in the
Eucharist. The events of the Old Testament are signs which prefigure the sacrament.

121–2]   The story of Abraham's readiness to sacrifice his son Isaac is told in Genesis 22:1–14.
figure ... lykned is renders 'in figuris praesignatur'.

123]   God's feeding of the people of Israel in the wilderness, Exodus 16:35, 'And the children
of Israel ate manna forty years, till they came to a habitable land: with this meat were
they fed, until they reached the borders of the land of Chanaan'. The poet transfers the
last line of the stanza of the hymn into the middle of this stanza in the poem in order
to be able to finish with a present tense reference to communion.

125–6]   Cf. note to line 98.

127–8]   Not in 'Lauda Sion'. The poet finishes with a present tense inclusivity with the
pronouns **We** and **oure**, and the act of corporate communion.

Poem 24. The Lessouns of the Dirige

The poem is a metrical paraphrase of the lessons and responses contained in the liturgical sequence, the 'Dirige' from 'The Office of the Dead'. The first three lessons are from Matins, first Nocturn; lessons 4, 5 and 6 are from the second Nocturn, and lessons 7, 8 and 9 are from the third Nocturn. The lessons are drawn from verses from Job. Lines 331–86 are a paraphrase of the responses in the liturgy after the last lesson, and not a tenth lesson as Kail's running headnote to this poem implies. The paraphrase bears very close resemblance to the Middle English version of the liturgy, see Littlehales, *Prymer*, Part 1. Lines 387–418 are the poet's addition to the liturgy; the stanzas repeat its fierce penitential warnings. Many lines in this section of the poem echo those of the earlier penitential lyrics in the sequence. The terrifying note on which the poem ends returns us to the blend of the secular and spiritual seen right at the start of the series.

24. The Lessouns of the Dirige

Lectio prima: Parce mihi domine

Almy3ty God, Lord me spare!
For soþe, my dayes werkys ben no3t;
My wittes on ny3tes wrong Y ware,
Þerof longe 3eres mon be wro3t.
Þenke man, þou ware born ful bare;   5
Into þis world what hastou bro3t?
Out of þis world whanne þou schalt fare,
Þou schalt bere with þe ry3t no3t.

What is man of gret renoun
That of hym self makeþ aldre mest?   10
Why settyst þou þy herte a3en resoun,
And sodeynly repreuest hem mest?
In þe dawenynge þou sou3test hem vpsodoun,
Contrary to Godis hest.
Þou purchasest þy saule helle prisoun,   15
For fleschely lust wormes fest.

1–32]   The first lesson is based on Job 7:16–21.

1–2]   Paraphrases 'Dirige', Littlehales, *Prymer*, p. 59/16, 'Lord, spare þou me, for my daies ben not'.

3–4]   These added lines stress the anguish of the speaker.

5–8]   These added lines are a reference to 1 Timothy 6:7, 'For we brought nothing into this world: and certainly we can carry nothing out'.

9–13]   Paraphrases 'Dirige', Littlehales, *Prymer*, p. 59/17–18, 'what is man, for þou magnefiest him? eþer what settest þou þin herte, towardis him./þou visitist him eerli; and sodeynli þou preuest him'.

10]   Differs from both Job 7:17 and the 'Dirige', Littlehales, *Prymer*, p. 59/17. Fein, *Pety Job*, line 15, has the same interpretation as Digby, 'That magnifyeth *himself* alway' (emphasis mine).

11]   **a3en resoun** is in neither Job, nor the 'Dirige'. Again, there may be influence of *Pety Job* which expands the verse to ask why God opposes himself to man since He 'hast [them] so dere bought' (Fein, l. 26).

13]   Not in Job or 'Dirige'. Both continue God's morning visiting with God's reproof which the Digby poet has already mentioned in line 12.

15–16]   Not in Job or 'Dirige'. The switch of address from God to humankind moralises the verse but diverts the sense of the lesson. **saule:** the only instance of Northern spelling of this word in the sequence. It is not needed for rhyme.

How longe sparest þou me noʒt
To swolwe my spotel bote it me gryue?
Þou keper of men, alle þyng hast wroʒt,
What shal Y do to þyn byhyue?   20
What hastou set me contrarie þy þoʒt
Þy holy lawe to repryue?
Lord, whenne my werkis mon be soʒt,
Dyspyce me noʒt in my myschyue.

Ful heuy to my self Y am maad withynne,   25
My werkes on me heuye isse.
Why takest þou noʒt away my synne,
And bere from me my wykednesse?
I slepe in dust, for we ben kynne,
For erthe claymeʒ me for hisse;   30
To seche me eerly, ʒif þou begynne,
I ne may withstonde þe ywisse.

Lectio secunda: Tedet animam meam

My soul of my self anoyed isse;
I shal leue my speche aʒens me,

18]   **bote it me gryue** is added. This is the only example of **gryue**; elsewhere the form is 'greue', Poem 2/41, 4/30/35, 10/113 and 17/162.

19-22]   Paraphrases 'Dirige', Littlehales, *Prymer*, p. 59/19-20, 'hou longe sparest þou not me, neþer suffrest þat y swolewe my spotele?/y haue synned, o þou keper of men, what shal y do to þee? whi hast þou set me contrarie to þee'.

20]   **byhyue**: *MED* 'beheve' (*n.*) is added.

21]   **þy þoʒt** is added for rhyme. Both Job and 'Dirige' have simply 'thee'.

22-4]   An addition to both Job and the 'Dirige'.

25-32]   Paraphrases 'Dirige', Littlehales, *Prymer*, p. 59/20-1, 'y am maad greuouse to my silf./whi doist þou not awey my synne? & whi takest þou not a-wey my wickidnesse? lo, now y slepe in poudur; and if þou sekest me eerli, y schal not abide'.

26, 30]   Cf. notes to Poem 1/116, 17/28 and 18/158.

29-30]   **we ben kynne** and line 30 are added. Cf. Genesis 3:19, 'In the sweat of thy face shalt thou eat bread till thou return to the earth, out of which thou wast taken: for dust thou art, and into dust thou shalt return'.

30]   **claymeʒ** repeated at line 271, and cf. line 186, 218, and note to Poem 16/117.

33-64]   The second lesson is based on Job 10:1-7.

33-40]   Paraphrases 'Dirige', Littlehales, *Prymer*, p. 59/1-2, 'It anoieþ my soule of my lyif; y schal lette my speche aʒenes me, y schal speke in þe bitternesse of my soule./y schal seie to god, "nyle þou condempne me; schewe þou to me whi þou demest me so"'.

33]   Cf. note to line 26, 30.

To my soul Y wole speke in bitternesse,   35
And Y shal saye to God so fre,
'Wyl noȝt dampne me fro blisse,
Shew me þe cause þat wolde I se.
Why demestou me þoȝ Y dede mysse,
Lord whether þe þynke good to þe?'   40

Ȝif þou chalenge my werk and bere me doun,
Me that am werk of þy hande,
And þou in consayl helpe ȝe moun,
To wykked men here synnes withstande,
Wiþ repentaunce and sorwful [fol. 125a] soun;   45
May launce hem from þe deuelys bande.
To ȝerde of loue Y moste me boun;
Lord, me chastice wiþ þat wande!

Wheþer þyn eyȝen ben fleschlye,
Or þou seest as man shal see,   50
Or þy dayes so sone syȝe
As other mennys dayes be,
Or þy ȝerys riȝt so hye,
As mennys tymes in here degre,

36]   **so fre** is added both to Job and 'Dirige' for rhyme.
41]   **my werk**, not in Job or 'Dirige'. It is possibly a scribal addition, anticipating **werk** in
       line 42 and the poet originally wrote 'me'.
42–4]   Paraphrases 'Dirige', Littlehales, *Prymer*, p. 59/3, 'wheþer it semeþ good to þee, if
       þou falseli chalengist & oppressist me, þe werk of þin hondis, & if þou helpe þe counseil
       of wickid men'.
43–4]   In order to meet the demands of the stanza form, the poet alters the direction of
       the verse from both Job and 'Dirige'.
45–8]   Not in Job or 'Dirige'.
46]   **bande**: only here and in line 238 is the Northern form of this word used. Cf. 'bonde',
       Poem 18/87.
47–8]   **ȝerde of loue**, cf. line 125 and Poem 1/83 and Proverbs 23:14, 'Thou shalt beat him
       with the rod, and deliver his soul from hell'.
49–54]   Paraphrases 'Dirige', Littlehales, *Prymer*, pp. 59–60/4–5, 'wheþer fleischli iȝen ben
       to þee? eþer as a man seeþ, also þou schalt se?/wheþer þi daies ben as þe daies of man;
       & þi ȝeeris ben as mannys tyme'.
51]   **syȝe**, i.e. perish, decline, *MED* 'seien' (*v*.); 2. The confected form secures rhyme.
54]   **in here degre** added to Job and 'Dirige' to secure rhyme.

For þou art God, shal neuere dyȝe,   55
For sorwe and deþ shal from the fle.

That þou seche my wykkednesse
And ransake my synne,
And wyte I haue noȝt doun mysse,
Bote hert and soule clene withynne,   60
Soþes, þer no man nesse,
May skape þyn hond and from the twynne;
Bote repentaunce and mercy kesse
Þat now ben frendis, Lord make hem kynne.

Lectio tertia: Manus tue fecerunt me

Thy hand made me man of þe soun,   65
And shope me al in compas,
And sodeynly þou cast me doun,
For knew Y noȝt what þou was.
Of me men sample take mowen,
Be ware lest þay folwe my tras.   70
I hadde lordschipe in feld and toun,
Now on a donghille is my pas.

55–6]   Not in Job or 'Dirige'.

57–62]   Paraphrases 'Dirige', Littlehales, *Prymer*, p. 60/6–7, 'þat þou enquere my wickidnesse & enserche my synne/& wite þat y haue do no wickid þing, siþen no man is, þat mai delyuere fro þyn hond?'

61]   **nesse.** The spelling secures the rhyme with **kesse** (l. 63). 'nes' is used elsewhere throughout the sequence, but not in rhyme position.

62]   **from the twynne** added to Job and 'Dirige' to secure rhyme.

63–4]   not in Job or 'Dirige'. **kesse** is the only instance of the Eastern form of this verb in the sequence. Elsewhere, the form is 'kys(se)', e.g. Poem 1/119, 8/37, 11/47, 17/15, 18/84 and 19/30. Line 63 repeats almost verbatim Poem 11/47. The line recalls Psalms 84:11, 'Mercy and truth have met each other: justice and peace have kissed'.

65–128]   The third lesson is based on Job 10:8–12.

65–8]   Paraphrases 'Dirige', Littlehales, *Prymer*, p. 60/8, 'Thyne hondis maden me, & han formed me al in cumpas; & þou castist me doun so sodeynli!'

65]   **of þe soun** Kail emended to 'resoun', but the MS reading makes sense if **soun** means earth/dust'; see *MED* 'sand' (*n.*); 2a. *MED* does record the form 'son'; the form in Digby used here to secure rhyme. In Poem 20/162 **soun** is voice, but this scarcely makes sense in this context.

68–9]   Not in Job or 'Dirige'.

72]   **donghille.** Job delivers his complaint sitting on a dunghill, Job 2:8, but the line may

Haue mynde on me Lord, and take hede;
Of fen of erthe þou dede me make,
Into dust aȝen þou shalt me lede,   75
My soule from þe body take.
My flesch is ful sleper atte nede,
And solpeþ my soule wiþ synnes blake;
Lord God, þy dome Y drede
Whanne þou comest, Y mon awake.   80

My hert shulde be stedefast;
Þou hast lopred [me] as mylk and slep in þouȝt,
Riȝt as chese þou croddest me fast,
I wyte my synnes þat Y wrouȝt.
Lord, alle my synnes away þou cast,   85
Bote wiþ my synnes cast me noȝt;
þou knowest how longe my lyf shulde last;
Þou sette my terme, Y passe it noȝt.

also be influenced by Job 20:6–7, 'If his pride mount up even to heaven, and his head touch the clouds: In the end he shall be destroyed like a dunghill, and they that has seen him shall say: Where is he?'

72–5]   Paraphrases 'Dirige', Littlehales, *Prymer*, p. 60/9, 'y biseche þee haue þou mynde þat þou madist me of cley, schalt brynge me aȝen in-to poudur'.

78]   **solpeþ my soule**, cf. Poem 11/74 and 21/106.

79–80]   Paraphrases the response to the third lesson, 'Dirige', Littlehales, *Prymer*, p. 60, 'Lord, whanne þou schalt come to deme þe erþe, where schal y hide me fro þe face of þi wraþþe? for y haue synned ful myche in my liyf. [V] I drede my trespassis, & y am aschamed to-fore þee: whanne þou schalt come to iugement, nyle þou condempne me'.

79]   Cf. Poem 7/18 and 24/353.

81]   Not in Job or 'Dirige'.

82–3]   Paraphrases 'Dirige', Littlehales, *Prymer*, p. 60/10, 'wheþer þou hast not softid me as mylk; and hast cruddid me to-gideres as chese'.

82]   **me**. Job 10:10 also has the pronoun 'me'. It is possible that its absence in line 82 is the result of compressed syntax, but its omission also creates the unfortunate suggestion that it is God that has curdled as milk. **slep in þouȝt** is an addition. **slep** is curdled milk, see *MED* 'slippe' (*n*.); 1b and hence is parallel to **mylk**.

84–6]   Not in Job or 'Dirige', but recalls the response, cf. note to lines 79–80.

87–8]   Cf. Job 14:5, 'The days of man are short, and the number of his months is with thee: thou hast appointed his bounds which cannot be passed'. These verses are part of the fifth lesson of the 'Dirige', Littlehales, *Prymer*, p. 64/5, 'þe daies of a man ben schorte: þe noumbre of his moneþis ben at þee; þou hast set hise termes, þe whiche moun not be passid'. The poet paraphrases them again lines 197–200.

Þou cloþedest me with flesch and skyn,
With bones and synewes made me togyder,   90
Lyf and mercy ȝaf me withyn,
As brotel vessel Y stonde slyder.
Þy sechyng haþ kepyd my gost with[ ]yn.
A! Lord, whenne þou comest hyder,
To deme al erþe þy domes to twyn,   95
Þouȝ I wolde fle, I not noȝt whyder.

To deme þe erthe whanne þou wendys,
Fro face of þy wraþþe whyder shal I go?
To hyde me wiþ angels aren Goddis frendys?
And God me hate, þay ben my fo.   100
And I hyde me in helle among fendys,
In pyne þay wolen tormente me so;
I haue synned [fol. 125b] riȝt moche, my synne me schendys;
Me thynke þay waxen mo and mo.

My trespas moche arn blamed   105
Bote repentaunce be mendement;
Byfore þe Y drede, Y am aschamed.
Whenne þou comest to iugement,
Þat weren wylde mon be tamed,
Al wopen of wraþþe mon be brent,   110

89–90]   Paraphrases 'Dirige', Littlehales, *Prymer*, p. 60/11, 'þou hast cloþid me wiþ skyn & flesch; þou hast ioyned me to-gideres wiþ bones & synewes'.

92]   An added line which intensifies the fragility of the speaker's plight, cf. Poem 4/7.

93]   Paraphrases 'Dirige', Littlehales, *Prymer*, p. 60/12., 'þou has ȝoue liyf and merci to me; & þi visitacioun haþ kept my spirit'. **withyn** the MS reads 'with wyn' which, as the paraphrase of 'Dirige' shows, is clearly an error.

94–6]   Paraphrases the response to the lesson in 'Dirige', Littlehales, *Prymer*, p. 60, 'Lord, whanne þou schalt come to deme þe erþe, where schal y hide me fro þe face of þi wraþþe? for y haue synned ful myche in my liyf'.

102–4]   Not in Job or 'Dirige'.

105–6]   Paraphrases the repetition of the response from 'Dirige', see note to lines 94–6.

107–8]   Paraphrases the versicle after the third lesson, Dirige, Littlehales, *Prymer*, p. 60, 'I drede my trespassis, & y am aschamed to-fore þee: whanne þou schalt come to iugement, nyle þou condempne me'.

109–12]   Not in Job or 'Dirige'.

110]   Cf. Jeremias 50:25, 'The Lord hath opened his armoury, and hath brought forth the weapons of his wrath: for the Lord the God of hosts hath a work to be done in the land of the Chaldeans'.

In bok of lyf, þo þat be named,
To ioye of heuene mon be sent.

Almyȝty God, Lord me ȝeme,
In thy mercy þou me lede
Whenne my soule is boden outfleme. 115
Helpe me, Lord, atte al my nede.
Whenne þou al þe world shal deme,
Dampne me noȝt after my dede;
Whenne þat angels blowen here beme,
Þenne alle folk may haue gret drede. 120

From worldis worschipe Y am shoue,
And broȝt abas from al astat;
My skyn is cloþed al on roue,
In pouerte and peyne my wyt is mat.
Lord, chastice me wiþ ȝerd of loue, 125
Þouȝ Y haue seruyd þe swerd of hat.
Wherto nyltou þy maystry proue
With suchon as I to make debat?

Lectio quarta: Quantas habeo

Als many wykkednesse and trespas,
And synnes withoute noumbre mo, 130
Shew me. Why hydest þy fas

111–12] Cf. Revelation 3:5, 'He that shall overcome, shall thus be clothed in white garments, and I will not blot out his name out of the book of life, and I will confess his name before my Father, and before his angels'.

118] Cf. line 243, and Poem 7/103.

121–8] Not in 'Dirige' or Job.

123] **on roue**: with scabs, see *MED* 'rove' (*n*.); 1 'a scabby condition of the skin; also, the scab of a wound'. The line may show influence of Deuteronomy 28:27, 'The Lord strike thee with the ulcer of Egypt, and the part of thy body, by which the dung is cast out, with the scab and with the itch: so that thou canst not be healed'.

125] **ȝerd of loue**, cf. note to lines 47–8.

126] May be suggested by Revelation 2:16, 'In like manner do penance: if not, I will come to thee quickly, and will fight against them with the sword of my mouth'.

129–68] The fourth lesson is based on Job 13:23–38.

129–31] Paraphrases 'Dirige', Littlehales, *Prymer*, p. 63/23, 'Hou grete synnes & wickidnessis haue y! schewe to me my felonyes & trespassis!'.

Fro me, and demest me þy fo?
Lord, þenkes þe solace,
This turment, and do me wo.
A drope of thy mercie, of oyle of grace,   135
Lord, graunte me er Y go.

I am slyme of erthe, haue in mynde,
Pore of matere, and dedely.
As a lef styrede with wynde,
On me þou prouest þy maystry.   140
Þou prouest þy my3t, and þat I fynde
O þe stubble þat is so drye;
Þou pursuest me and wylt me bynde,
Wiþ synnes in my 3ouþe þou wylt me stroye.

Lord, þou pursuest me fast,   145
For soþe a3ens me þou doest wryte
Bitternesse; bote swete is past.
I may no3t blenche whenne þou wylt smyte;
I trowe þat þou wolt me wast,
With synnes in my 3ouþe, do me endite.   150
Lord, on me þy wille þou hast,
My grete synne myself Y wyte.

131–2] 'Dirige', Littlehales, *Prymer*, p. 63/24, 'whi hidest þou þi face, & demest me þin enemy?'

133–6] Not in Job or 'Dirige'.

137–8] Not in Job or 'Dirige'. Cf. Genesis 2:7, 'And the Lord God formed man of the slime of the earth'.

139–44] Paraphrases 'Dirige', Littlehales, *Prymer*, p. 63/25–6, 'þou schewist þi power a3enes a leef which is rauyschid wiþ þe wynde, & þou pursuest drie stobil;/for þou writist bitternessis a3enes me, & wolt waste me wiþ þe synnes of my waxinge age'.

142]   **so drye** added to secure rhyme.

143]   **wylt me bynde** added to fill out the line and rhyme.

144]   Substitutes the sins of youth for those of old age, but cf. line 150. Fein, *Pety Job*, 260, reads 'And distroy me for my wyked dede'.

145–52]   The poet amplifies the first half of verse 26 from 'Dirige', already paraphrased in the previous stanza.

146–7]   Cf. Job 13:26, 'For thou writest bitter things against me, and wilt consume me for the sins of my youth'. There may be influence of Fein, *Pety Job*, 253–54, 'Thow wrytest, lord, ayenst me/Bytternesse, þat I shall rede'.

149–50]   See quotation from Job in previous note.

151–2]   An amplification to fill out the stanza.

In synn[u] þou settest my fot and hede,
And alle my werkes hastou soȝt,
And alle steppys Y euere ȝede;   155
Ȝe haue nombred alle my wordes and þoȝt,
And als þou hast taken hede,
Roten Y schal be wasted to noȝt,
As clothes þat moþþes on hem fede,
So shal my flesch with wormes [be] soȝt.   160

Wo me! So mon Y be,
For Y haue don moche synne;
I, wreche, whyder shal Y fle,
For wrechyd lyf Y lyued ynne?
My Lord, my God, noȝt bote to the,   165
God of mercie on me mynne;
Lord, haue mercie on me;
Let noȝt thy loue [fol. 126a] fro me twynne.

Lectio quinta: Homo natus

Man that is of woman born,
Lyuynge short tyme he is,   170

153–60]   Paraphrases 'Dirige', Littlehales, *Prymer*, p. 63/27–8, 'þou hast set my foot in a stok, and þou hast kepte alle my paþþis, & þou hast biholde þe steppis of my feet;/& y schal be wastid as rotenesse, & as a cloþ which is etun of a mouȝte'.

153]   **synnu**. MS reads 'synne', which is clearly in error. A more familiar word has been substituted for one less common; the final 'u' has been read as 'e', cf. *MED* 'sineu' (*n*.). The Vulgate reads 'nervo' at this point and Fein, *Pety Job* translates this as 'synew' (265). I have emended to restore what must have been the original reading.

154]   Added to fill out the stanza.

156]   **wordes and þoȝt** replaces the paths that the speaker has taken.

157]   An amplification which fills out the stanza and secures rhyme.

160]   **be**. Not in MS, but needed for the parallel with **be wasted**, line 158. The line is an addition to the 'Dirige' and may have been suggested by Isaias 14:11, 'Thy pride is brought down to hell, thy carcass is fallen down: under thee shall the moth be strewed, and worms shall be thy covering'.

161–7]   Paraphrases the response to the lesson, 'Dirige', Littlehales, *Prymer*, pp. 63–4, 'Woo is me, lord! for y haue synned ful myche in my lif. what shal, y, wrecche, do? whidur schal y flee, but to þee, my god! haue merci on me, whanne þou schalt come in þe laste dai!'

168]   Cf. Poem 17/85. The line paraphrases the versicle from 'Dirige', Littlehales, *Prymer*, p. 64, 'Mi soule is gretli troblid; bot þou, lord, socoure þou it'.

169–218]   The fifth lesson is based on Job 14:1–6.

Er his nauel be knytte and shorn,
Fulfilde with many wrechidnes,
Er he fro moder be forborn;
In peryl of deth bothe partie es.
ȝif flesch be lord, the soule is lorn,   175
Bote soule be lord, he leseth his blys.

Man geth out as don floures:
Corage, and strengthe, and fayre of hewe,
Makeþ moche of hymself, sayþe, 'al is oures',
And repeth þat he neuere ne sewe.   180
He is defouled be days and houres,
And fleeþ as shadow þat neuere grewe,
Dwelleþ neuere in þe self stat of ouris;
Encresceþ mo vyces þan vertew.

And þou holdest worthy to open thyn ey,   185
And come to me and clayme for rent,
To loke on such a wrecche as Y,

169–72] Paraphrases 'Dirige', Littlehales, *Prymer*, p. 64/1, 'A man þat is born of a womman, lyueþ schort tyme, & is fillid wiþ many wrecchidnessis'.

171] Added to fill out the stanza.

173–4] Amplifies the preceding and recalls Poem 22/11–13.

175–6] Not in 'Dirige' or Job. The poet's moralising recalls the frequent body/soul oppositions throughout the sequence.

177–84] Paraphrases and amplifies 'Dirige', Littlehales, *Prymer*, p. 64/2, 'which goiþ out & is defoulid as a flour, & fleeþ as a schadewe, & dwelliþ neuer parfitli in þe same staat'. **geth:** see note to line 335.

178] Human attributes all parallel to **Man** of line 177.

179–80] Cf. Matthew 25:26, 'Wicked and slothful servant, thou knewest that I reap where I sow not, and gather where I have not strewed'.

182] **þat neuere grewe** amplifies 'Dirige' and produces a powerful image of human powerlessness.

183] **of ouris** added for rhyme, but does capture the transitoriness of human existence.

184] The added moralisation repeats previous warnings about vices and virtue, e.g. Poem 1/143, 8/74 and cf. 24/191–2/352.

185–92] Paraphrases 'Dirige', Littlehales, *Prymer*, p. 64/3, 'and gessist þou it worþi to opene þin iȝen on siche a man, & to brynge him into doom wiþ þee?'

186] **clayme for rent** is added and continues the accounting imagery which has accompanied many of the poet's renditions of the Day of Judgement, e.g. Poem 1/39, 7/87, 8/100, 9/103, 10/196, 11/110–11.

187] **wrecche** is added and intensifies the pitiable state of the speaker.

And lede hym with the to iugement,
Þer al mankynde in company
Atte thy general parlement,   190
Vertues to heuen ther schul ʒe try;
The vyces in helle fyre be brent.

What man may make hym clene
Þat is conceyued in vnclene sed?
Ywhether þou art alone withoute mene,   195
To felowschipe þou hast non nede.
Short ar mannys deyes sene,
And the nombre of hys monthes in thy dede,
Þou hast sette his terme of fat and lene;
He passeþ it noʒt for no mede.   200

A! go away a lytel hym fro,
In mendement that he mow rest,
Tyl the day he ʒerned so,
A[s] of h[i]rde man come þat is best.
Lord, haue no mynde to do me wo,   205
Forber my synnes, wolde make me lest.

189–92]   Amplifies the reference to the Day of Doom in 'Dirige' and recalls the image in
Matthew 13:40, 'Even as cockle therefore is gathered up, and burnt with fire: so shall it
be at the end of the world'.

193–8]   Paraphrases 'Dirige', Littlehales, *Prymer,* p. 64/4–5, 'who mai make him clene þat
is conseyued of vnclene seed? wheþer not þou þat aloon? þe daies of a man ben schorte;
þe noumbre of his moneþis ben at þee; þou hast set hise termes, þe whiche moun not
be passid'.

195–6]   Amplifies God's single power of judgement to fill out the demands of the stanza.
mene, in the sense of 'company, fellowship, *MED* 'mene' (*n.*); 1.1b, is parallel to God's
having no need of **felowschipe**.

199–200]   Cf. note to lines 87–8. The diction recalls Ezechiel 34:20, 'Therefore thus saith
the Lord God to you: Behold, I myself will judge between the fat cattle and the lean'.
Fein, *Pety Job,* 355–6, also recalls the story of Ezechiel in its expansion of these lines.

201–4]   Paraphrases 'Dirige', Littlehales, *Prymer,* p. 64/6, 'þer-for go þou awey fro him a litil,
þat he haue reste, til þe mede disirid come; & his dai is as þe dai of an hirid man'.

204]   **A[s]:** MS reads 'A', most likely dittography from line 201. As the reading of Job and
'Dirige' help to clarify, the comparative 'as' is required. **h[i]rde:** MS reads 'harde', but as
the 'mercenarii' of Job 14:6 and 'hirid man' of 'Dirige' show, this is in error.

205–10]   Paraphrases the response and versicle to the fifth lesson, 'Dirige', Littlehales,
Prymer, p. 64, '[R] Lord, reherce þou not my synnes whanne þou schalt come to deme

Lord, whenne þou comest to deme so,
Al þe world be fyre, boþe est and west.
God in þy sy3t, þy way Y go
Ry3t ham in þy fayþ me fest.   210

Lord whenne þou demest alle þyng in ri3t,
Wher mercie shal no3t knawen be,
Ry3t leseþ no3t his my3t,
Þou3 mercie be in companye.
Mercy is euere in þy sy3t,   215
For mercie euere þyn ey3en se,
Whereuere þy dome is dy3t,
Ri3t claymeþ mercie for his fee.

Lectio sexta: Quis mihi hoc tribuat

Who 3eueþ to me þat Y me hyde
Tylle þy wraþþe in helle be past,   220
Withouten pyne þy dome to byde,
Tyl body and soule a3en be fast?
With arguments no3t me chyde,
Þou knowest how longe my lyf shal last,
Lord, lat mercie be my gyde,   225
And neuere fro þy face me cast.

þe world bi fier! [V] Mi lord god, dresse þou my weie in þi si3t, [Repeat] Whanne þou schalt come to deme þe world bi fier'.

208] **est and west**: a metrical filler.

210] **ham**, cf. note to Poem 2/23. Here, the Northern form is not needed for rhyme.

211–18] Not in Job or 'Dirige'. It expands on the previous stanza in its declarations that the force of justice is not weakened by the bestowal of mercy, and revisits the statements of earlier poems, e.g. Poem 1/135, 7/101 and 20/198.

212] **knawen**, cf. note to Poem 16/86. Here, however, the Northern form is not needed for rhyme.

218] Cf. note to lines 30 and 186.

219–50] The sixth lesson is drawn from Job 14:13–16.

219–34] Paraphrases 'Dirige', Littlehales, *Prymer*, p. 64/13–14, 'Who mai graunte to me þis, þat þou defende me in helle, & hide me til þi greet veniaunce passe, & þat þou ordeyne me a tyme in which þou haue mynde of me?/gessist þou not þat a deed man schal luye a3en? Alle þe daies in whiche y trauele now, y abide til my chaungyng come'.

221–3] An amplification to meet the demands of the stanza form.

224–6] Revisits lines 87–8 and 197–200.

Þou set me a tyme, couenant is tan;
Haue mynde on me what dome is diȝt,
Trowest þou ouȝt þat Y, dede man,
Shal haue aȝeyn man of myȝt,   230
And ȝelde rekenyng sen Y bygan.
With alle dayes þat Y now fyȝt,
[fol. 126b] Now I abyde þat I fro ran,
Tyl my folwyng come to myn insyȝt.

Lord þou shalt clepe me,   235
And I shal answere to þe werk of þyn hande,
Werk of þy riȝt hand take to þe,
Þou shalt not bynde it in helle bande.
Þou hast noumbred my steppes, how mony þay be,
How monye Y ran, how monye I stande;   240
Bot spare þou Lord to þe synne of me,
Ne wilne noȝt deme my werkes ȝe fande.

Deme me noȝt after my dede,
Lord, I byseche þe!

227]   Turns the question of 'Job' and 'Dirige' into a statement and recalls line 88 and 199.
couenant, cf. note to Poem 9/31. **tan**: a chiefly Northern form of the past participle of
'taken' cf. Poem 9/81.

229]   **Y**. Job and 'Dirige' have 'a' dead man at this point. It is possible that the text is in
error, but the substitution of the first person pronoun may also be a deliberate change
to emphasise the personal plight of the speaker.

231]   The need to give account of one's sins is added and continues a persistent theme of
the sequence. **rekenyng**, cf. note to Poem 1/29/35.

232]   **fyȝt**: closer to 'milito' of the Vulgate Job than 'trauele' in 'Dirige'.

233–4]   Redirects the sense both of Job and 'Dirige' to focus on the speaker's awareness
of the need to acknowledge his sins.

235–42]   Paraphrases 'Dirige', Littlehales, *Prymer*, p. 64/15–16, 'þou schalt clepe me, & y
schal answere þee; þou schalt strecche þi riȝt hond to þe werk of þin hondis./sikirli þou
hast noumbrid my steppis; but lord, spare þou my synnes!'

238]   An addition to 'Dirige' and 'Job'. **bande**: the Northern form is used for rhyme, cf.
note to line 46.

240]   Amplifies the previous line to fulfil the demands of the stanza.

242]   **fande**: 'to make trial of', see *MED* 'fonden' (*v.*); 1a. The Northern form is used for
rhyme, cf. line 266.

243–50]   Paraphrases the response and versicle to the lesson, 'Dirige', Littlehales, *Prymer*,
pp. 64–5, 'Lord, nyle þou deme me aftir my dede! y haue do no þing worþi in my siȝt.
þerfor y biseche þi maieste, þat þou, god, do awey my wickidnesse. [V] More-ouer,

I haue don in þy siȝt, and tok non hede,   245
Þerfore I praye þy mageste,
God, my wikkednesse away þou lede,
Myn vnryȝt away wasche ȝe,
Non more Lord at my nede;
Of alle my synnes clense ȝe me.   250

Lectio septima: Spiritus meus

My gost shalt þou be made [l]ewe,
My dayes shulle yshorted be;
My soule fro þe body mon remewe,
Alone a graue byleueth to me.
I haue non synne, no vices me sewe,   255
Myn eyen in bitternesse dwelle Y se;
Deliuere me Lord, and on me rewe,
And sette me bysydes the.

Whos hande þou wolt aȝeyn me fyȝt,
And þou proue þy stronge hande,   260
My dayes ben passed to withstonde þy myȝt,
I may noȝt bere þy litel wande.

god, wasche þou me fro myn vnriȝtfulnesse, & clense þou me of my trespas! for y
haue synned to þee alone. [Repeet] Þerfor y biseche þi maieste, þat þou, god, do awey
wickidnesse'.

245]   Alters the emphasis from doing no worthy thing in 'Dirige' to the speaker's having
taken no heed of his previous behaviour.

249]   An addition to fulfil the demands of the stanza.

251–82]   The seventh lesson is based on Job 17:1–3, 11–15.

251–74]   Paraphrases 'Dirige', Littlehales, *Prymer*, p. 68/1–3, 'Mi spirit schal be maad
feble; my daies schulen be maad schort; & oneli þe sepulcre is left to me./y haue not
synned; and ȝit myn iȝe dwelliþ in bittirnesse./lord, deliuere þou me, & sette þou me
bisidis þee'.

251]   [l]ewe. MS reads 'newe', which must be an error since it reverses the sense of the
lesson. The Vulgate has 'attenuabitur', which 'Dirige' translates as 'feble'. **lewe** has the
sense of weak, or frail, *MED* 'leu(e)' (*adj.*); 3.

259–66]   Paraphrases 'Dirige', Littlehales, *Prymer*, p. 68/3, 'and þe hond of whom euere
þou wolt, fiȝte aȝenes me!' and 11–13 'Mi daies ben passid. my þouȝtis ben scaterid,
turmentynge myn herte./þei han turned þe niȝt in-to dai; and efte aftir derknessis, y
hope, liȝt./If y susteyne, helle is myn hous; & y haue araied my bed in derknessis'.

262]   An addition to the verse.

My thou3tes ben wasted, turned [fro] ry3t,
Turmentynge my herte inwith [with] ande;
And turnyd day to þe ny3t,   265
After derkenesse I haue bedded my bed I fande.

I sayde to stynke and rotenesse,
'My fader and moder arn 3e!'
And to wormes, Y sayde þysse,
'My systren and brethern both be 3e,   270
And erthe claymeþ me for hysse!
Where þen now my bydynge to me?
My felynge þou art, and my God of blisse,
Drede of deth droueth me.

263] **turned [fro] ri3t**. Amplifies 'Dirige' to secure rhyme. The phrase means 'turned from
their natural course', cf. *MED* 'right' (*n*.) 3d. MS reads 'in', which reverses the sense of
the thoughts being scattered, and I have emended to bring the statement closer in line
to 'Dirige'.

264] **inwith [with] ande**. MS reads 'inwith and ande'. The scribe does not appear to have
understood the sense of the line which, in the Vulgate is 'torquentes cor meum'. *MED*
glosses 'inwith' when it collocates with 'herte' as 'internally in the heart', *MED* 'inwith'
(*adv*.); 2, and cites this example from Digby along with several others. The line must
have meant 'tormenting my heart inside with distress' (**ande**); a sense which is obscured
by the 'and' in the MS reading.

266] The poet omits the first half of verse 13. Line 266 looks to be corrupt; it is suspiciously
long. And while *MED* does record 'bedden bed' as to make one's bed, *MED* 'bedden'
(*v*.); 1b, which corresponds to 'araied' in 'Dirige', it is difficult to accommodate this
repetition with **I fande**. To read it as 'searched out', *MED* 'fonden; (*v*.); 6a, makes some
sense, but equally it might be a form of *MED* 'finden' (*v*.); 17d to furnish (for the form,
cf. note to line 242, and compare Poem 6/51).

267–74] Paraphrases 'Dirige', Littlehales, *Prymer*, p. 68/14–15, 'I seide to rotenesse: "þou
art my fadir"; & to wormes, "3e ben my modir & my sister";/þerfore, where is now myn
abidyng and my pacience? my lord god, þou it ert!'

267] **stynke** added for metrical requirements.

268] **moder** in 'Dirige', addressed to the worms.

270] 'mother' in 'Dirige', having already been used, is replaced by **brethern**.

271] Repeats line 30.

272] **bydynge** has the sense of 'expect', 'hope' for', *MED* 'biden' (*v*.); 7a; cf. 'abidyng' in
'Dirige'.

273] **felynge**, in the sense of 'to suffer', *MED* 'felen' (*v*.); 1.5c; cf. 'pacience' in 'Dirige'. **my
God of blisse** is added and is a paraphrase of 'þou it ert'.

274] Paraphrases the beginning of the response to the seventh lesson in 'Dirige', Littlehales,
Prymer, p. 68, 'Þe drede of deeþ trubliþ me euery dai'.

Eche a day synnyng,   275
And euere newe encres,
Neuere a day blynnyng,
Bote euere vertue waneles;
To repente no bygynnyng,
No3t bote gadre synne ay in pres,   280
In helle is no wynnyng,
Ne non a3enbyynge to pes.

Lectio octava: Pelli mee

My flesches ben wasted, don me refuse,
My bones cleuyn vnto þe skyn;
My lippes arn shronken out of syse,   285
Aboute my teth arn left atwyn.
Haue mercye on myn werk vnwyse,
Haue mercie on me, let mercie wyn,
Namly, my frendes, me no3t despyse,
Lordis hande hath towched me more and myn.   290

Why pursuye 3e me and on me syte,
And arn filled of my flesch and fel?
Who 3eueþ to þat wolde Y wyte?
Wordes in boke be ered wel,

275-82]   Continues the paraphrase of the response, 'Dirige', Littlehales, *Prymer*, p. 68, 'þe while y synne repente me not, for in helle is no redempcion. haue merci of me, god, & saue þou me!'

283-314]   The eighth lesson is based on Job 19:20-7.

283-329]   Paraphrases 'Dirige', Littlehales, *Prymer*, p. 68/20-1, 'Whanne my fleisch was wastid, my boon cleuyde to my skyn, & oneli lippis ben left aboute my teeþ./haue 3e merci on me, haue 3e merci on me; nameli, 3e my frendis! for þe hond of þe lord haþ touchid me'.

283]   **don me refuse**: make me defective, useless, added for metrical requirements.

287]   **werk vnwyse**. The addition fulfils the demands of the metre, but is also in keeping with the sequence's general concern with the consequences of sin and foolish deeds.

290]   **more and myn** added to fill out the stanza.

291-8]   Paraphrases 'Dirige', Littlehales, *Prymer*, pp. 68-9/22-4, 'whi pursue 3e me as god doiþ, & ben fillid wiþ my fleschis?/who mai graunte me þat my wordis be writun? who mai graunte me þat þei be writun in a bok,/wiþ an yrun poyntel, eþer wiþ a plate of leed, eþer wiþ a chisel be grauun in a flynt?'

291]   **on me syte** replaces 'as god doiþ' and intensifies the pursuit.

Or in a plate of led [y-wryte],   295
With an yren poyntel,
Or in a flynt grauen and [y-spyte],
By craft of werk with [a] chysel.

I byleue, [fol. 127a] þat soth Y say,
Myn aȝeynbyere lyuynge isse;   300
I shal rysen of þe erthe my laste day,
Bylapped in my flesch and skyn ywisse;
Byholde with myn eyȝen twey,
Se God my sauyour in blisse;
Non other eyȝen bote þes withouten nay,   305
Þe hope in my bosom yput vp isse.

The soule is in derkenesse from gostly syȝt,
Lord, ȝyue here rest and pees;
Withouten ende, ȝyue here lyȝt,
Euerlastynge lyȝt þat neuere shal sees.   310
Þou þat rered Lazar on hyȝt,
Out of þe graue stynkynge fro wormes pres,
Þy pauylon of mercy be on hem pyȝt,
To reste fro pyne make hem reles.

295, 297] ywryte … yspyte. MS reads 'wryten' and 'spyten', which destroys the rhyme.
While the infinitive **wyte** of line 293 could take a final 'n', this is not the case with the
present singular of **syte** line 291. The 'y' prefixed past participle is used in the sequence,
e.g. **yput**, line 306.

298] craft of werk added for metrical reasons **with [a].** MS reads 'without', which reverses
the sense both of Job and 'Dirige'. I have emended to restore the likelier reading.

299–306] Paraphrases 'Dirige', Littlehales, *Prymer*, p. 69/25–7, 'ffor y wot þat myn aȝenbier
lyueþ; & in þe laste dai y schal rise fro þe erþe,/& eft y schal be cumpassid wiþ my skyn;
& in my flesch y schal se god my saueour./whom y my silf schal se, and myn iȝen schulen
biholde, beynge not anoþir; þis is myn hope, & kept in my bosom'.

300] isse, cf. note to line 26, 30.

304] in blisse added to fulfil the demands of the stanza.

307–14] Paraphrases the responses and versicle to the eighth lesson, 'Dirige', Littlehales,
Prymer, p. 69, 'Lord, graunte þou hem endeles reste! & euelastynge liȝt, liȝtne to hem!
[V] Lord, þat reisidist stynkynge laȝer fro his graue, graunte hem reste! [Repeet] And
euerlastynge liȝt, liȝtne to hem'.

307] Amplifies the liturgy.

312] fro wormes pres added for rhyme and metre.

313–14] Amplify the request for eternal light, peace and rest.

Lectio nona: Quare de uulua eduxisti me qui &etc

Out of þe wombe why hastou me broȝt   315
þat wolde Y hadde be fordon?
Þanne hadde I be as noȝt,
Noon eyȝe hadde sene me after son;
Þan hadde I be as vnwroȝt,
Noȝt born from wombe to berelis doun,   320
Where my short dayes arn in my þoȝt,
Where þay shal noȝt be ended moun.

A! þerfore Lord, graunte me pes
To wepe and wayle, repente my synne;
Þat Y torne noȝt aȝeyn to erthe of derkenes,   325
To stryues of deþ be curyd þerynne.
Lond of wre[c]hes and þesternesse,
þer is shadew of deþ, noon oþer wynne,
Þer woneþ euerlastynge for hem lyued mysse,
Euere gryslyhede þat neuere schal blynne.   330

315–30] The ninth lesson is based on Job 10:18–22.

315–22] Paraphrases 'Dirige', Littlehales, *Prymer*, p. 69/18–20, 'Whi brouȝtest þou me forþ fro þe wombe? wolde god þat y hadde be wastid, þat noon iȝe hadde seie me!/þanne had y be as þouȝ y hadde not be; fro þe wombe ybore to þe graue./wheþer þe fewenesse of my daies schal not be endid in schort tyme?

318] **after son** added for the rhyme and the sense is uncertain, though the meaning of 'cry of pain, sorrow' is attested in *MED* 'soun' (*n.*); 3c, and the crying pains of childbirth would fit the context.

321] **in my þoȝt** added to secure rhyme.

323–30] Paraphrases 'Dirige', Littlehales, *Prymer*, p. 69/20–2, 'lord! suffre þou me, þat y weile a litil while my sorewe,/or y wende hennes, þat y turne not aȝen to þe derk lond, & keuerid wiþ þe derknesse of deeþ;/þe lond of wrecchidnesse and of derknesse, where þe schadewe of deeþ, & noon ordre, but euerlasting grisnesse dwelliþ inne'.

324] **repente my synne** added for rhyme, but also sustains the concern in the sequence as a whole for contrition.

326] Amplifies the previous line – the sense is 'to be rescued from the struggles of death'.

327] **wre[c]hes.** MS reads 'wrethes', which, even for this poet, is hardly likely as a form of 'wroth'. 'Dirige' has 'wrecchidnesse' at this point. It is likely that the scribe has mistaken 't' for 'c'. I have emended to restore closer sense to the liturgy. The sense is not identical: **wre[c]hes** means 'punishments', *MED* 'wrech(e)' (*n.*); 1b.

329] **hem lyued mysse** added for rhyme, but also stresses the consequence of sinful living.

Libera me domine

Delyuere me, Lord, fro endeles deþe
In þat grete dredful day
Where heuenys schullen be styred from erþe breþe,
Whenne þou shalt come to deme for ay;
To heuen or helle þat on he geþ,   335
Þe word be fyre and grete afray;
Þanne woo to the synful his soule sleþ,
And fendys claymen hym for here pray.

That day shal be a day of drede,
Of wraþþe, and myschyf, and wrechidnesse.   340
Þere may no man oþere rede,
Ne make amendis for his mysse;
For worldly witnesse of synful dede,
Gostly payne in bitternesse.
Þere helpeþ neþer counseil ne med,   345
Ech man for hymself to payne or blysse.

What shal Y say for shame and drede,
Or what to do, fool and nys,

331–86]   Paraphrases the responses and versicles to the ninth lesson.
331–38]   Paraphrases 'Dirige', Littlehales, *Prymer*, p. 69, 'Lord, delyuere þou me fro endeles
    deeþ, in þat dredeful dai, whanne heuenes & erþe schulen be moued; whanne þou schalt
    come to deme þe world bi fier!'
333]   **breþe** added for rhyme.
335]   Cf. Poem 11/62. **geþ**: the form is also used in line 177, not in rhyme position. Elsewhere,
    the form (not in rhyme position) is 'goth', Poem 4/5, 5/7 and 10/91.
336]   **grete afray** added for rhyme.
337–8]   Amplifies the liturgy, partly for metrical reasons, but the addition also stresses the
    ultimate fate of the sinful soul, cf. note to line 30.
339–46]   Paraphrases 'Dirige', Littlehales, *Prymer*, p. 69, '[V] Þilke dai is a dai of wraþþe,
    & of chalenge, & of wrecchidnesse; a greet dai and a ful bitter'. The amplification paints
    a chilling picture of the solitary helplessness of the sinner at the Day of Judgement.
345]   **counseil ne med**. The amplification shows that even when paraphrasing the liturgy,
    issues of secular government are not far from the mind of the poet – seen especially in
    the penultimate stanza of this poem.
347–54]   Paraphrases 'Dirige', Littlehales, *Prymer*, p. 69, '[V] Þerfore what schal y þanne,
    most wrechidful, þenke? what schal y seie, or what schal y do, whanne y schal schewe
    forþ no goodnesse to-fore so greet a iuge'.
348]   **fool and nys**: a metrical filler which is also consonant with the admonitions
    throughout the sequence against human folly.

Whanne Y shal schewe forþ no good dede
Byfore so gret iuge and wys?   350
Al folk on me woln take hede,
Wayte after vertue, and fynde vys,
Say God, 'Mercy, þy dome Y drede,
For in þe al mercy lys!'

Now Crist of þy mercie we craue;   355
Haue mercie on vs and leue noȝt,
We byseche þe þat come [fol. 127b] mankynde to saue,
To bye vs þou from heuene vs soȝt,
Oure herytage for vs to haue.
Þat wern lorn, þou hast boȝt,   360
Wyl noȝt dampne in helle kaue
Thy hondewarke þou hast wroȝt.

Þe brennynge soule in helle hete,
Withouten ende wepe thoo;
Allas oure synnes don vs bete,   365
Þay say, 'Wo, wo, wo!'
Here is no remedie to gete:

350]   **wys**. The addition points up the disparity between the wisdom of God and the folly of humankind, cf. previous note.

351-4]   The amplification turns the speaker into an exemplary figure and appropriates the trope in devotional lyrics, where Christ appeals to humankind to behold his suffering, see Woolf, *Religious Lyric*, p. 43. Lines 353-54 anticipate the opening words of the next versicle.

352]   **fynde** can hardly be from 'finden' in any of its senses given that the exemplum urges the forsaking of vice. Either 'to attack', *MED* 'founden' (*v.*); 1.3, or 'to confound', *MED* 'founden' (*v.*); 4, would make sense, but it is possible that the line is corrupt.

355-62]   Paraphrases 'Dirige' Littlehales, *Prymer*, p. 70, '[V] Now, crist, we axen þee, we biseche þee, haue merci on vs! þou þat come to aȝenbie hem þat weren lost, nyle þou dampne hem þat þou hast bouȝt'.

356]   **leue noȝt** added for rhyme.

359-60]   Cf. Poem 10/28.

361]   **helle kaue** added for rhyme.

362]   **hondewarke**: the Northern form is also used in line 407. Elsewhere the form is 'werk(e)'.

363-70]   Paraphrases 'Dirige', Littlehales, *Prymer*, p. 70 '[V] Brennynge soulis wepen wiþ-outen ende; þei wepen wiþ-outen ende, walkynge bi derknessis, and ech of hem seien, wo! wo! wo! hou greet ben þese derknessis'.

367, 369]   Apart from these amplifications, the stanza is a very close rendition of the versicle.

Þay walke in derkenesse to and fro,
Þe stynk and derkenesse is so grete;
Allas! in þysternesse we go.   370

God, that art shapere of al,
Of slyme of erthe þou me wroȝt;
Wiþ þy blod principal,
Wonderly þou haste vs boȝt.
Þouȝ my body now rote smal;   375
My soule to my body shal be broȝt,
Out of my graue reyse me þou schal,
To lyues man and fayle noȝt.

Blod and boon flesche and felle,
Here my prayer in parfitnesse,   380
At domesday comaunde my soule to dwelle
In Abrahamys bosum in thy blisse.
Whenne þou shalt delyuere me fram syȝt of helle,
Þou breke þe ȝates of helle ywisse;
Þou souȝtest helle in peynes felle;   385
Ȝaf lyȝt to hem in grete bryȝtnesse.

Alas! Y may be schamed sore,
At domesday stonde in drede,

371–8] Paraphrases 'Dirige', Littlehales, *Prymer*, p. 70, '[V] God, makere-of-nouȝt of alle creaturis, þat formedist me of þe erþe, and wondurliche wiþ þin owne blood hast bouȝt us, þouȝ my bodi rotte now, þou schalt make it rise out of þe sepulcre in þe dai of doom'.

378] Amplifies what is otherwise a very close rendition of the versicle. **lyues man** 'a living man', see *MED* 'lives' (*adj.*); a: 'alive, living'.

379] An amplification to fulfil the demands of the stanza. The rhyme on **felle** as 'skin' and as a verb **felle** (l. 385) is an example of rime riche.

379–86] Paraphrases 'Dirige', Littlehales, *Prymer*, p. 70, 'heere þou me! here þou me! þat þou comaunde my soule to be put in þe bosum of abraham, þe patriark, Whanne þou schalt come to iuge þe world bi fier! [R] Lord, delyuere þou me fro þe peynes of helle, – þou þat brak þe ȝatis of bras, & visitidist helle, and ȝaf liȝt to hem þat þei myȝten se, þat weren in peynes of derknessis'.

383] **fram**: the only instance of the Northern form. Elsewhere 'fro' or 'from' is used.

387–418] These lines have no direct source in the liturgy. They reiterate the fear of judgement and the need for repentance.

388] Identical to Poem 7/18.

I to come so gret a iuge byfore,
And shewe forþ no good dede,   390
Bote fardel of synnes gadred in store;
Þe fendes redy my rolle to rede,
Þe countretayle to shewe þe score,
þe leste steppe þat euere Y ȝede.

The good aungel on his ryȝt syde   395
Whenne he hem ladde with merye songe,
And whenne he wolde noȝt folwe hy[m], glyde
Out of the waye, he wente wronge;
In vertues he nolde abyde.
Þe good aungel mourned amonge,   400
'With þe soule nel Y chyde –
Y ȝeue þe vp for endeles longe!'

At domesday no man shal be excusyd:
Lord, ne lady, mayde ne knaue,
For wykked counsel scholde be refusyd,   405
And after good counsayle craue.
After warke þat þay vsed,
I shal hem deme or saue:

389–90] These lines reprise lines 349–50.

391] **fardel of synnes**. The same image is used in Poem 7/52. The line is the antithesis of Poem 21/104, and cf. Poem 22/43–4.

392] The same image is used Poem 9/63 and 11/111. See notes thereon.

393] **countretayle** repeats Poem 22/47 almost verbatim. For the image see note to Poem 4/235–6.

394] Repeats line 155 almost verbatim, and cf. line 239 and notes to 235–42.

394–402] These lines revisit the diction and scenario of Poem 22/41–8 and Poem 18/119–20.

397] **hy[m]**. MS reads 'hy'. I have followed Kail's emendation.

400–2] The poet reregisters speech more typical of the soul's rebuke to the body in Poem 20.

405–6] The axioms of following good counsel, and eschewing that which is wicked, reprise the diction of admonitions to those in secular government seen in earlier poems of the sequence. The first lines of the first poem start with this trope, Poem 1/1–2, and cf. Poem 2/78, 3/154, 5/1, 7/21 and 21/15. In Poem 24, attributing such statements to God on the Day of Judgement is a further example of the poet's fusion of heavenly and secular diction and also signals the importance he attached to this issue.

407–8] Repeats a formula used frequently in the previous poems, e.g. Poem 1/155, 2/22, 7/103, 10/195, 13/8, 19/103, 22/60 and 24/243. **warke** cf. note to line 362.

Þe sauyd excusyd, þe dampnyd accusyd,
As thay deseruyd echon haue.   410

Ech touche and mouynge with hys honde,
þe leste twynkelynge wyþ his ey3e,
His wronge worke, sitte or stonde,
Ryde or go, sitte or ly3e,
Þou3 he spede no3t þere he dede fonde,   415
Hys conscience wole hym bewrye;
Benefice, auauncement, hous or londe,
The leste bargayn þat he dede bye.

410] Cf. Poem 1/140 and 19/24.

411-12] The terrifying image of God's ability to judge every movement, even the twinkling
of an eye, recalls the statements in earlier poems that God can see everything, and that
no sin can be hidden from him, Poem 1/95/103/133–4, 12/93 and 14/71.

412] The diction is appropriated from 1 Corinthians 15:52, 'In a moment, in the twinkling
of an eye, at the last trumpet: for the trumpet shall sound, and the dead shall rise again
incorruptible: and we shall be changed'.

414] The asyndeton here and in line 417 emphasises the mighty power of God in judging
humankind's every action, and every worldly honour or achievement.

417] **benefice, auauncement.** The fierce penitential message of the poem is brought to
bear on those in clerical office, or in other positions of power. The sequence returns full
circle to the warnings of Poem 1.

418] Cf. Poem 1/30, 3/151, 7/83, 9/92, 10/196/210 etc. The sequence ends on a terrifying note
with a characteristic collation of financial and spiritual transactions.

Glossary

This is not a complete glossarial index; words are glossed if their sense is different from Modern English and/or if their spelling causes difficulty of recognition. The commonest spelling is treated as the headword; variants that may not be easily referable to the headword are entered in their alphabetical place with a cross reference. Where the sense of a word is obscure, the reader is directed to the discussion in the annotation to the poem. References take the form of the poem number followed by the relevant line after the forward slash. Variant spellings of vowels in a word are indicated by e.g. *i/y* in the headword. Where these variations are too numerous for a clean reading of the headword, a separate entry is given. Round brackets around letters e.g. *as(c)hamed* indicate that the word is found both with and without the *c*. Round brackets at the end of the headword indicate inflectional variation e.g. *assent(e)*. Headwords beginning with þ are included in their alphabetical place in the entry for *t*. Where it corresponds to Modern English *g*, ʒ is incorporated into the entry for *g* and where it corresponds to Modern English *y*, into the entry for *y*. *i* as Modern English *j* follows the entry for *i* as a vowel. Headwords beginning with *y* as a vowel follow *w* for ease of reference. The scribe uses *u* and *v* both as consonant and as vowel. These are sorted into modern usage. Conventional abbreviations are given for grammatical terms:

1.	first person	*pa.*	past
2.	second person	*pl.*	plural
3.	third person	*ppl.*	participle
adj.	adjective	*prep.*	preposition
adv.	adverb	*pres.*	present
comp.	compound	*sg.*	singular
conj.	conjunction	*subj.*	subjunctive
imp.	imperative	*superl.*	superlative
inf.	informal	*v.*	verb
n.	noun		

abas, *adv.* down 24/122
abate, *v. inf.* humiliate 13/123: *imp.sg.* remove 14/12
ableth, *v. 3.sg. pres.* ~ *refl.* makes worthy 1/52
abyde, *v. imp.sg.* endure 8/96
abye, *v. 3.pl. pres.* pay for 15/96; **aby3e** *2.sg. subj.* pay the penalty 10/210; **aby3ed** *pa.ppl.* revenged, paid back, incurred another's anger 5/29 *see note*
abyte, *n.* habit 18/46 etc.
acorde, *v. inf.* agree 20/63 **acordeþ** *3.sg. pres.* conforms 8/78; **acordid** *3.sg. pa.* ~ *wiþ* made a covenant with 20/97
adyte, *v. 3.pl. pres.* condemn 20/99
afflay, *v. inf. hem* ~ put them to flight 4/38
afray, *n.* commotion 24/336
agaste, *v. pa.ppl.* afraid 14/103
agaynes, *prep.* against 10/86 **a3eyn,** 24/230, 24/259; **a3eyns,** 18/56; **a3ens,** 3/33, 24/34, 24/146; **a3enst,** 13/76
a3eynbyere, *n.* redeemer 24/300
a3enbyynge, *ger.* making amends 24/282
agylte, *v. 1.pl. pres.* sin against 10/165
ayþer, *pron.* each 11/78
ake *v. 1.sg. pres.* ache 15/86
aknowe *v. pa.ppl. be* ~ confess 19/19
aldre, *adv.* ~ *mest* most of all 24/10
algate, *adv.* persistently 18/77
aly3ede, *v. pa.ppl.* incarcerated 13/103
als, *adv.* as 13/137, 24/129
alow, *v. inf.* assign 15/43
allowed, *pa.ppl.* belittled 16/26
amende, *v. inf.* reform 1/163, 13/3, 14/57, 17/178, 18/186; correct 11/13; *imp. sg.* 13/93; make amends 17/15; make restitution for 19/28; 9/135
amendement, *n. bringen in* ~ reform 14/79
amerous, *adj.* enamoured 20/125
amonge, *adv.* meanwhile 24/400
amonges, *prep.* among 21/70
amountes, *v. 3.sg. pres.* is worth, totals 4/233

amys, *adv. don* ~ sin 17/13; **omys** 7/74; with displeasure 8/36
ande, *n.* distress 24/264
anguysche, *n.* anguish 20/90
anoy(3)ed, *v. pa.ppl.* oppressed, harrassed 5/26; irked, grieved 24/33
answere, *v. inf.* make a defence 1/153; render account 8/16, 8/72
apayre, *v. inf.* slander 3/18; harm 9/41
apeche, *v. 2.sg. pres.* accuse of, charge 21/135
apele, *v. inf.* call upon 8/71; accuse 10/190; *3.sg. pres.* impeach 14/111
apere, *v. inf.* appear 10/192
apert, *adv.* publicly 12/54; in public 16/87; **opert** openly 18/96
appyl, *n.* apple 10/22 etc.
areue, *v. 3.pl. pres.* rob, plunder 18/62
ari3t, *adv.* correctly 9/63
array, *n.* verdure 2/2, apparel 2/10
arraye, *v. imp.sg.* put in order 3/151
articles, *n. pl.* ~ *of þe fay* articles of the faith 10/100
as(c)hamed, *pa.ppl. adj.* disgraced 3/4, 24/107; ashamed 20/173
ases(e), *v. inf.* cease 12/24; desist 3/21, 21/85; *3.pl. pres.* 3/30; *imp.sg.* put an end to 14/54; **asses** *inf.* cease 21/85; *3.pl. pres.* 3/30
askuse, *v. inf.* excuse, exonerate 4/83
aspi(3)e, *v. inf.* notice 3/45; observe 12/36; *imp.sg.* search out 6/62; *3.pl. pres.* reveal 20/66; **aspi3ed** *3.sg. pa.* observed 13/98; *pa.ppl.* sought for 5/28; discovered 12/66
assay, *n.* examination 2/77
assay(e), *v. inf.* try 4/30; test character 4/158; undertake 15/61; determine 17/57, *v. imp.sg.* examine 8/6
assaile, *v. inf.* overtake 7/12; *2.pl. pres.* attack 13/125; *3.pl. pres.* 3/116; rebuke, berate 2/75, 3/84, assail 4/237, 18/27
assent, *n. fals* ~ connivance 1/4; *on* ~ in full agreement 12/12, 13/2
assent(e), *v. 2.sg. pres.* yield, 22/40; *3.pl. pres.* 18/24

asses *see* **ases(e)**

assi/y/se, *n. euen* ~ fair-mindedness, justice 1/164, 3/13; *right* ~ justice 3/25, 6/29, *hold* ~ hold court hearing 9/65

assoyle, *v. 1.sg. pres.* free, absolve 20/206; *3.sg. pres.* provides solution 18/50

astat(e), *n.* public office 1/1, 4/165; social rank, position 4/151, 4/161, 4/191, 14/73, 20/76, 21/109; social class 4/241; high rank 6/23, 18/14, 18/153, 24/122; sovereignty 8/57; property, estate 21/93, 21/148; condition 15/121, spiritual state 16/107

aswage, *v. inf.* lessen, subside 13/117

ataynt, *v. pa.ppl.* convicted 13/61; **ateynt** 16/9

atent, *n. in good* ~ with proper attitude 11/108, 18/42, 22/34; intent 17/19

atwyn(ne), *adv.* in bits 24/286; *parte* ~ put asunder 18/144

atwoo, *adv. departed* ~ split apart 22/12

au3t, *v. 3.pl. pres.* should 13/151

auncetres, *n. pl.* ancestors 3/135; **aunsetres** 16/118

aungel, *n.* angel 18/119, 22/46, 24/395, 24/400

auntre, *v. 3.sg. pres.subj.* venture 15/140

auayle, *n.* profit 3/91

auaunce, *v. inf.* promote 2/44; *2.pl. pres.* 5/43; *3.sg. pres.* 21/122; *pa.ppl.* 14/85; benefit 7/25

auauncement, *n.* promotion 24/417

aueryce, *n.* avarice 21/14

auyse, *v. inf.* advise 4/88; *imp.sg.*~ *hym* reflect, take thought 1/141; consider 5/45; reflect on 22/68; *3.sg. pres.subj.* instruct 4/81; *3.pl. pres.* pause for thought 1/162

auysed, *v. pa.ppl. ful* ~ wholly acquainted with 20/125

auisement, *n. with good* ~ with due consideration, not rashly, prudently 1/7

auy3e, *v. imp.sg.* strive 18/67

avowe, *v. inf. make* ~ make known, reveal 4/87

awayte, *n. in* ~ in wait 16/83

awe, *n.* fear 4/18, 13/50, 14/90; awe 5/37, 11/83, 16/88; *holde* ~ power to excite fear 9/59

awen, *adj.* own 2/34, 7/120, 12/130 etc.

ay, *adv.* always 3/23, 4/169, 5/22 etc.

bad(e), *v. 3.sg. pa.* order, command 8/24, 8/64, 8/95, 23/125

bay, *sb brought to* ~ overcome, cornered 2/76, 4/238, *stonde to* ~ be cornered 8/54

bay, *v. inf.* to bark at? 9/21 (*see note*)

bayte, *v. 3.sg. pres.subj.* persecutes 16/82

bande, *n.* imprisonment 24/46, fetter 24/238

bank, *n.* slope, bank 2/5

bare, *adj.* naked 6/37, 24/5

bare, *v. 1.sg. pres.* bear 10/40, 11/103

barge, *n.* ship 1/65

batayle, *n.* battle 3/87/88, 4/186, 5/3, 9/143/145, 13/111, 18/25; *n. pl.* 11/53

be, *prep.* by 1/7, 3/82, 24/181, 24/208, 24/336

bed(e), *v. see* **bidden**

bedded, *v. pa.ppl.* make one's bed? 24/266 (*see note*)

bede, *v. imp.sg.* offer love 17/102

begeten, *v. 2.pl. pres.* produce 2/59

be/i/gyled, *v. pa.ppl.* betrayed 16/18, tricked 20/12/186

bekenyng, *ger.* summons 16/124

beme, *n.* trumpet 24/119

bende, *v. inf.* incline 4/34, 17/161/194; *2.pl. pres.* bend (a bow) 10/31; *3.sg. pres.subj.* bow 16/12; *imp.pl.* bow 18/105; *pa.ppl.* **bende**, bound 6/71; bent (a bow), **bent**, *v. 3.sg. pres.* 4/48 *pa.ppl.* 1/69, 1/81, 4/58, 20/94; *ppl.adj.* determined 7/74; set 12/10

berd, *n.* beard 14/53

berelis, *n.* burials, funeral 24/320

bere(n), *v. 3.sg. pres.* bears, carries 3/139/142, 15/60; *3.pl. pres.* 15/50, 15/59, *3.sg. pres.* endures 21/3, ~ *astate* holds rank, position 1/1, 1/97; ~ *here* behaves 20/40, *imp.sg.* ~ *on* accuse 6/44, ~ *good visage* put on a bold front 6/62

berkande, *pres.ppl.* barking 4/238

bersell, *n.* target 11/38

berþe, *n.* birth 18/53

besouȝt, *v. 3.sg. pa.* entreated 17/16

best, *n.* beast, animal 4/14, 7/80, 13/28; *pl.* 10/174, 23/76

bestayle, *n.* livestock 3/67

bysye(n), *v. inf.* ~ *hym* exert himself 16/42; *imp.sg.* ~ *þe* busy yourself 19/85;

besynesse, *n.* devotion, application to 15/28; preoccupation 18/13

bet, *comp.adj.* better 18/66; **betere** 10/63

bete, *v. imp.sg.* beat 6/55; *3.sg. pres.* 17/14; *pres.ppl.* **betyng** 10/136, *ppl.adj.* 20/114

beteres, *n. pl.* beaters 6/9 *see note*

beth, *v. 3.sg. pl.* are 1/26

betok, *v. 3.sg. pa.* prescribed, dictated 4/246

bewepe, *v. imp.sg.* weep tears over 22/67

bewrye, *v. inf.* ~ *hym* inform against him 24/416

bewte, *n.* beauty 17/66

beȝete, *n.* profit 13/12

bidden, *v. inf.* ask, command 4/189; *2.sg. pres.* 20/187; *3.sg. pres.* 4/115, 9/105, 17/193, 20/85 etc.; **bedeþ** 20/78; **byd** 20/23; *3.sg. pa.* **bed(e)** 1/22/70, 3/106, 7/63, 10/114, 17/34, 23/104 *etc*, *imp.pl.* 6/27; *pa.ppl.* 20/34

bidden, *v. 3.pl. pres.* pray 18/149

bille, *n.* formal charge 5/70, petition 12/109

biȝe, *v. inf.* buy 3/56

blasande, *pa.ppl. adj.* shining 2/12

blenche, *v. inf.* escape, dodge 24/148

blende, *v. inf.* make blind, deceive 13/82; *3.sg. pres.* 5/20

blent, *pa.ppl. adj.* blind 17/23, 23/54

blete *v. 3.sg. pres.* bleat like a sheep 9/158

blynne, *v. inf.* desist 15/85, 20/15, 24/330; *pres.ppl.* ceasing 24/277

blo, *n.* lustre 12/126

blome, *v. inf.* flower, flourish 1/62

bode, *v. 1.sg. pa.* lingered 2/1

boden, *ppl.adj.* commanded 24/115; *see also* **bede**

bo(o)n, *n.* bone 11/54, 15/49, 23/114, 24/379

bond, *v. 3.sg. pa.* bound 11/31

bond(e), *adj.* bound, in the state of a serf 4/197; under domination 21/32

bonde, *n.* *breke þe* ~ exceed propriety, limits 18/87

bonet *n.* auxiliary sail 7/28

boote, *adv.* outside 2/1

bord, *n.* table 2/25; *Goddis* ~ the Eucharist 9/73; *shippes* ~ on board ship 13/154

bore, *n.* opening, aperture 1/95

bore, *v. ppl.adj.* born 22/41

born(e), *v. pa. perf.* borne 8/13, carried 4/179 *see also* **beren**

borwe, *v. inf.* borrow 10/121, *3.sg. pres.* 14/75, *ppl.adj.* 1/138, 9/129

borwere, *n.* borrower 21/76

bost, *n. abate* ~ humble 13/123

boste, *v. inf.* boast 16/26; *3.sg. pres.* 21/43

bot(e), *prep.* except 10/148, 13/40, 24/18 etc.

bote, *n.* remedy 24/147

botemeles, *adj.* bottomless 15/82

boten, *v. 2.pl. pa.* bit 10/32

botme, *n.* bottom 4/99

boun, *adj.* ready, willing 12/6

boun, *v. pa.ppl.* obedient 24/47

bounden, *v. pa.ppl.* subject to 12/134

boundes, *n. passe þe* ~ exceed authority 4/212, 4/222 *see also* **bonde**

bounte, *n.* valour 12/18

boures, *n. heuene* ~ mansions of heaven 18/176

boyst, *n.* pyx 23/65

braken *v. 2.pl. pa.* fail to obey 10/31

breche, *n. spouse* ~ adultery 10/103

bred, *n.* food for the soul 7/61

brede, *n.* breadth 1/102, 13/158

brede, *n.* bread 9/182, 10/50

breme, *adv.* fiercely 3/62

bre/y/nne, *v. inf.* burn 12/115, 18/176, 22/63; *1.sg. pres.* 10/143; *3.sg. pres.* 3/62, 10/141; *3.pl. pres.* 7/37

brennyng(e), *pa.ppl.* burning 18/7, 22/26, 24/363

brent, *pa.ppl.* burnt 11/111, 24/110, 24/192; *ppl.adj.* 2/70

brest, *v. inf.* burst, fail 10/36, 12/133

breþe, *n.* breath 16/123

breþe, *n.* breadth 24/333

breþere, *n.* brothers' 21/34

breþered, *n.* brotherhood 10/167

brod, *n.* o ~ *to sprede*, spread out, extend 13/110

brondes, *n.* firebrands 7/37, staves 15/38

brotel, *adj.* fragile 24/92

broþelyng, *n.* scoundrel, rascal 10/191

browded, *pa.ppl. adj.* ornamented, embroidered 18/155

brydell, *n.* bridle 1/85

brynne(þ) *see* **brenne**

burgh, *n.* borough 3/34, 15/54

burnysche, *v. imp.pl.* polish 9/2

buske, *n.* wood 2/1

buxom, *adj.* eager 21/18

buxomness, *n.* humility 16/121

buyrnes, *n. pl.* men 2/5

by – shap *n. see note to* 9/155

byde, *v. inf.* stay 4/99, 20/136, 21/27; *2.pl. pres.* 18/129; remain *inf.* 9/85; dwell *inf.* 21/116; await 24/221

byddyng, *ger.* comandment 10/31, 21/82

bydynge, *ger.* expectation, hope 24/272

bye, *v. inf.* buy 7/20, 8/45, 24/358, 24/418; *3.pl. pres.* 1/121

byhe/i/nd(e), *adv.* behind 6/66, 10/209, 17/49/171, 19/16

byhyue, *n.* good, profit 24/20

byknowe, *pa.ppl. adj.* known 6/57

bylapped, *pa.ppl. adj.* clothed 24/302

bylde, *v. inf.* to lodge in 20/35; build 21/19, *pa.ppl.* built 21/63

byleue, *n.* religious faith 7/75, 23/46, 23/50, 23/56, 23/96; doctrine 23/71, 23/114 etc.

byleue, *v. 1.sg. pres.* believe 24/299; *3.pl. pres.* 1/125

byleueth, *v. 3.sg. pres.* is entrusted to 24/254,

byloued, *pa.ppl.* loved 4/148

byseche, *v. 1.sg. pres.* implore 24/244; beseech *1.pl. pres.* 24/357

bysyde, *adv.* moreover 9/84, beside 18/91; **bysydes** 24/258

byþenk, *v. imp.sg.* think hard about 22/42

byȝe, *v. inf.* buy 7/118, 10/98, 13/67

byȝete, *n.* spoils, booty 9/150

caas, *n.* snare, trap 20/194

cacche *v. 3.sg. pres.subj.* capture 20/148

cake, *n.* Eucharistic loaf 23/68

calde, *v. 3.sg. pa.* called 15/106; **calt** *pa.ppl.* 21/150

carayne, *n.* carcass 20/88

care, *n.* grief 6/36

cas, *n.* matter 9/42, situation 18/187

cast(e), *v. inf.* plot 13/66, plan 14/98; *3.sg. pres.* casts 20/79; ~ *a cheson* make an accusation against 13/76; *3.pl. pres.*, throw 12/38; *2.sg. pa.* cast 24/85; *imp.sg.* contrive 9/137, *~awey*, cast away 9/175; consider 12/82; expel 24/86; banish 24/226; *imp.pl.* use, apply 12/47; *pa.ppl.* thrown 16/4, got rid of 20/176; accused 20/194; **casten** cast out 10/134

catell, *n.* property 13/54

cause, *n.* cause 3/75/161/164, 18/156/160/162; reason 18/19, 19/14; legal charge 24/38,

certayn, *n. in* ~ inevitably 17/17

certeyn, *adj.* trustworthy 18/111

chace, *v. 2.sg. pres.* expel 18/189 *see also* **chas**

chalenge, *v. 2.sg. pres.subj.* find fault with 24/41

chambre, *n.* chamber 2/64, private council chamber 4/203, *pl.* rooms of state 20/35

champio(u)n, *n.* victor 18/25, military representative 12/78, *pl.* supporters 3/144

charge, *n.* responsibility 1/59, 8/17, 9/171, important matter 5/45, obligation, official duty 5/46

chargeth, *v. 3.sg. pres.* orders 3/3

charite(e), *n.* charity, benevolence 1/23, 9/122 etc., loving kindness 7/39, 9/140, holy love 18/70, 21/116

chas, *v. inf.* hunt 10/174, pursue 17/150; *3.pl. pres.* 19/61

chastyng, *ger.* punishment 10/139

chaunce, *n.* event, occurrence 1/73; lot, fate 3/167; *stonde to my ~* ride my luck 2/47

chef, *adj.* most important 15/15, head 20/36

chekkys, *n. pl.* checks 16/108

chep, *n. good ~ (adv)* at a low cost 9/53

chepen, *v. 3.pl. pres.* engage in bargaining 16/23

chere, *n.* spirit, demeanour 13/5

chery, *n.* cherry 3/145

ches(e), *v. inf.* choose 2/13, 13/153; *imp.sg.* 1/111; *3.sg. pa.* **ches** 3/54

chese, *n.* cheese 24/83

cheson, *n. cast a ~* make an accusation against 13/76

chete, *n.* reversion of property 9/118

cheualrous, *adj.* valiant 3/71

cheuenteyn, *n.* captain 4/193

chiste, *n.* chest 21/157

clepe, *v. inf.* call 24/235, **cleped** *pa.ppl. adj.* 21/83, 21/144

clete, *n.* small portion, bit, *at o ~* worthless 9/110

cleue, *v. inf.* split 20/117; *ppl.adj.* 17/197; **clyue**, *3.pres.subj.* break 23/89

cleuyn, *v. 3.pl. pres.* stick 24/284

cloos, *n. out of ~* freely 13/59

cochour, *n.* stay-at-home 2/23

coke, *v. inf.* fight 12/29

cokes, *n.* cook's 6/19

cokewold, *n.* cuckold 22/27

colege, *n.* endowed religious or scholarly body 8/58

coler, *n.* chain as badge of office 15/22

comon, *adj. ~ lawe* common law 14/67, 18/63

comone, *n.* commonweal 1/12

como(u)ns, *n.* third estate, 3/27, 3/29, 3/68, 3/117, 14/19, 12/137, 12/141, 13/33, 13/37, 14/78; parliamentary commons 3/99, 3/101, 3/103, 12/11, 12/143

comoun, *adj.* of the whole community, public, in common, 3/98, 4/17, 4/19, 4/155, 4/207

comounly, *adv.* regularly 4/127

compas, *n., in ~* altogether 24/66

consayl, *n.* counsel 24/43; **conseil** 1/60 *see also* **counsa/i/yl(e)**

conseile, *v. imp.* counsel 12/136 *see also* **counseil(l)e**

corayest, *v. 2.sg. pres. ~ fauel* curry favour 4/190

cors, *n.* body 16/120

cost, *n.* natural property 23/85

costage, *n.* cost, danger 14/103

couent, *n.* convent 18/44

couetys(e), *n.* covetousness 9/137, 14/54, 14/60, 17/38

counsa/i/yl(e), *n.* counsel 2/73, 3/82/89, 4/239, 5/1, 24/406; **counseil** 1/2, 2/78, 3/80 etc.

counseil(l)e, *v. inf.* counsel 7/43; *3.sg. pres.* 21/6; *3.sg. pa.* 13/135, 16/5; *imp. sg.* 7/36

countrefete, *v. inf.* simulate 9/38; emulate 18/128; *2.sg. pres.* 18/69; *3.sg. pres.* follows pattern of behaviour 20/152

countretayle, *n.* the other half of a tally stick 4/236, 22/47, 24/393

cracche, *n.* manger 20/146

craft, *n.* group of craftsmen, guild 3/33, 16/60; skill 12/75, 12/76; profession 14/43, art 24/298

craftes, *n.*, craftsmen 15/58

crafty, *adj. ~ folk* skilled craftsmen 14/35

crakowed, *adj.* pointed 20/138 (*see note*)

croddest, *v. 2.sg. pres.* to make into curds 24/83

croos, *n.* cross 20/116; **croys** 10/24, 22/52

crowele, *adj.* cruel 5/49

curatours, *n.*, priests, guardians of souls 8/71

cure, *n.* responsibility for spiritual welfare 8/17, 9/170, 10/132

curs, *n.* excommunication 21/107; *the ~* the formula said in church four times a year setting forth the various offenders which entailed automatic excommunication of the offender 9/49

cursen, *v. 3.pl. pres.* condemn 21/132, *3.sg. pres.* 21/96

curyd, *pa.ppl.* restored 24/326

custom, *n.* customary law 13/82, nature 16/117, *in ~* habitually 18/93

dagged, *pa.ppl.* decorated with slashes 20/137

dale, *n.* valley 12/14

dar, *v. inf.* dare 3/84; *2.sg. pres.* 10/83, 10/99; *3.sg. pres.* 4/9, 16/66; *3.pl. pres.* 4/144; *3.sg. pres.* challenge 2/75

dase, *v. 1.pl. pres.* be befuddled 15/90, 15/110

date, *n. in endeles ~* eternally 17/112

daunger(e), *n.* power 4/39; control 7/116; resistance 17/153

dawenynge, *n.* dawn 24/13

dawnted, *pa.ppl.* flattered 14/85

daynte, *n.* deliciousness 18/104

debat(e), *n.* conflict 5/25, 8/59; *maken ~* quarrel, dispute 4/149, 4/243, 6/21, 10/67, 20/80, 24/128

debate, *v. inf.* quarrel, argue, 17/106; *1.pl. pres.* 11/39, 12/33; *3.sg. pres* 15/125, 21/91

ded, *adj.* dead 7/58, 23/98, 23/115

ded(e), *n.* death 10/118, 13/20, 23/46 etc.

dede, *n.* deed, action 1/155, 2/20/22, 4/20, 6/58, 7/103 etc.; service 2/38; behaviour 7/119; *don his ~* follow his action 4/172; *don þy ~* perform your office 8/28; *do not þe ~* act 8/84

ded(e)ly, *adj.* mortal 3/149, 7/7, 15/150, 24/138 etc.

deef, *adj.* deaf 4/215

de(e)l, *n. euery ~* entirely 9/171; *eche a ~* everything 15/116

de(e)s, *n.* table 21/83; high table, 3/6

defame, *n.* slander 3/20

defame, *v. 3.sg. pres.* slander 12/73

defoule, *v. 2.pl. pres.* pollute 10/127; *2.sg. pa.* defaced 20/181; *pa.ppl.* destroyed 24/181

defowle, *v. 3.pl. pres.* violate 21/125

degre, *n.* rank 3/44, 4/151/161/191, 4/242, 14/1/3; ecclesiastical rank 8/58, 15/26, 18/15; position of hierarchy 1/20; condition 16/89; reward, position 9/131, 10/182, 13/39; *in foly ~* in a foolish way 3/39; *in no ~* in no way, not at all 14/18; *in that ~* in that way 16/69, 17/41; *in alle ~* in every way 18/2, 18/178; *in here ~* according to their nature 24/54

delices, *n. pl.* delights 18/143

dell, *n. neuere a ~* not a bit, not at all 13/97

delys, *n.* pleasure 1/44, 1/58, 8/79, 10/153, 20/171; bliss 11/63; fineries, luxuries 13/91

dene, *n.* din, noise 20/164

dent, *n.* blow, stroke, 13/120, 13/128

departe, *v. inf.* separate 5/14, *3.pl. pres.* 21/111; *inf.* leave 20/38; *3.pl. pres.* distribute, apportion 19/104

dere, *adj.* precious 17/190

dere, *adv.* dearly 8/45, 10/112; expensively 9/53; preciously 10/90; at a high price 15/96; *ful ~* at great cost 1/121

derne, *adj.* innermost 9/38; secret 12/94

derrere, *comp.adj.* at greater cost, 11/100, 19/12

des, *v. 3.sg. pres.* dies 3/134

despence, *n.* expenditure 18/121

despence, *v. inf.* spend time 18/123

despyse, *v. inf.* despise 24/289; *pa.ppl.* 15/147; **despuse**, *inf.* 5/35; **dyspyce**, *imp.sg.* 24/24

despi/y/te, *n.* hostility, contempt 10/115, 11/107; injury, harm 20/103

despit, *v. inf.* dispute 16/95

dest, *v. 2.sg. pres.* do 7/89

deuere, *n.* duty 16/114

deuyne, *adj.* divine 10/130

deuysed, *ppl.adj.* designed, constructed 15/145

deye, *v. 3.sg. pres.subj.* die 16/105

dirige, *n.* Office of the Dead 24/title

discomfites, *v. 3.sg. pres.* routs, vanquishes 18/26

di/y/3t, *v. 3.pl. pres.* prepare 13/138; *ppl. adj.* placed 3/11; decreed 7/103, 18/71, 19/103 etc.; assigned 19/99; dedicated 23/16; prepared 24/228

doo(e)l, *n.* pain, misery 16/105, *make ~* lament, wail in misery 15/114

doluen, *v. pa.ppl.* buried 4/102

domesman, *n.* judge, magistrate 3/26

donghille, *n.* pile of manure 24/7

dotard, *n.* fool 16/105

dou/w/ble, *adj.* deceitfully ambiguous 1/2, 1/71; twice as much 10/126, 16/78

drane, *n.* drone 2/60

dresse, *v. inf.* provide 2/55

dreuen, *v. 3.pl. pres.* drive 11/12

droneth, *v. 3.sg. pres.* torments 24/274

dure, *v. inf.* last 9/71

durked, *ppl.adj.* obscured 23/53

dyuerce, *adj.* distinct, separate, divergent, individual 23/51

echon, *pron.* each 5/30

eft(e), *adv.* often 4/88, 13/13, 13/83

eke, *v. inf.* increase 1/145, give 20/51

elne, *n.* measure of an ell 9/52

embrowdid, *pa.ppl.* embroidered 2/12

endite, *v. inf.* indict, accuse 24/150

entendement, *n.* meaning 1/2, 1/71

er(e), *conj.* before 1/55, 1/109, 1/110, 1/159 etc.

ere, *v. 3.sg. pres.* show mercy 3/103

ered, *pa.ppl.* inscribed 24/294

eren, *n. pl.* ears 15/109; **eryn,** 15/13

ese, *n.* peace of mind 4/209; pleasure 6/16; profit 8/33; comfort 10/154; **eys,** well-being 10/18

estre(n), *n.* Easter 23/28, 23/98, 23/100

euel, *n.* evil 2/66

euele, *adv.* badly 2/29

euelfare, *n.* misery, plight 20/30

euene, *adj.* equitable, fair, just 1/61, 1/164, 3/12, 3/13, 12/111, 13/71, 14/37

euene, *adv.* honestly 17/44; virtuously 17/94; *be ~* at peace 8/103

euenest, *superl. adv.* most honestly, fairly 17/124

eu/v/enhede, *n.* justice 1/6/14

euerydele, *pron.* everything 17/5

executours, *n.* executors of a will 4/232

falle, *inf. ~ to shame* result in slander, dishonour 4/202; *3.sg. pres.subj.* come about 1/73

fals(h)ed, *n.* corruption, treachery, fraudulence 1/62, 3/22, 4/93, 5/33, 12/67, 13/85, 16/9

fame, *n.* reputation 2/18, 6/61, 14/2, 20/100

famed, *pa.ppl. mis~* dishonoured, slandered 3/2

fande, *v. 1.sg. pres.* search out? 24/266 (*see note*); *2.sg. pres.* make trial of 24/242

fantasie, *n.* fiction, composition 20/5

fardel, *n.* bundle, pack 7/52, 24/391

fare, *v. inf.* depart, go 24/7; *1.sg. pres.* fare 20/129; *3.pl. pres.* 2/29; *2.sg. pres.* deal 10/121; *3.sg. pres.* goes 4/2; behaves, 10/9; *1.pl. pres. ~ wel* are well, comfortable 15/120

faring, *ger. wel ~* honourable, upright 2/51

fas, *n.* face 24/131

fauour, *n.* partiality 1/15, 13/9, 13/22, 15/46

fauoured, *pa.ppl.* made subject to partiality 1/156

fau3t, *v. 2.sg. pa.* fought 13/12

fawte, *n.* deficiency 3/27; lack 3/92, 13/28, 12/102

fawtes, *n*. errors of faith/conduct; 4/137; mistakes 14/70

fay, *n*. faith, belief 4/126, 8/86, 10/100, 23/20

fay, *adj*. dead 4/198

fayn, *adv*. willingly 21/54

fayn(e), *adj*. willing under duress 6/47; malleable, eager to please 4/221; glad 11/65

faytour, *n*. deceiver, imposter 2/63

fed, *n*. death, sentence of death 13/18

fe(e), *n*. fee 9/66; reward 10/162, 14/23, 19/24, 24/218; remuneration 15/52, 17/17

fele, *n*. many 8/52

fele, *adj*. great 21/2

fel(e), *adj*. stern 10/155; fierce 11/53; cruel 24/385

fel(le), *n*. skin 19/95, 22/50, 24/292, 24/379

felþe, *n*. filth 17/68

felyng, *ger*. perception though the senses 15/6, 23/113/115/117/119

felynge, *ger*. hiding place, refuge 24/273

fen, *n*. dirt, muck 24/74

fend(e), *n*. devil 4/39, 17/196, 19/61, 20/70, 21/88; enemy 2/75

fende, *adj*. devilish 7/54

fende, *v. inf*. defend against 15/35, 17/175

fende/i/y/s, *n. pl*. devils 1/55, 2/33, 1/87 etc.

fer, *adj*. distant 2/23

fer, *adv*. far 9/52, 17/18, 20/184

ferd, *n*. fear 13/7

ferd, *adj*. afraid 9/69

fere, *n*. companion, associate 10/108, 11/73, 20/182

ferly, *n*. wonderful thing 11/17

fern3er(e), *adv*. in previous times 11/65, 13/31

ferre, *n*. (deceptive) appearance 2/65

ferre, *n*. ~ with an army 15/138

f(i)erþe, *adj*. fourth 11/33, 16/116

fest(e), *n*. feast, 11/1, 21/56, 23/110, 24/16

fest, *v. imp*. fasten, lodge 24/210

fet, *v. 3.sg. pa*. fetched 11/19

feynt, *adj*. feeble 7/3

feynt, *adj*. deceitful 16/14

figure, *n*. prefiguration 23/122

filt, *ppl.adj*. filled 7/6

fit, *n*. eventuality 12/45

fleme, *v. imp*. drive out 18/116

flemed, *pa.ppl*. banished, exiled 14/86

fles, *v. 3.sg. pres*. flees 3/166

flet, *pa.ppl*. become separated, scattered 12/42; fled 20/25

fleye, *v. inf*. fly 20/208

fli/y3e, *v. inf*. fly 14/47, 20/82

flo, *n*. arrow 14/102

flon, *n. pl*. arrows 11/38

florische, *v. 1.sg. pres*. embellish 2/27

flynt, *n*. hard stone 24/297

flyt, *v. inf*. drive away 16/54; *imp.pl*. expel, banish 17/8

flyte, *v. inf*. argue, 7/93; rebuke 20/97

fode, *n*. food, 2/54, 23/58

fold, *n*. earth 16/113

fold(e), *n*. sheepfold 9/158

fold(e), *many a* ~ often, repeatedly 9/21

folde, *v. inf*. collapse, decay 17/125

foles, *n*. fools 2/35; 16/6

folwyng, *ger*. what comes afterward; consequence 24/234

foly, *n*. foolishness, stupidity 8/44, 10/21, 11/31 etc.; sinfulness 1/58, 16/104

folyes, *n*. foolish acts 16/15, 16/28

folyhede, *n*. foolishness 16/1

fomen, *n*. enemies 13/109

fo(o)n, *n*. enemies 3/140, 11/22, 15/35, 16/14, 17/175, 19/31, 21/86

fonde, *v. imp.sg*. have sexual intercourse with 6/51

forbed(e), *v. 1.sg. pres*. forbid 8/26; *3.sg. pres.subj*. 13/21; *3.sg. pa*. 14/41

forber(e), *v. inf*. be lenient towards 24/206; *imp.sg*. give up 19/52; *inf*. refrain from 19/63

forbode, *pa.ppl*. forbidden 16/65

forbore, *pa.ppl*. given up 18/139

forborn, *pa.ppl*. restrained, arrested 12/57

forborn, *pa.ppl*. born 24/173

forcast, *ppl.adj*. ~ *ded* sentence of death 13/20

fordon, *pa.ppl.* condemned to destruction 24/316

forgeþ, *v. 3.sg. pres.* plot 4/93, 14/97

forgo, *v. inf.* forsake 20/119

forlore, *pa.ppl.* given away 12/119, 17/88

fo(u)rme, *n.* appearance 9/182; 10/120

fors, *n.* make no ~ of, reject utterly 6/52

forswere, *v. 3.pl. pres.* repudiate 10/115

forsworn, *pa.ppl.* guilty of perjury 12/59

forþenke, *v. 3.pl. pres.* think about, dwell on 18/45

forþ/th/y, *conj.* therefore 9/16/144 etc. 13/47, 16/62

forȝete, *v. inf.* omit something 9/94; *imp.* forget 9/188; *pa.ppl.* lost 9/30; heedless 8/101

fostre, *v. inf.* feed 10/201

fraternite, *n.* common brotherhood 20/60

fraunchise, *n.* freedom 16/62

freek, *n.* man 16/99

frele, *adj.* weak, frail, easily corrupted 7/3, 11/50, 14/105, 15/126

frere, *n.* friar 10/5

fro, *prep.* from 1/42/44/58 etc.

ful, *adj. and intensifier* absolutely 1/38; absolute 1/106; full, replete 13/149, etc.

ful, *adv. intensifier* completely, fully, very 1/121, 4/142 etc.

fyere, *n.* fire 3/118

fylde, *pa.ppl.* defiled 21/57

fyled, *pa.ppl.* tainted, corrupted 21/105

fynde, *v. 3.pl. pres.* attack, confound? (*see note*) 24/352

fyne, *v. inf.* pay (a fine) 10/38

gadre, *v. inf.* accumulate 4/4; *3.sg. pres.* amass 21/104; store up 24/280

gadre/i/d, *pa.ppl.* assembled 13/1; laid up 24/391; *see also* **gedre**

gadryng, *ger.* assembly 23/5; acquiring of riches 21/14

ȝaf *see* **ȝeue**

game, *n.* sport 6/63; 10/113, *pl.* 16/40

gan, *v. 3.sg. pa.* did 10/98; *3.pl. pa.* 16/3; began 15/97

garner, *n,* foodstore 15/84

gat, *v. 2.sg. pa.* got, acquired 21/149

ȝate, *n.* gate 10/69, 11/36, 14/15, 17/110, 18/12; *pl.* 17/87, 21/45, 24/384

gates, *n.pl.* mode of behaviour, way 11/30

gawdy, *adj.* yellowish green 2/11

gay, *adj.* sumptuously, showy 2/12; well dressed 2/79

gay, *adv.* freely, openly 4/78; go ~ behave in a contemptuously pleasure-loving way 8/46

gayte, *n.* behaviour, conduct 16/81

geaunt, *n.* giant 10/146

gedre, *v. 3.pl. pres.* heap up; 3/38; *imp.sg.* grasp, seize 6/4; *see also* **gadre**

general(l), *adj.* common 18/148; all-inclusive 24/190

generale, *adv.* generically, not specifically 3/51; universally 4/41

gentyl(l), *adj.* noble 18/57/153; noble; honourable 18/184

gentyles, *n.pl.* noblemen 18/82

ges, *v. 3.sg. pres.* goes 3/14; *see also* **geth/þ/**

geson, *pa.ppl.* seen 13/77

gesse, *v. 1.sg. pres.* reckon 2/53

get(e), *v. inf.* 3/152; obtain, acquire, *1.sg. pres.* 2/50, *2.sg. pres.* 2/18 etc.; win, conquer 13/139

geth/þ/, *v. 3.sg. pres.* goes 24/177, 24/335; *see also* **ges**

getyng, *ger.* income 1/31, 8/7; profit 10/135

ȝeue, *v. inf.* give 10/186/207, 13/21; *3.sg. pres.subj.* 12/149; *imp.sg.* 4/25/26, 6/3; **ȝyue** 1/5, 14/49; *2.pl. pres.subj.* 7/29; *imp.sg.* 24/308/309; *1.sg. pres.* 10/67/120; *3.sg. pres.* **geueþ** 12/72; **ȝeueth/þ** 1/149, 4/164, 9/66, 12/89; *1.sg. pa.* **ȝaf** gave 10/118, 19/32; *3.sg. pa.* 10/22, 11/57, 13/23, 24/91; *pa.ppl.* **ȝeuen** 10/42; **ȝouen** 23/20/41

ȝifte, *n.* gift 4/182, 7/71; *pl.* 6/3

gilt(e)les, *adj.* innocent 1/166, 9/126; **gylteles** 13/70; **gulteles** 21/61

glade, *v.; inf.* cheer 23/127; *3.sg. pres.* 21/72; *2.pl. pres.* rejoice 9/9

glede, *n.*, live coal 1/110, 2/70, 13/14
glene, *v. inf.* acquire 2/68
glose, *n.* gloss 20/2
gloser(e), *n.* flatterer 2/47/57, 4/83 etc.;
7/22, 13/134, 16/51, 16/98; *pl.* 4/73 etc.
glosyng, *ger.* deceitful talk 2/42/49
glotry, *n.* surfeit, overeating 18/104
glyde, *v. 3.sg. pres.* slip 24/397
gnewe, *v. 3.sg. pa.* bit 10/23
gost(e)ly, *adv.* spiritually 5/23, 7/31 etc.
gostly, *adj.* spiritual 1/45, 4/107 etc.
goten, *pa.ppl.* acquired 1/117
gow, *n.* something useless 4/84 (*see note*)
grame, *n.* harm, injury 10/119, 16/78,
20/102
gras, *n.* grace 10/96, 17/148
gre, *n.* rank, position 7/15
gre, *n.* protection 10/72; favour, good
will 19/82
greceles, *adj.* lean 10/150
gref, *n.* distress, trouble 10/75
gren, *adj.* green 2/11
gres, *n.* fat 3/62
gres, *n.* grass 5/62
grese, *v. inf.* graze 14/46
gret(e), *adj.* great 2/86, 3/30 etc.
gret(e), *adv.* greatly 3/61, 9/86 etc.
gretter(e), *comp.adj.* greater 14/2/4, 9/27,
23/1
grettest, *superl.adj.* greatest 23/86
greua(u)nce, *n.* injury, damage 1/12, 1/91,
21/76; disease, harm, 3/164; upset 9/107
greue, *v. inf.* destroy, injure 1/74,
4/30; trouble 2/41, 4/35; offend, be
disobedient towards 17/162; *3.sg. pres.*
afflicts 3/101; suffers 4/76; displeases
8/46; *1.sg. pa.* harmed 10/43; *3.pl. pa.*
aggrieved 10/39; **gryue** *3.sg. subj.*
grieve 24/18
greues, *n. doth ~* afflicts 1/27
grounded, *pa.ppl* rooted 8/61
grucche, *v. 3.sg. pres.subj.* is grudgingly
reluctant 6/53
grynde, *v. inf.* grind grain 15/108
grype, *v. 2.pl. pres.* clasp 18/83
gryslyhede, *n.* misery 24/330

gryue *see* **greue**
gulteles *see* **gilt(e)les**
gyde, *n.* guide 13/78, 21/120, 24/225
gyed, *pa.ppl.* ruled 12/71
gyle, *n.* deceit, treachery 3/122, 4/93; *pl.*
14/97
gyle(þ), *v. 3.pl. pres.* cheat 8/39; deceive
10/152
gylt, *n.* sin 10/25, 13/67, 16/97; trespass
17/14
gylte/i/s, *n. pl.* sins 10/39/40, 11/103
gynne, *v. inf.* begin 7/2
gynnyng, *ger.* creation, foundation 9/110
gys(e), *n.* manners 6/31; fashion 13/91;
proper form 9/67, 10/128
gy3e, *v. inf.* guide 7/110

habergeoun, *n.* mailcoat 12/30
habyte, *n.* monastic rule 18/114
haldest, *v. 2.sg. pres.* hold 10/86, *3.sg.*
pres. 9/65
halt, *adj.* lame, deficient, 21/146
halwe, *v. inf.* consecrate 23/37
halwed, *pa.ppl.* reverenced, honoured
4/121
ham(e), home, 2/23, 24/210
han *v. see* **haue**
handles, *adj.* without hands 4/214
hap, *n. haue þurgh ~* happen to have
9/153
hardy, *adj.* valiant 2/76; brave 2/79; firm,
upright 3/76; bold 4/79
hardynes, *n.* bravery 13/95
harlotrye, *n.* crude immorality 10/109
hast, *v. see* **haue**
hastou, *v. 2.sg. pa + pron.* you have 24/6,
24/21, 24/154, 24/315
hastyng, *pres. pl.* hastening 10/138
hat, *v. 3.sg. pres.* is called 9/155/155, 16/116;
hatteþ 17/185
hat(e), *n.* hatred 1/3, 1/99, 1/165, 4/148,
5/27, 24/126 etc.
hate(e), *v. inf.* hate 10/68, 11/37 etc.; *2.sg.*
pres. 6/20, 10/81, 13/110; *3.sg. pres.*
15/123; *3.pl. pres.* 21/131
hatere, *n.* hater 18/20

hattere, *comp.adj.* hotter 7/37

haue, *v.inf.* have 1/29, 1/35 etc. **hauen**
1/132; *2.sg. pres.* **hast** 1/10, 2/17 etc.;
3.sg. pres. **hath/þ/** 1/25, 1/33 etc.; *3.pl.*
pres. **han** 1/123; *1 pl. pa.* 9/17; *2.pl. pa.*
13/105; *3.pl. pa.* 11/111 etc.

haunted, *pa.ppl.* scorned 4/127, 14/84

hauntest, *v. 2.sg. pres.* engage in, practise
10/80; *pa.ppl.* 9/163,

hay, *interj.* ~*3ol hayl* singing the refrain
of a carol 4/234

he, *pron.* *3.masc.sg.* he 1/27, 1/84 etc.;
3.masc.pl. they 17/54; *3.fem.sg.* **here**
her 6/55, 20/27/37/40; *3.sg. neut.* **hit**
it 1/27, 1/98, 2/18 etc. *3.pl.* **hem** them
1/70/77/91 etc.

hede, *v. 2.sg. pres.* protect, save 23/112

hedlyng, *adv.* headlong 8/52

hegge, *n.* hedge 3/127

heire, *n.* heir 3/123/125, 12/40

held, *pa.ppl.* reserved? 7/30 (*see note*)

held(e), *v. inf.* bend 5/60; *3.sg. pa.*
allied himself 2/8; *2.sg. pa.* wasted
7/84, 9/99

hele, *n.* prosperity 1/53, 10/11/159, 11/52,
14/106, 20/212; good health 5/51, 9/25,
10/186, 15/122, 19/71; salvation 8/69,
17/181; *soule* ~ spiritual profit 21/6

hele, *v. inf.* conceal 4/47; keep silent 4/155

helþe, *n.* salvation 23/38

hem, *pron. see* **he**

hemself, *refl.pron.* themselves 4/7, 9/173

hende, *adj.* gracious 21/84

henne, *adv.* from hence 8/103

herbe/o/rwe, *n.* shelter 1/150; 17/36

herberweles, *n. pl.* homeless 6/38

herd(e), *v. see* **here** *v.*

herde, *n.* shepherd 23/112 *see also* **hurd**

here, *v. inf.* hear 1/51, etc., *3.sg. pres.*
hereþ 12/110, 18/38; *1.sg. pres.* **herde**
20/5; *pa.ppl.* **herd** 4/223

her(e), *poss.adj.* *3.pl.* their 1/123, 1/125,
2/6, 3/74, 3/102 etc.

here, *pron. see* **he**

hereon, *adv.* on this 7/48

herkne, *v. inf.* listen to 18/107

hernes, *n. pl.* corners 3/5, 4/157, 12/74

herre(re), *comp.adj.* higher 14/1/3, 15/140,
18/61

hertely, *adv.* carefully, 22/1

heryed, *v. 1.sg. pa.* harrowed 10/60,
22/52

heryng, *ger.* hearing 15/13/89/109

heryeng(e), *ger.* rejoicing, praising 23/17,
23/22

hery3e, *v. imp.sg.* praise 23/9

hest, *n.* commandment 24/14; *pl.* **hestes**
21/36, 22/37

het, *pa.ppl.* touched 15/22

het(e), *n.* heat 1/109, 3/60, 13/15, 15/69,
15/119

hete, *v. imp.sg.* hit 13/15

hete, *adj.* hot 20/77/157, 24/363

heþen, *n.* heathen 12/123

heued, *n.* head 15/9/18

heuy(e), *adj.* heavy 11/79, 24/25/26

hewe, *n.* colour 4/12/53, 11/119, 24/178

hey(3), *adj.* high 3/128, 13/39; *superl.*
heyest 13/42

hi/y/der, *adv.* here 4/2, 12/27, 24/94

hire, *n.* payment for hire 9/66

his, *poss. pron.* his 1/26/33/50 etc.; **hi/**
y/sse 1/116, 17/28, 18/158, 19/32, 24/30,
24/271; **hesse**, his own 5/53

hit, *pron. see* **he**

hi3e, *v. inf.* approach 4/115; **hy3e**, advance
7/46

hi/y/3e, *adj.* high 3/44/71; 4/155/132, 7/46,
11/26, 14/47, 15/53, 15/70, 18/4/22/99,
20/89; *superl.* **hi3est** 13/34, 18/8

hi3t, *n.* joy 23/10

hi3t, *n. on* ~ on high 20/10, 21/156,
23/109, 24/311

ho/o/d, *n.* hood 2/83, 18/155

hoke, *v. inf.* stoop 5/60

hold(e), *v. inf.* regard 4/27; keep 4/51,
9/106; maintain 9/20; sustain 13/129;
1.sg. pres. consider 16/45/71/77; regard
20/121; *2.sg. pres.* 9/148; maintain
11/114; *2.sg. pres.subj.* observe 11/81;
2.pl. pres. consider 10/152; *3.pl. pres.*
keep 21/10; *imp.sg.* keep 21/36, 22/25;

holdest 2.*sg. pres.* withhold 10/70; regard 24/185; **holdeþ** 3.*sg. pres.* stays 3/166; considers 20/87; **holden** 3.*pl. pres.* keep 11/59; *pa.ppl.* obliged 13/45; considered 16/99

hordyng, *ger.* hoarding 1/31, 8/7

holi/y/day, *n.* holy day 4/121/122

holl, *adv.* whole 23/70

hom, *adv.* home 12/1, 20/77

homly, *adv.* familiarly 16/24

hond(e), *n.* hand 18/83, 21/28, 22/56, 23/117, 24/62, *pl.* **hondes** 4/135, 15/36

hondewark, *n.* handiwork 24/362

honge, *v.* 3.*pl. pres. remain* 16/83; **hongeþ** 3.*sg. pres.* hangs 3/165

hony, *n.* honey 2/59/62

hoo, *v. imp.* stop 1/109, 14/54

hool, *adj.* intact 14/10

hool, *adv.* wholly 3/51; whole, unbroken 23/62; *makeþ ~* heals 17/192

hoot, *n.* heat 20/34

hoot, *adj.* hot 20/205

hord, *n.* treasure store 10/87; *in ~* locked up; undisclosed 9/75/84; *in ~* in memory 13/156

hospytal, *n. holde ~* give hospitality to 15/31

hostry, *n.* inn, public house 6/9

hoteþ, *v.* 3.*sg. pres.* promises 20/75

houre, *n.* service at canonical hour 23/11

housell, *n.* holy communion 23/128; **howsel** 15/72

how, *v. imp.sg.* take heed of 21/73

hurd, *n.* shepherd 21/10; *see also* **herde**

hyde, *n.* skin 4/53

hye, *v. inf. in ~* invade quickly 12/37

hyne, *n.* servant 10/45, 15/66, 19/38

hyng, *v. inf.* hang 14/45

hyre, *n.* wage 6/2, 10/9

hy3e, *adv.* high 14/47, 20/84

ilke, *adj.* same 17/1

incertayn, *adj.* ignorant 22/58

insy3t, *n.* judgement 24/234

inwith, *prep.* within 24/264

isse, *v.* 3.*sg. pres.* is 24/26/33/300/306

ianglest, *v.* 2.*sg. pres.* wrangle 20/163

iape, *n.* joke, trifle 6/63

ielous, *adj.* jealous 22/23

iewel, *n.* jewellery 18/155, *pl.* jewels 18/141

ioly, *adj.* cheerful 23/24

iour, *n. ~ delay* a day's delay 8/16/24 etc.

ioye, *n.* joy 7/46 etc.

ioyed, *v.* 3.*pl. pa.* rejoiced 23/22

iuge, *n.* judge 12/96

iugement, *n.* judgement 1/5

iustice, *n.* justice 3/10, 3/11, 18/177

kaue, *n.* pit 24/361

kay(e), *n.* key 4/118/230, 21/133

kele, *v. inf.* become cool, dampen 22/15; **kelde**, *pa.ppl.* cooled 5/61

kenne, *v. inf.* know 7/115, 8/101, 12/113, 23/43

kep, *n.* heed 10/208

kepe, *v. inf.* protect 1/76, 9/157; maintain 3/144, 10/47; keep 11/34, 13/151,18/141;defend 12/13 etc.; obey 14/94, 22/65; preserve 18/182; 3.*sg. pres.* keeps 15/44; holds 15/119; *1.pl. pres.*; **kepen**, keep 23/104; 2.*sg. pa.* **keped**, kept 22/14; 3.*pl. pres.* maintain 12/21; 13/44; *imp.sg.* hold 12/151; protect 15/143; keep 19/69; observe 19/89; *imp.pl.* cherish 9/183; continue 11/95; preserve 12/3; defend 13/108; **kept**, *pa.ppl.* observed 1/63, 3/15; **kepyd**, kept 24/93

kerue, *v. inf.* carve 2/84; cut 16/22

kesse, *v.* 3.*pl. pres.* kiss 24/63

knaue, *n.* servant 1/55, 4/109, 17/142, 19/80, 20/47; labourer 10/9; wastrel 10/191; boy 24/404; *pl.* villains 21/151

knawe(n), *v. inf.* know 16/86; 24/212 (elsewhere **know(e)**)

knet, *v. inf.* knit 12/44

knete, *ppl.adj.* knit 20/27

knoweleche, *n.* knowledge 19/64

knowelechyng, *ger.* becoming acquainted with 4/68

knowleche, *v. imp.sg.* confess 20/195

kyd, *ppl.adj.* known 14/19, 21/153

kyd(de), *v. 1.sg. pa.* showed 20/178/190
kylde, *pa.ppl.* killed 21/61
kynde, *n.* by nature 2/74, 18/21; natural
  disposition 3/76; *in ~* natural, healthy
  15/146; rank 15/151; natural world 23/33
kynde, *adj.* faithful, true 9/31; generous
  10/61; lawful 13/114; normal/natural
  15/119
kyndel, *v. inf.* kindle 3/118
kyndenes, *n.* generosity, graciousness
  11/105

lad(de), *v. 3.sg. pa.* led 10/44, 24/396;
  pa.ppl. led 3/82
laft, *pa.ppl.* disregarded, abandoned 3/35;
  left 19/13
lamed, *pa.ppl.* injured, slandered 3/5
lane, *adj.* lean 2/63
large, *adj.* lax 1/67, 8/19
lasse, *v. inf.* lessen 7/40; *3.sg. pres.* **lasseþ**
  weaken, diminish 23/92
lasse, *adj.* less 13/38, 14/27, 23/30
lat, *v. imp.sg.* let, allow 14/59; 18/63
launce, *n.* lance 2/45
launce, *v. inf.* spring, release 24/46
lauȝhe, *v. 3.pl. pres.* laugh 12/147 *see also*
  lawhe
lauȝt, *pa.ppl.* obtained, acquired 9/189
lawhe, *inf.* laugh 2/36; **lawheþ** *3.sg. pres.*
  4/93; **lawhen** *3.pl. pres.* 16/63
lay, *n.* law 4/246
lay, *v. imp.sg.* apply 17/191
lay(e), *adj.* fallow, uncultivated 4/142,
  7/62
layd, *ppl.adj.* calm 7/27
layne, *adj.* secret 4/220
leche, *n.* healer, physician 10/52, 12/79,
  21/22
leche, *v. inf.* to heal 8/23
lef, *n.* leaf 24/139
lef, *adj.* desirous 1/51; dear, precious
  10/77; pleasing 20/141; glad 21/18
leman, *n.* lover 3/121, 4/228
leme, *n.* limb 12/106, 13/17 *see also* **lymes**
lene, *n.* deprivation, need 24/199
lene, *v. inf.* distribute 21/75

lene, *adj.* weak 2/71
lent, *pa.ppl.* aimed 1/83
lent(e), *v. 1.sg. pa.* gave 10/19, 19/64; *3.sg.*
  pa. 14/74; *pa.ppl.* loaned 7/82; given
  5/65; granted 23/50
lenton, *n.* Lent 16/103
lere, *v. inf.* learn 1/49, 10/7, 13/41, 16/44,
  21/26, 23/36
lerneþ, *v. 3.sg. pres.* teaches 17/97
lernyng, *ger.* teaching, lesson 21/title
les, *n.* snare 3/150
les, *n.* pasture 10/150
les, *n. pl.* lies 3/46
les, *adj.* less 16/122
les(e), *v. inf.* 2/38, 12/126, 17/164; *3.sg. pres.*
  3/86, 12/101; **leseþ/th/** 23/92, 24/176,
  24/213; *3.sg. pres.subj.* 7/108; *3.sg. pa.*
  lost 16/62; *2.pl. pres.* 13/155; *3.pl. pres.*
  18/47
lesyng, *n.* lie 7/86; *pl.* 4/73, 21/135
let, *v. imp.sg.* cease 20/69
lette, *n.* obstruction 20/78
lette(n), *v. inf.* neglect 9/60; thwart 12/7;
  disregard 12/60; prevent 18/147; *3.sg.*
  pres. disregard 16/53; *pa.ppl.* **letted,**
  obstructed 8/14
leue, *n.* permission 2/43, 17/171; leave
  14/15, 18/84
leue, *v. inf.* believe, 9/109, 11/113, 24/34;
  3.sg. pres. 8/49; *3.pl. pres.* 4/74; *3.sg. pa.*
  leued 9/113
leue, *v. inf.* live 3/38
leue, *v. inf.* leave, abandon 10/203, 11/51;
  imp.sg. 17/95, 24/356; *3.sg. pres.* 5/8/24
  etc; 10/209, 21/70
leue, *3.sg. pres.subj.* allow 15/149
leuere, *comp.adv.* better 17/44
leuynge, *ger.* living 21/title
leues, *n. pl.* leaves 17/188
lewe, *adj.* feeble, faint 24/251
lewed, *nom.adj.* unlettered 6/22
ley, *v. inf.* lay 20/53
liche, *adv.* likewise 1/116
li/y/f, *n.* life 3/161, 7/20, 9/29, 23/110 etc.
ligge, *v. 3.sg. pres.* lies 4/142; *3.sg. pres.*
  subj. 10/169

li/y/kne, *v. 1.sg. pres.* compare 2/57, 15/9/17/25/34 etc.

li/y/kned, *pa.ppl.* compared 17/187, 21/152, 23/122

list, *v. 3.sg. pres.* please 2/44 *see also* **lust**

li/y/te, *adj.* little 1/82, 7/90, 17/115

li/y/ʒe, *v. inf.* lie 7/30, 7/62, 8/47, 10/206, 20/86; *3.sg. pres.subj.* 24/414; lie sick 1/149

liʒe, *v. inf.* tell lies 7/86; *2.sg. pres.* 6/6; *imp.sg.* 17/92

li/y/ʒtly, *adv.* easily 10/96, 12/140, 19/82

loke, *v. imp.sg.* ensure, take care 1/59, 5/42, 6/10 etc.

loken, *pa.ppl.* locked 3/95

lomb, *n.* lamb 23/126

lon, *n.* loan 11/110

longeþ, *v. 3.sg. pres.* belongs 19/106/108

loo, *interj.* lo 2/13/16

lo(o)s, *n.* reputation 3/5, 13/57

loos, *adv.* loose 9/126

lopred, *pa.ppl.* curdled 24/82

lore, *n.* learning 12/116; teaching 17/82, 21/98; knowledge 17/97

lore, *pa.ppl.* lost 12/86

lorn, *ppl.adj.* lost 8/15, 12/145, 24/175, 24/360

loþ, *adj.* disinclined 6/42, 10/1/7; hateful 11/11; reluctant 20/119

loþes, *v. 3.sg. pres.* loathes 20/141

lust, *n.* pleasure 24/16; *pl.* **luste/ i/s** 6/56/64, 17/195, 18/54, 19/84, 20/42/69/95, 22/71

lust, *v. 3.sg. pres.* please 20/6

ly(e), *v. inf.* lie 6/46, *3.pl. pres.* 6/38; **lyþ** *3.sg. pres.* lies (down) 20/146

lyge, *adj.* liege 12/15

lyk, *adj.* like 9/98, 17/11, 19/6/8, 22/18

lym, *n.* mortar 15/53

lymes, *n.pl.* limbs 15/39/99/123 etc. 19/76

lynage, *n.* lineage 6/50, 22/22

lys, *v. 3.sg. pres.* belongs 2/39, 19/109; rests 3/99, 4/165, 17/22, 24/354; lies 9/139, 11/61, 13/165, 14/61, 16/75; exists 23/62

lytel, *adj.* little 12/28,

lytel, *adv.* little 24/201

lyther, *adj.* wicked 20/52

lyueliche, *adj.* living 23/18

lyuen, *3.pl. pres.* live 18/73; **luyeþ**, *3.sg. pres.* 21/7/12/98

lyuer(e), *n.* living person, 2/73/75, 3/77 etc., *pl.* 18/9/10/66

lyuyng(e), *n.* church living, benefice 8/34, 14/26; wages 15/78;

lyuyng(e), *ppl.adj.* living 3/76; alive 24/170; *ger.* life 22/42

lyʒtnes, *n.* purity 10/109

ma(a)d, *pa.ppl.* made 15/1, 23/25, 24/25

mad, *v. 1.sg. pres.* made 10/107, 17/114; *3.sg. pa.* 13/127, *3.pl. pa.* 12/123

madde, *v. 2.pres.subj.* behave foolishly, act in a headstrong fashion 17/145

mageste, *n.* majesty 24/246

make, *imp.sg.* match 17/43

maked, *pa.ppl.* made 8/2, 20/98

making, *ger.* poem, composition 8/*title*

maladye, *n.* suffering 7/38

manere, *n.* fashion 7/56; kind of 16/2

maneres, *n. pl.* behaviour 18/78

manhed(e), *n.* manhood 10/166, 13/118, 19/8, 19/108; **manhode**, 3/119

manne/y/s, *poss.adj.* man's 1/17/137; 3/18 etc.

marchaundes, *n. pl.* merchants 3/69

marchaunt, *n.* merchandise 18/139

marche, *n.* boundaries, frontiers 13/108

martyres, *n. pl.* martyrs 18/31

maryage, *n.* marriage 6/52, 22/24

masouncraft, *n.* masonry 14/42

mat, *pa.ppl.* overcome, checkmated 16/108; confounded 24/124

matere, *n.* substance 8/2, 22/2, 24/138; ~ **meue**, stir up trouble 1/77

maþ, *v. 3.sg. pres.* makes 3/159

mau/w/gre, *adv.* despite, notwithstanding 4/13, 18/56

mayde, *n.* girl 24/404

maynt, *pa.ppl.* mixed 13/63

maynten(e), *v. inf.* uphold, support 2/48, 3/143, 12/63, 13/12, 16/30; *3.sg. pres.subj.* 9/68, *3.pl. pres.* 3/104, *imp.sg.* 6/11; *imp. pl.* 12/8/56/136

mayst, *v. 2.sg. pres.* may 7/27, 8/30

mayster(e), *n.* master 8/93, 10/10, 15/77, 20/47, 21/147, *pl.* **maystres**, 15/79

maystershepe, *n.* mastery 20/169

maystri/ʒ/e, *n.* victory 9/145; cunning 4/139; **maystry(e)**, power, sovereignty, 24/127/140; upper hand 12/39; *n. pl.* **maystryʒes**, honourable deeds 12/121

med(e), *n.* payment 24/345; wages, 9/165; financial gain 6/12; material reward, worldly gain 2/8/etc.; reward 1/43, 4/11, 7/71; bribery 1/68, 4/118, 7/20

medle, *v. inf.* mingle 20/98; *3.pl. pres.* meddle 3/39; *pa.ppl.* blended 1/135, 7/101

meked, *v. 1.sg. pa.* humble 19/17/49; *pa.ppl.* 21/112

mekely, *adv.* humbly 18/105, 20/211

mekenesse, *n.* humility 10/168, 18/97, 20/59

mekere, *comp.adj.* more humble 18/61

mele, *n.* meal, food 15/118, 17/7/35

membres, *n. pl.* body parts 15/*title*

mende, *v. inf.* reform 4/134, 5/22, 12/46; correct 4/137; atone 16/112; *2.pl. pres. subj.* 10/56; 21/54; *inf. 3.pl. pres.* 9/115, *imp.sg.* 20/195

mendement, *n.* correction 22/38, 24/106, 24/202

mendid, *pa.ppl.* corrected 17/118, 23/1

mendi/y/s, *n. pl.* amends 14/37; compensation 16/78

mene, *n.* intermediary 9/3

mene, *n.* company, fellowship 24/195

mene, *adj.* poor 2/10

mene, *v. inf.* intend 2/66; *pa.ppl.* **ment** meant 7/85

mennys, *poss. n.* men's 4/130, 8/68 etc.

mercyable, *adj.* forgiving, compassionate 21/65

meriest, *superl.adj.* most prosperous 16/57

merkis, *n. pl.* marks 9/175

merþe, *n.* happiness 12/2, 20/130

mes, *n.* affliction 3/78

messager, *n.* messenger 3/9; *pl.* **messageres** 19/99

mest, *superl.adv.* most 11/3, 24/10/12

mesure, *n.* equity 1/61; fairness 3/3; measurement 9/54, 14/68; moderation, temperance 14/39, 15/118/119

met, *pa.ppl.* acquainted 15/71; met 20/65

mete, *n.* food 1/150 etc; *pl.* **metes** 18/104

mett, *n.* proper, due amount 14/68

meue, *v. inf.* speak 4/79; *3.sg. pres.* dislodge 18/64; *3.pl. pres.* ~ **matere** stir up trouble 1/77; **moueþ**, *3.sg. pres.* stirs, moves 10/166; **myue**, *inf.* alter 18/91

mirre, *n.* myrrh 10/119

miʒt, *v. 1.sg. pres.subj.* might 10/62

mo(o), *adj.* more 3/114, 4/31, 7/36, 18/126/186, 19/43 etc.

moche, *adj.* much 2/7/15/31/50 etc.

mochil, *adj.* great 20/193

moder, *n.* mother 22/6/11, 24/173/268; *poss.* 20/149

mon, *v. 3.sg. pres.* must 4/195/231, 5/5; *2.pl. pres.* 5/59; *3.pl. pres.* 1/119

mon(e), *n.* moan, complaint 11/46/70, 19/25

mone, *n.* moon 15/91

mony(e), *adj.* many 3/125, 4/73, 21/20/150, 24/239/240

mood, *n.* mind 17/145, 19/35; spirit 18/61/157

morn, *n.* morning 8/10

morneþ, *v. 3.sg. pres.* mourns 21/33

morning, *ger.* contrition 9/38

morþere, *n.* murder 12/94

mortkyn, *n.* carcass of an animal killed by disease or accident 20/86

morwe, *n.* next morning 10/122, 11/67

mot, *v. 3.sg. pres.* must 1/38, 4/67, 5/31, 7/118; **mote**, 21/49/80; *2.sg. pres.* 8/76, 9/33/87, 13/41

moþþes, *n. pl.* moths 24/159

moun, *n.* memory 24/322

mouynge, *ger.* movement 24/411
mow(e), *v. 3.sg. pres.* may 24/202; *1.pl.
pres.* 17/76; *2.pl. pres.* 3/48/64, 11/25,
12/46/83, 13/123, 18/23/147; **moun** 24/43;
mowen, *3.pl. pres.* 24/69; **mown**, *2.pl.
pres.*; must *2.sg. pres.* 1/49; *3.pl. pres.*
9/123
mowe, *v. inf.* mow 4/63, 19/23
mowntayne, *n.* mountain 14/17
mownten, *v. 3.pl. pres.* climb 20/84
myche, *adj.* much 18/159
mylde, *adj.* merciful 20/33/162, 21/17
mylle, *n.* mill 15/108
mylt, *n.* spleen 10/26
myn(e), *poss.adj.* my 2/4, 8/44, 10/45 etc.
mynne, *v. inf.* record 16/16; make
mention of 16/57; *3.sg. pres.subj.* think
upon 24/166
mynstrallis, *n. pl.* minstrels 4/82
myrrour, *n.* mirror 3/133
mys(se), *n.* criminal act 1/161; wrong 13/3;
sin 7/44/93, 9/115, 17/178, 18/88, 21/143;
wickedness 1/103, 9/135, 19/28, 20/195,
24/342; evil deeds 21/119
mys, *adj.* wrong, awry 8/7, 14/57; wrong
21/54
mys, *adv.* incorrectly 23/1; improperly
20/107; wrongly 24/39; wickedly
24/59/329
mysbede, *v. inf.* oppress, mistreat 3/31;
3.sg. pres.subj. 13/46/54
mysche/y/ue, *n.* harm 1/76; distress
24/24; **myschyf**, misery 24/340; *n.
pl.* **myscheues** miseries 1/124, 21/32;
misfortunes 3/100
mysdede, *n.* wrongdoing 21/34, 23/106
mysfamed, *3.sg. pa.* slandered 3/2
myst, *pa.ppl.* missed 4/231
mysvsed, *pa.ppl.* misused 14/107
myue, *v. inf. see* **meue**
my3t(e), *n.* power, strength 10/145, 11/18
etc.
my3t(e), *v. 2.sg. pres.* may 5/50, 7/91 etc.;
3.sg. pres. 12/137, 13/22; *1.pl. pres.* 17/132;
my3test, *2.sg. pres.* 11/115, 17/104
my3ty, *adj.* robust 15/122; powerful 15/124

namly, *adv.* especially 24/289
nan, *pron.* none 21/120
nas, *v. 3.sg. pa.* was not 19/12
nauel, *n.* navel 21/171
nay, *adv.* no 2/28, 4/91, 6/5, 8/94, 10/102,
24/305
nayled, *pa.ppl.* nailed 20/115
ne, *conj.* nor 1/62, 1/156 etc.
nede, *n.* necessity, need, 1/94, 2/78/86,
4/173, 7/23/71, 9/60/192, 10/200, 17/174,
18/110, 19/70, 21/38
nede, *v. 2.pl. pres.* are in poverty 9/183;
3.pl. pres. 9/125/167
ne(e)de, *adv.* needs 1/38, 5/31
nede/i/d, *v. 1.sg. pa.* needed 11/101; *3.sg.
pa.* was necessary 10/18
nedeles, *adj.* unnecessary 13/91, 21/75;
adj. n. not in need 7/69, 14/109,
16/94
nedy, *adj.* in need 7/65/67, 14/109
nel(e), *v. 1.sg. pres.* will not 20/197,
24/401; *2.sg. pres.* **nelt** 17/105/141;
3.sg. pres. 9/20/106/109/174, 16/85/106,
21/26/109; **nelle**, 18/52; *3.pl. pres.*
nelen 4/106; *see also* **nyl**
neme, *v. inf.* take 10/18
nempned, *v. 3.sg. pa.* named 23/3
nerre, *comp.adv.* nearer 15/144, 19/68
nes, *v. 3.sg. pres.* is not 10/148/188, 11/55,
13/40, 18/156/160/162, 23/70; **nesse**,
24/61
neþer, *conj.* neither 24/345; **noþer** 4/18,
15/130
newe, *adj.* new 9/76, 11/116, 13/29 etc.
newe, *adv.* afresh 4/15, 9/19/115, 18/117,
21/14; anew 10/28; newly 20/135
newefangyl, *adj.* fickle, inconstant 13/32
ney3(e), *adv.* near 12/26, 14/44, 19/69
noblay, *n.* nobility 12/86
nolde, *v. 3.sg. pres.* would not 10/36/41,
20/38/160, 24/399; *2.sg. pres.* **noldest**
2/72, 19/83
no(u)mbre, *n.* number 24/130/198
no(u)mbred, *ppl.adj.* numbered 1/133,
24/156/239
non, *adj.* no 1/54/86, 3/5 etc.

non, *pron.* none 4/208, 9/163 etc.
none, *n. hiȝe* ~ 3 o'clock 15/70
noo, *adj.* no 8/28; noon 24/318
nost, *v. 2.sg. pres.* do not know 5/50,
    8/98, 11/109, 22/57
noþer, *conj. see* neþer
nouellerye, *n.* contrivance, malpractice
    3/63
no/u/ȝt, *n.* nothing 4/227, 7/65/67/68, 8/3,
    10/15 etc.
no/u/ȝt, *adv.* not 4/58, 9/188, 11/101,
    13/26/51, 20/109 etc.
nouȝten, *n.* nothing 7/81
nowþe, *adv.* now 7/51
noys, *n.* noise 4/17
noyȝe, *n.* grievance, affliction 3/42
nyce, *adj.* extravagant, dissolute 18/122;
    see also nys, *adj.*
nyl, *v. 3.sg. pres.* will not 1/63, 3/15 etc.;
    3.pl. pres. 4/90; nyll(e) *3.sg. pres.* 10/8;
    3.pl. pres. 5/4, 18/94; nylt, *2.sg. pres.*
    17/101; nyltou, 24/127; *see also* nel(e)
nys, *v. 3.sg. pres.* is not 1/37, 3/4, 3/131,
    4/11 etc.
nys, *adj.* foolish 1/45, 8/77, 10/151, 14/63,
    16/77; dissolute 2/34, 8/43, 11/60, 14/3,
    18/24; wicked 13/162, 18/77; *see also*
    nyce
nyȝe, *v. inf.* torment 6/70, 8/99; nyȝed,
    pa.ppl. afflicted, assailed 13/101

o, *ind. art.* a 1/14, 9/17/110/142, 13/41,
    23/63/64; *pron. num.* one 10/163, 15/91,
    17/49
o, *prep.* on 13/110; of 9/182, 18/18,
    23/68/128; ~ *day* on a day 4/193;
    ~ *ferre* afar 15/138; ~ *hast* in haste
    4/179; ~ *side* aside 20/130; ~ *tway*
    in two 4/70; ~ *two* 5/69, 20/20; ~
    twynne in two 7/111, 17/85, 19/56,
    20/13, 21/111
obley, *n.* communion wafer, bread 23/65
occupacioun, *n.* possession,
    preoccupation 18/11
office, *n.* appointed duty 17/18; offys
    4/164

offryng, *ger.* sacrifice 23/121
oftere, *comp. adv.* more often 9/95
omys, *adv. see* amys
ones, *adv.* once 7/94, 12/43, 17/69, 23/4
oo(n), *num.* one 3/50, 4/241, 5/13, 12/68,
    16/115
opert, *adv. see* apert
orda/e/yned, *pa.ppl.* established,
    instituted 13/4; appointed 14/58;
    decreed 18/137; provided 22/20
ordeyne, *v. 2.sg. imp.* govern, control
    9/135
ordi/y/naunce, *n.* ordinance, law 1/75,
    23/36; provision 3/159; plot 12/30,
    13/138; religious service 23/26
oreson, *n.* prayer 18/164
ost, *n.* Eucharistic bread, wafer 23/38/83
oþes, *n. pl.* oaths 20/139
ouerhope, *n.* excessive hope,
    presumption 1/129, 7/97, 8/47, 20/201
ouertylt, *v. inf.* overthrow, destroy 13/65
outeray, *v. 3.pl. pres.* exceed, surpass
    11/84
outfleme, *v. inf.* cast out 24/115
outrage, *n.* extravagance 9/100, 18/121
ouȝt, *v. 3.pl. pres.* ought 17/10
ouȝt, *pron. adv.* anything 7/66, 15/8/132,
    19/16, 24/229
ouȝte, *v. 3.sg. pres.* owns, possess
    17/122
owe(n), *adj.* own 10/136; 1/33, 4/38/45 etc.
owe, *v. inf.* own, possess 21/19; *3.sg. pres.*
    subj. 21/27; oweth *3.sg. pres.* 1/27
oyle, *n.* compassion 24/135

palays, *n.* palace 11/68
palfrey, *n.* riding horse 2/14
pape, *n.* pope 10/192
parage, *n.* lineage 13/116
paramour, *n.* love 4/125
parauenture, *adv.* perhaps 18/187
parcel, *n.* part 12/16
parchemyn, *n.* parchment 17/182
parfitnesse, *n.* perfection 24/380
parfyt, *adj.* perfect 17/27/70, 18/2/21
parischen, *n.* parishioner 9/174

parlement, *n.* parliament 3/97, 13/4/9, 24/190

part(e), *v. inf.* separate 18/144; *inf.* divide 19/56; *2.sg. pres.* 5/69; **parten** 17/85; *3.sg. pres.* 7/111; *3.sg. pres.subj.* distribute 23/84

parted, *pa.ppl.* separated 20/13, 22/12; divided 20/20; fragmented 23/70

partnere, *n.* co-ruler 12/107

pas, *n.* state 24/72

paske, *adj.* ~ *lomb* paschal lamb 23/126

passe, *v. inf.* pass beyond 4/222; *3.sg. pres.subj.* 4/212; *3.sg. pres.* **passeþ** goes beyond 24/200; surpasses 13/147, 23/14; turns 23/42

passing, *adv.* exceeding 14/76

past(e), *adv.* over, finished 15/111, 24/220; beyond 14/101

pater, *n.* ~ *noster* Lord's Prayer 6/15

pauylon, *n.* tent, protection 24/313

pawe, *v. inf.* manhandle 4/21

payed, *pa.ppl.* satisified, content 9/179, 12/131

pa/e/yne, *n.* torment 24/344/346; punishment 4/218; distress 24/124; *n. pl.* **pa/e/ynes** torment 16/111, 19/73, 24/218/385; *see also* **pyne**

paynte, *v. 2.sg. pres.* colour, ameliorate 9/43

pece, *n.* piece 12/42, 23/86; *n. pl.* **peces** 23/69/90

pe(e)s, *n.* peace 3/8/16/24/ etc. 24/308

penyworth, *n.* smidgeon 14/38

pere, *n.* equal 5/21, 10/3/107, 11/75, 17/186, 20/180

perfeccyone, *n.* completeness 12/102

peri/y/l(e), *n.* danger 14/43/101, 15/27/51, 16/48/75, 18/86, 22/12, 24/174

pete, *n.* fart 9/142

pilage, *n.* extortion 2/68

plas, *n.* place 10/97, 17/152

plaster, *n.* poultice 7/107

playn, *n.* field, green 4/100

playn(e), *v. 3.sg. pres.* make complaint 20/7, *2.pl. pres.* 15/113; *3.sg. pres.* **pleyneþ** 16/77

pla/e/ynt, *n.* complaint, grievance 12/110, 13/60, 16/10, 20/9/109/161/167/185; *n. pl.* **playntes** 13/43

plente, *n.* plenty, abundance 15/56, 19/67

plesande, *ger.* pleasing 20/75

plete, *v. inf.* plead 9/62, 18/181

pleye, *v. imp.sg.* play 15/99

plyt, *n.* state, condition 15/40

ply3e, *v. inf.* swerve 7/102

pondryng, *pres.ppl.* multiplying 16/111

pore, *adj.* poor 1/89/138/145, 3/103 etc.

post(e)les, *n. pl.* apostles 8/21, 11/26

pouert(e), *n.* poverty 10/158, 11/90, 15/30, 19/65, 20/62/211, 21/3, 24/124

pouste, *n.* power 12/20, 23/31/92

poynt, *n.* swordpoint 10/27, point 13/34

poyntel, *n.* stylus 24/296

poyntes, *n. pl.* articles 9/116; items 16/79

pray, *n.* livelihood, food 4/150, 8/14

pray, *n.* victim, quarry 6/7, 24/338

pray, *n.* request 17/73, 24/338

pra/e/y(e), *v. inf.* pray 4/174, 15/97/148; *1.sg. pres.* 24/246; *3.pl. pres.* 13/148, 18/38; *2.imp.sg.* 22/69; *2.sg. pres.* **preyest** 23/39; *3.sg. pres.* **preyeþ** 20/104; *1.sg. pres.* ask 2/15; *3.sg. pa.* **preyed** begged 15/85

prelat, *n.* clergyman 16/65; *n. pl.* **prelates** high-ranking clergy 3/148

prented, *v. 3.sg. pa.* stamped 17/183

pres, *n.* trouble 3/38; crowd 3/158; *in* ~ increasing 24/280; mass 24/312

pres, *v. inf.* hasten 21/87

presone, *v. inf.* imprison 21/78

preso(u)n, *n.* prison 2/30/52, 4/14, 6/45, 13/103

presoned, *pa.ppl.* imprisoned 21/61

presoner(e)s, *n. pl.* prisoners 6/39, 9/126

prest, *n.* priest 9/3/34, etc. 14/25, 23/67/83/89; *n. pl.* **preste/i/s** 4/81, 9/162

prest, *adv.* ready, prompt 15/29

presthod, *n.* priesthood 15/26

preue, *v. inf.* prove 7/73, 13/87; *2.pl. pres.* 4/33; *3.pl. pres.* 1/79, 5/47, 7/11, 9/173, 13/164, 14/63; *3.sg. pres.* **preues** 1/125, 3/98; **preueth/þ** 2/34/88; **proue** *inf.* 11/25, 17/187, 24/127; *2.sg. pres.* 24/140/141; *2.sg. pres.subj.* 24/260

preue(y), *adj.* secret 1/3/99, 5/27, 14/44

preue/y/te(e), *n.* secret, private 4/203/213, 14/20, 16/87

preuyly, *adv.* privately 12/54; inconspicuously 21/8

preyer(e), *n.* prayer 4/183, 7/114, 15/29, 18/37/164; *n. pl.* **preyers** 18/39, 23/3

preyse, *v. inf.* praise 4/50, 6/32; *3.sg. pa.* **preysede** 2/7

principal, *n.* the best 17/72

principal, *adv.* foremost 17/60

pri/y/nci/y/pal, *adj.* chief 15/14, royal 24/373

pri/y/s, *n.* price 17/102; worth 4/162; value 10/22, 16/73; prize 13/133/167; benefit 23/64; *o ~* most precious 11/15, 18/18, 20/175

professed, *ppl.adj.* admitted to religious order 18/44

profre, *v. 3.sg. pres.subj.* offer 19/62; *3.sg. pres.* **profreþ** 11/40, 17/15

profyt, *n.* advantage 1/4, 14/52, 17/20/28/37, 21/60; gain 2/60; benefit 13/42, 17/22/160; *n. pl.* **profytes** 3/100

profytable, *adj.* charitable 21/69

profyte, *v. inf.* benefit 17/154

propre, *n. in ~* in private 18/59; private property 18/141

prow, *n.* fortune 19/83; benefit 23/101

puple, *n.* people 1/10/19/21, 3/130 etc.

purpos, *n.* sense, significance 3/92; proposal 4/91

pursue, *v. 3.pl. pres.* take to law 21/124

pyke, *v. 3.pl. pres.* plunder 4/140; *3.sg. pres.* **pykeþ** steals 12/64

pyked, *ppl.adj.* long and pointy 20/138

pyn(e), *n.* pain, torment, punishment 1/28, 7/40, 8/5, 10/203. 11/107 etc.; *n. pl.* **pynes** 11/45, 20/205, 22/13; *see also* **pa/e/yne**

pyne, *v. inf.* torment 4/21

pynne, *v. 2.pl. pres.* lock, fasten 17/87; *3.pl. pres.* 15/83, 21/45

pyt, *v. inf.* thrust 10/87 *see note*

py3t, *pa.ppl.* pitched 24/313

quantite, *n.* capacity, mass 15/50

quaue, *v. imp.sg.* tremble 23/88

qued, *n.* evil 7/60

queme, *v. inf.* please 13/163

quere(lle), *n.* quarrel, dispute 3/87, 9/139, 13/96/117, 21/116/123; **queryle** grounds for dispute 13/113

queynt, *adj.* ingeniously wrought 7/1

quod, *v. 3.sg. pres.* said 15/87/89/90, *3.pl. pres.* 15/95

quyk, *adj.* alive, living 4/198, 23/18/68/100

quykeneþ, *v. 3.sg. pres.* springs to life 20/3

quyte, *v. imp.sg.* repay 1/40, 9/132; *2.sg. pres.* **quytest** repay obligation 17/48

raft, *ppl.adj.* plundered 16/58; lost 16/62; forcibly deprived 20/14

rage, *v. inf.* to have sex with 6/53

rank, *adj.* abundant 2/2

ransake, *v. 2.sg. pres.* search, examine 24/58

raue, *v. inf.* behave senselessly 1/53; *1.sg. pres.* speak derangedly 20/43

rauenere, *n.* plunderer 14/108

raysed, *pa.ppl.* stirred up 12/129

recche, *v. inf.* care 4/24/72; *3.pl. pres.* 4/128; *3.sg. pres.subj.* 4/136; *imp.sg.* 4/40; *3.sg. pres.* **reccheþ** 13/97

reche, *v. 3.sg. pres.* extend, share 21/20

recheles, *adj.* reckless 14/110

rechelesly, *adv.* recklessly 4/141

red, *n.* command, bidding 13/23, 23/104

red(e), *v. inf.* advise 2/78, 24/341; *1.sg. pres.* 1/109, 8/102, 9/8/24/63; *imp.pl.* 18/108

red(e), *v. inf.* read 24/392, *2.pl. pres.* 9/63

refuse, *adj.* defective, 24/283

reherce, *v. inf.* recite a list of charges 13/83

reioys(e), *v. inf.* enjoy 21/30; *imp.sg.* rejoice 23/12

rek(e)ne, *v. inf.* count 9/92; account 21/148; *3.pl. pres.* calculate 4/233; *imp. sg.* account for; 9/39, give account 10/210

rekened, *pa.ppl.* accounted 1/118

rekenyng, *ger.* accounting, judgement 1/29, 1/35, 7/83, 10/196, 11/110, 14/31, 16/125, 24/231; *n. pl.* accounts 3/151

rele/i/geon, *n.* observance of religious rule 18/3/17/22/25/29/169

rele/i/gous, *n.* those in religious orders (monks) 18/13/147/149

relige/ious, *adj.* in accordance with religious rule 18/60/139/142

reles, *n.* transfer of property, rights 3/126; forgiveness 24/314

relygyoun, *n.* religious orders 12/142

reme, *n.* realm 12/19/32, 13/95/106/161 *see also* **rewme**

remewe, *n.* restlessness 21/16

remewe, *v. inf.* remove 24/253; *imp.pl.* 18/74

renne, *v. inf.* run 8/52, 15/75; operate, be 23/47; *2.sg. pres.* fall 9/103; *2.pl. pres.* accumulate 8/100; *3.pl. pres.* go 22/61; *2.sg. pres.* **rennest** run wild 10/104; *3.sg. pres.* **renneþ** 20/81

renou/w/n(e), *n.* reputation, fame 12/126, 24/9

rente, *n.* fee 7/87; income 13/52; *n. pl.* **rentis** revenues 3/102

repe, *v. inf.* reap 4/63, 19/23, 21/128; *3.sg. pres.* **repeth** 24/180

repref, *n.* rebuke, reprimand 10/2

repreue, *v. inf.* rebuke 4/77, 7/34, 11/115, 19/3; *2.sg. pres.* **repreuest** 24/12; *3.sg. pres.* **repreueth** rebukes 13/74; upbraids 20/137 *pa.ppl.* **repreued** 14/6; *inf.* **repryue** challenge 24/22

rerage, *n.* arrears, debt 8/100, 9/103, 11/111

rered, *v. 3.sg. pa.* raised 24/311

res, *n.* emergency 3/70; rashness, madness 12/7

resceyue, *v. inf.* receive 1/140, 9/181, 11/66, 23/82; *2.pl. pres.* 23/128; *3.pl. pres.* 1/98; *imp.sg.* 2/20, 6/58, 9/133, 9/171; *3.sg. pres.* **resceyueþ** 9/74; *pa.ppl.* **resceyued** 11/77 *see also* **ressayue**

reson, *n. as adj.* reasonable, equitable 9/130

reso(u)n, *n.* wisdom 1/102, 12/134; good sense 4/34; reason 4/107/110, 11/50, 13/74, 15/45, 20/179, 22/18, 24/11; justice 20/46; *do ~* exercise justice 14/33; *of ~* according to reason 19/5

ressauye, *v. 2.pl. pres.* receive 8/73; *imp. sg.* 8/87, 14/7; *3.sg. pres.* **ressauyeþ** 3/126, 8/33/36, 23/4, 23/73

ressayuour, *n.* receiver, communicant 23/61

reue, *n.* steward 18/60

reue, *v. inf.* steal, rob 6/13; *3.pl. pres.* 5/38; *inf.* take by force 11/89

rewe, *v. inf.* repent 1/92, 11/117, 16/106; *1.sg. pres.* have pity 10/160; *imp.sg.* 19/73, 24/257; *3.sg. pres.* **reweþ** 21/74

rewme, *n.* realm 1/74 *see also* **reme**

reyse, *v. inf.* raise 24/377

ri/y/g/ʒ/ht, *n.* justice 1/135, 3/9/138, 12/65, 23/105; equity 3/10/143, 7/101; lawful conduct 10/147; right 9/60, 13/33, 10/142; rights, heritage 13/140 etc; nature 24/263

riʒt, *adj.* right 6/29, 9/67/139, 11/23, 22/56, 24/395; just 4/20; legitimate 12/40; true 23/53 etc.

ri/y/ʒt, *adv.* just as 8/37, 20/39; right 7/51, 9/44; rightly 10/147, 21/152 etc.

ri/y/ʒtwi/y/s, *adj.* righteous 8/65, 9/90/138, 12/96, 13/7, 16/90/106, 17/93, 19/106, 20/15

ri/y/ʒtwisnes(se), *n.* righteousness, justice 19/106, 20/105/197, 21/50/113

rode, *n.* rood 10/98, 17/116, 19/18; **rood** 19/37

rolle, *n.* document roll of accounts 24/392; *n. pl.* **rolles** 9/63, 11/111

roo, *n.* roe deer 14/110

rosted, *ppl.adj.* roasted 23/126

rote, *v. 3.sg. pres.subj.* rot, decompose 24/375

roten, *ppl.adj.* decomposed 24/158

rotenesse, *n.* putrefaction 24/267

roue, *n.* scab, *on* ~ with scabs 24/123

rouþe, *n.* pity 16/37 *see also* ruþe

rouȝt, *v. 3.sg. pa.* cared 4/159

rowe, *v. 3.sg. pres.* row 4/3

rowne, *v. inf.* speak 12/54

ruþe, *n.* pity 10/78 *see also* rouþe

ruyde. *adj.* foolish, ignorant 21/25

ryht, *n.* right 1/36

rys, *v. 3.pl. pres.* prevail 1/143; *inf.* rysen rise 24/301

ryue, *n.* reef sail 7/28

sad, *adj.* sober 6/33

salue, *v. inf.* heal with ointment 7/109; *3.sg. pres.* salueþ 10/164

salue, *n.* healing ointment 9/178

sample, *n.* example 10/185, 24/69

sare, *adv.* sorely 10/39

sarmon, *n.* sermon 10/5

sat, *v. 3.sg. pa.* afflicted 19/11

saue/y/our, *n.* saviour 23/9; 24/304

saule, *n.* soul 24/15

saued, *pa.ppl.* explained 23/96

sauyd, *n. pl.* saved souls 24/409

sauȝt, *n.* rest 9/191

sauȝten, *v. inf.* to be reconciled 9/179; *pa.ppl.* sauȝte 11/35

sawe, *n.* law 5/34, 9/109, 13/55, 14/93

sawt(e)nyng, *ger.* reconciliation 11/25/33/41

sayn(e), *pa.ppl.* seen 4/98/223

sayþ(e), *v. 3.sg. pres.* says 13/55, 17/177, 20/95/140, 24/179; sei/yþ 10/15, 20/43/143/177; *2.sg. pres.* seyst 10/102

schendi/y/s, *v. 3.sg. pres.* destroys, damns 14/107, 24/103

schewe, *inf.* confess 9/83, ~ *forþ* recount 24/349

schold(e), *v. 3.sg. pres.* ought 24/403; *3.pl. pres.* 1/100; schuld(e) *2.sg. pres.* 22/69; *3.sg. pres.* 9/94

schul, *v. 2.pl. pres.* shall 24/191; *3.pl. pres* schullen 24/333

sclaundre, *n.* slander 16/101, 18/94/95/190

sc/k/ol(e), *n.* school 7/9, 16/101, 20/92; *pl.* scoles 2/33

se, *v. inf.* see 3/133, 17/68/109, 20/200, 24/38 etc.; *1.sg. pres.* 10/92, 19/101; *3.pl. pres.* 3/37, 4/46; *1.sg. pa.* seyȝe 15/92

seche, *v. inf.* seek 4/77, 24/31; *2.sg. pres.* 24/57; *imp.sg.* 9/47; *2.sg. pres.* sechest 10/105; *3.sg. pres.* secheþ 3/5, 4/158, 12/74

sechyng, *ger.* seeking 24/93

sed(e), *n.* seed 4/141, 24/194

sed(e), *v. inf.* seeds 1/62; *3.sg. pres.* 13/142

seiþ *v. 3.sg. pres. see* sayþ(e)

sek, *n.* sack 7/5

seke, *v. imp.sg.* seek 7/50

selde, *adv.* seldom 15/71

selue(n), *n.* self 1/9, 2/85, 3/54, 6/40, 9/12, 11/108, 12/97

selue, *adj.* same 13/116

semblaunt, *n.* appearance 3/122

sen, *v. inf.* see 23/88

sen, *prep.* since 8/10; *conj.* 24/231

sene, *pa.ppl.* seen 24/197/318

sengyl, *adv.* exclusively, distinctively 23/66

sercle, *n.* circle 12/10/41

serkis, *n. pl.* shirts 9/172

seruage, *n.* enslavement 20/182

serue/y/d, *pa.ppl.* deserved 8/5/11, 24/126

seruyse, *n.* service 10/130

ses, *v. inf.* stop 3/102, 19/46

seson, *n.* season 13/79

sete, *n.* seat 9/102, 17/139, 18/99, 20/159; city 14/17; throne 18/177; sitting 23/63

sewe, *v. inf.* follow 16/115, 18/78; *3.pl. pres.* 18/119, 24/255

sewe, *v. 3.sg. pa.* sowed 21/128; *pa.ppl.* 24/180

seyn, *v. 3.pl. pres.* say 8/41, 9/90, 16/63

seyntes, *n. pl.* saints 9/102, 17/67/140, 18/127, 23/109

sey3e, *see* **se**

shad(e)w(e), *n.* shadow 23/39, 23/32, 24/328

shaft, *n.* pole 16/64

shame, *n.* shame 2/21, 3/23/83, 4/47/202, 6/60, 9/45, 10/83, 12/75, 14/5, 16/8; disgrace 16/76, 18/95, 20/68, 21/110; harm 18/190; *do* ~ revile 10/117, 20/104

shame, *v. inf.* revile 13/80

shameles, *adj.* as *n.* modesty, decent persons 4/127, 14/84

shamely, *adv.* reproachfully 10/124, disgracefully 13/85

shap, *n.* shape? 9/155 *see note*

shapere, *n.* creator 24/371

sharp, *adj.* bitter 18/174

sharpe, *v. inf.* whet 10/171

shaue, *v. 3.pl. pres.* shave 14/53

shede, *v. inf.* spill 2/62; separate 10/142; scatter 13/86; *2.sg. pres.* shed 1/118

sheldis, *n. pl.* shields 10/143

shende, *v. inf.* destroy 13/8/90; *3.sg. pres.* **shendes** 5/23; *pa.ppl.* **shent** destroyed 1/66, 12/137, 14/77, 20/96

shep, *n.* sheep 14/46; *pl.* 9/157, 10/150

sheteþ, *v. 3.sg. pres.* shoots 4/58

shew(e), *v. imp.sg.* show 2/15, 19/20, 24/38/131; *pa.ppl.* **shewed** shown 13/118, 21/64

shidre, *v. inf.* break rank, disperse 5/4

sholde, *n.* shallows 13/146

shon, *n. pl.* shoes 20/138

shon, *v. 3.sg. pa.* shone 11/118

shop(e), *v. 3.sg. pa.* created 17/11, 24/66

shorn, *pa.ppl.* cut 24/171

shoue, *pa.ppl.* pierced 17/189; shoved, excluded 24/121

shoures, *n. pl.* distress 18/174

shrede, *n.* thread 1/30

shrewes, *n. pl.* rascals 21/21

shri/y/ft(e), *n.* oral confession 4/180, 7/53, 18/35/123

shronken, *pa.ppl.* shrunk 24/285

shrynes, *n. pl.* shrines 17/67

shul, *v. 2.pl. pres.* shall 21/131; *3.pl. pres.* 11/86

shuld(e), *v. 2.sg. pres.* 10/207; *3.sg. pres.* 7/34/35; *2.pl. pres.* 5/62, 10/47; *3.pl. pres.* 1/162, 4/78; **shulle** 24/252; *3.sg. pres.subj.* 2/43; *2.sg. pres.* **shuldest** 19/51

shuldres, *n. pl.* shoulders 15/33

shynynges, *ger.* radiance, brilliance 23/53

signyfye, *v. inf.* signify, mean 12/9; *3.sg. pres.* **signyfye**þ 12/17

sikirnes, *n.* safety 7/42 *see also* **sykernes(se)**

singulere, *n.* selfish gain, profit 16/59

siþ, *conj.* since 5/55/69, 7/10/111, 11/95, 21/9

skape, *v. inf.* escape, elude 24/62

skatre, *v. inf.* scatter 3/153; *1.sg. pres.* 10/144; *pa.ppl.* **skaterid** 12/23

skille, *v. 3.sg. pres.subj.* to distinguish 5/54

ski/y/lle, *n.* fairness 5/46; justice 12/111, 13/71; reason 16/102; logical argument 18/50; discrimination 20/46; *n. pl.* **ski/y/lle/i/s** equity, fairness 4/107; reasons 1/90, 7/33

skippe, *v. 3.sg. pres.* skips 16/101

skol, *v. see* **sc/k/ol(e)**

skorn(e) *n.* contempt 9/78, 18/36, 20/68; derision 12/147, 16/63

skorn(e), *v. 3.sg. pres.* treat contemptuously 16/74; *imp.sg.* 5/58; *2.pl. pres.* deride 2/35; *3.sg. pres.* **skorne**þ 13/73

skornes, *n. pl.* dung 4/129

skornyng, *ger.* deception 9/55

skourged, *pa.ppl.* scourged 20/155

skourges, *n. pl.* scourges 10/136, 20/114

slake, *v. inf.* cease 20/187/215

slau3t, *n.* execution 13/18

slay, *n.* part of a loom 4/6

sle, *v. inf.* kill 10/186, 11/54, 21/139; *3.sg. pres.* **sle(e)s** 3/22, 20/89; **slee**þ 20/2

slep, *n.* curdled milk 24/82

slepe, *v. inf.* sleep 15/87, 22/69; *1.sg. pres.* 24/29; *3.sg. pres.* 13/149

sleper, *adj.* vile, treacherous 24/77

slet, *n.* sleet 15/69

slete, *v. 3.pl. pres.* pursue, attack 9/22

sley3t(e), *n.* deceit 20/12/186
slidre, *adj.* treacherous 5/2
slo(o), *v. inf.* destroy, kill 3/117, 14/62, 21/94; *1.sg. pa.* slow 10/33; *3.sg. pa.* 10/180; *3.pl. pa.* slowen 12/124; *pa.ppl.* slon 11/14
slouþe, *n.* sloth 13/13, 16/42
slow, *adj.* sluggish, slothful 16/44
slyde, *v. imp.sg.* backslide 9/82
slyder(e), *adv.* perilously, precariously 4/7, 24/92
slyme, *n.* slime, muck 24/137/372
smal, *adj.* little 14/26
smal, *adv.* into little pieces 24/375
smerte, *v. 3.sg. pres.* feel pain 16/21
smyt(e), *v. inf.* strike 1/84, 7/95, 17/117, 20/101, 24/148; *3.sg. pres.* 16/97, 12/79; *imp.sg.* 13/15
snapere, *v. inf.* stumble, trip 4/90
socour, *n.* protector 13/45
sodeyn, *adj.* sudden 5/54, 8/101, 9/26, 13/18
sodeynly, *adv.* suddenly 24/12/67
soget, *n.* subject 4/219, 5/21; suget 1/102, 17/165; *n. pl.* sogettis 16/7
soget, *adj.* subject 1/20
solempne, *adj.* solemn 11/1
solempnyte, *n.* religious celebration 23/25
solpeþ, *v. 3.sg. pres.* defiles, pollutes 24/78; sulpeþ 21/106; *pa.ppl.* sulpid 11/74
son, *n.* cry of pain, sorrow 24/318
sonde, *n.* ordinance 9/37
sondes, *n. pl.* sands 4/132
sone, *n.* son 5/12, 14/41, 20/16/25 etc; sones, *poss.n.* 19/107; *see also* sun(ne)
sone, *adv.* soon 4/74, 5/50/52, 11/109, 12/137 etc.
sonere, *comp.adv.* sooner 3/37
sonne, *n.* sun 11/118
sooles, *n. pl.* purpose 16/8
sopere, *n.* supper 23/19/34
sore, *adj.* bitter 19/73; grievous 20/106
sore, *adv.* bitterly 10/95, 21/33; severely 12/114; grievously 19/11; wretchedly 24/387

sorefull, *adj.* as *n. pl.* afflicted 21/71; sorwefull, *adj.* as *n. pl.* wretched 21/72
sorw(e), *n.* sorrow 6/33/36/47, 9/33, 10/126, 16/115 etc.
sorwful, *adj.* contrite 24/45
soth/þ/e), *n.* truth 3/46, 4/104/120/224, 8/50, 24/299; soþes, *n. pl.* 24/61; *for ~* truly 17/136, 24/2/146
soþfast, *adj.* true 23/31
sotyl(le), *adj.* intricate, delicate 7/1; cunning, deceitful 13/81, 21/60
sotyly, *adv.* cunningly 13/63
souera/e/yn, *n.* sovereign 2/43, 4/219, 15/10; *n. pl.* 16/7
soun, *n.* voice 20/162; sown(e), sound 12/86/110
soun, *n.* sand, dust 24/65
souned, *pa.ppl.* resounded 23/23
soure, *adv.* bitterly 17/131
sowke, *v. inf.* suck 21/150
so3t, *v. 2.sg. pa.* sought 24/358; *pa.ppl.* 24/23/154; as company 24/160
spak, *v. 3.sg. pa.* spoke 11/27
speche, *n.* 2/65, 3/65, 8/21, 12/74, 18/132, 21/132, 24/34
speci/y/ale, *n.* intimate acquaintance 4/43; *in ~* specifically 3/49; individually 18/146
specyall, *adj.* specific, special 23/17
spede, *v. inf.* prosper 1/46, 4/175, 11/87, 16/32, 18/167; further, forward 17/31/172; *3.sg. pres.subj.* 9/146, 13/126, 24/415
spere, *n.* spear 2/45, 10/53, 17/189, 20/117
spettes, *v. 2.sg. pres.* spits 20/72
spices, *n. pl.* species 23/51/52; spys 23/60
spille, *v. inf.* wither 5/6; die 5/62; kill 12/106; destroy 19/60
spirituale, *n.* religious life 18/150
spiritualte, *n.* spirituality 15/28, 16/68, 18/8/9
spirytuall, *adj.* spiritual 10/129
sponnen, *pa.ppl.* spun 21/64
sporne, *v. inf.* trip, stumble 11/86
spotel, *n.* saliva, spittle 24/18
sprad, *ppl.adj.* spread 15/131

sprede, *v. inf.* spread 13/110

sprong, *v. 3.sg. pa.* sprang 12/122

spyled, *pa.ppl.* impoverished, despoiled 21/59

spys, *see* **spices**

spyse, *v. 2.sg. pres.subj.* see, spy 6/30; *3.sg. pres.subj.* 7/54

spyseþ, *v. 3.sg. pres.* despises 21/108

spyten, *pa.ppl.* tooled 24/297

squyers, *n. pl.* squires 3/69, 15/36

sta(a)te, *n.* spiritual condition 7/115, 18/34, 20/48, 24/183; proper condition 11/34, 14/10; office, rank 15/151; nature, composition 23/91

stad, *pa.ppl.* separated 15/129

stakes, *n. pl.* rope stakes 14/99 *see note*

stal, *v. 3.sg. pa.* stole 6/44

stalworþe, *adj. as n.* powerful 12/38; *adj.* robust 15/122

stalworþly, *adv.* resolutely 6/11

stant, *v. 3.sg. pres.* stands 4/140

stature, *n.* physical composition 23/91

staunche, *v. inf.* staunch, stop, prevent 4/17

sted(e), *n.* place 3/11; home 10/48; space 23/119; stead 23/127

stede, *n.* horse 1/142, 2/14

stedefast, *adj.* constant, resolute 24/81

steke, *v. inf.* thrust 17/110; **styke** stick 14/100; *1.sg. pres.* seal 3/1; *imp.pl.* 18/130; *2.sg. pres.* **stekest** thrust 10/69; *2.pl. pres.* **steken** close 17/87; *pa.ppl.* **stoken** lodged 3/93; locked 4/117; fettered 11/5; placed, put 23/65

stekenyng, *ger.* choking 16/123

stel, *n.* steel 20/124

stele, *v. inf.* hide 4/153, 10/161/188, 11/55; catch unawares 15/128; *3.pl. pres.* steal a march 21/8; *imp.pl.* thieve, rob 4/214, 17/92; *2.sg. pres.* **stelest** 4/190

stere, *v. imp.pl.* manage, move 15/108; *3.sg. pres.* **stereþ** steers, guides 1/65; *pa.ppl.* **styred(e)** tossed, twirled 24/139; steered away 24/333

sterne, *adj.* harsh, brutal 21/138

sterue, *v. inf.* starve 2/87

steryng, *ger.* guidance, admonition 10/*head*

stille, *adv.* still, yet 10/80

sti/y/lle, *adv.* quiet 4/51, 10/6

stoden, *v. 3.pl. pa.* stood 4/7

stok, *n.* tree, tree trunk 11/86

stoken *see* **steken**

stoles, *n. pl.* stools 16/4

stomble, *v. inf.* stumble 4/89; *3.pl. pres.* 9/26

ston, *n.* stone 11/86, 15/53/76, 20/124

stonde, *v. inf.* stand 2/47, 7/18, 13/33, 15/74, 18/63; *1.sg. pres.* 24/92/388; *2.sg. pres.subj.* 11/83; *3.sg. pres.* 18/91, 24/413; *2.pl. pres.* 18/81; *3.pl. pres.* 8/54 13/50; *3.sg. pres.* **stonde/i/s** 5/37, 12/77, 13/6, 15/40, 21/67

storble, *v. inf.* impede, take away 9/60

store, *n.* granary 3/67; treasure 9/181; preciousness 10/14; value 12/28; keeping 17/86, 19/13; possessions 18/141; merit 21/104; *in* ~ saved, supply 22/43; stored up 24/391

stoute, *adj.* bold 21/73; violent 21/138

straunge, *adj.* strange 16/34

stray, *n.* enclosure 4/14; *out of* ~ morally astray 4/110

stre, *n.* stalk of grain 2/26; straw 4/89; *pl.* 3/118

strete, *n.* road 9/166

stroi/y/e, *v. inf.* destroy 1/158, 2/62, 24/144; **stroyʒe** 2/60; *3.sg. pres.* **stroyeþ** 21/122; *1.pl. pres.* 12/130; *3.sg. pres.* **striʒeþ** vanquish 23/32; *pa.ppl.* **striʒed**, destroyed 5/31

stryf, *n.* conflict, discord 9/76/107, 13/86, 14/89, 21/123, 23/75; *pl.* **stryues** ~ *of* deþ struggles with death 24/326

strype, *v. inf.* strip, peel 2/26

stryue, *v. inf.* contend 9/13/37; *3.pl. pres.* **stryuen** 11/26

stye, *v. 3.sg. pres.* ascends 20/159

styf, *adj.* mighty, valiant 1/142; *comp.* **styffere** more unyielding 20/124

style, *n.* stile 3/127, 4/90; *pl.* rungs of a ladder 14/99 *see note*

styred(e) *see* stere
suchon, *pron.* such a one 24/128
suffre, *v. inf.* endure, suffer 11/101;
　3.sg. pres. suffreþ 14/81/83; *1.sg. pa.*
　10/58/60; *2.sg. pa.* 19/20; *3.sg. pa.*
　20/62/113, 22/51; *imp.sg.* allow 8/91
suget, *see* soget
sulpeþ/id *see* solpeþ
sum, *pron.* some 4/9/185, 11/105, 20/33;
　pl. summe 1/83/84, 3/46, 4/131/132/139,
　14/27 etc.
sumtyme, *adv.* formerly, once
　4/121/123/126, 20/22
sumwhat, *pron.* somewhat 2/16, 9/177,
　20/63
sun(n)e, *n.* sun 11/76, sun/Son 23/31; *see
　also* sone
suppose, *v. 1.sg. pres.* state as belief 23/83
suspende, *pa.ppl.* prohibited 16/68
susspescioun, *n.* suspicion 18/88
suste/y/naunce, income 14/39; livelihood
　3/156
swerd(e), *n.* sword 1/84, 3/139, 4/196,
　5/39, 10/141, 13/120 etc. *pl.* swerdis
　10/143
swere, *v. inf.* proclaim 4/219; pledge,
　promise 6/48; *2.sg. pres.* declare, assert
　6/6; *imp.sg.* swear oaths, profane 19/75
swerue, *inf.* get up, rise 2/82
swete, *v. inf.* sweat 9/134, 13/13, 15/117
swete, *n.* bliss 17/131, 24/147
swete, *adj.* sweet 17/53/90
swetnes, *n.* sweetness 17/66
swolwe, *v. inf.* swallow 24/18
swyn, *n.* pig 10/201
swynke, *v. inf.* toil 9/134, 15/117
sybbe, *n.* relative, kin 17/77
syde, *n.* side 3/116, 11/43 etc. *pl.* sydes
　15/44
syk, *adj.* sick 17/191, 18/73; *adj. as n.* 6/39,
　9/125
syk, *adv.* sick 15/126
syknes(se), *n.* sickness 5/52,
　10/76/160/164, 11/90, 19/65, 20/211
syker(e), *adj.* sure, confident 5/51; robust
　11/95

sykernes(se), *n.* peace of mind,
　confidence 4/71; free from danger 5/55;
　security 18/160; *in* ~ securely 8/34; *see
　also* sikirnes
symonye, *n.* simony 14/81/92
symple, *adj.* whole 12/104
synewes, *n. pl.* sinews 24/90; *see also*
　synnu
synguler(e), *adj.* selfish, individual 1/4,
　5/28, 8/60, 14/52, 17/37, 21/60, 21/93
syngulerte, *n.* personal gain, advantage
　13/81
synnu, *n.* sinew 24/153
syr, *n.* sir 2/17
syse, *n.* assise 1/61
syse, *n.* normal condition 24/285; *in* ~
　properly 15/75
syt, *v. inf.* sit 16/53; *3.pl. pres.* 5/15
syte, *v. 2.sg. pres.* lie in wait for 24/291
syþes, *n. pl.* times 9/89
sy3e, *v. 3.pl. pres.* perish, sink 24/51
sy3t, *n.* sight 4/153, 11/21/76/89 etc.

table, *n.* food 21/71; eucharistic table
　23/19/26/27
tacche, *n. in* ~ characteristically, by
　nature 20/150
tan, *pa.ppl.* taken 9/81, 24/227
tan, *v. inf.* declaim 8/83 *see note*
tapestis, *n. pl.* carpets 13/134
tauerne, *n.* tavern 6/19
telyeþ, *v. 3.sg. pres.* tills, cultivates 7/61
temperal(e), *adj.* worldy 10/135, 18/152
temperalte, *n.* worldly goods 8/60, 16/67;
　worldly matters 18/11
tenauntes, *n. pl.* tenants 13/43
tent, *n.* heed, attention 12/13
teres, *n. pl.* tears 10/94
terme, *n.* appointed time 24/88/199
teth, *n. pl.* teeth 24/286
tey3e, *v. inf.* tie 4/113
th/þ/an, *adv.* then 1/64, 3/21/28, 21/11 etc.;
　th/þanne 7/106, 16/112, 20/81, 21/73
thar, *v. 2.sg. pres.* need 9/134; *3.sg. pres.*
　17/170/176; *2.pl. pres.* 1/80, 3/180, 9/142;
　3.pl. pres. 4/24, 11/93, 18/85

th/þ/ede, *n.* people 1/158, 13/22

th/þ/eder(e), *adv.* thither 4/2, 13/5/122

thee, *v. inf.* prosper 16/85

th/þef, *n.* thief 4/9, 10/71

th/þ/enk(e), *v. 1.pl. pres.* think 1/82;
3.pl. pres. 4/16; *imp.sg.* 7/48, 8/10/92,
18/53/58, 22/57, 24/5; *2.sg. pres.* þenkes
24/133; *3.sg. pres.* th/þenketh/þ 2/61/81,
9/78, 10/3 etc.

þens, *adv.* from thence 4/92

þerout, *adv.* outside 6/38

þertille, *adv.* thereto 20/44

þeryn(ne), *adv.* therein 7/36, 10/80, 19/66,
21/43/109, 24/326

th/þes, *dem.art.* these 1/119, 9/128, 23/126,
24/305

þesternesse, *n.* darkness 24/327

thies, *n. pl.* thighs 15/49

þirled, *v. 3.sg. pa.* pierced 10/32

þi/u/rst, *n.* thirst 15/68, 21/63

th/þo, *pron.* those 1/151, 4/87, 9/92, 12/103,
16/16, 18/77, 18/135, 19/98, 21/23/119,
22/37, 23/86, 24/111; þoo 22/14

tho, *adv.* then 6/45; thoo 24/364

thonder, *n.* thunder 10/187

thong, *n.* whip, scourge 16/22

th/þ/onke, *n.* thanks 2/15/31/45/55, 13/16,
16/76

þoȝt, *n.* thought 24/21/156/321

þral(le), *n.* slave 8/91, 20/171

þraldom, *n.* slavery 9/28, 18/19

þrawe, *n.* conflict, strife 9/108; *see also*
thro

threp, *n.* conflict, strife 14/78

th/þ/ret(e), *v. inf.* threaten 7/94, 9/46,
17/141, 16/27, 20/73; *3.sg. pres.* 3/58

thretyng, *ger.* threats 10/140

th/þ/ridde, *adj.* third 3/41, 11/25, 16/116

thrift, *n.* savings 21/58

thro, *n.* conflict, strife 14/78; *see also*
þrawe

þrong, *n.* crowd 6/9, 10/144

thryue, *v. inf.* prosper 6/70, 16/85; *3.pl.*
pres. 4/146

th/þ/urgh, *prep.* through 1/95/103, 4/255,
8/44, 9/153, 10/26/44, 11/18, 15/20, 17/189

thursten, *v. 3.pl. pres.* thirst after 21/50;
3.sg. pres. thurstes 21/53

þursty, *adj.* thirsty 9/123

þysse, *dem.pron.* this 24/269

tike, *n.* hound 9/157

ti/y/l, *conj.* until 3/102, 4/205, 6/47, 7/50,
12/68/69, 13/103/142, 16/10/118, 20/116,
21/28, 22/38/40; tyll(e) 7/50, 24/220

tille, *prep.* to, towards 19/62

tixt, *n.* text 20/1

tobroken, *pa.ppl.* broken into pieces
12/50

togedere, *adv.* together 2/59, 4/4; togyder
24/90; togydre 11/35, 12/67, 15/18,
17/128, 19/93, 20/18

tok(e), *v. 1.sg. pa.* took 2/68, 17/79, 19/8,
24/245; *3.sg. pa.* 17/130, 20/58; *3.pl. pa.*
16/48, 18/46

tokene, *n.* sign, commemorative action
23/48/94

tokenynges, *ger.* signs 23/51

toles, *n. pl.* tools 16/2

ton, *see* too

tong(e), *n.* tongue 13/100, 17/91, 21/133;
tunge 4/113

too, *n.* toe 15/37, *n. pl.* to(o)n, 11/102,
15/74

torne, *v. 1.sg. pres.* turn 24/325

toun, *n.* town 3/34/124, 4/206, 9/166,
15/54, 24/71

toure, *n.* tower 17/129; *pl.* toures 13/49

tow, *adj.* tough 10/35

towche, *n.* touch 18/88; *pl.* towches 18/93;

towched, *v. 3.sg. pa.* touched 24/290

tras, *n.* trace, tracks 24/70

trauayle, *n.* work 2/23/38, 18/29

trauayle, *v. 3.pl. pres.* 15/67

trauaylyng, *ppl.adj.* labouring 2/9/29

tre, *n.* tree 10/21, 15/60, 17/116, 19/18, 23/2

trede, *v. 2.pl. pres.* tread 1/134; *3.pl. pres.*
13/134; *3.sg. pres.* tredeþ 20/80

treso(u)n, *n.* treason 12/69/94, 13/20/61;
pl. 14/61

tresory(e), *n.* treasury 3/66, 7/19

tresour(e), *n.* treasure 5/9, 12/40, 13/44,
17/133

trespas, *n.* sin 9/45, 10/95/172, 24/105; offence 18/185, 24/129; **trespac/s/e** 12/51/63

trespas, *v. inf.* offend 19/63, 20/196; *2.sg. pres.* sin 17/117

trespasour, *n.* offender 1/163

trest(e), *v. inf.* trust 4/226; **triste** 16/17; *imp.sg.* 14/47; **truste** 7/113

trete, *n.* treaty 13/124/155, 16/17

trete, *v. inf.* negotiate 3/120; *2.sg. pres.* 17/143; *2.pl. pres.* 13/137/139/140; plead *2.pl. pres.* 9/head/8/16/24 etc.; *2.pl. pa.* 9/17; *imp.pl.* 3/152; *inf.* discuss 18/179, 23/59; *3.sg. pres.* **treteþ** handles 11/45

treuth, *n.* truth 1/78

trewe, *adj.* true 2/38, 17/127; *comp.* **trewere** 17/132; *superl.* **trewest** 22/23

trewes, *n.* truce 9/20

triȝe, *v. imp.sg.* separate 7/14; *pa.ppl.* **tried** 12/69; *inf.* **try** adjudicate 24/191

trouth/þ/(e), *n.* truth 3/4, 4/10, 12/69, 13/30 etc. *gen.sg.* **trouþes** 4/113, 13/100

trowe, *v. inf.* trust 4/60; *1.sg. pres.* believe 2/86; *2.sg. pres.* 24/229; *pa.ppl.* 16/25; *1.sg. pres.* avow 7/76, 20/32, 24/149

trussen, *v. inf.* pack up 12/140

trusty, *adj.* trustworthy 4/60

try *see* **triȝe**

tunge *see* **tong(e)**

turment, *n.* torment 20/90, 24/134

turmentest, *v. 2.sg. pres.* torment 19/41; *pres.ppl.* **turmentynge** 24/264

tway, *n.* two 4/70; **twey** 24/303

twyggis, *n. pl.* branches 12/119

twyn(ne), *v. inf.* separate 4/70, 17/168, 18/94, 24/62/95/168

twynne, *n.* two 7/111, 17/85, 19/56, 20/13, 21/111

twyȝe, *adv.* twice 7/94

tyde, *n.* holy office, divine service 23/11

tylyers, *n. pl.* tillers 15/62

tyrauntri/y/e, *n.* tyranny 1/3, 10/110, 14/62

tyme, *n.* theme 23/17

tyþe, *n.* tithe 8/20

tyȝed, *pa.ppl.* tied 13/100

vnbende, *v. 3.sg. pres.* shrinks, attenuates 15/7; *3.sg. pres.subj.* slacken 12/87

vnbynde, *v. inf.* release 10/59, 15/150, 18/19; untie 17/136; *2.sg. pres.* 7/52

vnclene, *adj.* sinful, dirty 24/194

vndercrepe, *v. 3.sg. pres.subj.* creep in stealthily, infiltrate 22/71

vndir, *prep.* underneath 23/68

vneuene, *adv.* erroneously, illogically 8/49

vnhende, *adj.* discourteous, rude 4/27

vnkonnyng, *adj.* lacking in knowledge, uneducated 13/37

vnkynde, *adj.* ungrateful, uncharitable 10/11; rebellious, sinful 11/39; unhealthy, unnatural 15/106; ungrateful, indifferent 19/3

vnkyndely, *adj.* excessive, immoral 14/84/91

vnloken, *pa.ppl.* proclaimed 11/2; expounded 12/53

vnneþe, *adv.* scarcely, hardly 4/128

vnryȝt, *n.* sinfulness 24/248

vnstable, *adj.* irresolute, fickle 13/32

vntyme, *adv.* unseasonably – *i.e.* uncharacteristically 13/13

vnwetand, *pres.ppl.* unwittingly 4/213

vnwroȝt, *adj.* unmade 24/319

vnwys, *adj.* as *n.* the ignorant, unlearned 9/167

vnyte, *n.* unity 1/13/21, 3/130, 8/63, 13/106

vp, *adv.* up 9/82, 14/99, 18/39, 20/168, 21/146, 24/306/402

vpbreydeþ, *v. 3.sg. pres.* upbraids 20/139

vp(p)on, *prep.* upon 4/218, 7/54, 16/113, 17/22

vpsodoun, *adv.* upside down 24/13

vs, *pron.* us 1/81, 4/44, 11/4 etc.

vse, *v. 3.sg. pres.* use 5/33; *2.pl. pres.* 5/42; *imp.sg.* 22/66; *3.pl. pa.* **vsed** 4/123, 24/407; *pa.ppl.* 15/151, 20/123

vsurye, *n.* usury 14/83

vtteremore, *adv.* further away 13/107

vanyte, *n.* vanity 18/13/102/108/130, 20/172

vaunsement, *n.* advancement 17/21

vauntage, *n.* benefit 12/103; advantage 13/132

venyale, *adj.* venial 9/85

vertew, *n.* virtue 24/184

vilonye, *n.* wickedness, shamefulness 4/124

visage, *n.* countenance, appearance 6/62

vowtrye, *n.* adultery 20/174

voyde, *v. inf.* leave 4/189; *3.sg. pres.* **voydeþ** disregards 4/95

voys, *n.* voice 4/19/155

vyage, *n.* journey 13/119,

vylenye, *n.* wrongdoing, wickedness 20/68

vyne, *n.* vine 10/49

vys, *n.* vice, sin 1/42, 8/74, 11/10, 13/89, 18/20/75, 19/111, 20/169, 24/352

vysement, *n.* prudence 13/93

vysite, *v. imp.sg.* visit 9/125

wacche, *n.* vigil 18/113

wan, *v. 2.sg. pa.* obtained 7/84, 9/99; *3.sg. pa.* won 13/136; *pa.ppl.* ~ *in* begotten 22/4

wande, *n.* stick, rod 24/48/262; *n. pl.* **wandes** branches 15/60

wane, *adj.* absent, lacking 2/61

waneles, *adj.* hopeless, despairing 24/278

wanen, *v. 3.pl. pres.* diminish 19/44

wanhope, *n.* despair 1/131, 7/99, 10/91, 20/203

wanton, *adj.* badly-behaved 12/113

war, *adj.* aware 1/1, 4/29, 5/1; aware, prudent 9/79; wise 14/8 etc.,18/81, 19/33; **warre** 14/head, **ware** 24/70 careful

warde, *n.* charge *or* cell 18/41

ware, *v. 2.sg. pa.* were 24/5

ware, *v. 1.sg. pa.* wear out, exhaust 24/3

warke, *n.* work 24/407; *see also* **werk**

warnestor, *n.* defending force 7/13; military provision 13/122

wary, *v. inf.* complain, fulminate 20/133

wasche, *v. inf.* wash 9/172; *imp.pl.* 4/135, 24/248

waste, *adj.* prodigal 9/100

wast(e), *n.* pointless 4/177; *in* ~ futilely 13/124; extravagant expense 14/76

wast(e), *v. inf.* waste 4/166, 20/165; *1.sg. pres.* 20/56; *3.pl. pres.* 15/148; *inf.* destroy 24/149; *ppl.adj.* **wastyng** dwindling 10/137

wasted, *pa.ppl.* destroyed 23/70; decomposed 24/158; corroded 24/263; shrivelled 24/283; **wastede** 3/119 squandered, exhausted

wastours, *n. pl.* idle spendthrifts 13/92

waxe, *n.* candle wax 18/175

waxe, *v. 1.pl. pres.* grow 15/110; *imp.sg.* become 13/58; *3.sg. pres.* **waxeþ** 15/126; *3.pl. pres.* **waxen** 19/43, 24/104; *pa.ppl.* 20/135; *see also* **wexe**

waye, *v. 3.pl. pres.* weigh 9/51; **weye** *imp. sg.* 1/14

wayle, *v. inf.* wail 24/324

wayte, *v. inf.* wait 16/70; *3.sg. pres.* 5/30; *3.pl. pres.* 15/127; *imp.pl.* 9/151

wayueþ, *v. 3.sg. pres.* disregards 16/100

waȝtes, *n. pl.* weights 9/51; *see also* **wyȝt**

web, *n.* woven fabric 4/6

wede, *n.* clothing 1/150, 2/54, 10/204, 13/30, 16/120, 18/161

wede, *v. inf.* weed 4/143

wede, *v. inf.* go 16/3

weder, *n.* weather 2/57

weel, *adv.* thoroughly 9/34

weet, *n.* wet 15/67

welde, *v. inf.* possess 5/63; *3.pl. pres.* handle, dispose 10/4

wele, *n.* joy 4/66; prosperity 5/49, 10/184; wealth 8/68, 9/27, 10/4, 11/94, 14/108, 16/3; bliss 10/65; health 10/157

wele, *adv.* well 1/40, 4/head, 9/135, 15/120, 17/33

welfare, *n.* good fortune 6/34

welþe, *n.* wealth 15/55

wend(e), *v. inf.* go 4/37, 6/68, 8/22, 20/144/216; *2.pl. pres.* 18/107; *3.pl. pres.* 17/51; *2.sg. pres.* **wendys** 24/97; *3.sg. pres.* **wendes** 5/18; *inf.* 12/85 turn out

wene, *v. inf.* believe, suppose 1/132, 4/147, 7/100, 12/61, 18/92; *1.sg. pa.* **wende** assumed, concluded 15/91; *pa.ppl.* deemed 1/36/68

went(e), *v. 3.sg. pa.* went 13/5, 24/398; gone 18/48, 20/92, 23/52

wer(r)e, *n.* war 2/67, 3/72/104/136/160/168, 10/86, 12/125, 13/127/129, 15/142, 16/29, 20/93, 21/85/88/90

were, *v. inf.* wear 18/52

were, *v. inf. vs* ~ defend ourselves 15/93

wer(e)n, *v. 3.pl. pa.* were 24/109/360

werk, *n.* deed 4/154/156, 8/76/78, 14/23, 18/136; action 13/94; handiwork 24/41/42/287; creation 24/298; *n. pl.* **werke/i/y/s** acts 17/34; deeds 1/79/87, 4/160, 5/47, 24/26 etc.; *see also* **warke**

werkman, *n.* labourer 9/165

werne, *v. inf.* deny 17/146

werreþ, *v. 3.sg. pres.* fights 3/113

werryours, *n. pl.* warriors 9/138

werye, *adj.* weary 18/30

wes, *v. 3.sg. pa.* was 3/142

wet(e), *v. inf.* know 3/97; *3.pl. pres.* 3/101

wete, *v. inf.* wet 9/174

wexe, *v. 3.sg. pres.subj.* grow 1/159; *3.pl. pres.* **wexen** 4/31; *see also* **waxe**

wey, *n.* way, path 3/128; *n. pl.* **weyes** 23/8

weye, *v. see* **waye**

weylaway, *interj.* woe, alas 8/70

whan, *conj.* when 2/29/82, 3/33 etc.; **whanne** 1/65, 3/25, 7/89 etc.

whel, *n.* wheel 22/11

wheron, *prep.* on which 10/25

wherto, *adv.* to what end 24/127

whet, *3.pl. pres.* sharpen 20/67

whete, *n.* wheat 3/47, 9/182

whidre, *adv.* to where 5/7 *see also* **whyder**

whirlewynd, *n.* whirlwind 10/144

whoche, *rel.pron.* which 3/36

whule, *conj.* while 14/26

whyder, *adv.* to where 4/5, 24/96/98/163

whyder, *prep.* whether 18/129

widre, *v. inf.* wither 5/5

wi/y/le, *n.* plot, stratagem 4/95, 7/104

willis, *n. pl.* desires 4/105

wi/y/lne, *v. imp.sg.* wish 17/75, 24/242; *2.sg. pres.* **wi/y/lt** 17/106/118, 19/46/60/78; 24/143/144/148; **wi/y/ltow** 17/119/152

wi/y/st(e), *v. 3.sg. pres.* knows 5/9/17, 7/35/41; *2.sg. pres.* 19/81; *2.sg. pres.* **wost** 6/36, 8/4/97, 10/82; *1.sg. pres.* **wot** 4/5; *3.sg. pres.* 1/25/97, 16/32/41; *inf.* **wyte** 1/49, 17/119; *1.sg. pres.* 24/84/152/293; *2.sg. pres.subj.* 24/59; *3.pl. pres.* **wyten** 13/27, 23/97

wi/y/t, *n.* reason, good sense, wisdom 1/25/57, 2/61, 3/85/89/92, 4/65, 5/18, 10/91, 18/24/72 etc.

wiþal, *adv.* by means of 14/28; in addition 15/12

with/þ/outen, *adv.* without 24/221/309/364

with/þ/outen, *prep.* without 12/138, 23/20

witles, *adj.* senseless, devoid of reason 3/38; **witteles** 3/90

witnes, *n.* witness 13/94

wittes, *n. pl.* senses 9/39, 22/68; wits 24/3; *in* ~ wise 3/71

wo, *n.* trouble 1/146, 16/58; misery 4/66, 6/47, 8/11, 18/190, 20/113; *do me* ~ punish 24/134/205; *see also* **woo** 1/108, 5/66, 10/65 etc.

wo, *adj. be* ~ in trouble 14/8 etc.

wo, *interj.* woe 24/366

wod, *adj.* mad 16/3, 20/43; **wood** 10/55, 20/81; furious 17/149; illogical 19/39

wode, *n.* wood 12/14

wol(e), *v. 1.sg. pres.* will 2/32/56, 10/56, 17/141; *2.sg. pres.* **wolt** 24/149/259; *3.sg. pres.* 1/29/35, 3/57/70/81/82, 4/30; **wolle** 16/20; *3.pl. pres.* 2/22, 4/37; **wolen** 1/152, 24/102; **woln** 24/351; desire, wish *3.sg. pres.* 1/57; *2.pl. pres.* 1/23/49

wold(e), *v. 1.sg. pres.* wish 2/77, 4/217; *2.sg. pres.* 1/115, 4/244; **woldest** 2/67, 20/192; *2.sg. pres.* would 17/155; *3.sg. pres.* 1/131; *3.pl. pres.* 10/73, 3/21 etc.;

wolward, *adv.* dressed in wool, penitential clothing 20/23

wombe, *n.* womb 6/51, 24/315/320; belly
    10/178; stomach 13/149, 15/81 etc.
won, *n.* home 11/94, 15/55; *n. pl.* 17/17,
    23/8
wonde, *v. inf.* hesitate 4/199; forbear 18/85
wonder, *adj.* miraculous 11/21
wonderly, *adv.* miraculously 24/374
wondryng, *ger.* derision 16/109
wone, *v. inf.* dwell 18/140, 20/144; *2.sg.*
    pres. **wonest** 10/80; *3.sg. pres.* **woneþ**
    17/200, 24/329
wonne, *pa.ppl.* won 8/65; **wonnen** 13/133
woo *see* **wo**
wood *see* **wode**
wopen, *n. pl.* weapons 24/110
worche, *v. imp.sg.* work 1/7; *3.sg. pres.*
    worche/i/þ 5/8/10/24/32/40, 16/100
worchip(e), *n.* honour 3/57, 4/32;
    worschep 8/26; **wors(c)hip(e)**, 1/99,
    2/21, 3/24/83/86, 4/171/185, 8/22/73,
    10/117, etc.
worchyng, *ger.* working 13/head
wors, *comp.adv.* corruptly 9/51
wors(c)hip(e), *v. inf.* honour, respect
    13/77; *imp.sg.* 1/101; *pa.ppl.* **worschiped**
    3/6
worschipful, *adv.* reverently 23/26
wost *see* **wist(e)**
wot *see* **wist(e)**
woþes, *n. pl.* lamentations 20/143
wounden, *pa.ppl.* wrapped 16/61
wowe, *v. inf.* woo 20/120
wrake, *v. inf.* wreak, wage 16/29
wrappid, *pa.ppl.* wrapped 11/6
wrastle, *v. inf.* wrestle 15/76
wraþþe, *n.* wrath 9/107
wrec(c)he, *n.* wretch 24/163/187
wrecched, *adj.* accursed 15/88; **wrechyd**
    wretched 24/164
wrecchednes, *n.* wretchedness 22/8;
    wrechidnes(se) 24/172/340
wreche, *n.* vengeance 10/56/126/171,
    12/77/78/79, 16/70; misery 10/105
wreches, *n. pl.* punishments 24/327
wreke, *v. 3.sg. pres.subj.* vent 18/134; *3.sg.*
    pres. **wrekeþ** avenges 21/68

wreten, *pa.ppl.* written 22/48
wro, *n. from ech a ~* from every nook
    and cranny 14/86
wroken, *pa.ppl.* avenged 4/116, 11/4, 12/55
wrongwys, *adj.* unlawful 4/20, 21/62
wrot, *v. 3.sg. pa.* wrote 4/245, 9/93, 17/181
wroþ, *adj.* angry 11/9
wro(u)ȝt, *v. 1.sg. pa.* did 24/84; made
    10/17, 20/181; *3.sg. pa.* 17/42; *pa.ppl.*
    13/29, 15/4/134, 17/62, 20/179, 22/3,
    24/4/19/362/372, done 4/156; performed
    17/94
wrye, *v. inf.* turn away 6/54
wyd(e), *adv.* wide 15/84, 20/118
wyf, *n.* woman 9/79, 23/73; married
    woman 21/125
wyft, *n.* threads, weft 21/64
wyke, *n.* candlewick 18/175
wyket, *n.* gate 15/83, 22/4
wylde, *adj.* wild 1/53, 7/57, 14/110, 20/37,
    21/23, 24/109
wyldernes, *n.* wilderness 23/124
wyle, *n.* trick 4/95
wyn, *n.* wine 15/72, 23/37/44, 24/288
wynd(e), *n.* wind 2/58, 4/3, 7/27, 9/29,
    15/3, 22/19, 24/139; breath 7/53, 12/51,
    13/127, 15/148, 20/56, 23/37
wynne, *v. inf.* win 1/114, 3/57, 6/12, 7/4
    etc.; *2.pl. pres.* 13/155/157; *2.sg. pres.*
    wynnest 1/130, 7/98; *3.sg. pres.* **wynneþ**
    gains 16/93
wynnyng, *ger.* gain 13/135, 15/52, 19/77,
    21/37/93, 24/281
wys, *adj.* wise 1/45/47/60/79/141, 2/37 etc.
wyse, *n.* end 1/98
wyseman, *n.* sage 14/41
wysse, *v. inf.* guide, instruct 23/7
wyst(e), *see* **wi/y/st(e)**
wyte(n), *see* **wi/y/st(e)**
wyþ, *prep.* with 24/412
wyȝt, *n.* weight 14/68 *see also* **waȝtes**

Y, *pron.* I 1/90/109, 2/13/15/16/32 etc.
ydel, *n. in ~* vainly 3/90, 8/12
yfere, *adv.* together 17/192
yliche, *adj.* alike 23/74

yliche, *adv.* alike 14/35, 23/87; **ylyk** 9/159

ylle, *n.* wickedness 13/68, 16/106; evil 19/58

ylle, *adj.* wicked 10/2

ylle, *adv.* wickedly 5/22

ymage, *n.* image 9/98, 17/11/114, 19/6, 20/181, 22/18

ymagenyng, *v. pres.pl.* planning 15/15

ympnes, *n. pl.* hymns 23/11

yn(ne), *n.* inn, lodging 10/121, 21/47

ynne, *adv.* in 10/173, 17/93

ynne, *prep.* in 3/113, 16/61, 24/164

ynnere, *adj.* inner 11/36

ynow(e), *adv.* enough 1/151, 10/29, 20/114

yput, *pa.ppl.* put 24/306

yren, *adj.* iron 24/296

yrnes, *n. pl.* containers 23/65

ys, *v. 3.sg. pres.* is 5/28, 23/5/65; **ysse** 13/1

yse, *n.* ice 17/24

yshorted, *pa.ppl.* shortened 24/252

ywis(se), *adv.* certainly 13/147, 24/32/302/384; **ywist** 4/229; **ywys** 1/29

3e, *pron. 2.pl.* you 1/6/23/43/49/80 etc; **3ou** 18/119; **3ow** 1/76, 2/34/83, 3/107 etc.

3ede, *v. 1.sg. pa.* went 24/155/394; *3.pl. pa.* 16/118

3ee, *adv.* yes 2/28, 4/91

3e(e)r(e), *n.* year 9/19/50, 10/50, 13/29; *pl.* 24/4; **3erys** 24/53

3elde, *v. inf.* yield 3/58, pay 9/97, 10/196, 11/110; give 17/108, 24/231

3eme, *v. inf.* rule 13/161; *imp.sg.* 24/113; *3.pl. pres.* **3emen** 15/37; *inf.* observe 18/114

3eme, *v. inf.* 13/19 tolerate (*see note*)

3erd(e), *n.* rod 1/83, 12/114/115/117, 24/47/125

3erde, *n.* yard 9/52

3erne, *adj.* eager 21/77

3erned, *v. 1.sg. pa.* desired 19/9; *3.sg. pa.* yearned 24/203

3et, *adv.* yet 7/87, 16/83; **3ut** 1/39, 7/39, 10/77, 17/13, 18/182; *see also* **3it**

3if, *conj.* if 1/51/73/161, 3/17 etc.

3it, *conj.* yet 3/41, 12/133, 17/49, 20/63; *see also* **3et**

3ol, *n.* refrain of a song 4/234

3ong(e), *adj.* young 1/5; *as n.* 9/23, 13/131, 14/65, 17/121

3ool, *n.* Yuletide 16/103

3ore, *adv.* of old 3/65, 12/117, 18/137, 19/9, 20/110

3ouen *see* **3eue**

3our(e), *poss.adj.* your 1/20/87, 2/35/36/83, 3/105 etc.; *pron.* **3oures** 1/19, 3/131, 13/51

3owthe, *n.* youth 7/49

3ut *see* **3et**

Index of proper names